Voices from Haskell

Voices from Haskell
Indian Students between Two Worlds, 1884–1928

Myriam Vučković

UNIVERSITY PRESS OF KANSAS

All photographs are courtesy of the
National Archives and Records Administration.

© 2008, 2024 by the University Press of Kansas
All rights reserved

Published by the University Press of Kansas (Lawrence, Kansas 66045), which was organized by the Kansas Board of Regents and is operated and funded by Emporia State University, Fort Hays State University, Kansas State University, Pittsburg State University, the University of Kansas, and Wichita State University

Library of Congress Cataloging-in-Publication Data
Vučković, Myriam.
Voices from Haskell : Indian students between two worlds, 1884–1928 / Myriam Vučković.
p. cm.
Includes bibliographical references and index.
ISBN 978-0-7006-1617-6 (cloth)
ISBN 978-0-7006-3684-6 (paperback)
ISBN 978-0-7006-3685-3 (ebook)
1. Haskell Institute—History. 2. Off-reservation boarding schools—Kansas—Lawrence—History. 3. Indian students—Kansas—Lawrence—History. 4. Indian students—Government policy—Kansas—Lawrence. 5. Indian students—Cultural assimilation—Kansas—Lawrenc   I. Title.
E97.6.H37V83 2008
371.82991'411—dc22   2008021377

British Library Cataloguing-in-Publication Data is available.

To all the students of Haskell—

past and present

Contents

Preface to the Paperback Edition   ix

Acknowledgments   xxi

Introduction   1

1 Beginnings   11

2 Coming to Haskell   30

3 Living by the Bell   59

4 The Curriculum   91

5 Rituals and Recreation   128

6 Health and the Body   179

7 Accommodation and Resistance   211

8 Life after Haskell   247

Notes   279

Bibliography   309

Index   317

A photograph section follows page 165.

Preface to the Paperback Edition

In the sixteen years since *Voices from Haskell* was published in 2008, the American Indian boarding school experience has received more attention from academics, Indigenous activists, and policymakers than ever before, reflecting the pivotal role boarding schools play in the ongoing discourse surrounding historical trauma and its repercussions on Native individuals and societies. In this new preface, I will give an overview of new scholarship in this field, discuss contributions of the Native American Rights Fund and the National Native American Boarding School Healing Coalition, and outline recent United States government efforts and initiatives to address the history and impact of the schools on Indigenous peoples.

Since I researched and wrote the book in the early 2000s, several significant scholarly publications have emerged on the topic. Their authors, many of them Indigenous scholars, offer varied perspectives, historical analyses, personal narratives, and insights into the legacy of American Indian boarding schools. They contribute to our understanding of this oftentimes traumatic chapter in American history and its effects on Indigenous communities in the United States and beyond, navigating the complexities of honoring the diverse array of student experiences, while acknowledging and analyzing the deep-seated injuries inflicted by the schools.

One of the most notable publications, *Indian Subjects: Hemispheric Perspectives on the History of Indigenous Education* (2014), edited by Brenda J. Child and Brian Klopotek, explores the history of Indigenous education in the Americas, focusing on the experiences of Native American communities in the United States and Indigenous peoples in Latin America. The book adds a new dimension by providing a nuanced understanding of the challenges faced by Indigenous communities within the broader context of colonialism, modernity, and the politics of education throughout the hemisphere.

Unsettling the Settler Within: Indian Residential Schools, Truth Telling, and Reconciliation in Canada (2010) by Paulette Regan and *Our Shared Future:*

Windows into Canada's Reconciliation Journey (2020), edited by Laura E. Reimer and Robert Chrismas, examine the impact of truth-telling and reconciliation processes, offering insights into tangible ways of healing and justice for Indigenous communities in Canada that also have relevance for Indigenous peoples and policymakers here in the United States.

In *Away from Home: American Indian Boarding School Experiences, 1879–2000* (2016), Margaret Archuleta, Brenda Child, and K. Tsianina Lomawaima offer diverse perspectives on the 121 years of the U.S. American Indian boarding school experience and its lasting impacts. In the spring of 2018, the *Journal of American Indian Education* published the *Special Issue: Native American Boarding School Stories*, which is a fantastic collection of twelve articles by K. Tsianina Lomawaima, Bryan McKinley Jones Brayboy, Teresa L. McCarty, Janet Cantley, Rayna Green, Brenda J. Child, Jon Reyhner, Jeffrey Ostler, Matthew Sakiestewa Gilbert, Louellyn White, Patty Talahongva, Khalil Anthony Johnson Jr., and Charles M. Roessel.

The collection covers a wide range of topics and includes Brenda Child's influential piece "The Boarding School as Metaphor," originally written for the above mentioned 2014 book *Indian Subjects: Hemispheric Perspectives on the History of Indigenous Education*. Child's article explores the concept of the American Indian boarding school as a metaphorical space that represents larger themes in Native American history and experiences. Through this metaphorical lens, she highlights how the boarding school system was emblematic of the broader efforts of colonialism to dismantle Indigenous cultures, languages, and identities. Child emphasizes the lasting impact of this assimilationist policy on Native American communities and the intergenerational trauma it caused but also draws attention to the resilience and agency of Native peoples in the face of these adversities. Despite the traumatic experiences of boarding schools, she underscores the ongoing efforts of Indigenous communities to reclaim, preserve, and revitalize their cultures, languages, and traditional knowledge.

In addition to these publications, works by Hayes Peter Mauro (2011), Lee Miller (2012), Diana Bahr (2014), Marie Battiste (2014), Melissa Parkhurst (2014), Peter Cozzens (2016), Jacqueline Fear-Segal and Susan Rose (2016) and Mary A. Stout (2017), have all provided important new insights into the boarding school experience by focusing on both the historical context and contemporary repercussions, including firsthand accounts of the experiences and traumas endured within these institutions.

Specifically on Haskell, the recent book *Embattled Lawrence Vol. 2: The Enduring Struggle for Freedom*, edited by Dennis Domer (2022), contains six chapters on the evolution of the school, including a reprint of my first chapter from *Voices from Haskell*, works by Kim Warren and Martha K. Robinson, as well as Haskell professor Eric P. Anderson's exploration of Haskell's history through the school newspaper *The Indian Leader*, Jeanne Klein and Charles Haines's chapter on Haskell's Cemetery, and Daniel R. Wildcat's personal reflections and vision for Haskell's future as a faculty member of thirty-four years: "Haskell: From Grade School to International University."

In addition to these scholarly works, the Phoenix-based Heard Museum's exhibition *Away from Home: American Indian Boarding School Stories* has attracted thousands of visitors since its opening in 2000—back then under the name *Remembering Our Indian School Days: The Boarding School Experience*. This powerful exhibit presents "works of art, archival material, first-person interviews and interactive elements in an immersive setting to encourage visitors to have a personal and visceral connection to the topics explored."[1] In print and on television, several recent articles in the *New York Times*, *Washington Post*, and other leading newspapers, as well as PBS documentaries, news segments, and talk shows—including the hour-long special "Unspoken: America's Native American Boarding Schools" (2016)—have brought the topic to a nationwide audience and provided context and commentary on current efforts for reparation and reconciliation.

All these scholarly publications, news articles, TV programs, and museum exhibits have no doubt significantly contributed to recent discussions about decolonizing education systems that have historically oppressed Indigenous cultures. They give voice to the survivors and their descendants, and illuminate the complexities of cultural survival, resilience, and the ongoing struggle for self-determination and cultural revitalization, which is happening not only throughout Indigenous communities and advocacy organizations, but also in our nation's courts, government departments, and legislatures.

A prominent Indigenous organization in this effort is the National Native American Boarding School Healing Coalition (NABS), which was established as a nonprofit organization in June 2012, following a gathering of leaders from the United States and Canada in 2011. Inspired by the work of the Canadian Truth and Reconciliation Commission, these leaders recognized the urgent need for a similar initiative in the United States. NABS was founded with the goal of creating and executing a nationwide strategy to raise public awareness and facilitate healing for the trauma inflicted upon individuals, families, communities, and Native American and Alaska Native Nations caused by the U.S. government's adoption and implementation of the Boarding School Policy of 1869. Initially, NABS operated under the fiscal sponsorship of the Native American Rights Fund (NARF) until it achieved financial independence in 2015. The organization's mission is: "To lead in the pursuit of understanding and addressing the ongoing trauma created by the U.S. Indian Boarding School policy."[2]

In 2013, NARF published a legal review about the history of the Indian boarding schools. In the review, NARF stated that the schools were part of a federal effort to erase Native identities through a "deliberate policy of ethnocide and cultural genocide."[3] NARF called for a commission to address the injustices committed in the boarding schools, like the Canadian Truth and Reconciliation Commission (TRC). The TRC on the Indian residential schools was established to address the historical injustices and abuses inflicted upon Indigenous children who attended residential schools in Canada. The TRC was officially launched in 2008 as part of the Indian Residential Schools Settlement Agreement, which aimed to address the legacy of the residential school system. The commission was tasked with documenting the history and impacts of the residential schools, hearing testimonies from survivors, and making recommendations for reconciliation between Indigenous and non-Indigenous peoples in Canada.

Over the course of its mandate, the TRC heard from thousands of survivors of residential schools, as well as from their families and communities. It collected statements, documents, and other evidence related to the operation and effects of the residential school system. The TRC also conducted research and organized public events to raise awareness about the history and legacy of the schools. In 2015, the TRC released its final report, which included a summary of its findings, recommendations for action, and a detailed account of the abuses suffered by Indigenous children in residential schools. The report called for acknowledgment of the harm done, apology, and reparations, as well as long-term efforts to address the ongoing impacts of colonialism on Indigenous communities. The TRC's work was a significant step in Canada's efforts to confront its colonial past and work toward reconciliation with Indigenous peoples. However, many of the Commission's recommendations remain to be fully implemented, and the process of reconciliation is ongoing.[4]

In January 2023, the Canadian government announced that it will pay 2.8 billion Canadian dollars in compensation to hundreds of Indigenous communities for decades of abuse suffered by First Nations, Métis, and Inuit children in residential schools. The settlement, which was approved by Canada's Federal Court in March 2023, is the result of a class action lawsuit by 325 Indigenous groups. The payout will be placed in a not-for-profit trust, independent of the government, and used to "revitalise Indigenous education, culture, and language—to support survivors in healing and reconnecting with their heritage."[5]

In 2015, the Native American Rights Fund issued a challenge to prominent church denominations, urging them to disclose the extent of their involvement and shed light on historical events. In a partial response to this call, the Friends or Quakers organized a conference in November 2016, titled "Quakers, First Nations, and American Indians from the 1650s to the 21st Century," featuring research contributions from various scholars. According to NARF, until 2019, neither the U.S. government nor other major churches that worked on the government's behalf had taken formal responsibility for the harm caused by the boarding school system.[6]

In 2019, NARF continued its work on the boarding school experience with the extensive literature review "Trigger Points: Current State of Research on History, Impacts, and Healing Related to the United States' Indian Industrial/Boarding School Policy," intended to provide "accurate and comprehensive information to the United States government, Indigenous Peoples and the American public about the purposes and human rights abuses of boarding school policies." The aim of the review was to show the links between the federal boarding school policy and modern impacts, to explain why past abuses are still important today, and to highlight promising approaches to mitigate the negative impacts of the schools. According to NARF, the publication was intended to "turn back institutionalized ignorance of what happened . . . [and] simply begin to uncover the truth of what has happened," serving as a resource for Indigenous communities, lawyers, and policy makers.[7]

During the past five years, several important developments took place that provide a glimmer of hope for Indigenous communities. In April of 2022, Pope Francis formally apologized for the Roman Catholic Church's involvement in the system of Canadian boarding schools that abused Indigenous children for 100 years, saying that he felt sorrow and shame for the role that

Catholics played "in the abuses you suffered and in the lack of respect shown for your identity, your culture and even your spiritual values." His apology was the first apology to the Indigenous people of Canada from a pope and was a reversal of Francis's earlier position.[8]

Recently, the U.S. government has taken a more active role in response to the historical trauma inflicted on Native American communities through the boarding school system. In June 2021, Secretary of the Interior Deb Haaland, the first Native American to serve as a cabinet secretary and a member of the Pueblo of Laguna, announced the Federal Boarding School Initiative, a comprehensive review of the troubled legacy of federal boarding school policies. She directed her department to identify boarding school facilities and examine potential burial sites near the schools, as well as the identities and tribal affiliations of the students who were taken to the schools. The initiative was prompted by the discovery of the remains of 215 children at the Kamloops Indian Residential School in British Columbia, Canada. According to Haaland,

> The Interior Department will address the inter-generational impact of Indian boarding schools to shed light on the unspoken traumas of the past, no matter how hard it will be. . . . I know that this process will be long and difficult. I know that this process will be painful. It won't undo the heartbreak and loss we feel. But only by acknowledging the past can we work toward a future that we're all proud to embrace.[9]

The work of the initiative comprised several phases, including the identification and collection of records and information related to the Department of Interior's own oversight and implementation of the Indian boarding school program; formal consultations with Tribal Nations, Alaska Native corporations, and Native Hawaiian organizations to clarify the processes and procedures for protecting identified burial sites and associated information; and the submission of a final written report on the investigation to Secretary Haaland by Assistant Secretary for Indian Affairs Bryan Newland. In this effort, the Department of the Interior partnered with the National Native American Boarding School Healing Coalition,[10] using NABS historical research to prepare the first comprehensive, 106-page-long Federal Indian Boarding School Initiative Investigative Report, which Assistant Secretary Newland submitted on April 1, 2022. In his letter to Secretary Haaland he writes:

This report, as I see it, is only a first step to acknowledge the experiences of Federal Indian boarding school children. It notes a desire from people across Indian Country and the Native Hawaiian Community to share their individual and family experiences within the Federal Indian boarding school system and the resulting impacts today. This report also presents an opportunity for us to reorient our Federal policies to support the revitalization of Tribal languages and cultural practices. This reorientation of Federal policy is necessary to counteract nearly two centuries of Federal policies aimed at the destruction of Tribal languages and cultures. In turn, we can help begin a healing process for Indian Country and the Native Hawaiian Community, and the United States, from the Alaskan tundra to the Florida everglades, and everywhere in between.[11]

On May 18, 2023, the Truth and Healing Commission on Indian Boarding School Policies Act (S.1723), cosponsored by Senator Elizabeth Warren (D-MA), was introduced in the U.S. Senate. If passed, the bill would establish the Truth and Healing Commission on Indian Boarding School Policies in the United States to investigate the impacts and ongoing effects of the Indian Boarding School Policies. According to the bill, "the commission must develop recommendations on ways to (1) protect unmarked graves and accompanying land protections; (2) support repatriation and identify the tribal nations from which children were taken; and (3) discontinue the removal of American Indian, Alaska Native, and Native Hawaiian children from their families and tribal communities by state social service departments, foster care agencies, and adoption agencies."[12]

The Truth and Healing Commission would conduct a full inquiry into the assimilative policies[13] of U.S. Indian boarding schools by examining the location of children, documenting ongoing impacts from U.S. Indian boarding schools, locating church and government records from the 521 known Indian boarding schools in the United States—408 of which have been directly funded or supported by the federal government, including 21 schools in Alaska and 7 schools in Hawaii—holding culturally appropriate public hearings to collect testimony from survivors and descendants, gathering institutional knowledge from subject matter experts, sharing findings publicly, and providing a final report with a list of recommendations for justice and healing.[14]

The National Native American Boarding School Healing Coalition (NABS) strongly supports the bill and has been working with members of Congress to reintroduce and pass the Truth and Healing Commission on Indian Boarding School Policies Act. In June 2023, the bill was amended and passed unanimously out of the Senate Committee on Indian Affairs led by Senators Brian Schatz (D-HI) and Lisa Murkowski (R-AK). Currently, S.1723 is being prepared for a full Senate vote. According to the NABS, "We are currently waiting for the House bill to be introduced, which is being led by Rep. Tom Cole (R-OK) and Rep. Sharice Davids (D-KS). Once it is introduced, the bill will need to be passed out of the House Committee on Natural Resources before going to the House floor for a full vote."[15]

NABS stresses the urgency of the bill, as

> we have a limited amount of time to hear directly from survivors and record their stories. A congressional commission will help ensure that accounts of Indian boarding schools—told by survivors, families, and presently undisclosed records—are preserved. It is essential that our children who were forced to attend these schools are not forgotten, and that this assimilative era of U.S. Indian policy is acknowledged so that future generations may understand the impact that this trauma has had in their community. Ultimately, we must know the truth so that we ensure that this never happens again.[16]

Since *Voices from Haskell* was published in 2008, Indigenous communities, scholars, organizations, and activists have tirelessly worked to raise awareness, address the injustices, and support survivors, descendants, and relatives of the boarding school experience. The U.S. government has finally committed itself to engaging in a nation-to-nation consultation with tribal nations, seeking their input and collaboration in these investigations and healing efforts, and to provide support services for affected communities, including mental health resources, cultural preservation programs, and other forms of support for survivors and their descendants. And in Congress, discussions about allocating funds and resources to support these initiatives and provide restitution for the harm caused by the schools are ongoing.

Collecting and sharing the stories of boarding school students and the counter voices of Indigenous peoples is an essential part of healing and reconciliation—the process by which Indigenous communities, families, and individuals create meaning and grieve from boarding school experiences.[17] As one of the Bureau of Indian Affairs' major off-reservation schools and the premiere tribal university in the United States, Haskell played and continues to play a central role in this experience and the stories and voices of Haskell's students—past and present—deserve to be heard. Haskell Indian Nations University's Vision 2020 states that "Haskell is a unique and diverse inter-tribal university committed to the advancement of sovereignty, self-determination, and the inherent rights of tribes."[18] Preserving and sharing Haskell's history and student experiences are an integral part of this vision, and it is my sincere hope that this paperback edition of *Voices from Haskell* will reinvigorate interest in this topic and make Haskell's fascinating story, filled with heartbreak as well as triumphs, accessible to a larger audience and new generation of readers.

Myriam Vučković, PhD
Washington, DC
June 2024

Notes

1. From the museum's website: "Away from Home," Heard Museum, accessed February 2, 2024, https://heard.org/exhibition/away-from-home-american-indian-boarding-school-stories/.
2. "About Us," National Native American Boarding School Healing Coalition, accessed February 3, 2024, https://boardingschoolhealing.org/about-us/.
3. Native American Rights Fund, quoted in "Trigger Points: Current State of Research on History, Impacts, and Healing Related to the United States' Indian Industrial/Boarding School Policy" (Boulder, CO, 2019), 1.
4. See Reimer and Chrismas, *Our Shared Future*.
5. National Indigenous Times, "Canadian Government to Pay $3 Billion in Compensation to First Nations, Métis and Inuit Survivors of Residential Schools," January 24, 2023, https://nit.com.au/24-01-2023/4792/canadian-government-to-pay-3-billion-in-compensation-to-first-nations-metis-and-inuit-survivors-of-residential-schools; CBC News, "$2.8-Billion Settlement Reached in Class Action Lawsuit over Residential Schools," updated January 21, 2023, https://www.cbc.ca/news/canada/british-columbia/residential-school-band-class-action-settlement-1.6722014.
6. Native American Rights Fund, "Trigger Points," 1.
7. Native American Rights Fund, "Trigger Points," 1–4.

8. Elisabetta Povoledo and Ian Austen, "'I Feel Shame': Pope Apologizes to Indigenous People of Canada," *New York Times*, April 1, 2022, https://www.nytimes.com/2022/04/01/world/europe/pope-apology-indigenous-people-canada.html.
9. "Secretary Haaland Announces Federal Indian Boarding School Initiative," Department of the Interior, updated February 15, 2023, https://www.doi.gov/pressreleases/secretary-haaland-announces-federal-indian-boarding-school-initiative.
10. Memorandum of Understanding Between the U.S. Department of the Interior and National Native American Boarding School Healing Coalition, December 7, 2021.
11. Assistant Secretary Bryan Newland, "Federal Indian Boarding School Initiative Investigative Report," U.S. Department of the Interior, April 1, 2022, p. 3.
12. Truth and Healing Commission on Indian Boarding School Policies Act, S.1723, 118th Cong. (2023–2024), May 18, 2023, https://www.congress.gov/bill/118th-congress/senate-bill/1723.
13. Specifically, the 1887 Dawes Act, which sought to integrate Native American tribes into mainstream American society by parceling tribal lands into individual plots, promoting private land ownership and agriculture. The Dawes Act led to significant loss of Indigenous land due to coercion and manipulation. Federal Indian Boarding schools were aligned with the Dawes Act as part of a broader assimilation strategy, aiming to forcibly assimilate Native American children into mainstream culture, erasing their Indigenous identities, and preparing them for lives as individual landowners as mandated by the Dawes Act.
14. NABS, Factsheet on the Truth and Healing Commission on Indian Boarding Schools Policy Act, updated April 18, 2024, https://boardingschoolhealing.org/truthcommission/.
15. NABS, Status of the Bill, updated April 18, 2024, https://boardingschoolhealing.org/truthcommission/.
16. NABS, Factsheet on the Truth and Healing Commission on Indian Boarding Schools Policy Act, updated April 18, 2024, https://boardingschoolhealing.org/truthcommission/.
17. Native American Rights Fund, "Trigger Points," 1–4.
18. "Mission Statement," Haskell Indian Nations University, accessed February 4, 2024, https://haskell.edu/about/vision/.

Works Cited

Archuleta, Margaret L., Brenda J. Child, and K. Tsianina Lomawaima. *Away from Home: American Indian Boarding School Experiences, 1879–2000*. Tucson, AZ: University of Arizona Press, 2016.

Bahr, Diana Meyers. *The Students of Sherman Indian School: Education and Native Identity since 1892*. Norman, OK: University of Oklahoma Press, 2014.

Battiste, Marie, ed. *Reclaiming Indigenous Voice and Vision*. Vancouver, BC: University of British Columbia Press, 2014.

Child, Brenda, and Brian Klopotek, eds. *Indian Subjects: Hemispheric Perspectives on the History of Indigenous Education*. Santa Fe, NM: SAR Press, 2014.

Cozzens, Peter. *The Earth Is Weeping: The Epic Story of the Indian Wars for the American West*. New York: Vintage Books, 2016.

Domer, Dennis, ed. *Embattled Lawrence Vol. 2: The Enduring Struggle for Freedom*. Lawrence, KS: Douglas County Historical Society Watkins Museum of History, 2022.

Fear-Segal, Jacqueline, and Susan D. Rose. *Carlisle Indian Industrial School: Indigenous Histories, Memories, and Reclamations*. Lincoln: University of Nebraska Press, 2016.

Lomawaima, K. Tsianina, Bryan McKinley Jones Brayboy, and Teresa L. McCarty. "Editors' Introduction to the Special Issue: Native American Boarding School Stories." *Journal of American Indian Education* 57, no. 1 (2018): 1–10. https://doi.org/10.1353/jaie.2018.a798593.

Mauro, Hayes Peter. *The Art of Americanization at the Carlisle Indian School*. Albuquerque: University of New Mexico Press, 2011.

Miller, Lee. *From the Heart: Voices of the American Indian*. Lincoln: University of Nebraska Press, 2012.

Native American Rights Fund. "Trigger Points: Current State of Research on History, Impacts, and Healing Related to the United States' Indian Industrial/Boarding School Policy," Boulder, CO, 2019.

Parkhurst, Melissa. *To Win the Indian Heart. Music at Chemawa Indian School*. Corvallis, OR: Oregon State University Press, 2014.

Regan, Paulette. *Unsettling the Settler Within: Indian Residential Schools, Truth Telling, and Reconciliation in Canada*. Vancouver: University of British Columbia Press, 2010.

Reimer, Laura E., and Robert Chrismas, eds. *Our Shared Future: Windows into Canada's Reconciliation Journey*. New York: Lexington Books, 2020.

Stout, Mary. A. *Native American Boarding Schools*. Charleston, SC: Arcadia Publishing, 2017.

U.S. Department of the Interior. "Federal Indian Boarding School Initiative Investigative Report." Washington, DC, 2022.

Acknowledgments

Many individuals and institutions have contributed to this book, and in the course of researching and writing I have benefited from the help and advice of numerous wonderful and insightful people. First, I would like to thank my advisers and professors at the University of Kansas, who initially encouraged and supported my curiosity of Haskell and Indian educational history and gave me invaluable advice and guidance along the way: Bill Tuttle, Norm Yetman, Joane Nagel, Lucy Tapahonso, Cheryl Lester, Donald Fixico, and Sandra Grey. I would also like to thank my current academic home, Georgetown University, and particularly Bernhard Liese, for generously supporting the last stages of this project.

I also owe my gratitude for the help and support of archivists and librarians at the following institutions: the National Archives in Kansas City and in Washington, D.C., Haskell Indian Nations University, the Doris Duke Collection at the University of Oklahoma, the Kenneth Spencer Research Library at the University of Kansas, and the Kansas Historical Society in Topeka. I am particularly grateful for the criticism, encouragement, and valuable suggestions of two scholars who generously gave of their time in reading the manuscript: David Adams and Clyde Ellis.

Lastly, I want to express my heartfelt gratitude to my family and friends for their unwavering support, encouragement, and patience throughout the journey of bringing this book to fruition. To my parents and sister, whose belief in me and support during my graduate studies at the University of Kansas have been invaluable. To my incredible KU friends, whose camaraderie made the years of research and writing in Lawrence both productive and very enjoyable. And to my husband, Robert, and my sons, Ben, Lukas, and Patrick, whose love and inspiration infuse purpose into everything I do.

Introduction

> My school life began in the government boarding school at Blackrock, New Mexico. When I reached the sixth grade I decided to enter Haskell Institute, to receive a better education in order that I might be a help to my Indian people. My hopes and ambitions are to be a carpenter and a mechanic. My future plan is to return to my home and make use of my trade and show my people what a returned student can do.[1]
> Warren Ondelacy, Zuni

Voices from Haskell is the story of Haskell's boarding school years during the late nineteenth and early twentieth centuries. By drawing as much as possible from the students' voices as transmitted in letters and oral accounts, this book paints a detailed picture of daily life at the school. Indian children at boarding schools such as Haskell lived in "total institutions," designed to remold them both culturally and psychologically. At its core, the history of federal off-reservation boarding schools is the story of indigenous youth struggling to retain a sense of dignity and Indian identity. As Haskell's records reveal, many of the children refused to be victimized and created a subculture of accommodation and resistance that bears testimony to their enormous creativity, adaptability, and perseverance in the face of the federal educational crusade. I hope that this exploration of Haskell's past will help all of us to remember this powerful chapter in human history. For those who stop and listen, the voices of Haskell's students, past and present, reveal a century of hope, loss, struggle, and triumph for the indigenous peoples of the United States.

This study is built upon the narratives of individual lives, but it is guided by a wide body of cultural theory. Understanding the Indian boarding school experience in theoretical terms is a multidimensional endeavor. On the one hand, one needs to look critically at the role of boarding schools as "total institutions," as tools and tactics of the federal government, employed to dominate and reeducate American Indian children. The phenomenon of the boarding school as a hegemonic structure has to be placed in the context of broader political, economic, and cultural developments during the eighteenth, nineteenth, and early twentieth centuries, marking the shift from a mercantile economy to an industrial system. On the other hand, one needs to examine critically the gap that existed between government expectations and the realities at schools such as Haskell, Chilocco, and Carlisle. Analyzing questions related to cultural construction and cultural survival, as well as to the formation of ethnic identities, can give valuable insights into the complex and sometimes conflicting experiences of Indian boarding school students. The theoretical works of Joane Nagel, Stephen Cornell, James Scott, Michel Foucault, Antonio Gramsci, Raymond Williams, and others shed light on the complex cultural processes involved and help to explore questions related to hegemony, discipline, resistance, assimilation, cultural survival, and the construction of ethnic identities.

Even though Indian policymakers and boarding school administrators had clear goals in mind—assimilation, education, and subordination—federal educational policy rarely achieved its goals and encountered multiple layers of resistance. Investigating the students' responses to their schooling reveals that contrary to government expectations, there was no single boarding school experience. Although Indian educators' strategies, tactics, and goals were aimed at turning indigenous children into obedient and productive members of the rural and urban working class, students were everything but passive victims in the government's assimilation campaign. Indian boarding schools such as Haskell did not merely serve the interests of domination and inequality; they were important arenas of contestation and resistance, where Indians and whites engaged in complex cultural encounters and constantly negotiated cultural and ethnic boundaries.

Looking at the Indian side of the story supports this argument. Indigenous students' reactions ranged from complete rejection to enthusiasm, and most felt ambivalent about their boarding school years. They were constantly forced to negotiate their adherence to tribal values and practices that were an integral part of their identities as American Indians and that often had no currency in the dominant Anglo-American world. Few students readily accepted the civilization-savagery paradigm promoted by Haskell's administrators, and ultimately the school was not able to destroy their Indian identity. Many students' family ties remained strong, and individual students made choices about which aspects of white civilization and education they would accept and which they would not. Even students who adapted willingly to the regimentation of the school adopted a dual identity, often acting as culture brokers throughout their lives. Haskell students had bittersweet memories of their school years and recalled negative as well as many positive aspects of their experience. The boarding school experience cannot be understood simply in terms of acculturation and resistance. It was not an "either or" phenomenon but needs to be understood in terms of the students' conflictual identities composed of both subordinate and dominant values and practices. The responses of individual students depended on a variety of factors such as the length of their stays at school, their ages at the time of entrance, and, especially, their family backgrounds. It made a great difference whether the children attended the school voluntarily with the support of their parents or whether they were forced to attend. Also, students who had attended other schools before their arrival at boarding schools suffered less from culture shock than those who came directly from an Indian-only environment. Children of boarding school alumni had the greatest advantage, knowing already from their parents what to expect and usually benefiting from stronger family support.[2]

Some earlier studies of the boarding school experience have treated the issues of assimilation and resistance as somehow separate, even devoting distinct chapters to each topic. In order to come to a more comprehensive understanding of the students' struggles, however, an integrative approach is required. To understand the conflicts experienced by indigenous students, it is helpful to recognize that the assimilation processes that took place in some spheres of students' lives did not rule out ethnic resilience in others. Boarding schools were important sites of cultural contact and negotiation, where more often than not Indian students selectively incorporated those aspects of Anglo-American culture that would ensure their individual and collective survival and well-being.

In the context of the boarding school experience, a constructionist approach to the understanding of ethnicity and culture proves useful in explaining the survival of native cultures and identities under extreme assimilationist pressure. Sociologists such as Joane Nagel and Stephen Cornell interpret ethnic identification, organization, and action as dynamic, situational, and fluid processes. Ethnicity, which serves as a means for the construction of internal and external boundaries and the production of meaning, is socially constructed. Ethnic boundaries, identities, and cultures, the basic building blocks of ethnicity, are defined, negotiated, and produced both by ethnic group members themselves and by external processes and actors. Ethnic group formation and change are products of human action, social circumstances, and historical events. Therefore, ethnicity is constantly undergoing reconstruction and redefinition.[3]

With this theoretical framework in mind, we can see the question of whether indigenous students became acculturated or assimilated through white schooling, or whether they resisted, in a new light. Certainly the boarding school experience changed Indian students. But in many instances it changed them according to Indian needs and traditions. It would be wrong to assume that students who willingly accepted the school's dominant ideology lost all their "Indianness" in the course of doing so. The integration of foreign customs, new technologies, and new modes of thought already had a century-long tradition among indigenous peoples, who in the face of European encroachment were constantly forced to balance cultural change with cultural continuity. Again and again, indigenous people used federal Indian education to further their own needs, including the preservation of identity, and proved more receptive to learning and more creative in culturally appropriating their education than white policymakers ever imagined.[4]

It is difficult to imagine, though, how any child could have withstood the influence of the dominant ideology completely. The testimonies collected in this and other studies give insight into the hegemonic processes taking place and reveal how difficult the negotiation between boarding school ideals, Indian heritage, and real life choices could be. The extent to which the children experienced internal conflicts between their desires to be "Indian" versus "white" depended on numerous factors such as family ties, age, personal experiences with teachers, fellow students, and modern life in general. Many children became bicultural, at least on a functional level, and over time, the boarding school experience came to be regarded as an integral part of the Indian experience and of American Indian culture in general.

Contemporary critics of the boarding schools claimed that Indians did not become "civilized" through their schooling and that upon returning to their reservations they went "back to the blanket." What policymakers and school authorities had not anticipated was that Indian students were active participants in the acculturation drama. The nature of student responses was far less predictable than educators had originally assumed or were ready to admit. Indigenous youth resisted victimization and developed a subculture of resistance and accommodation that helped them to mentally survive an alien and often hostile environment. The result was that Indian students not only survived and successfully retained elements of their tribal cultures but also created something new—a boarding school culture that helped to break down traditional barriers to a common Indian consciousness. As Indian Commissioner Thomas Morgan accurately pointed out in 1889, the boarding school environment "breaks the shackles of tribal provincialism."[5] Morgan had anticipated, however, that the discouragement of tribal ties and indigenous cultural activities would automatically lead to complete assimilation into white society. He did not predict that many cultural practices would survive "undercover" and develop into new cultural forms such as the Native American Church, as well as into an Indian political consciousness as expressed in the formation of the first intertribal political organization of the twentieth century, the Society of American Indians.[6]

The students' reactions toward the dominating power of school officials and to the military-like routine are much in line with our present knowledge about power relations, hegemony, resistance, and subordination in general.[7] Haskell's strict discipline and regimentation strengthened and mobilized the students' agency, expressed through their active and passive resistance, their loyalty to their families and their fellow students, the retention of tribal identities and memberships, and the evolution of a supratribal sense of identity.

The National Archives in Kansas City, Missouri, hold countless valuable records on Haskell's early history, but few scholars have so far taken advantage of these documents. *Voices from Haskell* is the first book-length study of the school from its founding through the first quarter of the twentieth century. For more than 124 years, Haskell has touched the lives of tens of thousands of Indian students and their families. *Voices from Haskell* is dedicated to all of Haskell's students, to their strength and resilience and their contributions to the school's prominent place in Native American history. Since the introduction of the school's commercial department in 1895, Haskell has offered more to Indian students than most government schools. During the early twentieth century, the school's business, normal, and nursing programs gave Native American students the opportunity to advance beyond a work life as domestic servants and laborers. Indigenous students and their families valued these opportunities, and many alumni chose to send their own children back to Lawrence, a testimony of their positive boarding school experience. Generations of Haskellites have helped to transform the school from its assimilationist beginnings into a visionary place that celebrates Native American cultures and integrates the perspectives of American Indian and Alaskan peoples into the curriculum. Haskell is the only former government boarding school that has evolved into a four-year university, offering bachelor degrees in American Indian studies, environmental science, business administration, and elementary teacher education. Through the years, the school has maintained its unique intertribal character, providing a culturally diverse learning environment for more than 1,000 Indian students from 150 tribes each year. For more than a century, Haskell alumni have assumed positions of political, economic, and intellectual leadership in their communities and tribes. Building on the achievements of generations of former students, Haskell Indian Nations University strives to "empower American Indian and Alaska Native scholars for leadership and service to sovereign first nations and the world," and it is the school's vision to assist "tribal constituents in their efforts to address social, cultural, educational, and environmental development for the twenty-first century."[8]

Voices from Haskell focuses on the early period of the institution, from its beginnings in 1884 as an elementary school, the United States Industrial Training Institute, to the 1920s, when a high school curriculum was introduced and Haskell became the first and for several years only Indian boarding school to offer a full four-year high school education. The book is organized along thematic lines rather than chronologically, allowing for an in-depth analysis of topics that directly affected the students, such as the school's curriculum, health issues, gender differences, the children's extracurricular activities, accommodation and resistance, and the children's life after Haskell.

The task of writing a social and cultural history of Haskell's boarding school years from 1884 to the 1920s would have been impossible without the rich resources of the National Archive–Central Plains Region (NACPR) in Kansas City, Missouri. The written documents on Haskell's past comprise an intimidating total of 530 cubic feet of boxes.[9] The most interesting and helpful files to understand Haskell's history are the Individual Student Case files, as well as most of the Correspondence Files, holding many of the letters between students and parents, administrators and students, and administrators and parents or reservation agencies. In many cases theses letters contain private information on the students' experiences at Haskell and on their home environment; their relationships with parents, teachers, and school employees; their health; and their lives after Haskell. A smaller but similar collection of Haskell documents and photographs is housed at the National Archives in Washington, D.C. (NADC), including the annual inspection reports of the school, which reveal important details about conditions at the school.[10] In addition to the National Archives, Haskell Indian Nations University holds all published yearbooks in Haskell's history and a complete set of the school's newspaper, the *Indian Leader*, which provides an inexhaustible, though not unbiased, resource for detailed information on the school's activities and population. Another source of information on the school is local newspapers such as the *Lawrence Daily Journal* and documents in the Kansas Collection of the Kenneth Spencer Research Library at the University of Kansas as well as at the Kansas State Historical Society in Topeka, Kansas.

The time frame of this study precluded personal interviews with Haskell alumni of the period, even though an objective of the study was to uncover as much of the feelings, attitudes, and actions of the students as possible. Clearly, not every aspect of the students' lives can be gathered from written documents or the few published memoirs of boarding school alumni alone. Recorded interviews conducted with Haskell alumni from 1967 to 1970 therefore provided a valuable resource, adding to our understanding of how former students have remembered and negotiated their boarding school past. These interview transcripts belong to the Doris Duke Oral History Collection, part of the Western History Collection at the University of Oklahoma, and include a number of firsthand accounts of Haskell alumni who attended the school during its early period. As historian David Wallace Adams has rightly pointed out though, *experiencing* an event is quite different from *having experienced* it. As historians we constantly face this dilemma and can only hope that by skillfully combining as many relevant sources as possible, we get as close to the children's experiences as possible.[11] Building the narrative around the students' voices allows the reader to have access to Haskell's history through the everyday life of its inhabitants. Throughout this book, the children's actual names were used as much as possible. Although this is a sensitive issue, especially since living memory runs deep in indigenous communities, individual identities and forgotten records are crucial to Haskell's story. Using people's names and biographical data gives dignity to the people who lived through the boarding school experiences; it makes them the agents and actors of this book, rather than mere objects of a scholarly investigation. In some instances, however, where medical and legal issues are involved, names were either omitted or pseudonyms used, in order to protect the students' and their families' privacy.[12]

Considering that off-reservation boarding schools have affected thousands of Indian children and must be regarded as a major influence in shaping the Native American experience and identity during the late nineteenth and early twentieth centuries, they have until recently received comparatively little scholarly attention. Since the late 1980s, however, the study of American Indian boarding schools has developed into one of the richest fields in Native American history. The books and articles that have appeared since 1988 have contributed substantially to our understanding of the boarding school's place in Indian lives and in the study of American Indian history. Since the 1980s, David W. Adams, Robert A. Trennert, Frederick E. Hoxie, Basil H. Johnston, and Margaret Connell Szasz, among others, have pointed the way to important new approaches for examining Native American education. Their works go beyond discussions of facts and policy and recognize the need to place Indian education in its broader cultural and historical context. These authors—and even more so scholars such as K. Tsianina Lomawaima, Clyde Ellis, Brenda J. Child, Scott Riney, Sally Hyer, Benjamin G. Rader, Jacqueline Fear-Segal, Kim Warren, Esther Burnett Horne and Sally McBeth, and Michael C. Coleman—have placed the Indian students and their families at the center of their discussions and have skillfully combined oral histories, long-neglected memoirs, and photographs with historical narratives to produce a more inclusive understanding of schooling's complex cultural consequences. Many questions concerning the dynamics of culture formation, the construction of ethnic identities, and the legacy of the boarding school experience still remain open, however, and the stories of some major institutions, including Haskell, remain practically untold. Apart from Brenda Child's sensitive 1998 account, *Boarding School Seasons,* and Theresa Milk's 2007 study on Haskell's earliest years, the only academic studies on Haskell have been written by graduate students as part of their degree requirements.[13] *Voices from Haskell* is meant to fill this important gap in Native American scholarship. The goal of this book is to give a comprehensive and sensitive account of the life of Haskell's students from 1884 until the late 1920s and to tell the story of the cultural encounters and contests that occurred at one of the nation's most prominent federal Indian boarding schools.

CHAPTER ONE

Beginnings

> When this work shall be completed the Indian will cease to exist as a man, apart from other men, a stumbling block in the pathway of civilization; his empty pride of separate nationality will have been destroyed, and in its place the greater blessings which he or his friends could desire will be his,—an honorable absorption into the common life of the people of the United States.
> *Herbert Welsh, executive secretary*
> *of the Indian Rights Association, 1882*[1]

From the time Europeans began to colonize the North American continent, the introduction of formal, European-style education became an integral part of their attempt to "civilize" and subdue the continent's indigenous population. Europeans acted upon their conviction that among American Indians, an education system had not previously existed. To them, indigenous peoples were heathens and savages, whose souls needed to be saved and whose pagan beliefs and customs had to be destroyed. The assumption that Native Americans neither educated their children nor had anything to teach was devastating to native peoples.[2] In Indian societies, learning was regarded as a lifelong, holistic process that included the oral tradition, the concept of learning by observing and doing, and especially the exposure to the words and lessons of the tribe's elders. Values, moral instructions, traditions, and a sense of history were passed down from generation to generation through storytelling and the children's participation in tribal ceremonies.[3] This combination of listening, observing, and hands-on experience did not fit the European definition of formal education, and as early as the 1600s, French, Spanish, and British missionaries and colonists established formal schools for indigenous children along the eastern and western seaboards. Throughout the colonial period and the first half of the nineteenth century, however, Indian education was never truly systematized. Apart from the educational systems among the southeastern tribes,[4] native schooling was administered by churches and missionaries and reached only a limited number of indigenous children. This rapidly changed in the second half of the nineteenth century as the federal government became increasingly involved.[5]

During a time when American society experienced a great influx of immigration, assimilation and the concept of "Anglo-conformity" seemed to provide the solution for a country that was becoming more and more pluralistic. In order to preserve Anglo-Saxon hegemony, the threatening "other," immigrant and Indian alike, had to become Americanized.[6] Protestant ideology, the civilization-savagism paradigm, and the continuing hunger for Indian land provided the ideological backdrop for the nation's emerging Indian education policy. Protestant ideology consisted of a mix of religious and economic core values and beliefs that included Protestantism, individualization (capitalism), and Americanization (republicanism). Schools were seen as the natural environment where Indian children would absorb these core values and beliefs. The civilization-savagism paradigm reinforced Protestant ideology by expressing the belief that Indians were a doomed race and could be saved only by embracing American civilization. Native American children were regarded as savages but were thought to be capable of progress once removed from their home environment and exposed to white schooling. Schools, and especially off-reservation boarding schools, were thought to be able to speed up the evolutionary process, civilizing Indians within one generation, while leading to their complete political and cultural subjugation.[7] The new federal Indian policy that emerged after 1870 had three major components that reflected Protestant ideology, the civilization-savagism paradigm, and the desire to further dispossess Native Americans of their land: compulsory education, allotment of tribal lands, and religious replacement.

Up to this point, the federal government had left the task of educating Indian children mostly to missionaries, churches, and private organizations. Only in the wake of the "campaign to assimilate the Indians"[8] did the federal government assume a major role in Indian education. By 1879, eight years after the treaty-making period had ended, an estimated 500 teachers in 292 day and 64 boarding schools already taught 13,343 students: a little more than a third of all school-aged Indian children at the time. That same year, after experimenting with the education of Indian prisoners at Fort Marion in Florida and Hampton Institute in Virginia, General Richard Henry Pratt founded the first off-reservation boarding school for Indians in Carlisle, Pennsylvania. In the following years, Carlisle Indian School served as a model for a number of boarding schools, including Genoa Indian School in Nebraska, Chilocco Indian School in Oklahoma, and Haskell Institute in Kansas.[9]

The federal Indian boarding schools aimed to remedy the "flaws" of the reservation day schools: their proximity to the children's communities and the daily exposure of the students to the "savage ways" of their people. Removal from the home environment and separation from their families were hence regarded as prerequisites for the children's successful assimilation. In the 1880s and 1890s, many children were forced to leave home against their and their parents' wills and were taken to boarding school at a very early age, sometimes as young as three, four, or five years old. During this period, the government especially targeted tribes participating in the Ghost Dance religion, which had spread across the Great Plains.

The boarding schools were supposed to "kill the Indian and save the man," as Richard Henry Pratt proclaimed during the 1880s.[10] Besides basic academic education, most schools focused on agricultural, industrial, domestic, and manual training in various arts and crafts. In addition, the children had to learn the "white man's ways" and manners. The children were expected to renounce their Indian origins and to succumb to a strict, military-like routine. For many children the boarding school experience was traumatic, and even though some students emerged from the boarding schools as eminent Indian spokespeople, many others could not find their way in either culture and became a "lost people." For many graduates, going back to the reservation was no real option. They had lost their ability to speak their native languages and had become alienated from life in a communal society. On the other hand, Anglo society provided very few opportunities for Indian youth.[11] Despite those problems, for many poor or orphaned children the boarding schools provided the only hope for a home and an education. Many students have bittersweet memories of their school years and recall negative as well as positive aspects of their experience. The sense of community among the children was very strong, and in many cases indigenous cultural practices were kept alive "under cover" and against all odds.[12] An unexpected outcome of intermixing children from diverse tribal and cultural backgrounds was the development of a shared identity as American Indians that transcended tribal boundaries. English as a common language allowed students to exchange their experiences and to gain a wider perspective of their own identity. Intertribal marriages became more frequent, and new ideas and beliefs, such as the Native American Church, spread across tribal boundaries and wide geographic distances. The irony of the boarding school experience lies in the fact that the very institutions trying to destroy Indian cultures and identity also contributed to their strengthening and survival.[13]

The second component of the new federal Indian policy, the allotment of tribal lands, was intended to break up traditional tribal structures and to speed up the dissolution of the western reservations. Under the General Allotment Act of 1887, also known as the Dawes Allotment Act, each family head was eligible for a 160-acre plot of land. In addition, each single adult would receive 80 acres and each child 40 acres of land. The allotment policy had severe, irreversible effects. It led to a drastic reduction of land owned by indigenous people, and it can be regarded as a major step in the history of white encroachment on native lands. Between 1887 and 1933, more than 90 million acres of Indian land were lost, reducing the native land base from 150 million to a mere 53 million acres. The intended effect of making Indians self-sufficient did not occur. On the contrary, Indian agriculture even declined and led to a period of economic deterioration.[14]

The last pillar of the federal government's attempt to assimilate indigenous people was the replacement of indigenous religions and worldviews with Christianity. Previously the work of missionaries had been instrumental in dealing with Native Americans; by the 1870s, however, Christianization became a federal policy. Under President Ulysses S. Grant (1869–1877), each reservation was assigned to a different denomination responsible for the spiritual life of its inhabitants. A Code of Religious Offenses outlawed the practice of Indian religions and forbade the performance of traditional rituals such as potlatches or the annual Sun Dance. But as with the boarding school experience and allotment, the effects of religious replacement were not always as expected and hoped for by reformers and policymakers. Many traditional customs and rituals lived on and were performed in secrecy. In addition, many new forms of both syncretic or traditional origin, such as the Native American Church and the Ghost Dance religion, were created and attracted thousands of followers.[15]

During the last decade of the nineteenth century, the original assimilationist ideas of many Christian reformers,[16] based on the universalist assumption that American Indians could indeed become civilized and equal citizens, became increasingly contested. This shift in public attitudes, as well as federal Indian policy, resulted from several factors. On the one hand, the assimilation campaign had not worked as expected. As the new century approached, Native Americans were still largely poor, uneducated, and in many ways traditional. They had not assimilated into white America within one generation, as reformers such as Richard Henry Pratt had anticipated. On the other hand, the closing of the frontier, industrialization, imperialism, and the spread of scientific racism and social evolutionism led to a different sentiment toward Indians and minorities in general. Many saw American Indians as a vanishing race and as part of the national heritage that evoked a feeling of nostalgia for the old pioneer days and a Wild West that was gone forever. Indigenous peoples were "backward but beautiful."[17] The described attitudinal shift found its expression in a series of policy changes, court decisions, and laws that led to further loss of native land.[18]

In the field of Indian education, it led to the lowering of expectations and to a change in emphasis. After the turn of the century, many schools replaced their academic syllabi with curricula stressing vocational training. Estelle Reel, who became superintendent of Indian education in 1898, was a strong adherent of social evolution and believed that indigenous children, just like African American and other nonwhite children, did not have the same intellectual capabilities as white children. She promoted an education focused on manual training. According to Reel's vision, the children would spend most of the day outside the classroom, learning trades such as shoemaking, carpentry, plowing, livestock raising, cooking, and cleaning. They would only receive a basic education in English and mathematics and the average period of school attendance would be reduced to only six or seven years. Although Reel's policies certainly reflected her limited view of Indian capabilities, she did introduce a number of positive changes with regard to teaching methods, including object lessons and English language instruction that was not solely based on recitation or memorization. She encouraged teachers to find out about their students' interests, home lives, and personal characteristics and also showed more respect for the children's native languages than her predecessors. In 1905 she wrote that "the child's natural love for his mother tongue must be respected" and that "no child shall be forced to drop out or forget the language of his ancestors."[19]

These changes did not come about without criticism. Former superintendent of Indian education Thomas Jefferson Morgan strongly objected to the shift in educational emphasis, regarding it as a condemnation to permanent inequality. Morgan's outrage illuminates the distance between the assimilationist ideas during his administration and the new "realism" of Estelle Reel. By 1912, however, most Indian schools had adopted a new curriculum centered around vocational training in order to prepare students for a working-class life on the margins of American society.[20]

It should be noted, though, that this development fell in line with the larger educational debate taking place in America at the time. Educators and philosophers such as John Dewey and David Snedden, both professors at Columbia University, debated about the virtues and dangers of tracking students into vocational training classes, a strategy that affected not only Indian students but also—disproportionately—children from immigrant, African-American, and rural backgrounds.[21] By the 1920s, the belief in the big "melting pot" had vanished. The meaning of the term *assimilation* had shifted from full integration to "knowing one's place and fulfilling one's role," in order to preserve a social order that granted minorities only a marginal place.[22] Indigenous peoples, just like African Americans and many of the new immigrants, had found their place in American society, a place filled with poverty, hardship, and suffering, as the 1928 Meriam Report revealed.

The Meriam Report was based on investigations conducted in 1926 by the Institute for Government Research at Johns Hopkins University at the request of Secretary of the Interior Hubert Work. It became known by the name of the principal investigator, University of Chicago professor Lewis Meriam. The staff included an agricultural economist, a medical doctor, a social worker specializing in women and family life, and Winnebago educator and Yale graduate Henry Roe Cloud as "Indian advisor" as well as Will Carson Ryan Jr., a Swarthmore College professor and advocate of progressive education who was instrumental in preparing the Indian school section of the report. The group visited sixty-four of the existing seventy-eight government boarding schools and concluded that most boarding schools did not even provide minimum standards of care for their students—a fact that Indian parents and students had known for decades. The report strongly criticized the philosophy underlying the boarding school system. It concluded that "to take Indian children, even very young children, as completely as possible away from their home and family life, is at variance with modern views of education and social work, which regard the home and family as essential social institutions from which it is generally undesirable to uproot children." The Meriam Report called for the establishment of more community schools and the support of native cultures and criticized boarding schools for being inferior to the "standards set by reasonably progressive white communities." The report argued that through their discipline and routine, boarding schools actually destroyed the students' independence and initiative instead of promoting it.[23] The Meriam Report had a major influence on policymakers in the following years, leading to many of the reforms introduced during the Indian New Deal under Commissioner of Indian Affairs John Collier from 1933 to 1945.

Ironically, the campaign that was designed to assimilate Native Americans into white America helped to create a more pluralistic society instead. Through their marginalization, indigenous nations were able to survive and to develop modern incarnations of their traditional cultures.[24] Also, it should be emphasized that despite the rhetoric of the federal government, only a fraction of all school-aged Indian children attended government schools. Schools were especially scarce in the West, and in 1901, for instance, fewer than 10 percent of all Navajo children attended schools. The U.S. Congress did not provide the necessary funds to develop a comprehensive Indian school system, thereby indirectly preventing the outright extermination of many indigenous cultures. Despite the efforts of the U.S. government, missionaries, and teachers to eradicate them, native languages, religious practices, and social and political forms were not only continued by indigenous communities but passed on from generation to generation. Contrary to federal desires and rhetoric, considerably more Indian children were educated, however secretly, through indigenous rather than Anglo-American institutions until a point well into the twentieth century.[25]

The immediate success and great publicity surrounding General Pratt's educational experiment at Carlisle led policymakers to support the opening of similar off-reservation boarding schools across the western and central part of the United States. In 1880, only one year after Carlisle opened its doors, a second school in Forest Grove, Oregon, known as Salem Training School, was established. It was followed in 1883 by a third school, the Howard Institute in Fort Stevenson, North Dakota. On May 10, 1882, the Forty-seventh Congress passed the Indian Appropriation Bill for the fiscal year 1883. This bill appropriated $115,000 for the three nonreservation schools already in existence (Carlisle, Howard, and Salem) and designated another $150,000 for the establishment of three more schools in Genoa, Nebraska; Chilocco, Indian Territory (Oklahoma); and Lawrence, Kansas.[26]

The selection of Lawrence as one of the sites resulted from the lobbying efforts of Dudley Chase Haskell, representative for Kansas's Second Congressional District and chairman of the House Committee on Indian Affairs. Congressman Haskell's brother John ran an architectural firm, Haskell & Wood of Topeka, which was well known for the design of institutional buildings. The firm had planned Chilocco Indian School the previous year and was therefore the natural choice for the design of a Lawrence-based school. Even though Congressman Haskell had obvious personal motives for the promotion of his hometown, Lawrence also held a great appeal to Washington's politicians and philanthropists. Founded by New England abolitionists amid the Bloody Kansas turmoil of the 1850s and 1860s, the town had distinguished itself from other western settlements through its liberal, cultured, and intellectual atmosphere. Home of the state university since 1865, Lawrence prided itself as the Athens of the West,[27] and even Carlisle founder Pratt, who generally opposed the location of Indian schools in the West, conceded that Lawrence might be the only western city devoid of the typical prejudices against Indians so prevalent in this part of the country.[28] Lawrence was centrally located, had access to the major railways, and benefited from its proximity to Kansas City as well as to the state capital, Topeka. Northeastern Kansas was located in the wheat-, corn-, and stock-raising section of the Midwest, and with the exception of Carlisle, a school based in Lawrence would be located closer to the center of population in the United States than any other nonreservation boarding school. In addition, Lawrence was close enough to Indian Territory (Oklahoma) and several reservations such as the Kickapoo, Sac and Fox, Potawatomi, Iowa, and Ottawa to have access to a large Indian population while keeping transportation costs low.

Although Kansas had only recently emerged from an era of Indian-white warfare, Lawrence citizens, as well as the local press, were generally in favor of the new Indian school.[29] In 1882, the federal government agreed to Congressman Haskell's proposal, provided the city of Lawrence donated enough land for an adequate campus. As early as 1882, a subscription fund established by the *Lawrence Daily Journal* bore fruit and received nearly $10,000 from local citizens. With the money, a 280-acre plot 1 mile southeast of town was purchased from local businessman Colonel E. Learnard, who in 1889 would come to serve as Haskell's fourth superintendent. As expected, Haskell

& Wood was selected to design the new school, proposing plans quite similar to the work it had done at Chilocco. Another Topeka firm, Smith & Sargent, was entrusted with the construction side of the project, and work on the proposed buildings began in August 1883. The opening date was planned for March 1884, but a shortage of funds delayed the work during the winter. This precarious funding situation epitomized the financial problems that would plague Haskell during its first years of operation. Once Congress had freed the necessary funds, construction resumed on March 1, and the three limestone and pine buildings were finally finished by July 1884, when Superintendent of Indian Schools Major Haworth officially accepted the structures.

The buildings were located in the northwestern part of the campus, the school building occupying the middle of the site, flanked by the girls' dormitory to the west and the boys' dormitory to the east. The school building provided six classrooms and an assembly hall. The administrative offices, the shoe shop, and the quarters for the male employees were located in the boy's building. The kitchen, dining room, and sewing room, as well as the quarters for female employees, were placed in the girls' dormitory. Each dormitory contained a room for sick pupils, bathrooms, a cistern, storerooms, and sitting rooms. The other buildings on campus included a barn, a tool house, a boiler house, a blacksmith shop, a bakery, a horse barn, and a large shed for lumber storage.[30]

After the sudden and unexpected death of Congressman Haskell on December 17, 1883, the school was frequently referred to as Haskell Institute. When this name was officially adopted is not clear, but by late 1884 it had become the school's official title, in honor of the man who had brought the institution to Lawrence. Dr. James Marvin, a minister and former chancellor of Kansas University, was appointed first superintendent of Haskell Institute. According to a study of Haskell's early years, Dr. Marvin "embodied the missionary idealism of an older age; his educational experience appealed to the reformist spirit of the new Indian crusade. Accordingly, his tenure at Haskell focused on imparting Christian morality as the key to knowledge and understanding of the white world."[31]

But before Marvin could begin this great "humanist" endeavor, the school had to be prepared for the students' arrival. With the help of a small task force consisting of a farmer, his assistant, a carpenter, and six Indian boys who had been transferred to Lawrence from Chilocco Indian School, the school was getting ready for its opening in early September. The group cleared the school grounds; planted 400 fruit trees; seeded the garden with sorghum, oats, millet, and potatoes; cleaned the buildings; and transported materials from the railway station to the school.[32] The use of the children's labor even before the school had opened its doors reflects the deeply held belief in the values of industrial training as well as the economic philosophy on which Indian boarding schools were founded. Institutions such as Carlisle, Chilocco, and Haskell depended heavily on their students' labor for the schools' maintenance and operation.

On September 1, 1884, the first Haskell students arrived, consisting of twelve Ponca boys from the Ponca Agency in Indian Territory (Oklahoma). They were joined by two of the Chilocco boys who had been working at the school for the past few months. On September 16, five girls and three boys from the Ottawa reservation in Kansas arrived. These twenty-two students participated in Haskell's official opening ceremony on September 17, 1884, an occasion witnessed by many prominent Lawrence citizens who expressed their great enthusiasm and support for the school. During the ceremony, Kansas University chancellor Joshua A. Lippincott, who had served as Carlisle's chaplain for three years, dedicated the school, and Superintendent Marvin explained to the public the underlying educational philosophy and how Haskell would guide Indian youth along the road to "civilization." Marvin emphasized the importance of the English language as well as Christianity and further stated that the school would provide: "instruction to coming farmers and mechanics and housekeepers."[33] Marvin and Lippincott appealed to Lawrence's citizens to support and help Haskell's great endeavor in every way possible. They echoed Carlisle founder Pratt's belief that schools could do a lot to "civilize" Indian youth but that their work would be successful only if America's citizens welcomed the graduates in their midst and let them "stay in civilization." Marvin reassured concerned citizens that the methods used to recruit pupils were honorable and that "the pupils come as volunteers."[34] Lawrence's press was enthusiastic about the new school and repeatedly encouraged the town's citizens to support Haskell and to make its mission a great success. On September 21, the *Lawrence Daily Journal* wrote: "The presence of several hundred Indian children in our city should give our citizens an increased interest in this method of dealing with the red man who has for so long been wronged by our people and our government."[35]

Within the next few days, a group of approximately 100 Cheyenne, Pawnee, and Arapaho arrived at Haskell from Indian Territory. The group included small children as well as some of the children's parents. The adults accompanied their children to assure their safety, and some of them stayed at Haskell over the winter, sharing the dormitories with the students. By the end of the year, thirty-two children between the ages of three and nine were enrolled in the school as well as sixty students over the age of eighteen. During Haskell's first decade, its administrators admitted a much larger proportion of young children than in later years, when the school primarily recruited students over the age of fourteen. Upon Haskell's opening, Superintendent of Indian Schools Major Haworth had requested that the Cheyenne and other tribes send their younger children to Haskell, in order to test the possibility of training younger pupils, and especially girls, away from traditional influences.[36] This policy was typical for the early boarding school period and reflected white educators' stereotypes concerning the role of women in indigenous societies.

During the following months, more and more children arrived at Haskell, increasing the attendance figure to 280 by the end of the year. In early January 1885, the student body consisted of 219 boys and 61 girls. Haskell's first few months were marked by difficulties and tragedies, which would have a lasting impact on the school's enrollment figures. Owing to a shortage of funds, the boiler house was not completed until late November, leaving students without heat during an unusually cold fall. Many children developed respiratory infections, pneumonia, and diphtheria, forcing Superintendent Marvin to hire a full-time nurse to care for the sick. In mid-November, six-month-old Harry White Wolf died. He was one of the babies who were part of the Cheyenne/Arapaho group that had arrived in late September. During that first harsh winter at Haskell, ten more students succumbed to diseases, and eight of the children were buried in a small cemetery on the eastern side of the campus. In 1893, Haskell's fifth superintendent, Charles Francis Meserve, recommended that the cemetery should be closed and that the children's graves should be moved to the city cemetery. He argued that "it would not be very interesting for white parents who were visiting an educational institution to spy in some secluded corner the graves of those who were formerly members of the school. What the effect is upon the minds of the untutored Indian parents when they visit Haskell Institute can well be imagined."[37]

Despite his plea, the cemetery remained at Haskell, where it still stands as a grim reminder of the government's assimilation campaign against indigenous peoples. Soldiers no longer fought the battles, but the casualties remained high. Altogether, the names on twenty-nine graves do not appear in the school's records, meaning that some deaths occurred without being properly recorded. During 1886, for instance, ten new gravesites marked the little cemetery, even though that year's annual school report does not indicate any deaths at Haskell. Instead of recognizing the bad conditions at school, Haskell's superintendents tended to put the blame on the students, requesting that in the future, reservation agents should exercise greater care "in selecting pupils of sound health."[38] Naturally, many white employees suffered from exactly the same diseases caused by the unhealthy living conditions at the school. During the school year 1885–1886, 587 instances of illness or injury occurred, and one of the first structures added to the campus was a two-story hospital building that could accommodate up to thirty patients at a time. Indian parents became anxious about their children's well-being, and several asked to have their children sent home. Sick students wanted to leave the school, and many children deserted.[39]

The problems of the first winter led to a serious drop in enrollment figures over the course of the spring and summer. In July 1885, an ailing and frustrated Dr. Marvin resigned and was replaced by Colonel Arthur Grabowskii. In his only annual report, Marvin summarized his observations and impressions about his Indian students:

> The Indian pupils are obedient. Very few cases of insubordination have occurred. Severe punishments have not been required to secure observance of general rules. Exceptions to these statements have been rare. The characteristics of Indian pupils are quickness to observe through the eye and ear, slowness to manifest any emotion, reticence in the presence of strangers or of others whose confidence they have not proved. They are imitative; teachable in the use of tools and in methods of work. They are very sensitive to ridicule, quick to observe any personal slight, and to resent any apparently unjust discrimination. Close attention to every word and motion of a teacher is a marked fact in the schoolroom. Penmanship, drawing, and descriptive lessons are favorites, while abstruse problems of arithmetic have few admirers.[40]

Under Colonel Grabowskii's superintendence, however, Haskell's reputation did not improve. In addition to the ever-present health and funding problems, Grabowskii became quickly feared for his excessive disciplinary measures. Whereas under Dr. Marvin the denial of privileges and the threat of extra work had kept students in line, Grabowskii introduced a military-like system that divided students into five companies of cadet battalions that served to break up tribal groupings and any kind of resistance to school rules. Corporal punishment, as well as the introduction of a school prison, reflected the superintendent's strict reign. Even though praised by some, Grabowskii's methods triggered much resentment. The *Lawrence Tribune,* for instance, criticized him for his brutality and general cruelty toward the students. Many students refused to be treated that way and deserted from the school; others wrote letters home, complaining about their treatment. During Grabowskii's first year in office, the average attendance stood at about 310, 40 less than the 350 that Haskell could accommodate at the time. By the end of the following year, enrollment was at an all-time low, having dwindled to 260 students. During all of 1886, only 43 new students enrolled in the school. As John Williams, agent for the Cheyenne and Arapaho, explained, the decline in enrollment was directly related to Grabowskii's authoritarian leadership: "There is a deep-rooted prejudice in the minds of the Indians against Haskell Institute, caused in part by the death of some of their children there, but I think more particularly on account of the rigid discipline of the school, as the pupils from this agency are continually writing to their people of the severe rule, etc., of the school."[41] Grabowskii alienated not only Indian students and parents but also many of Lawrence's citizens who had been avid supporters of the school.[42]

Following Superintendent Marvin's success in procuring pupils, the U.S. government had allotted $63,000 for the academic year 1886–1887, money that was intended for the completion of the school. Grabowskii's plan included the purchase of 40 additional acres of arable land, construction of a separate dining hall and kitchen, completion of the hospital, more farm structures, cottages for the superintendent and Haskell's employees, four additional dormitories, a boys' gymnasium, and several industrial shops. It was the superintendent's goal to increase Haskell's capacity to 500 students, making it the second largest school after Carlisle. Many of the proposed additions, though, such as the gymnasium and the employee cottages, would not be built for many years to come. Several of the projects were finished, however, and the installation of a lighting system, as well as the addition of basic fire equipment and playgrounds for the children, improved living conditions at the school.[43]

The sharp drop in enrollment figures and the strained relationship with Lawrence's most prominent sponsors put pressure on Grabowskii to resign. In early 1887, former Kansas governor Charles Robinson, a prominent abolitionist and experienced educator, became Haskell's third superintendent. He was deeply convinced of the worthiness of the institution:

> When three hundred and fifty children of any tribe or nation demonstrate by actual experiment that they can do all the work, under proper supervision, required for their daily subsistence, all the work necessary to farm almost 500 acres of land, to erect several substantial buildings of both wood and stone, and also manufacture a great variety of articles in a neat and satisfactory manner, besides attending school one half of each day, such children are well worthy of the attention, the time, and the money expended on their behalf.[44]

If the school were to survive, however, Robinson would have to eliminate the shortcomings of the past and convince Indian parents that Haskell was after all a good place for their children to be. After only two and a half years of operation, Haskell had already faced severe funding, health, and reputation problems, and it would be a difficult task to restore public and, especially, Indian confidence in the school. Under Robinson, life at Haskell did not change in any dramatic way, but some improvements were made. The former governor was successful in improving relationships with the local community, and his goal of regaining the trust of native leaders was achieved to some degree. After his first winter at Haskell, Robinson visited Indian Territory in order to recruit new students. He carried a letter from former Cheyenne and Arapaho agent Williams, telling Indian parents about the important changes that had been taking place at Haskell:

> When Dr. Marvin resigned another man was chosen, Col. Grabowskii. I did not ask you to send your children to him for the reason that I did not believe him to be a proper person to have charge of them. The "grand" Col. is gone. I am glad that I can to day unhesitatingly advise and urge you to give your children to the man who shall present this letter to you. Governor Robinson . . . will be a father to them and will make the best use of the authority and means at his disposal given by the government for the benefit and advancement of your children.[45]

Despite these words of praise, it was not an easy task to convince parents to let their children leave home or even to convince reservation school agents to send their older students to Haskell. The latter attitude frustrated the ex-governor, who believed that "if all the children of the reservation could be put in reservation schools till twelve or fifteen years of age, and then be sent to an industrial school till taught some industry, the Indian question would be solved in one generation."[46] Robinson was an avid supporter of compulsory education for Indian children. Despite initial difficulties, he gradually succeeded in increasing the school's enrollment and was able to maintain discipline with methods less abusive than those of his predecessor. Despite these successes, students' ill health and a high number of desertions remained two of the most serious problems faced by his administration. By the end of the 1886–1887 school year, attendance was up to about 400 students, leading to overcrowded conditions in the dormitories and classrooms. During the 1887–1888 term alone, seventeen students died, many of them as the result of pneumonia and tuberculosis.[47]

Despite the students' bad health and the crowded conditions, life at Haskell became more bearable under Robinson's superintendence. The children were allowed to interact socially two evenings each week, the Haskell band was established, a school library was opened, and in response to the students' requests, the school started subscriptions to all regional newspapers.[48] In general, students liked Superintendent Robinson much better than his predecessor, and some expressed their support for the school directly to him, as in Teresa Tucquinn's 1888 letter: "I think it is nice here. I think it is a better place to be here than to be home. You treat us very kind and thank you for your kindly care."[49]

During the 1887–1888 school year a three-story shop building, housing seven industrial departments, was added to Haskell's campus. Male students would now be able to receive training in blacksmithing, tailoring, carpentry, painting, wagon and harness making, printing, tinsmithing, and shoemaking as well as in farming, baking, and engineering. Girls were taught domestic arts and sciences in the new sewing and laundry facilities, which were included in the recently finished boiler house. New dormitories and a new dining hall were under construction, and all other land was "utilized for garden, field, meadow, and pasture."[50] Not all these trades were offered right away, however, and some of them, including printing, would only be taught several years later. Students still performed a great number of menial tasks that served to keep down the school's operational costs. Superintendent Robinson held on to his predecessors' vision of Haskell as a place where Indian youth would be taught the values of self-discipline and hard labor. In the summer of 1888, Robinson introduced Haskell's outing program, a system inspired by Carlisle's founder General Pratt. Under the annual summer "outing," Haskell's students were to be placed among white families to work either as farm hands or, in the case of the girls, as domestic servants. The purpose of the program was to teach students "Anglo-civilization" firsthand and to immerse them into the dominant culture. Many Indian parents were reluctant, though, to have their children leave the school and especially feared for their daughters' safety. Haskell's outing program got off to a rather slow start and only gained momentum in the course of the following decades.

After two years in office, Superintendent Robinson resigned, leaving the post to Colonel Oscar E. Learnard, the Lawrence attorney and businessman who had sold the original plot of land to the school. Local newspapers lauded Robinson's hard work as "an important factor in saving the race to humanity, to civilization, and from decay and annihilation." According to the *Lawrence Daily Journal,* "Haskell is the crowning work of a noble and well spent life. His efforts have always been on the side of the oppressed and the weak. It is the under-dog in the fight that commands his sympathy."[51]

Learnard made it clear from the beginning that he would only serve until a permanent replacement could be found. Busy with all his other business affairs, he did not consider Haskell a priority. Nevertheless, he remained in office for a full nine months, and despite his preoccupancy, he seemed to have managed the school successfully. During an 1889 inspection visit, Daniel Dorchester, superintendent of Indian education, had noted that Haskell's industrial shops were small and overcrowded, the sanitary conditions were horrible, the school still relied on windmills to guarantee its entire water supply, and the students' health had not improved much over the previous year.[52] Superintendent Learnard successfully addressed several of these problems, and Haskell's campus was further expanded under his administration. The introduction of the post of chief matron meant an improvement for the lives of homesick boys and girls. According to the superintendent of Indian education, the chief matron should provide "motherly oversight of the boys, large and small, as well as the girls—one to whom they will look for counsel—a woman of culture and high ideals, of practical wisdom and tact, to exert the best refining womanly influence upon even the oldest of pupils."[53] The first lady to hold the position was Harriet Kelsey Haskell, the widow of Congressman Haskell. Even though the matron could certainly not be a surrogate mother to all children, Harriet Haskell was well liked for her kindness and positive influence on the students.[54]

With the appointment of Thomas Jefferson Morgan as commissioner of Indian affairs in 1889, the government's Indian education program received more attention than ever before. Morgan introduced a standardized curriculum for Indian schools, made education for Indian children compulsory, and did much to systematize and professionalize the field of Indian education. These changes on the highest level affected Haskell in many ways, making the school a more stable and permanent institution. During the 1890s, Haskell adopted a standardized curriculum, expanded its size, increased enrollment and tribal diversity, and fortified its relationship with the community of Lawrence. By the mid-1890s, the once-ailing institution had gained new support among both Indians and whites and was second only to Carlisle in capacity and size.[55]

In September 1889, Charles Meserve, an old acquaintance of Commissioner Morgan, became Haskell's fourth superintendent, freeing Colonel Learnard to pursue his pressing business activities. Meserve, an educator from Massachusetts, supported all of Commissioner Morgan's policies and molded Haskell according to Morgan's ideals. Like Superintendent Robinson before him, Meserve showed a universalist and egalitarian approach to Indian education and deeply believed in the possibilities and capabilities of Indian students. He increased the school's emphasis on teaching patriotism, expanded industrial training capacities, and supported a possible extension of Haskell's program to include a high school curriculum. As in the preceding years, though, students spent more time working in the school's industrial departments than studying in the classroom. In the early 1890s, the U.S. Congress refused to raise the yearly allocations for the school, thereby crippling Meserve's high school plans. Owing to the lack of funds, Haskell continued to offer academic training at the primary and grammar school level, with classes mainly focusing on the three Rs, American history, and basic sciences such as biology. Instead of investing in academics, Congress appropriated almost $10,000 for the purchase of additional farmland—testimony to the government's belief in the virtues of industrial training and self-sufficiency. Under Superintendent Meserve, Haskell's students did extensive work on the school's buildings and structures, so that when Superintendent J. A.

Swett took over Meserve's post in late 1894, he was able to report: "The thirty-eight buildings comprising the institute are all in an excellent state of repair, and beyond the ordinary care and occasional job work, need cost but little for years to come."[56] Fire was a constant threat during the school's early years until Haskell received electricity in 1897 (the telephone arrived in 1908). The city water line, finished in 1890, only reached up to the school gate, and it was another two years before the school installed indoor plumbing. During the dry season, the water came directly from the Kansas River, making it too polluted for consumption. The school had to cope with its share of disasters, such as the 1891 damage inflicted by a severe tornado and an 1893 fire that destroyed a barn as well as several stables and horses. Life at Haskell had certainly improved over the school's first five years, but it was by no means comfortable, safe, or easy.

The school's enrollment had increased from 425 students in late 1889 to 538 students in 1893 and 660 students in 1894. By the mid-1890s, students from more than thirty-five tribes attended the school, making Haskell second only to Carlisle in ethnic diversity in Indian schools in the nation. A big change in Haskell's curriculum occurred in 1894 and 1895, with the introduction of a normal department and a commercial course. After years of training that prepared students for manual labor, Haskell's pupils would finally be able to become teachers, clerks, accountants, typists, and stenographers. Most of the graduates of these two programs would be hired by the Indian Service to teach in Indian schools or work in the growing administration of the Office of Indian Affairs.[57] Initially, only a few would venture out into the white world, but the introduction of these two programs was a first step toward more equal opportunities for indigenous students. In the following years, several more programs and departments were added, such as the domestic science department in 1898 and the domestic arts department in 1900. By the turn of the century, Haskell's curriculum had become more diversified as well as more specialized, offering students broader choices than in the previous decade. By 1900, music and art teachers had been hired, a new gymnasium had been completed, regular gymnastics classes were introduced for all students, and Haskell's soon-to-be-famous football team had started practicing.[58]

In 1898, Harvey B. Peairs became Haskell's superintendent, a post that he would hold until 1910, and then once more from 1917 until his retirement in the late 1920s. Peairs had served as Haskell's disciplinarian since 1887, as principal of the school since 1892, and as assistant superintendent since

1896. His leadership style and educational philosophy markedly influenced Haskell's character and development during the first two decades of the twentieth century. Unlike his predecessors, Peairs stayed at Haskell for a long time, giving the school an element of stability. When he took office, Haskell had an enrollment of 619 students, with an average attendance of 500, and the campus had grown to include forty buildings and structures.

At the dawn of the new century, Haskell had grown into the nation's second-largest Indian training school. The institution that American Indian students found in the early 1900s differed markedly in size, diversity of programs, and quality of life from the school that the first twenty-two Ponca and Ottawa children had entered in 1884. Nevertheless, the philosophy and purpose of Haskell Institute had remained constant during all these years: to destroy indigenous cultures and to elevate Indian children from the "savagery" of their people's past to a brighter future of American citizenship and civilization.

CHAPTER TWO

Coming to Haskell

Odanah, Wis., July 24, 1907

Dear Sir;

Having heard of your Institute, my friend Margaret Beauregard and myself would like to go to Haskell, on condition if we can take up the sewing course only and not school studies. I also would like to know if you will let us come home if we pay our fare to Haskell. I hope you will let us know as soon as possible if you can agree to our terms or not. Will close hoping to receive a favorable reply.

I am yours truly,
Sophia La Pointe[1]

Superintendent Peairs replied that he was willing to admit the girls on their own terms, as long as they paid for their transportation. In that case they would be able to spend the next summer vacation at home. He added that, if they were both of sufficient age, arrangements could be made to give their entire time to sewing.

As the new century progressed, students and parents showed a growing interest in Haskell's program. Requests like Sophia's were not unusual and bear testimony to the students' agency in planning their own education. They obtained information from catalogs that the school sent out to reservation agents, day schools, and reservation boarding schools, and they listened to the reports of their friends and families. By the early 1900s, Haskell was well known for its domestic arts and science, business, normal, and engineering departments, and indigenous people from all parts of the United States showed a growing appreciation for the school. As Sophia's letter indicates, prospective students were aware of school policies and were determined to tailor their stay at Haskell to their own needs and expectations. This does not mean, however, that all parents were eager to place their children in the care of the school, that students were usually able to negotiate the terms of their enrollment, or that Haskell no longer depended on the active solicitation of prospective students. It merely suggests that there is no single answer to the question of why students attended Haskell. Students' motivations for or against schooling were influenced by personal motives and cultural and environmental factors as well as the opinions and experiences of kin and peers.[2]

Economic considerations were among the key factors leading to the enrollment of native children in off-reservation boarding schools. During the allotment era of the early twentieth century, boarding schools such as Haskell and Flandreau, for instance, were a safe haven for Ojibwe students, who faced terrible poverty and starvation on their Minnesota reservations. Parents unable to provide for their children saw in the schools a last resort to ensure their offspring's survival.[3] Esther Burnett's autobiography supports this harsh reality. After the death of her white father in 1922, Esther Burnett and her five siblings moved from Idaho to Green River, Wyoming, to live near her mother's Shoshone relatives. The children's mother had great difficulties coping with the death of her husband, and soon after his death the family was in financial trouble. Burnett recounts her and her siblings' lack of supervision during that time. As she points out, "things had fallen apart—our family no longer had a mother and father, and we children were left to take care of ourselves and hadn't fared so well. The wheels were set in motion through the Wind River Indian Agency to enroll us at Haskell Institute."[4]

In a sense, poverty was as much a coercive factor as federal authority when it came to school attendance. In the early years of the boarding school system, involuntary recruitment by coercion or starvation was a common practice. Indian agents and reservation police would "collect" students during recruitment raids, forcing parents to comply by threatening to withhold food rations necessary for survival or by arresting parents unwilling to cooperate with government policies. Opposition to white schooling was prominent in many indigenous communities, and several native autobiographies support this view.[5] As the twentieth century progressed, involuntary recruitment became less of a factor. In Indian Territory (Oklahoma), for instance, education was largely a desired commodity, and many Indian families favored Chilocco

Indian School over the oftentimes racist public schools in the area.[6] The same holds true for Haskell. During the core period of this study, 1900–1920s, the school did not have to force students to attend; on the contrary, year after year Haskell had to turn away large numbers of students owing to overcrowding. In August 1909, nineteen-year-old Adelia Sandoval from Taos Pueblo wrote to Superintendent Peairs:

> I will tell you that the blanks you send me are full and there are still some more pupils that want to go to school at Haskell. Their parents are anxious to send their children to Haskell to school. The people that come here to my home tell me that they know a boy or girl that come from Haskell. They said that no boys or girls that come from other schools are dressed as good as those who come from Haskell.[7]

Adelia Sandoval, who attended Haskell from 1903 to 1907, was one of many Haskell alumni who promoted their former school among friends and family back home. Superintendent Robinson had successfully relied on the recruitment skills of student representatives as early as 1887, sending his best and brightest students out to their tribes in order to inform tribal leaders about Haskell's advantages. During the 1900s and 1910s, Haskell started to profit from a growing number of second-generation boarding school students, whose parents or other relatives had attended the school and regarded Haskell as a formative and—in many instances—positive experience in their lives. As Adelia's letter indicates, a number of parents were eager for their children to attend Haskell. In a later communication, the girl added that Taos parents did not want their children to attend Santa Fe Indian school, since they considered it inferior to Haskell. In her second letter, Adelia Sandoval asked Peairs to send a ticket for her younger brother, and explained her own reasons for staying in Taos:

> Mama wants my brother to go back to school again, he came home this vacation. . . . He is very very anxious to go back to Haskell; he says he will learn more at Haskell in one week than he would here in ten years. Jessie wants to go back to school for three more years, he is fourteen years old. . . . Mama is anxious for him to go back to Haskell again. I would go too. But my mother is getting old and I have to stay with her. Not because I don't like Haskell. I know it's a good school to go to. I have been there

for six years, and I often wish I could go for another six or more years. God bless the good school![8]

Adelia's letters convey the girl's emotional attachment to her former school and her positive attitude toward Superintendent Peairs. It would be wrong to assume that all students had such a close relationship with the school's administrators, but Adelia's letter is certainly no exception. Many students kept in touch with Haskell after they left the school, and Superintendent Peairs corresponded with former students on a regular basis over an extended period of time.

In his letters to Adelia, Peairs alluded to the competition among off-reservation boarding schools for students from particular locations. Peairs pointed out that the Santa Fe Indian School recruited students from Taos and other pueblos and that it was therefore difficult for Haskell to enroll students from New Mexico.[9] Adelia's messages support this view, explaining that the local Indian agent even refused to sign Haskell enrollment forms, trying to coerce the parents to send their children to Santa Fe instead. Apart from these restrictions, the Southwest was in many ways an untapped reservoir for Haskell, a vast area with few educational facilities and thousands of school-aged children. Despite the high transportation costs arising for students from Arizona, New Mexico, and Utah, Superintendent Peairs was very much interested in recruiting Navajo children. In a letter to Navajo agent W. R. Johnson, Peairs expressed his deep conviction in Haskell's right and ability to transform Indian societies and to uplift the students under the school's care. He emphasized the high quality of care that would be provided for the children, the superiority of Haskell's teachers, and especially the provisions taken to guarantee the children's physical health and safety.[10]

Despite Peairs's assurances, in 1905 Indian schools were neither the healthiest nor the safest places to be, and once-healthy children were crowded into dormitories and classrooms with students suffering from active, contagious tuberculosis. As Haskell's records reveal, many children suffered from tuberculosis, measles, trachoma, pneumonia, typhoid fever, and other infectious diseases. Haskell's student cemetery stands as a sad reminder of this troublesome truth, and many Indian parents saw their children return home only to witness their suffering and death soon after. Parents in faraway places such as the Southwest were especially reluctant to send their children halfway across the continent to attend school. The correspondence between Raymond

Bonnin, a Haskell alumnus working among the Ute tribe, and Superintendent Peairs underscores this sentiment:

> I have been among the Ute Indians for five years and have never ceased trying to influence them to send their children to Haskell. So far I have had little success. The main reason for failure in this has been due to the fact that these Utes have not had the advantage of other Indians and are so isolated that they are not aware of the immense advantage that it would mean to them as a tribe to send their children to some good non-reservation school (such as yours) to have them educated in the better ways of the whites. They feel that their children will not return or that they will come home sick and never recover.... They are very backward and suspicious of the whites, thereby making it very difficult to deal with them.[11]

Haskell's administrators and many of the school's alumni worked hard both to counter these fears and to convince Indian parents that an education at Haskell would benefit their children rather than expose them to any dangers. And sometimes, students' health could actually turn into an argument *for* Haskell, as demonstrated by the following letter from the Kaibab Indian School in Arizona:

> Dear Sir: I am enclosing applications for the enrollment of two boys in your school.... Ordinarily these boys should have gone to Phoenix or Riverside, but one of the pupils from here died at Riverside a couple of years ago. These Indians have become prejudiced against schools in warm climates, without a real cause. After considerable consideration, the boys selected your school.[12]

In general, though, Haskell's enrollment records indicate that the majority of students came from places closer to Lawrence than the Southwest. Even though many different tribes were represented at Haskell, students from Oklahoma, Kansas, Nebraska, the Dakotas, Minnesota, Michigan, and Wisconsin made up the bulk of the student population. The states were more accessible than other parts of the country, transportation costs were lower, and many parents living in these areas had already been exposed to the dominant culture and the principles of formal schooling. Consequently, they were more willing to let their children travel the distance to Lawrence than parents residing in the remote areas of the Southwest or the Great Basin.

Over time, even Haskell's leadership became more reluctant to recruit students from the Southwest, as this 1914 statement reveals: "The truth is, as I have learned from personal observation, Indian children from that section do not ordinarily prosper very well at schools of the East like Haskell, Chilocco or Carlisle. Yet, if they come in sound health and take good care of themselves I do not believe they would run any great risk of deterioration in health."[13] From 1911 on, Haskell's student population changed because of a new ruling that once more allowed children from the Five Civilized Tribes (Cherokee, Choctaw, Creek, Seminole, and Chickasaw), who had previously been excluded from enrollment, to attend the school. Students from these tribes flocked into Haskell and Chilocco, and Superintendent Peairs lamented in 1917 that this "has made it impossible to take as many from other reservations as is desirable" and that he wished to "once again increase the number of students from the Dakotas and the Upper Midwest in order to balance the tribal composition of Haskell's student body."[14]

Despite the large number of students from these areas, resistance and fears were also encountered in indigenous communities in Oklahoma and the Midwest. In one instance, Superintendent Peairs was aware of prejudices against Haskell on the Menominee Reservation in Wisconsin and encouraged his recruiter to "spend a few days getting acquainted and presenting the advantages offered by Haskell."[15] Similar difficulties were reported from Ponemah, Minnesota, where several youngsters were willing to go to Haskell but "the parents are not willing to let them go." According to the local teacher, Mary Lawrence: "The old Indians held a council and made the parents promise that they would not allow their children to go away to school, so the young people that are ambitious and bright enough to go, are prevented from going."[16]

This statement reveals how deeply rooted, and at times even organized, the resistance to off-reservation boarding schools could be and how different generations disagreed on the subject. Whereas many of the younger people were eager to attend Haskell, their parents and especially grandparents feared for their physical and emotional health as well as for their tribe's cultural survival. Many elders were what whites called "traditionalists," determined to preserve their culture and to keep their families together. In indigenous societies, grandparents oftentimes fulfilled the role of primary caretakers for the young. They were the bearers of the tribe's history, ceremonies, and language, teaching the children the ways of their people. From the stories revealed in Haskell's records, it is apparent that grandparents had a crucial influence on whether a child would be allowed to attend the school. A Haskell recruiter in Oklahoma poignantly described this reality: "There are four or five children who are to go with us unless the parents back out, or their grandparents steal them before we can start."[17] Parents and grandparents were concerned not only about their children's safety and health but also about their emotional well-being and moral development, as the superintendent of the Kiowa Indian Agency in Oklahoma pointed out in 1917: "A great number of our parents are taking the position that they will not allow their children to go away to non-reservation schools because they feel that the damaged character of the pupils have been returned is due to lack of discipline at the schools."[18] This seems surprising considering the strict military-like routine found in the schools of this time. One should remember that many students were expelled for offenses such as drinking alcohol or deserting, however, and that most parents were not happy when their children got into trouble or were returned to the reservation in disgrace. The schools were strict indeed, but as later chapters will show, students found many ways to circumvent, bend, and break the rules.

By the early 1900s, the Indian education system was more structured and better organized than in previous decades. Rules were ever developing, however, and policies and regulations drafted in Washington were often not followed in the field. During the late 1880s and early 1890s, Commissioner of Indian Affairs Thomas Jefferson Morgan had been instrumental in reforming the system of Indian education, especially with regard to off-reservation boarding schools. His vision was to bring day schools, reservation boarding schools, and off-reservation schools into a systematic relationship and to create a system that would allow students to progress from one institution to the next according to their achieved level of education. The primary education was supposed to be the responsibility of the various reservation schools, whereas secondary education would be pursued at off-reservation boarding schools. High school classes were only to be offered at selected institutions such as Carlisle, Santa Fe, or Haskell. In 1890, Commissioner Morgan drafted a course of study for Indian schools that included a complete list of textbooks to be used, placing major emphasis on English language training, academic subjects, moral training, and especially industrial training.[19] Morgan encouraged school administrators to solicit students from diverse backgrounds: "Special pains should be taken to bring together in the large boarding-schools members of as many different tribes as possible, in order to destroy the tribal antagonism and to generate in them a feeling of common brotherhood and mutual respect."[20]

At Haskell, Morgan's ideas were shared and supported by Superintendent Robinson, as well as Superintendents Meserve and Peairs. But despite some improvements at Haskell, Morgan's larger vision of a reformed Indian education system did not become reality for another twenty to thirty years, and as late as 1915, most off-reservation boarding schools did not offer courses beyond the primary eight grades. Haskell was one of the exceptions, offering its students normal and business courses that provided Indian youths with an opportunity to advance beyond an eight-year education. Haskell's business course attracted many graduates from other off-reservation schools, and the school's leadership actively recruited students from places such as Chilocco or Carlisle. Haskell's administrators regarded the business department as one of the school's most important and advanced programs. Eager to attract the best students for the course, they aimed at increasing the average attendance age at the school by filling up the business course. By offering a degree that would allow students to gain experience in a white-collar field that held the promise of steady employment and decent salaries, Haskell offered far more to indigenous youth than most of the other off-reservation boarding schools. But even Haskell did not become a fully accredited high school until 1921, and only a few students actually graduated. It is thus important to emphasize that apart from its rather slow implementation, Morgan's (and after 1901, Estelle Reel's) standardized curriculum did not guarantee student success. Especially before 1900, graduation rates were extremely low, and as late as 1920, only a small percentage of students received their diplomas.[21]

From the 1880s onward, the question of whether school attendance should be made compulsory was an important issue. On March 3, 1891, Congress finally empowered the commissioner of Indian affairs "to make and enforce by proper means such rules and regulations as will secure the attendance of Indian children of suitable age and health at schools established and maintained for their benefit."[22] The "proper means" were further specified in 1893, when Congress authorized the Indian Office to "withhold ration, clothing, and other annuities from Indian parents or guardians who refuse or neglect to send and keep the children of proper school age in some school a reasonable portion of each year."[23] As mentioned earlier, agents made use of this power, and many families became victims of coercion and police pressure. Nevertheless, because of the lack of schools in remote areas such as the Southwest and the limited capacity of existing schools, school attendance rates rose slowly. The authority given by Congress benefited mainly reservation schools, where the relative closeness to Indian families allowed Indian agents to keep track of reservation youth and to enforce attendance by a variety of means.

For off-reservation schools such as Haskell the situation was more difficult. Having no authority on the reservations, they depended on recruitment, including sending delegations of teachers and other employees to the reservations in order to recruit students by going door to door, relying on current and former students to solicit children from their families and communities, and sending out catalogs and brochures. Haskell's administrators engaged in extensive correspondence with administrators from reservation boarding schools, encouraging them to send their older and most promising students on to Haskell. In some instances, reservation school staff transferred students to Haskell in order to remove them from what they considered to be negative home influences. Often, though, reservation boarding schools were reluctant to send their students to Haskell, being eager to fill up their own ranks with "quality" students. One reason for the stiff competition between the different schools was the system of school financing. Indian schools received funds from three sources: appropriations provided for by treaties, government funds resulting from the sale of Indian lands, and annual appropriations made by the U.S. Congress. Since school appropriations depended solely on attendance, superintendents were naturally eager to fill their schools to capacity and beyond.[24] Without enough students, schools would have inadequate resources to provide for the student population. Haskell's records attest to this problem, containing numerous letters expressing the administration's concerns about attendance. Haskell's student population fluctuated, owing to a variety of reasons. Students left for health reasons and because of issues arising in their families, such as the sickness or loss of a parent that required them to return home. In addition, a high number of desertions plagued Haskell as much as any other Indian boarding school. Students from areas close to Lawrence especially tended to go back and forth between the school and their home, as Peairs lamented in a letter to Chilocco's superintendent: "The Pottawatomies come and go every year because they live so near!"[25] Due to the pressure faced by school officials to fill their annual student quotas, it was not unusual to find representatives from several missionary, on-reservation, and off-reservation boarding schools simultaneously soliciting students on the same reservation. In the summer of 1907, a female Haskell representative traveling in Wisconsin wrote Superintendent Peairs about her difficulties recruiting students: "Mr. Compton of

Tomah [Indian school] is here, and a Catholic Father is soliciting for Chilocco. Carlisle is represented by pupils, and Mr. Pierce of Flandreau is expected in a day or two."[26] Peairs encouraged Marion Kidder to "get out onto the reservation and get in touch with former pupils and get pupils' and parents' signature" and present the blanks to the agent for his signature. A couple of days later, Kidder reported that she had been out every day from morning until night but was accomplishing little and was only able to enroll four students owing to the competition.

Despite their effort to solicit as many students as possible, Haskell's administrators frequently reminded their representatives in the field to abide by the rules laid out by the Indian Office. Among these rules was the 1893 established law that superintendents and Indian agents were not allowed to enroll a child in an off-reservation boarding school without the "full consent" of his or her parents, the signature of the responsible Indian agent, and a physician's certificate attesting to the student's health. As mentioned earlier, school attendance was compulsory. That did not, however, apply to off-reservation boarding schools such as Haskell. Indian parents had to send their children to school, but they no longer had to consent to have them taken off the reservation. In reality, though, Haskell's records are full of stories of students attending Haskell without parental consent and of parents not agreeing with Haskell's administrators on the original terms under which their children had been admitted. A recurrent point of confusion concerned the duration of their term. Originally, students signed a contract for a term of three years. After the turn of the century, this rule was changed, causing conflicts between Haskell and the students' parents. In October 1901, Mr. Hill complained to the Commissioner of Indian Affairs about what he considered to be an unlawful attempt of the school to retain his son Eli after his term had expired. As in many other instances, however, the Indian Office sided with Haskell:

> In your report on Eli Hill you state that during the summer of 1898 a new ruling with reference to the term of years for which pupils might enter Haskell Institute was made, and was: pupils 18 years of age entered for three years, 17 for four years, 16 years or under five years; that this ruling was published in application blanks and in circulars sent out at that time, and has since been followed; that under this ruling Mr. Hill sent his son and he was enrolled for five years; that it is possible however, he did not understand the matter as custom previous to that time was that pupils

were enrolled for three years only; that as Eli is now only eleven years of age and a very small boy, you recommend that he remain in school. Your recommendation is approved, and you may so inform the boy's father.[27]

As Eli's case illustrates, many Indian children entered Haskell at a very young age, especially during the 1880s and 1890s. Washington's lawmakers, as well as Haskell's early superintendents, believed that the advantages of taking small children away from the "negative influences" of traditional communities would outweigh the problems created by admitting them and fully backed this policy. According to section 14 of the 1898 Indian School Rules, "when kindergarten facilities are provided, with the consent of the Commissioner of Indian Affairs, children may be enrolled at 4 years of age."[28] In later years, however, Haskell's administrators tried to reduce the percentage of younger children, limiting their number to one class per kindergarten and primary school grade, in order to provide Haskell's normal students with the opportunity to gain firsthand experience in teaching younger children. Even though Commissioner Morgan had envisioned an educational system in which only older students with previous training would be admitted to off-reservation boarding schools, the actual implementation of this rule did not occur until 1909, when the Indian Office in Washington informed superintendents to stop accepting children younger than fourteen. The upper limit for admitting students was eighteen years. Of course, students were allowed to stay in school beyond that age in order to finish their course of study. Students over the age of twenty-one, however, needed the explicit consent of the commissioner of Indian affairs in order to remain at Haskell. If the school wished to admit students above or below these age limits, special permission from the Indian Office was required. In most cases, though, obtaining the commissioner's consent was a mere formality, and up to the 1920s, Haskell's enrollment records show many students in their mid- and late twenties as well as under the age of fourteen.

Besides age, "degree of Indian blood" was an important enrollment criterion. In theory, Indian schools were intended to serve "the real Indians"—referring to full-blood Indians from the nation's 141 reservations.[29] In reality, however, many Haskell students had only one parent, one grandparent, or even one great-grandparent with indigenous background. In March 1902, Indian Commissioner W. A. Jones quoted from a special agent report on Haskell: "The present enrollment is said to be 675, of which number 120 are

$^1/_4$ and $^1/_8$ bloods. He further observes that many children are being given free education and support at the expense of the government who have but the slightest trace of Indian blood in their veins, and the majority of whose parents are well able to take care of them, but send them to government schools through purely mercenary motives; that a larger part of these pupils live in towns and cities where there are free school advantages."[30] One of the tools the Indian Office used to monitor field operations was the delegation of special agents and inspectors who visited Indian schools, agencies, and reservations regularly, reporting back to the commissioner of Indian affairs. The commissioner then informed the school superintendents of the findings and any changes deemed necessary. The report mentioned above considered Haskell to be "in such excellent condition that little comment is necessary." Nevertheless, the issue of student recruitment and the "racial" composition of the student body instigated a critical response from the special agent in charge. Commissioner Jones appealed to Superintendent Peairs to "weed out of the school the so-called 'White Indians,' that is, Indians with less than $^1/_8$ Indian blood in their veins."[31] Jones's successor, Francis E. Leupp, was even clearer about how to deal with eligibility and attendance questions. In 1905, Haskell was ordered to drop almost 100 ineligible students from its roll. The discussion surrounding degree of Indian blood had sharp racial undertones that reflected the "scientific racism" and belief in social evolutionism of the time. In the early twentieth century, Indian educators took it for granted that the students' intellectual abilities and scholastic success were directly related to their degree of Indian blood. Haskell's inspection reports attest not only to the increasing bureaucratization of the Indian education system but also to the meticulous control exercised over individual Indian students and their families. Through its agents, school superintendents, supervisors, and inspectors, the Office of Indian Affairs kept track of indigenous people and their "rights" and perceived responsibilities. In his 1909 inspection report, Supervisor L. Davis discussed the blood degree question in greater detail:

> From my personal knowledge of the sentiment prevailing among the real Indians, the full bloods of the reservations, I do not hesitate to say that the presence of these "near whites" in the non-reservation schools causes much dissatisfaction and deters some from going to the larger schools. The full bloods cannot keep apace the mixed bloods in academic work, and the various features of the school wherein mental activity is brought

in competition. This means the mixed bloods secure the places of prominence, get more privileges, receive more commendations, while the full bloods fill the "back seats." The full blood Indian is always easily discouraged, and the distinctions arising in these ways cause many to become discontent and return home as soon as they can.[32]

Davis's allegations of mixed-blood favoritism and full-blood apathy reflect the prevalence of racial prejudices in the Office of Indian Affairs and at Haskell as well as on the reservations. The belief in social evolution and whites' superior intellectual abilities were deeply ingrained in the Indian Service. It pervaded every line of argument put forth by Indian educators and certainly influenced indigenous people's perception of themselves. Whether the "real Indians" felt the way Davis claimed is difficult to know. It is clear, though, that school administrators expected less academically from full-blood students than from their "whiter" counterparts.

Native Americans on and off the reservations were certainly aware of the distinctions U.S. officials made based on their degree of Indian blood, and they had to deal with the underlying assumptions. Even if they did not believe in the superiority of Indians with mixed ancestry themselves, the consequences of these beliefs were real and had to be acknowledged. Since colonial times, government policies and attitudes had fueled divisions among indigenous tribes and had led to deep splits in Indian communities. In many tribes, such as the Cherokee or the Choctaw nations, mixed bloods had advanced to positions of tribal leadership in disproportionate numbers. This was partly due to the fact that whites treated Indians with mixed ancestry differently and that mixed-blood families were able to benefit from the government's prejudices when it came to the education of their children. As Haskell's records demonstrate, off-reservation boarding schools did indeed admit a large number of children with predominantly white ancestry—students whom school administrators described as particularly "desirable." On the other hand, there was a constant attempt to purge boarding schools of ineligible students, as Supervisor Davis's report indicates. Though generally responsive to their superiors' criticism, Haskell's superintendents did not hesitate to justify the presence of students they considered worthy of Haskell's guardianship. In a 1912 letter to the commissioner of Indian affairs, Superintendent John R. Wise went into great detail to justify the enrollment of students of less than one-fourth Indian blood. This is vividly depicted in the case of Fannie Gullet who, like many others, had her status questioned by Washington: "*Fannie Gullet*—One-eight blood Cherokee from Quapaw Agency, sent, enrolled September 3, 1909 for three years, has no home and has accordingly been continued on the rolls. Is in 7th A grade, has completed no domestic course. Is not prepared to earn her own living and we would be at a loss to know where to send her, if discharged."³³

Wise refused to send away students who had no other place to go, whose families did not live in the vicinity of a public school, or who were close to finishing their coursework at Haskell. According to him, though, he had always "made the necessity for government help in getting an education the first test and, other things being the same, the boy or girl of full or nearly full blood has invariably been given preference."³⁴

Throughout the 1910s, Haskell received many more applications than it could accommodate. Despite already being filled to capacity, Haskell accepted more than 100 additional students from Carlisle after that school's closing in the summer of 1918, contributing to the overcrowded conditions at Haskell. During the academic year 1918–1919, Haskell's enrollment had risen to an all-time high of 1,130 students, with an average attendance of about 800 pupils.³⁵ By the second decade of the twentieth century, the school was well known throughout indigenous communities, and even though students' experiences were not always positive, enough native families felt comfortable sending their children to Lawrence to fill the school to its capacity of more than 1,000. In theory, off-reservation schools intended to "elevate" the most deserving and "backward" Indian students by taking them out of their reservation environments. In reality, though, many students had grown up outside of reservations, had attended public schools, and had at least one parent who belonged to the majority culture—all factors that influenced their experience at Haskell.

Whether students were eligible to attend, however, did not depend solely on their age or degree of Indian blood. One rule that was strictly enforced concerned the status of students who had deserted or who had been expelled from another government boarding school. Policymakers in the Office of Indian Affairs believed that once a student had forfeited his or her "privilege" of attending a government boarding school by being expelled, no other school should admit him or her. Students could be expelled on the grounds of serious violations of the school's rules, such as repeated desertion, the consumption of alcohol, or crimes such as theft, forgery, or arson. But the same rule applied to students who had been expelled owing to their insufficient degree of Indian blood. It was quite common for students who had been expelled or had deserted from one school to try to enroll in another school. Often, neither they nor Haskell's administrators were aware that the students had violated the rules of the Indian Office, that is, until the Indian Office followed up on the case or until Haskell received a letter from another school searching for students who had either deserted or had not returned after summer vacation. There was an ongoing confusion about the terms of enrollment, and some students, believing that their terms at one school had actually expired, enrolled for a new term in another school. Haskell often received inquiries from Chilocco and other boarding schools concerning the whereabouts of deserted or absent students. At the same time, Haskell's superintendents frequently contacted other schools in search of missing pupils. Considering that annual funding was determined on the basis of attendance, it becomes clear why superintendents were so eager to retain their students as well as to have them returned if the superintendents considered the students' absence to be in violation of school rules. In addition, any bending or breaking of the rules was considered detrimental to the school's discipline. Students were very much aware of the whereabouts and actions of their fellow pupils. They shared information among each other and across the miles, and they certainly influenced each other's behavior: whether to stay and adapt, to resist, or even to run away. The presence of friends or siblings and the closeness to one's home, as well as rumors about the special qualities of a certain school, could all influence a student's decision to try to enroll in another institution. School officials were aware of this and tried hard to keep what they considered illegal movements between schools to a minimum.

In 1908, the Indian Office announced that nonreservation boarding school agents would no longer be allowed to recruit students directly on the reservations. This new rule made the retention and return of already enrolled students even more of a priority for Haskell.[36] Commissioner of Indian Affairs Leupp was strongly opposed to the schools' recruitment activities, since he believed that school superintendents were prone to fill their schools with little or no regard to the children's health or welfare. He even compared the practice with the African slave trade and publicly decried this "regular system of traffic in these helpless little red people."[37] In the future, Indian parents would be allowed to decide for themselves whether they wished to send their children to an off-reservation school. If they decided to do so, they could apply through their reservation superintendents. Leupp, an outspoken critic of off-reservation boarding schools, believed that over time these changes in the regulations would lead to the closing of the majority of schools. He did not expect institutions such as Haskell to keep up their attendance figures without actively recruiting students, and he did not believe that Indian parents would choose off-reservation schools if they were no longer coerced into doing so. Superintendent Peairs was less than pleased by the new rules and feared that he would not be able to fill Haskell to its capacity. In a letter to one of his Oklahoma recruitment agents, he lamented:

> We are now in the hands of our enemies or friends as it may be. . . . The only thing we are allowed to do under the new regulation is to send out advertising matter and make an attempt to get parents to ask the 'Lords' of the reservation schools to send them to non-reservation schools. Time will tell what results will be. Of course I cannot send you or any one else out after pupils under the present conditions.[38]

The issue was the subject of many conversations among school administrators, revealing not just the superintendents' disagreement with the policy change but also interesting details about indigenous families' resistance to school rules that infringed upon their traditional way of life. A letter from Flandreau's superintendent illuminates this reality:

> You know as well as I do that Indians are never ready to start school in the fall of the year, they wanting to pick berries, make hay, pick rice, etc., before they are ready to come, which is usually about the time cold weather starts in and they need better clothing and more food. The average superintendent and agent in charge of reservations is not inclined to hurry pupils into a non-reservation school, giving them all the time that they desire to complete their work. Now it seems to me that we are going to be seriously deficient in our first quarter's attendance, which is based on the month of September.[39]

This statement shows native parents' pragmatism when it came to their children's school attendance. In late summer, the children's labor was needed at home, and Indian parents did not privilege government policies or school rules over their immediate needs. They refused to compromise their traditional yearly activities by sending away their children in the middle of the fall harvest. Haskell's records show that Indian families tried to keep their children at home as long as possible after the summer vacations and that students had their own agendas when it came to determine their departure date for the school. C. E. Birch, long-time principal teacher and head of Haskell's business department, informed Superintendent Peairs from his 1907 recruiting trip to Minnesota that "the boys will not agree to going until a little after the 1st of September as they are bound to take a hunt first. None of these have any desire to attend any other school however."[40] School rules were strict, but they were bent constantly. Knowing that Indian families were eager to stretch the rules according to their own needs, Peairs and his colleagues were afraid that the end of active recruitment and student roundups would make it harder for Haskell to reach its annual attendance figures.

It is interesting to note that the superintendents' worries proved unwarranted, and Leupp's prediction that off-reservation schools would disintegrate proved inaccurate. Despite the new ruling, Haskell did not have any problems filling its ranks. As the century progressed, students applied in ever-greater numbers, and Haskell had to turn down many applicants. Peairs's reaction, though, hints to another reality of the emerging Indian education system: the people working in the field felt contempt for many of the policies and rules implemented by the Office of Indian Affairs. As the education system became increasingly centralized and systematized, they felt restricted in their ability to make their own decisions.

One important change that met the approval of Peairs, however, was the inclusion of the Indian school system under the civil service. Beginning in the late 1890s, the positions of school superintendent, assistant superintendent, teachers, matrons, physicians, clerks, industrial teachers, carpenters, cooks, laundresses, seamstresses, and disciplinarians received civil service classifications. This led to a certain standard of quality among boarding school staff and increased the level of accountability. At the same time, it meant that tenure and advancement in the Indian Service depended on personal performance as well as on the success of their respective institutions, as indicated by enrollment and graduation rates.[41] One of the positions created to facilitate the monitoring of Indian schools was the post of superintendent of Indian schools. The superintendent was to inspect all Indian schools and make recommendations for their improvement to his or her superiors, the commissioner of Indian affairs and the secretary of the interior. H. B. Peairs was appointed to, and gladly accepted, the prestigious position of superintendent of Indian schools in April 1911, after having served as Haskell's superintendent for thirteen years. In April 1917, however, he returned to Haskell once more and remained the school's superintendent until his retirement in the mid-1920s.

By 1900, the Indian Office operated 147 reservation day schools, serving 5,000 students; 81 reservation boarding schools, with 9,600 pupils; and 25 off-reservation boarding schools attended by 7,430 students. In addition, 32 contract and 22 mission schools existed, serving a student population of about 4,075 students.[42] At the same time, the number of employees in the Indian school service had risen from a mere 114 in 1877 to 1,936 in 1897.[43] These figures indicate that a true "system" of Indian education was emerging—a system in which Haskell's students played a central part.

How did these developments affect prospective students, their families, and their communities? Did indigenous students in any way profit from these changes? Did they receive better care? Did it become easier for them to make their own choices? The centralization and bureaucratization of the education system certainly made it more difficult for parents to avoid sending their children to school altogether, and educating children traditionally in their own cultures became less of an option. At the same time, though, schooling choices became wider and more complex, allowing many indigenous families to use the government system to their own advantage. As demonstrated earlier, many native students had clear ideas and high expectations concerning their stay at Haskell. These students consciously chose Haskell over any other school, sometimes because of a particular course of study such as the business or the engineering course, sometimes because their siblings or parents had attended the school, and sometimes because they simply liked the brochures or the things they had heard from recruiters or friends. In the early 1900s, education was compulsory, but attendance at Haskell was not. Haskell's records attest to the initiative hundreds of students took when it came to their own education. Even though their letters tell only part of the story, they are nevertheless an important testimony to the children's agency. Commissioner Leupp's prediction that Indian parents would no longer send their children to Haskell once the coercion factor was gone simply proved wrong. Why? What appeal did the school have for indigenous families?

Although poverty, the loss of one or both parents, the lack of school facilities close to home, and other pressing circumstances can be regarded as coercive factors, choosing Haskell over other schools was in many cases a conscious decision. In the early 1900s, education had become a valued commodity across America, and it would be wrong to assume that Indian parents and their children did not value quality schooling. Even though indigenous and European concepts of education differed in many ways, education itself was highly valued among native peoples. And although the values Indian children were taught at home could differ substantially from those promoted by white educators, tribal cultures were certainly not devoid of values concerning privilege, status, and the power of knowledge. Knowledge was often linked to social, cultural, political, and economic institutions as well as to gender. Through knowledge, people asserted their authority and status, and oftentimes specific rights and powers were attached to this status. Schooling could become a way to affirm these values, cultural ideals, and practices. For some families and returned students, schooling became a means to assert their traditional sense of authority within their tribes. One should also bear in mind that in the early 1900s, Native Americans had already experienced 300 years of contact with non-Indian societies. At the turn of the twentieth century, native communities had been touched and changed by white missionaries, traders, merchants, soldiers, land speculators, settlers, policymakers, and teachers. For centuries, Indian cultures had adjusted to the changing circumstances and had adopted certain aspects of European cultures. By 1900, many Native Americans parents and even grandparents had been exposed to some form of Western education and had witnessed poverty, the breach of treaties, the loss of land, and the negative effects of the government's allotment policy. Many Indian parents regarded schooling as a necessity in a rapidly changing world, and like all parents, they hoped that their children would have a better life in the future. Even though letting their children go could be a heartbreaking experience, many Indian families believed that their children should be educated for a new way of life that was slowly but surely replacing the old one. The trauma that the separation caused was real. But so was the need for skills in a world that made it impossible for indigenous communities to sustain themselves based on their former way of life. The reasoning of a Pueblo student, even though expressed in 1997, reflects thoughts that native families at the turn of the century certainly harbored as well. Justifying what he called the "Anglo curriculum" of his Indian high school, the boy explained: "The reason they teach it is that we have to have it to live with a dominant race. If we don't have it, people will just run right over us. If we don't know what they are talking about, we won't be able to defend ourselves."[44]

By the late 1880s, several Indian leaders publicly supported Haskell. In February of 1888, a group of six Cheyenne and Osage leaders visited the school and encouraged the students to embrace education in order to save their people from extinction. Split Ax, an Osage leader, told the children: "White people's ways are not our ways, but we are trying to follow. . . . Our old customs are being done away with. Now is your chance to learn white people's ways."[45] One of the Cheyenne chiefs, Red Wolf, reiterated the government's rhetoric and urged the students to conform to the dominant society.[46] Wolf Face, another Cheyenne leader, praised Superintendent Robinson for his work: "Haskell is a very good school since the Governor took hold of it. It is now noted among the Indians in the territory. Indians all call him a very good man. You young men, as you receive instruction here, you must not forget you must help us when you come home." Wolf Face added that he had seen many schools in the East, but that none of them was as good as Haskell. Voicing the concern of many Indian parents, he warned Haskell's employees to "teach my people in the right way, and do not abuse them."[47] That same summer Red Wolf made a similar request to Robinson, promising him support in the collection of new pupils but at the same time urging him to send any sick child home to his or her parents. In the light of high death rates during the 1887–1888 school year, the support of so many influential Indian leaders was quite a tribute to Robinson and a sign of growing indigenous interest in the institution.

By the early twentieth century, even tribal leaders who had once fiercely fought for their peoples' independence supported the idea of schooling. Haskell, for instance, admitted several boys from Geronimo's Apache band who were under arrest at Ft. Sill, Oklahoma. The boys came to Haskell voluntarily and were supported in their decision by their elders. Geronimo's nephew, Asa Daklugie, who attended Carlisle, paraphrased his uncle's pragmatism: "Without this training in the ways of the White Eyes, our people could never compete with them. So it was necessary that those destined for leadership prepare themselves to cope with the enemy. I was to be trained to become the leader."[48] Many Indian leaders shared Geronimo's sentiments and expected the young people to learn reading and writing in order to understand treaties and other documents so that they could act as culture brokers between the dominant culture and the tribes. Indian youth often attended white schools in order to serve their people. Their elders did not expect them to assimilate or to lose their own culture but to acquire skills and an understanding for Anglo ways that would help their tribes to survive as distinct entities. Many indigenous people exhibited a modern, adaptive "tribal patriotism," accepting certain elements of white civilization in order to defend their tribal identity rather than to be assimilated into American society.[49]

Of course, not all parents and elders felt this way. In the early 1890s, Superintendent Meserve observed "on the part of a large majority of the parents a feeling that their children are drifting away from them," leading to "opposition to the schools."[50] Sometimes, opinions were divided within the family and the community, leading to bitter controversies among kin. Haskell's records abound with letters reflecting divisions between children and their families. Sometimes a child was eager to go to Haskell, but one of the parents was strictly opposed; sometimes students left without the consent of their parents. As one of Haskell's recruiters in Oklahoma put it: "I do not wish to be pessimistic but it seems to me if a parent is willing, the child is not, and vice-versa."[51] In a 1967 interview, Mary Poafpybitty Neido, a Comanche/Arapaho woman from Oklahoma, recalled that in 1908, when she was thirteen years old, her parents did not consent to the agent's attempt to enroll her at Haskell: "My mother wouldn't sign the papers and my dad wouldn't let me go. 'No we don't want her to go up there. She might run off or she'll freeze to death or somebody might kill her on the road.' . . . Both of my brothers went. I didn't go. They were younger than I am and they went. And my mother said, 'No she's not going but you boys could go. Boys are tougher than the girls.' That's what she told my brothers so they went."[52] Poafpybitty Neido's parents were not alone in their reluctance to send their daughter to Haskell, where she would be far away from her family's supervision. In the fall of 1909, Lizzie Fuller, an Ojibwe student from Red Lake, Minnesota, wrote to Superintendent Peairs:

> Just a few lines to answer your question. . . . I thought I would surely go to Haskell this fall and now I see I can't go any place this fall. Dear me. I wish I could go over there—my mother would let me go but my father wouldn't let me go. But I know I can't go without my father's name. I am always to go to Haskell because I heard Haskell is the highest school and best of all. . . . So if you tell me what to do, I will try to go next summer again, that is if I live that long.[53]

Lizzie Fuller's letter shows Haskell's good reputation and high ranking among the children of a particular native community. It also shows how much the girl really wanted to attend Haskell and how unhappy she was about her father's opposition. Apparently she had corresponded with the school before and was not planning to give up her dream of coming to Haskell, even though she did not dare to leave against her father's will. In other cases, students managed to circumvent the parental consent clause by taking advantage of their extended family's positive attitude toward Haskell as well as the absence of their parents. According to the rules of the Office of Indian Affairs, children under the age of eighteen could not be transferred from "any Indian reservation to a school beyond the State or Territory in which said reservation is situated without the voluntary consent of the father or mother of such child if either of them are living, and if neither of them are living, without the voluntary consent of the next of kin of such child."[54] Sometimes it was difficult for Haskell's administrators to know who a child's legal guardian was and who was eligible to sign the child's application form. In 1906, W. E. Hudspeth from Pine Ridge, South Dakota, sent the following telegram to the president of the United States:

> The President, Washington.
> Myrtle, my 17-year old daughter, quarter-blood Indian, has been taken to Lawrence, Kansas, placed in Haskell Institute, without my consent. Have appealed to Superintendent of Haskell for her return; can get no satisfaction. Law says Indians should not be moved without consent parents. I am her father; want her returned where she can have my protection. All appeals to other authority have been fruitless. Am informed you can, through proper authority return my daughter Pine Ridge. Please answer at my expense, as the suspense I am subjected to is awful. W. E. Hudspeth.[55]

In order to clarify the situation, Myrtle gave her version of what had happened in the following statement:

> My mother has been dead for six years. I have attended the Mission school for three years at Pine Ridge. . . . Last December I went to Pine Ridge to my aunt Fannie Janis' place. Last March Mr. Balmer was getting pupils for Haskell. I gave my consent to go. My aunt Fannie Janis also gave her consent to have me go. The last twelve months my father has been at Buffalo Gap, S.D. I went to Haskell with my own free will and was anxious to go.[56]

According to Haskell's representative, Janis had told him that she was the girl's legal guardian and he did not question her since Myrtle was very eager to attend Haskell. In her statement to the local Indian agent, Fannie Janis supported her niece's story and said that Myrtle "cried and took such a spell that we signed her paper." She added that the girl had threatened to "run away with an Indian buck or kill herself if I did not let her go to school."[57] Pine Ridge's Indian agent explained to Superintendent Peairs that in his opinion the girl would be much better off at Haskell than on the reservation since her home influences were very bad. He doubted Myrtle's father's sincerity in requesting his daughter's return and advised Peairs to keep the girl at Haskell against her father's will.[58] In response to all these statements and explanations, the commissioner of Indian affairs ruled in favor of the girl's father: "The correspondence you submit would indicate that the girl's best interests would be subserved by her remaining at Haskell Institute. Notwithstanding this, the law is very plain on the subject, and you will take the necessary steps to return her to her father."[59]

Myrtle Hudspeth's story is one of many preserved in Haskell's records that reflect the students' strong initiative, the parents' determination to decide what was best for their children, and the government's patriarchal way of dealing with these issues. Commissioner Leupp's ruling to return the girl to her father's care is unusual in that it overrides the recommendations of several other officials involved. In many other cases, parents' requests were the last to be considered, giving preference to the judgments of white Indian agents and school superintendents. Often, students were retained in schools despite the law calling for parental consent. It was easy for the Indian Office to declare parents unfit for their own children's upbringing, and many parents wrote to supervisors and Indian agents in vain. Myrtle's father took his request to the last resort—he sent a telegram to President Theodore Roosevelt and invoked the rule of law. His prior pleading had been to no avail, but this desperate last attempt to have his daughter returned proved successful. Rarely did parents go that far in their quest for justice, but Myrtle's story is a vivid example of the conflicting interests and high emotions involved in this first stage of the boarding school drama.

Whereas some parents went through much effort and pain to keep their children out of school or to have them returned home, others went to great lengths to make sure that their children could enroll at Haskell and would receive exactly the kind of education that they had in mind for their offspring.

In reality, though, the school had the last word when it came to deciding which course of study a child was allowed to follow, whether the student was permitted to spend vacations at home, or whether the child was allowed to leave Haskell before the official term of enrollment had expired if the parents so desired. Many relatives expressed their and their children's wishes to the school before signing the enrollment forms, as the following letter shows:

> Dear Sir, I will write to you in order to let you know that I am going to send my sister up there to school, but I want ask this before I send her that you let her come home every vacation or any time when we need her happen to be one of our folks should be sick that you let her come. You know some Superintendents say they do that but they never do. I know how they talk just to get the children into their school once she goes there for three years. Answer my letter and let me know.[60]

Parents and relatives were very much aware of the practices boarding schools used to retain students in school. They were suspicious and cautious when it came to the school's promises. Superintendent Peairs's answers to their requests were usually short and evasive. He explained to them that the children could go on a thirty-day summer vacation if the families would deposit enough money for transportation. He also stated that if a student should be required to go home during the school year, a formal request to the Indian agent had to be made. Only with his endorsement and a travel deposit could a leave of absence be granted. Peairs avoided making any promises that were against Haskell's rules and hoped that the parents would sign the application blanks without any further inquiries.

Parents quickly found out that Haskell was less than willing to accommodate their wishes, once the children had entered the school. Ultimately, the school decided whether a student would be allowed to go home and whether the reasons given by the parents were sufficient to warrant a leave of absence or even a student's discharge. Like all Indian boarding schools of the period, Haskell consciously and deliberately took away the parents' fundamental right to determine what was best for their children.

Students had their own agendas for applying to Haskell and often did so without their parents' knowledge or support. Some came to enroll in a particular program, some to join friends or siblings, some to escape from their home environment or to flee parental control, some because they were attracted by Haskell's intertribal environment, and some because they wanted to play in the band or on one of Haskell's famous athletic teams. Jesse Rowlodge, an Arapaho born in Indian Territory in 1884, attended Haskell from 1904 until 1910. In an interview he gave in 1968, Rowlodge explained his reasons for coming to Lawrence:

> You know the reason I left, really—the purpose I left was I used to get in lots of girl trouble. I'd sooner get out of one trouble than I'd get in another. So I just thought, "Well this ain't gonna last forever, so I'm gonna go off to school. Anyhow, I wanted to go to school. Be a good way to get away from this girl's trouble around here, you know." . . . So I actually run off from home to go to school, instead of the other ways [laughs]![61]

In a later part of the interview, Rowlodge elaborated why he chose Haskell:

> When I grew up I told my dad that I wasn't going to go to Carlisle. I didn't care for it. They were a military school; you know at Carlisle—had white uniforms. I told him, "I don't take to these uniforms, so I'm going to go to Haskell, where some of these pretty well educated Indians came from." That's in Lawrence, Kansas. That's where the best educated Indians come out from . . . that's where I studied. They had good courses in practical schooling, you know, and they teach commercial and all subjects. . . . That's where all these clerks at the Agency, now, that have worked up, you know—office clerks. They're agents now. The Commissioner of Indian Affairs—all those employees in Indian offices, were educated at Haskell.[62]

Rowlodge's recollections reflect the personal reasons that motivated students to come to Haskell and the perceptions of Haskell in a particular Indian community. Jesse Rowlodge joined Haskell's band and various athletic teams and excelled in his academic performance, graduating from the business course in 1910.

That same year, Charles McGilbery from Oklahoma wrote to Superintendent Fiske: "Dear Sir—I am a full-blood Choctaw Indian. I am 17 years old, in 8th grade, and am in good health. I beg to be your student. I could be valuable to the school in football and baseball. Will you please send me a Blank so I might fill it out and enter the Institute next September. I beg to be your student. Charles McGilbery"[63] Charles was certainly aware of Haskell's great reputation in athletics, and he saw the school as an opportunity to play against some of the country's best football teams. For most Indian boys, Haskell's or Carlisle's football, baseball, and basketball teams were the only chance to play their favorite sports on a collegiate level.

Other students were eager to continue their education in a particular program, as indicated by Patrick O'Neil's 1910 letter from the Wind River Reservation in Wyoming:

Dear Sir,

I find no better time than now to make arrangements with you. I would like to take a thorough course of engineering, both steam and electrical. I was a student at Carlisle Indian School; I served a time of five years there. I spent most of the time under the outing system. I have only been away from school about six months, and I never did have a fair chance of mastering a trade. I would like to devote all my time to engineering. I would like to hear from you soon. I will pay my own fare to school. Please answer without delaying.

Yours Respectfully, Patrick O'Neil.[64]

Whereas Patrick O'Neil had very clear ideas concerning his future career, sixteen-year-old John Taylor from Minnesota looked to Haskell for a new home, where he would be cared for after the death of his mother:

Dear Sir,

I will inform you with these few lines that I would like to be one of your students. I wanted to go to school there. My poor mother she has been dead for about a month. I am the only one left alone. I haven't got any home after my mother died. I am full blood Santee Indian. I am only 16 years of age. I have been gone to country school. I have heard Haskell Institute was a nice school. I would like to come to school. . . . Hoping to hear from you.

Yours truly. John Taylor.[65]

As these letters indicate, most students who took the initiative to write to Haskell's superintendent had already been exposed to several years of schooling and were familiar with the school's rules and routines.[66]

In the twentieth century, Haskell had become a "continuing" school, and only few students enrolled without any prior schooling. Whether students came of their own free will and with the support of their families or whether they were coerced to attend could substantially influence their adjustment to life at Haskell. A pro-school family did not necessarily produce a well-adjusted Indian student, however, nor did a child's initial wish to attend the school. On the other hand, many students who were forced to come to Lawrence eventually got to like the school and decided to continue their schooling after their first term had expired. Although boarding schools created many problems for Indian students and their communities, they also offered solutions to some of their most immediate concerns. Even though Native Americans at times resented boarding schools, they also found them useful. In times of economic hardship or family crisis, Indians could turn to boarding schools for support.[67]

No matter what their background or initial motivation was, once the children left home, they embarked on an unknown and oftentimes frightening journey into a new world. Saying good-bye to friends and families could be heartbreaking, and in their autobiographies, former students recall the trauma of being separated from home and family. Esther Burnett described the emotional departure from her mother, as she and her two siblings left their Wyoming home for Haskell: "As we clung tearfully to our mother, she reminded us, 'If you run away from school, you'll go back faster than you came home.' It must have been heart wrenching for her to say this, but it was her way of protecting us from the dangers that she knew we would encounter if we ran away. It sounded harsh to us, but she had our best interest at heart."[68] Especially in the early boarding school days, parents were afraid they might never see their children again, a fear that became a reality for far too many families. Visits from parents were rarely encouraged, and most parents could not afford to travel to Haskell in order to see their children. Even though children stayed in touch with their families through monthly letters, Christmas packages, and news carried by word of mouth from friends and relatives, the good-bye at the end of the summer usually meant a very long separation—sometimes for several years at a time. Letting young children travel to a place several hundred or even thousands of miles away was as frightening for the parents as it was for their offspring. Stories of children who got lost on the way abounded, and parents' fears proved well founded.

The trip could be long and bewildering, and younger children and students who had never left their reservations before were often bedazzled by the experience. For some children, the trip lasted several days and was quite an adventure, as the Indian agent's route description for two boys from northern Arizona illustrates:

> These Indians live 150 miles from a railroad and only one of these boys has ever seen a railroad train much less ridden on one. It will require three or four days to make the trip from here to Marysvale. Just now there is 4ft of snow on the mountains we must pass over so will have to wait until a good road is opened. The trip will require us to have at least 4 nights of lodging before we take the train at Marysvale. Only one train a day leaves Marysvale, that in the morning. I can take the government team from here to Marysvale and save at least $30 on stage fare. There will be at least two train changes between Marysvale and Lawrence. I am of the opinion that these boys will need an escort, as I do not believe that they will be able to make the trip alone.[69]

Superintendent Wise, however, did not think an escort was necessary, as long as the boys were well instructed and would receive a card for the train conductor explaining their route and final destination.

In general, however, Haskell tried to have students travel in groups and with designated escorts, especially if the students were girls. Older students, as well as students who had made the trip before, were usually allowed to travel by themselves. One can only imagine how the two Arizona boys must have felt, traveling for several days, experiencing a train ride for the first time, and entering a part of the country and a landscape that they had never seen before. In their autobiographies, former students recalled their fears and amazement during their first trip to boarding schools in the East. The children were terrified when they realized that the row of "houses" they were sitting in was beginning to move—they had never seen a train before—or when they discovered that the "house" they entered was actually a boat. Some students from the South saw snow for the very first time; some were amazed to see cities, towns, villages, and farms pass by; many were terrified by the way whites stared at them in the train depots; and some disliked the unfamiliar food they were offered during the trip. Esther Burnett vividly recalled her first trip to Haskell that took her and her two siblings all the way from Wyoming to eastern Kansas:

I remember that it was a long, long way.... The conductor showed us points of interest as we traveled through the flat, treeless plains. It might have been much more frightening had we not known that someone on the train was responsible for us, and the conductor seemed to have taken that responsibility very much to heart. As he walked back and forth tending to his own duties, he would joke with us and ask how we were. I was not terribly scared. We ate our meals in the dining car; the flower on the table and the concern of our fellow passengers made us feel quite sophisticated as we began our journey into the unknown.[70]

The students' feelings veered between excitement and fear, between confidence and regret. By the 1900s and 1910s, most of the children had already been exposed to a certain amount of white culture and schooling. Only a few of them would have experienced the trip to Haskell in ways as dramatic as the students during the school's early days. Nevertheless, the voyage to Lawrence was an exciting part of the great adventure that was about to begin—their life at Haskell Institute.

CHAPTER THREE

Living by the Bell

After a long and tiring trip, the children finally arrived in Lawrence, anxious to begin their new life at Haskell Institute. Many children were homesick and frightened; others were excited and curious about their new school. But no matter what their initial mindset was, little prepared them for the harsh realities of boarding school life. Esther Burnett remembered her first traumatic hours at the school:

> We were worn out and disheveled from our travels and leery of what new changes were about to take place. . . . One of the first places they took us was to the dormitories. I have a vivid recollection of the long row of white cots on the sleeping porches in the dormitory at Haskell; they reminded me of the crowded hospital ward where my father died. I was grief-stricken and frightened, and I can still visualize myself standing there, feeling lost and alone. . . . I thought, "I hate this place; I will never be happy here." I wondered which direction my home was.[1]

Their arrival at Haskell was a moment that most children would remember for a lifetime. The new surroundings, the unfamiliar faces, the impressive structures, and the foreign languages—all these impressions were confusing and in many cases frightening for the students. The children's age and prior exposure to white culture certainly influenced their immediate response to their new home, but even children who had been reared off the reservation or had attended other schools before were overwhelmed by the experience. Arrival at Haskell meant entering a world that had very little in common with the students' home environment. It was a place designed to change the children completely: to alter their outer appearance, their language, their habits, their way of thinking, and their demeanor. This assault on the children's culture and on their Indian identity began immediately after they arrived on the Haskell campus. Culture shock awaited even acculturated youngsters. Lucille Winnie, who was part Seneca and part Cayuga, had grown up with parents working as Bureau of Indian Affairs teachers, had relatives who were Haskell alumni, and had even visited the campus before her enrollment. Lucille was twelve years old when she arrived in 1912 and had come to the school voluntarily. Nevertheless, her first day at Haskell was a painful and "never-to-be-forgotten" experience. Lucille was "keenly disappointed" that she would not be allowed to share a room with her sister and "wanted to go home at once." During the night she lay on her uncomfortable bed and wondered why she had "been so stupid" as to exchange her room at home for the impersonal and cold Haskell dormitory. She tried hard to hold back the tears, but her high expectations of Haskell had been shattered that very first day.[2] Even though Esther Burnett and Lucille Winnie would eventually come to enjoy their stay at Haskell, the transition to boarding school life required students to go through a number of painful changes and rituals that were designed to transform them into "civilized" Christian Americans.

One of the most distinctive and pervasive characteristics of federal Indian boarding schools was the military regimentation. The children were closely controlled around the clock, living by the bell almost every minute of the day. Boarding schools such as Haskell comprised a tightly controlled space that served to discipline, compartmentalize, and individualize the students. Haskell was laid out like a military camp, a world filled with squares, corners, and lines: square or rectangular desks, tables, and beds (all carefully arranged in straight rows) filled square or rectangular classrooms, dormitories, and dining rooms.[3] The same was true for the school grounds, where the Western concept of human dominance over nature became apparent in contoured gardens, cured lawns, and trimmed trees. The students were constantly under surveillance, and their daily routine was characterized by a relentless regimentation. Every aspect of their daily life—sleeping, eating, learning, working, singing, and praying—was rigidly scheduled. Bells gave the rhythm for a seemingly endless number of required responses. One of the most important instruments of discipline was the clock. The division of every practice into quarters of an hour, minutes, and seconds came to increasingly govern their life. The students were expected to comply with white conceptions of time, obedience, and military forms of training. Their behavior was constantly recorded and under surveillance, and their progress was subject to meticulous examination. Noncompliance led to various forms of punishment, ranging from corporal punishment such as whipping to isolation through confinement in a school jail or guardhouse. Frequently school officials employed punishment techniques that were directly related to the disciplinary lessons they were hoping to teach. Boys were forced to march for long periods of time; girls had to cut the school grass with scissors or were assigned extra chores such as scrubbing the floors or cleaning up the school grounds.[4]

Haskell's second superintendent, Colonel Grabowskii, was instrumental in establishing the school's military system. Like other Indian educators of his time, he was of the opinion that the only way to house, feed, teach, and especially control several hundred "savage" youngsters was through strict discipline and harsh punishments. Grabowskii introduced a cadet system, dividing students into a battalion of five companies, organized by age and gender, which were supposed to break up tribal groupings and any student resistance. He required students to sleep in dormitories and to sit in the dining hall with their assigned companies. He also established Haskell's prison, a structure that would be used to punish unruly students for decades to come. The preferred method of controlling students was the platoon system of organization for mass movements of the children from the dormitories to the dining halls, dining halls to the classrooms, and from the classrooms to the work details.[5]

Disciplinary power and surveillance works not only from the top to the bottom but also laterally. Even though one can distinguish between the dominant and the dominated, it is not the dominant but the apparatus as a whole that produces power. During the late 1880s, Superintendent Charles Robinson exercised less overt disciplinary power than his predecessor, but he was instrumental in establishing the court-martial system of lateral surveillance.[6] Robinson granted Haskell's students a degree of autonomy without relinquishing any of the school's power. By making the students responsible for enforcing the code of conduct, he made them an intricate part of the system, "supervisors perpetually supervised." According to a 1909 report, the court-martial system was quite effective in keeping students in line, even though sometimes students were too lenient with some offenders and too strict with others. Also, some pupils were reluctant to recognize the justice of their punishment. Despite these shortcomings, the system was used at Haskell for many years.[7] Esther Burnett's memoirs from the 1920s show how little had changed during the preceding thirty years:

> We were divided into companies by grade and sex; the company officers—captain, lieutenant, sergeant, major—were students who were responsible for drilling the companies. There was a competition between the companies not only in the drill exercises but also for good citizenship—meaning good behavior—especially in our detail. There was a group called the "awkward squad" by the staff, and actually all of us! They were those kids who couldn't master the technique of marching, and they needed extra drill.[8]

Haskell used a demerit system, giving students the power to give demerits to their fellow students for offenses such as sloppy detail work or loitering in the halls on their way to class. Students had to work their demerits off by doing menial tasks such as cleaning the toilets or polishing the assembly hall. If they accumulated too many demerits, punishment could be even harder and could include the loss of one's privilege to go to town or the movies. Company officers were responsible for random checks and white-glove inspections in the students' dormitories—the boys in the female quarters and the girls in the boys' quarters. Esther Burnett became an officer herself. Her recollections attest to the inner conflicts Haskell's students experienced once they became actively involved in the school's disciplinary system:

> It became a matter of honor for me to be able to discipline my best friend or relative. It was not easy for me to hand out demerits, and it often created hard feelings. I realized that we officers were being used by the school, but like student governing bodies today, we were aware that we were being taught self-discipline. . . . Occasionally, student officers would get so caught up in their own ego trips that they would try to throw their weight around in order to get even with someone whom they had a grudge against. Haskell terminology for someone who acted in this way was a suitcase. Nevertheless, it was an honor to be chosen as an officer, and most of us had great pride in the military.[9]

Burnett's interpretation of Haskell's military practices shows the children's awareness of the deeper meaning and purpose of the system. Students knew that discipline was a means to re-educate them culturally and that through the officer system, the school used them to control and transform each other. But Burnett's account also shows that she willingly accepted parts of the dominant ideology, seeing an intrinsic value in a system that taught her what she considered important lessons for her life. Over the years, Haskell's system of student government was expanded and an honor roll system introduced that granted students certain privileges as a reward for good behavior. The honor roll system was regarded as an important method to prepare students for the duties of citizenship, which would be extended to them upon graduation.[10]

Even though the power exercised over American Indian children appears less violent than that formerly exercised against their parents and grandparents on the battlefield, it was nonetheless corporal in a multitude of ways. Their bodies were the very targets of transformation: their hair, their clothes, their way of movement, their diet, their medical practices, their forms of personal hygiene—in short, all bodily practices were made part of the educational assault. The children were expected to change not just their appearance but also their demeanor. At boarding school they were required to stand at attention with eyes straight ahead. This was not simply a change in stance but also an indication of a forced change in attitude for Indian children who might have been taught at home that an indirect stance was an indication of respect. In the mind of Indian educators, the children's bodies had to be transformed, subjected, used, and improved, to make them "civilized," docile, and productive members of American society or, more specifically, the American working class. As one student recalled, "The supervisors were all non-Indian, and I suppose they felt that the Indian was dirty and filthy; and so they gave us brushes and we scrubbed the floors until there was no varnish or finishing on them."[11] At the time, good health, neatness, politeness, self-confidence, and the ability to concentrate were all attributed to strict discipline, hard physical labor, and the military regimen. Indian educators believed that military training could teach Indian girls and boys everything from obedience to patriotism and the Protestant work ethic.

The underlying assumption was that Indian children were wild and savage, products of cultures devoid of discipline, order, and self-constraint. Indian educators of the time believed that Indian parents "generally exercise very little control over their children and allow them the utmost freedom."¹² This, of course, was not true. Esther Burnett argued that even though Shoshone values differed from white values, discipline was far from absent in her family: "Some of our people, too, have gotten the idea that Indians didn't discipline their children. My mom would have disagreed with that. Indian children were taught to obey by example, and they were taught to be quiet. . . . The way we disciplined our children was through touch and firm but gentle words."¹³

The ways Indian parents taught their children were certainly different from those of the dominant society. Nevertheless, indigenous societies had many ways of teaching their children obedience and culturally appropriate behavior. Instead of punishing children physically or forcing them to do certain things, Indian families would rather employ techniques such as teasing and allowing the children to learn by observation and experimentation.¹⁴ Many indigenous families taught their children to "stand-in" rather than to "stand-out." They expected them to behave in noncompetitive ways and to place the communal good over their individual desires. These teachings stood in contrast to the rugged individualism, aggressiveness, and competition promoted in much of American society. While at Haskell, students constantly had to negotiate the opposing expectations and worldviews that were now part of their lives. Esther Burnett believed that despite the pressure to assimilate, Haskell's students were successful at retaining their Indian values:

> While we were encouraged to compete as individuals and to vie with other students for privilege and favor, we also managed to maintain a sense of responsibility to our fellow students. This responsibility to community is a part of the Indian way. . . . We nurtured a sense of community among ourselves, which helped us not only to survive the boarding school experience but to grow in it and learn from it.¹⁵

But indigenous cultural teachings could also help the children to master their new environment. As one boarding school student explained, "we had been trained to respect authority, and that is the secret of a successful apprenticeship to military life."¹⁶ Respect for kin, training to endure hardships, and conditioning to accept discipline were all part of tribal teachings and made the transition to Haskell easier. According to Sally Hyer, Pueblo cultural teachings of perseverance and tolerance allowed students at Santa Fe Indian

School to survive an extremely repressive environment through passive resistance.[17] Looking at Pueblo cultures more closely supports this view. Traditionally, the Hopi approve of the person who is a hard worker, who is good-natured, and who causes no trouble. The ideal for the "good life" is a state of harmony in which the person has peace of mind and only good thoughts, devoid of anxiety and hatred. Hopi parents expect their children to perform household work in well-defined gender roles, to respect property rights, and to avoid conflicts.[18] These teachings were certainly beneficial to the students' adaptation to boarding school life.

The same holds true for the Navajo, whose worldview has as its goal the preservation and restoration of universal harmony, expressed in the Navajo term *hozho,* which is a combination of many ideas, including beauty, harmony, well-being, goodness, and happiness. In Navajo society, a child was cut off from the maternal relationship at an early age, when an older sibling took over the youngster's care. This cultural pattern could have helped children feel more comfortable in a boarding school environment that left them with only their peers as primary relationship partners. In Navajo society, control of the individual is achieved primarily by "lateral sanctions" rather than sanctions from above. This characteristic, which can be found among other tribes as well, might have facilitated the students' adaptation to the student officer and court-martial system propagated at Haskell.[19]

For other students, the school's emphasis on hierarchy and discipline did not oppose their tribal values but actually provided venues to reaffirm their traditional beliefs. This was especially true for students from the Plains tribes, who came from societies that distinguished their members according to social rank, attaching specific rights and privileges to a person's or a family's status. Many students carried their values and notions of status over to the boarding school setting and used Haskell's disciplinary structure to their own advantage, by asserting their traditional sense of authority over children from other tribes and especially their own tribe. Obviously, students did not come to Haskell as "blank sheets" or "empty vessels." Each individual brought along a rich cultural and personal history that equipped him or her to deal with the many challenges of boarding school life.

For most students, it took time to get used to the discipline and regimentation, but sooner or later the military regime became an integral, and often accepted, part of their daily lives. The bell regulated their days, and every minute of their time was appropriated to a certain task. From six o'clock in the morning on, the children were on a tight schedule that changed little over the course of weeks, months, and years. To Indian children who were oftentimes used to much greater freedom, the adaptation to Anglo concepts of time was especially hard. The expression "being on Indian time" in contrast to "Anglo time" is often used in a humorous context. Nevertheless, to this day there is some truth in this comparison, as the recent explanation of a Pueblo student illustrates: "In the non-Indian world I am constantly pushed to do things at a certain time. I have to get to my first class on time. Eat lunch after fifth period and before sixth. We all have time limits when things are done in a non-Indian way. In the Indian way we do things when we think they should be done. There are no times set on when we do things. We work during the day until the sun sets in the West."[20] Many studies mention differences in Indian versus white conceptions of time—sometimes as "circular" versus "linear," sometimes as "natural time" as opposed to "clock time." Clearly, for Indian students the cultural and psychological distance separating these two orientations was substantial. For many children, promptness and punctuality, highly valued in Western culture, must have been difficult concepts to grasp. Indian educators believed that by constantly drilling and marching, the mechanical, clocklike movements on the drill field would carry over to other areas of student behavior.[21] Students did not always agree with this view, and many youngsters held the white man's clock, as well as the drilling field, in disdain. Lucille Winnie, who attended Haskell in the 1910s, strongly objected to the military system: "All this shouting of commands and marching was a lot of nonsense to me. I felt then, and still do that the army is no place for a woman. Due to my firm belief I was never popular with the officers or matrons, and in seven years at Haskell my rank was 'buck private.'"[22] Even though Lucille complained about the cold and bullying staff that resembled army superiors rather than mentors, she spent many years at Haskell. Her account is typical of the ambivalence students experienced during their boarding school years. Despite her strong critique, she adjusted to the routine and succeeded academically. Lucille remained convinced in her later life that her education at Haskell had changed her life for the better and had opened the world to her.[23]

On the other hand, there were students such as Esther Burnett, who took pride in the school's military regimen and felt empowered by participating in its rituals: "By the time that I left Haskell, I had obtained the rank of major and was sometimes responsible for drilling the whole platoon of companies on Sunday afternoon when townspeople from Lawrence would visit the campus and watch us go through what was called a silent manual, or silent drill. We were trained so well that we could drill without any commands being given. It must have been an interesting sight to see us Indian kids marching around in military formation."[24] Burnett might have been less critical of Haskell's philosophy than many other students, but she saw a clear connection between the lessons learned at school and her Arapaho identity: "My husband-to-be—whom I met at Haskell—and I used to talk about the military regime in the boarding school. We were grateful for that military experience because it taught us self-discipline for our later lives. That's what it did for us. It may not have done that for everybody, but we both knew that self-control was one of the strongest of the Indian values."[25] Many students felt like Burnett and participated eagerly in the school's military training, which became an entertainment in itself: as part of the graduation exercises, Haskell annually organized competitive drills between six companies of cadets, which were judged by high-ranking military personnel invited from nearby military bases.[26]

Boarding school life was full of conflicting experiences, and even students who disliked the military regimen often developed nostalgia for the "order" of their school days. The regimentation was certainly hard to get used to. Nevertheless, it provided a structured and in many ways safe environment for young people who frequently came from poverty-stricken homes or broken families. Haskell was certainly not heaven, but it could become a safe haven for children who lacked structure or care during a difficult historical period.

Changing the children's "savage" outer appearance was the first step in the long process of stripping them of their tribal identities. On arrival, the children were required to take a bath, an experience that was frightening and humiliating for many youngsters. The older students washed themselves; staff members scrubbed the younger ones. All students were disinfected and treated for lice. The assumption that all Indian children needed sanitizing and delousing was humiliating to many children, who were ashamed and shocked by the presumption that their home environments were dirty.[27] Keeping the children clean certainly benefited their health and the overall sanitary conditions at Haskell. Nevertheless, the assumptions underlying the rigorous sanitation regimen were as much cultural as practical. Controlling and changing the children's "uncivilized" bodies was a first step in the long process of assimilation. Ojibwe student Mattie recalled that upon arrival at Haskell, "we were stripped of our clothing, we were given baths and haircuts and fine combs. It was to make us more or less easier to handle. At school, who's going to stop and braid your hair?"[28] The older girls had their hair trimmed and were expected to wear one of the modest and tidy Western hairstyles of the day. Many younger girls had their hair cut shorter, as pictures from the period indicate. Sometimes girls lost their braids for disciplinary purposes, as a punishment for running away or repeated offenses of the school rules.[29] Cutting the children's hair took on a distinctly cultural dimension when it came to the boys' hair. It was one of the school's transforming rituals to crop off the boys' long hair, thereby destroying one of the children's most visible symbols of their tribal identity. Educators considered long hair a sign of savagery, and removing it was central to the new identification with civilization. In many Indian cultures hair cutting was associated with mourning, and for many of the boys the loss of their braids was a traumatic experience. But resistance proved futile, and the staff defused the boys' opposition by taking the children out of the classroom one-by-one. To Indian students the loss of their hair meant more than a simple change in style. It signified a very real assault on their identity as indigenous people and the beginning of a transformation that would change them for good.[30]

After being cleaned and trimmed, the children experienced the next step in the civilization process: They had to exchange their personal clothes for the uniforms and dresses that the government in Washington provided for them. Most children arrived at school with little or nothing in the way of personal possessions, many of them because they were poor, others because the school hardly provided any space for the students to store their belongings. To Lucille Winnie, the clothes given to her at Haskell looked like "prison garb" and were much inferior to the beautiful dress and underwear that her mother had made for her before she left for school.[31] Her description testifies to the fact that by the early 1900s, students did not usually arrive at Haskell in buckskin dresses, leggings, or blankets, even though that had often been the case in the school's early years. For students who were used to traditional clothing, the change to "citizen's clothes" could be difficult. Many boys disliked the feeling of coarse trousers, and students complained about scratchy woolen underwear and heavy, ill-fitting boots.[32] The dress code at boarding schools violated the students' sense of individuality and was another aspect of the school's mission to mold them into carbon copies of white Americans. Ironically, as symbols of total conformity rather than expressions of individuality and personal freedom, school uniforms reinforced the communal values that policymakers had intended to destroy. Nevertheless, "dressing-up as white men" seems to have been less traumatic to the children than losing their hair, and some children appear to have enjoyed the excitement of wearing the unfamiliar garments.[33]

According to Indian Service rules, each boy received two plain suits and an extra pair of trousers, and each girl received three dresses. In some instances, boys were also provided with a Sunday suit of better quality. The annual clothing ration also included the necessary underwear, nightclothes, and boots.[34] For poor families, the fact that the school provided clothing could be an incentive to send their children to Haskell. Moreover, school uniforms had an equalizing effect since they softened economic differences among the students and allowed students with no or very little money to attend school properly dressed. At the same time, though, parents and students frequently complained about the insufficient number and poor quality of clothes given to the children. When Superintendent Meserve arrived at Haskell in the early 1890s, he found that "there was a great lack of clothing both for boys and girls, as well as sheets, etc. for the beds."[35] The clothing promised by Indian Service regulations did not always reach the students. Sometimes the school did not have enough money to buy the necessary materials, sometimes the materials ordered turned out to be of inferior quality, and Haskell often lacked the sheer manpower to produce the large amount of garments necessary to fulfill its students' needs. Even though the students were employed in the making of their own clothes, it was almost impossible for the girls and boys to manufacture adequate supplies for a student body of several hundreds. When in the summer of 1903, Superintendent Peairs asked the Indian Office for some relief, his request for additional help in the tailoring department was denied. Instead, his superiors pointed out the educational value of the students' work and requested them to work even harder to "thus receive the benefit of the experience." In the end, Haskell's students had to carry the burden of this argument: they did not receive adequate clothing at the beginning of the term, and they had to manufacture even more clothes than Haskell's superintendent considered humanly possible.[36]

Haskell's leadership acknowledged the inferior quality of some of the issued articles and allowed students to purchase their own things if they could afford it. In 1908, Superintendent Peairs explained Haskell's policy to one of the Indian agents:

> I have to advise you that the school furnishes one uniform, one school suit of gray cashmere, and all necessary working clothes to the boys. Under such circumstances, I do not think it necessary for any of them to spend much money for clothing. . . . The shoes furnished by the government are very coarse and rough and nearly all the boys, who can possibly do so, buy their Sunday shoes at least and I believe if I were in their place I would do the same thing.[37]

According to Superintendent Fiske, the same was true for the girls who preferred to buy their own shoes with pointed toes at downtown stores. At Haskell it was common practice for students to supplement the government's provisions with their own clothes. Haskell's records abound with letters from students requesting money from their parents or agencies to buy clothes. What becomes evident in this endless exchange of correspondence between agents, school staff, parents, and students that followed many of the children's requests is the meticulous control that was exercised over every aspect of the children's lives. Although many students were critical of the clothes provided for them, others remember this aspect of their boarding school experience in positive terms:

> The uniforms at Haskell were much nicer than at Flandreau. They looked sharp. We made our own striped ticking dresses for working, and were given very nice white blouses and pleated skirts for our school uniforms. The boys had uniforms, with pants and jacket, for school, and for work they wore coveralls. Some of the boys wore work pants that were like the Levi's you wear today. We called those "half-cuts" because they didn't have a top. The half-cuts were considered more stylish.[38]

Unlike the boys, Indian girls suffered under the Victorian cult of domesticity. Haskell's administrators and matrons forced on them heavy bloomers, high boots, chaste collars, and uncomfortable corsets, in an outright attempt to control their female bodies and banish the girls' sexuality. In 1914, Superintendent Wise told a concerned Wisconsin agent: "The Matron informs me that practically all the girls now wear corsets, and she thinks the large majority do so even before coming here. Only a few of our youngest girls under 14 do not wear them."[39] The girls' habits were closely watched and controlled, leaving little room for "uncivilized" appearances or "unchaste" behavior. In 1913, their wardrobe got a little bit more comfortable, when their unpractical shawls were finally replaced by sweaters, which the girls liked much better. It would take many more years, though, until the girls were allowed to express themselves freely when it came to fashion.

Over the years, Haskell's dress code changed little, and uniforms remained an important part of the students' wardrobe, since Haskell's superintendents believed in the value of military-style clothing for the maintenance of discipline and as an expression of American patriotism. The styles and colors of the students' clothes were altered according to the availability of materials and reflected to some extent national fashion trends, but in general the clothes were rather plain, very modest and functional. According to Esther Burnett, "there were advantages in dressing alike. Those of us who didn't have money to buy nice clothes never had to feel inferior to those who could."[40] Indeed, Haskell's students came from very diverse economic backgrounds, and whereas a majority had only limited resources, some children, in particular among the Osage and Quapaw of Oklahoma, who had become rich through oil revenues, had a lot of money to spend. Arapaho Jesse Rowlodge recalled that while he attended Haskell in the 1900s, Osage boys wore "Tibbitz every day, you might say—black Tibbitz suits—that's fancy cloth, you know—they make suits out of it. They wore it."[41] Esther Burnett remembered that in the mid-1920s, her Osage roommate Mary Rose wore Saks Fifth Avenue clothing, which she generously lent to the other girls on occasions when the students were allowed to wear their own clothing. In 1920, the guardian of a Choctaw boy who had recently deserted from Haskell wrote the commissioner of Indian affairs, criticizing the students' extravagant behavior:

> Mr. Peairs is doing a great work there with the boys, and I do not wish to criticize, but in my visits to the school, I find the boys are wearing entirely too many silk shirts, twenty dollar shoes, etc. I think that perhaps this comes from the boys in what is known as the "oil territory," but it engenders a desire for these things in the minds of the boys that cannot afford them.[42]

Haskell's administrators had repeatedly discussed the issue and had, again and again, tried to limit student purchases of clothing. In his reply to a 1910 inspection report, Superintendent Fiske voiced his concern about the negative effects of too much spending money:

> It has caused very great dissatisfaction in the past among many of the poorer pupils, and I have had a number of instances of deserters, who, when brought back, gave as their reason for deserting that they had no money to spend and could not wear nice clothes like other pupils.[43]

Fiske's analysis is supported by Jesse Rowlodge's recollections about his time at Haskell from 1904 to 1910. When his interviewer asked him in 1968 whether students got homesick or decided to leave the school, Rowlodge explained:

> Well, most of that happened this way: Some of the boys like to dress—not Oklahoma boys, but other state boys and girls—they hate to fall back, way that they dress, you know—clothing. Whenever their clothes get old, why then they started, you know—just didn't feel in the right place among the rest of us. They'd write home—get discouraging letters, you know—family sickness, and that sort of discouraged them. I know I gave one boy a suit of clothes one time.[44]

Rowlodge said that the children could have worn school clothing, but that most students preferred to wear their own things. He remembered the kind of clothes he liked to wear:

> I wore good civilian clothes. I wore a suit all the time. Costume I wore was gray, or fawn, tan, mostly—those colors. And on other occasions I would wear blue serge, but I had a nice dress suit, black for something like banquets and like that . . . I pay for them myself. When I come home in the summertime I'd always go to Oklahoma City or El Reno and go to a tailor and pick out the kind of clothes I want.[45]

According to Rowlodge, students from Oklahoma were generally better dressed than children from other parts of the country. He explained that they usually had more money and easier access to towns where clothes could be purchased. Talking about students from outside of Oklahoma, Rowlodge said: "You know those peoples are sparsely settled, their reservations—long ways to go and they don't have towns like we have. And most of them are full-bloods, and their parents weren't educated, and they didn't go to barber shop regular like we do here in Oklahoma."[46] He added that students with little money tried to keep their clothes as clean and neat as possible. They would wear government clothing during the weeks, especially when working in the printing shop, dairy, and on the farm, and save their suits for the weekends and special occasions. Rowlodge's memories illustrate the many differences between Haskell's students—their diverse economic backgrounds, various degrees of Indian blood, and different home environments that all influenced their personal experiences at the boarding school. For students, clothing was an important topic that occupied their minds and influenced their physical well-being as well as their perception of life at Haskell. Even though often ignored, students frequently voiced their demands as well as their dissatisfaction. Through their clothes, the students defined their place at the school, so much so that dissatisfaction with their wardrobe could become an incentive to reject Haskell altogether and run away. "White men's clothes" could certainly act as agents of assimilation, but they could also spark opposition and work as a medium of resistance.

In many regards a more serious assault on tribal identity came in the form of the school's English-only policy and the assignment of Anglo-American names. Especially for students who did not speak English, the first weeks and months at Haskell were extremely difficult. Haskell did not allow children to use their native languages, and it enforced the rule under the threat of severe punishment. Through exclusive use of English, teachers intended to weaken tribal bonds and suppress "profane" (i.e., Indian) language and conduct. Many former boarding school students remember being beaten or locked up, or having their mouths washed with lye or soap, for breaking the rule. Students recall praying and speaking in native tongues when unsupervised, but considering the strict supervision, the intertribal character of the school, and the tight daily schedule, there were not many opportunities for students to socialize with children from their own tribe.

Haskell was a distinctly intertribal environment, making English a much-needed vehicle for communication. Even though students did not necessarily give up the use of their tribal languages in private, English certainly took over as their everyday means of communication. After five or more years at boarding schools, younger children especially lost some of their ability to speak in their native tongues. Students recall how they could not speak with their parents and grandparents upon their return home, a painful and alienating experience. Many had to relearn Ojibwe, Lakota, Creek, or Cheyenne in order to communicate with their own families.[47] Boarding schools had a long-lasting impact on the decline of tribal languages, affecting not just the generation attending the schools but also their children and grandchildren. Many indigenous people who attended boarding schools during the first decades of the nineteenth century refused to teach their own children their native language, fearing negative effects for their offspring.[48] The suppression of tribal languages was a key aspect of forced assimilation. Destroying native languages meant destroying native cultures—their storytelling traditions, their histories, their songs, their religions, and their ceremonies. If the children would lose their language, they would lose the connection to their people's past as well as to their own families. As Vine Deloria has stated: "Language is the first glue that links people together . . . it is the key to cultural survival and cannot be considered in isolation; it is and must be the substance of self-determination."[49]

Like other government schools, Haskell taught Indian children to be ashamed of their tribal languages and sometimes even forced them to adopt new names. Renaming the students in the Anglo-Christian tradition was an assault on a highly visible symbol of their tribal identity. Indian educators argued that the children's traditional names were unpronounceable, pagan, and sometimes even improper. Another reason for the renaming policy was the government's attempt to force Indians to adopt Anglo surnames. According to Commissioner Morgan, allotment and the advance of property ownership among native peoples required clear documentation of family members and lines of inheritance. Morgan pointed out that the lack of family names would hurt the Indians and could easily result in the loss of their property. Assigning surnames was an important step in the government's attempt to destroy tribalism and to transform Indians into self-reliant property owners.[50]

At Haskell, administrators followed several renaming patterns: The Cheyenne children sent to the school by Black Kettle in the mid-1880s received new first names Ernie, Starr, Malcolm, and Nathan and kept Black as their last name. Some students were named after their white guardians, such as Cheyenne student Suzie Walker, whose traditional name was His-to-be-yoe. If no English name could be derived from the immediate family or the students' surroundings, school personnel picked a name that they considered appropriate. The *Lawrence Gazette* explained: "When pupils are received they are given English names and Henry Ward Beecher, Henry Clay and other celebrities have namesakes there. The difference between the Indian names and the new ones is ludicrous: Roman Nose alias Joshia Patterson, Howling-from-Above alias Paul Rodney." Many names on Haskell's roster reflect heroes of Western culture, including names of Haskell's superintendents. During the 1880s and 1890s, Julius Caesar, Napoleon Bonaparte, Grover Cleveland, Charles Meserve, and H. B. Peairs all attended the school.[51] Having to answer to a new name could be emotionally difficult, and many students were alienated by the procedure. Others, however, enjoyed the selection of an English name and seemed to have taken the change more lightheartedly, as Lucy Logan Griggs (Sac and Fox) recalled in a 1969 interview:

> I was so proud to have an English name when I got to school. They gave me the name of "Lucy." Of course, I didn't have any English name. Of course Indians don't ever have no English names until the government comes in and gives you an English name. So my grandfather was given the name of General John A. Logan. And he was a general I think in the Union Army, so my grandfather got the name of this big general, and he was just a little old short fellow and it was just real comical [laughs]. So when he gave him that name, so naturally, why I took the name of Logan after him. And so when I got the name of Lucy I was really proud that I had an English name. I just had an Indian name then. So I been Lucy ever since.[52]

In indigenous societies, the naming process was deeply connected to the process of cultural transmission and the formation of identities. Names were used to stimulate a person's self-improvement, to reward a particular action or achievement, and to transfer the traits of an honored tribal figure or relative to a child and thereby to the next generation. The giving of names was often embedded in an elaborate ceremony, and it was common to rename Indian youth at crucial times in their development, for instance, when a young man accomplished his first brave deed and became a warrior. Tribal naming practices were rich in cultural meaning and gave native youth ideals to live by. It is difficult to judge how Indian children experienced the renaming process at Haskell. To some it might have been acceptable and even enjoyable as a rite of passage, indicating the new stage of their lives they were entering. For others the oftentimes randomly picked names meant a loss of cultural meaning and identity. Some students liked their new names and found a historic or biblical meaning in them that would become a guiding principle for their life; others despised their new names and asked the school staff to have them changed.[53] But no matter what the students' reaction was, Haskell's renaming policy constituted a serious assault on native identities.

All facets of the children's lives, including discipline and the military routine, sanitary practices, clothes, and language, were areas of contestation that produced positive as well as negative responses. The same holds true for the food the students were fed and the dormitories they lived in. At Haskell, everything happened according to schedule, including the meals. There was never much variety in the menu or in the daily mealtime routine. Food had to be eaten at precise intervals of the day and in a certain manner. For some students, the food they received at school was more plentiful and diverse than what they had eaten at home. Jay Black, a Cheyenne who attended Haskell from 1895 to 1898, recalled in a 1967 interview that he was well taken care of: "Oh, they treat us pretty good—new clothes, and plenty to eat, rooms to stay in. Boy they treat us pretty good."[54] To others, however, Haskell's diet was a constant source of discontent, invoking the students' resistance and sometimes even their outright rejection of the school. At many boarding schools, the children's diet was inadequate, and a large number of students were malnourished and overworked.

In general, boarding schools spent little money on the children's nutrition. The 1928 Meriam Report found that, on average, schools only allowed eleven cents per student per day, twenty-four cents less than the report considered necessary in order to feed the children properly. The food situation differed from school to school, and it appears that larger schools such as Haskell or Carlisle did better than smaller or more remote boarding schools. One point of criticism was that boarding school students subsisted on a diet high in starch and meat and that despite the cultivation of fruits and vegetables in the schools' gardens, students did not profit from their own farming efforts. The same was true for milk. Most schools operated a dairy, but students only received small amounts of milk or butter. In 1915, Haskell's superintendent claimed that his school made every attempt to provide ample food. In addition to fruit, vegetables, and dairy items that the students produced, the school purchased "fish, sausage meats, chicken, [and] raisins on a regular basis."[55] A look at Haskell's actual January 1916 "Bill of Fare" reveals that this statement was not entirely accurate:

BILL OF FARE FOR HASKELL INSTITUTE
January 1916

Breakfast
   Cereals (Oatmeal gruel, Cornmeal Mush, or Milk Toast). Butter (about twice a week). Brown Gravy or hash. Coffee, with cream and sugar (Every morning)

Dinner No.1.
   Roast beef. Mashed potatoes. Brown gravy. Cornstarch pudding (once a week). Bread.

Dinner No. 2.
   Vegetable soup. Soda crackers. Plain boiled potatoes. Roast beef. Brown gravy. Pickled beets. Bread

Dinner No. 3.
   Roast beef. Milk gravy. Mashed potatoes. Chow chow (Our own make) Ice cream. Bread
   At other dinners during the month we have cabbage, turnips, carrots, tomatoes, rice, dumplings.
   Milk and tea about twice a week.

Sunday dinner.
   Either roast pork, Frankfurter sausage, or pork link sausage. Mashed potatoes. Brown gravy, Cucumber pickles (our own make) Pie. Bread. Coffee or cocoa.

Supper No.1.
   Fried potatoes. Cold sliced beef. Brown gravy. Dried fruit sauce. Cinnamon rolls. Tea and bread.

Supper No.2.
   Baked beans with pork gravy. Corn bread. Syrup and butter. Bread and milk.

Supper No.3.
   Meat pie. Brown gravy. Ginger bread. Fruit sauce. Bread
   At other suppers during the month we had Irish stew, baked hash, fried mush, hominy macaroni, baked, boiled, or creamed potatoes, hot rolls, coffee, ginger or spice cookies.

Sunday Supper.
>Either bologna, cold sliced beef, or salmon. Brown gravy. Buns. Cake. Grape jam, or canned fruit. Tea. Sometimes fried potatoes. Potato salad, or bean salad.[56]

Although Haskell's diet was more varied than at many other schools, from the meal plan it becomes apparent that the students received few vegetables and practically no fresh fruit. Milk and butter were given out sparingly, and fish or chicken did not make their way into the January fare. The children's diet was based mainly on beef, potatoes, gravy, and bread. In her autobiography, Lucille Winnie recalled Haskell's reputation as the Gravy College, attesting to the students' critical attitude toward the school's cuisine.[57] A 1919 menu shows a bit more variety, including chicken dishes, sauerkraut, dried corn, canned peas, and canned apples. Fresh fruit and vegetables were still only provided seasonally and in small amounts. It appears, though, that Haskell's diet got better over the years, as funding improved and methods of preserving and processing foods became more advanced. But even in the 1920s, students still complained about Haskell's inadequate diet.

Haskell's superintendents occasionally complained to the commissioner of Indian affairs about the difficulties they faced in providing the students with a well-balanced diet. In December 1902, for instance, Superintendent Peairs reported to Washington:

> I have to report that the supply of dried fruit of all kinds was entirely exhausted at the end of the last quarter, September 30th. We have been without any kind of fruit for the pupils since that time and are in very great need of a supply. . . . It is a very difficult matter to provide a variety of food for a family of 750 pupils even when the supply of rations is all on hand and without the fruit it becomes much more difficult. I therefore trust that some steps may be taken immediately, to enable me to secure fruit for the pupils.[58]

If Peairs was aware of the value of fruit for the children's diet, one could ask, though, why it took him until December to write to Commissioner Leupp, considering that the supplies had run out in September. In general, though, the Indian Office was reluctant to accommodate either the students' or the superintendents' wishes. The commissioner of Indian affairs expected his field staff to make do with what it had and to stop complaining about any shortcomings. In his views, the Indian Office did everything necessary to keep the schools running properly. According to Commissioner Leupp, criticism did not point to mistakes made by the Indian Office but to the inability of the schools' superintendents to find their own solutions. Considering the Indian Office's attitude, it must have been difficult for Haskell's superintendents to improve their students' diet—even if they themselves wished to do so.[59]

Sometimes, Indian educators defended the absence of fresh food and milk in their menus by claiming that Indian students did not care for fresh vegetables, milk, and eggs. But even though dairy foods were indeed not a traditional food among indigenous cultures, that certainly did not apply to fruits and vegetables. Many tribes were dedicated agriculturalists, growing corn, beans, squash, and even peaches. All Indian societies harvested wild foods that could be found in their region, such as berries, mushrooms, turnips, and wild rice, supplementing their diets of meat and fish.[60]

For the students, meals at Haskell meant another important facet of "civilized" life to get used to. Eating three meals a day at exactly the same times felt unnatural to many children, who were used to eating when they were hungry. The kinds of foods provided, as well as the Euro-American dining etiquette, made things even more difficult. The school forced students to give up their traditional foods, while adjusting to Victorian table rituals and cooking styles. Many children complained about the food they were fed, the way it was prepared, and the insufficient amounts they received. Jesse Rowlodge recalled that it took him quite a while to get used to Haskell's fare, even though he eventually did:

> Things that I didn't like to eat at home—like I didn't like coffee. I didn't like beans. I didn't like syrup. I didn't like cornbread. Some things I had to eat up there and I got used to them. I wouldn't eat pork, but after I got up there and got used to it, that's all that—I like it better than other foods I used to eat before. Prunes—I wouldn't eat prunes, and when we got to studying, you know—and the good of those things like prunes, cornbread. But I never did take much to syrup. I'm thankful for that because I am not diabetic. I never did like candy.[61]

Rowlodge remembered that when he was a senior, his cousins from Oklahoma came to visit and that on this occasion they ate traditional Arapaho foods such as "fry bread, steak, boiled meat, soup—things like we have at home. You know we ate that way while they were there."[62] After almost sixty years, Rowlodge still remembered this visit, an indication of how important this occasion was for him back then. It did not happen often that students were allowed to enjoy a piece of home while at school and being able to indulge in home cooking was a memorable event.

If they had any money, students supplemented their diets with Sunday dinners in town, shopping trips to nearby stores or diners, or visits to the bakery. But these occasions were few, and not all students had the means to purchase food off campus. Neither did the school encourage the sale of supplemental food to the students. The school supported its own eatery, the Haskell Institute Young Men's Christian Association (YMCA) restaurant, which was attached to the school and run by the school's employees. For five years, Tom Ross, who was finally evicted for unsanitary conditions and bad influence on the students, operated this restaurant. After Haskell took over the restaurant in 1911, Ross continued to conduct his business from the basement of his house, a place that Haskell's disciplinarian found less than suitable for the students: "The size of his place is about 10x12 feet and it was considered an unfit place for girls to go, so they were forbidden to trade there. The boys, however, were allowed to patronize him until January 6th, last, at which time an order was issued that no pupil would be allowed to go to this place except upon the boys' regular town day, when they might patronize him the same time as other merchants in town." Haskell's principal, Mr. Birch, supported this view and added, "I have seen boys going and coming to and from his place not only on Sundays but at other times when they should not have been away from the school grounds. I have frequently had boys come to school late, giving as their excuse that they were at Mr. Ross's place and did not know that it was time to go to school."[63] For students, Ross's basement store and restaurant was a space where they enjoyed eating, socializing, and escaping from the watchful eyes of Haskell's staff. Obviously, the boys enjoyed much greater freedom than Haskell's girls, for whom leaving campus was made even more difficult.

While on campus, working in the kitchen or on the farm could provide an opportunity for extra treats. Esther Burnett recalled that "the boys who worked in the bakery sometimes brought their girlfriends or other chums a fresh loaf of bread. That was always such a treat—to share fresh baked bread!"[64] During their home economics classes, the girls learned how to cook and bake pies, but usually they were not allowed to taste their own creations:

We would have so liked to have a pie to eat, or to share with our friends. The teacher must not have been aware of the kinds of food we ate daily—she frequently just let those pies go stale. Once in a while, we'd manage to abscond with one of those pies and treat some of our friends to the wonderful taste of hand-made pie. I always thought that it was cruel of that teacher—not to give the pies to the kids who had made them.[65]

During the summer months, the students' diet was more diverse, as they profited at least a little bit from the abundance in the school garden, even if not in a "balanced" way:

During harvest, big baskets of tomatoes for us to eat were available in the back of the dormitory. I ate so many one time that I got a terrible case of hives; my eyes were swollen shut when I woke up the next morning—a reaction to eating all of those tomatoes.[66]

Food preparation and service, seldom a high priority in government schools, followed a military routine. As a result, hot food had generally cooled by the time the children had marched into the room and said their prayers.[67] At Haskell, the students were divided by age, gender, and military organization:

There were two dining rooms: the Prevo for grades one through six, and the Big Dining Room for the older students. The boys ate on one side of the dining room and the girls on the other. We were assigned seats by company. It was the responsibility of the girls to serve the food, clear the tables, and wash the dishes. The dinner meal was served at noon. Employees supervised the students whose "tour of duty" was to work in the kitchen. The cooking for the hundreds of students was done in enormous steam vats.[68]

In 1887, the *Lawrence Gazette* described how bells regulated the behavior in the dining room, indicating when the students were allowed to sit down and when they were allowed to start eating. According to the article, one boy oversaw the behavior of the whole table, while other boys waited on the students.[69] In Haskell's early years, many more boys than girls attended the school, requiring boys to perform "female" chores such as serving food. Despite the regimentation in the mess hall, students were expected to acquire the food rites of civilized society. They had to learn how to eat with spoons, forks, and knives and how to use napkins, and the dining room became a classroom for instructing Indian children on the basics of middle-class table manners.[70]

Children at Haskell were expected to adopt white middle-class standards of cleanliness, beauty, and orderly behavior. The discipline expected in the dining room extended to the dormitories, classrooms, and school grounds. During Haskell's first decades, the school suffered from serious funding problems and overcrowded conditions.[71] Haskell's superintendents struggled to provide enough living space for the children, and dormitories were filled to the rooftops, with students sometimes sharing beds, squeezing together on 36-inch by 40-inch mattresses. The children's quarters were neither safe nor comfortable. In order to accommodate more children in the dormitories, Haskell added sleeping porches, which were considered beneficial to the students' health since they provided more fresh air than the regular dorm rooms. During harsh Kansas winters, however, these porches were very cold places and might have contributed to the many respiratory illnesses reported at Haskell.

In the early 1920s, the girls' dormitory with porches had room for 450 students; the boys' dormitory accommodated 550 students. Until the 1920s, twenty to thirty children usually slept in one room; in later years, the rooms were split up into smaller units of two students each. In 1890, Superintendent Meserve had already tried to break up the large wards into smaller rooms. An outspoken proponent of assimilation, Meserve was convinced that the "massing of 20 or 30 students in one room savors too much of the reservation idea."[72] But it would take another thirty years until this plan became a reality. In 1911, there were two dormitories for the boys and one dormitory for the girls, and the rooms were divided by age group and military company. No matter how uncomfortable or crowded the dormitories were, students got used to them and made them their home. In her journal, Burnett had written: "In all this world of buildings rare, few of them to this castle compare." She added, "It may sound a little corny to refer to my dormitory as a castle, but many of the buildings on the Haskell campus were ivy-covered, and they became our homes over the years. Five or six girls would share a room. Everyone had a drawer, and we shared tables to study on. We kept our clothes and nightgowns there but slept on large sleeping porches."[73]

Matrons kept a watchful eye over the girls and the smaller boys; the disciplinarian was responsible for the discipline in the older boys' dormitory.

There was one head matron in charge of all the children, and an assistant matron supervised each dormitory. Students did not enjoy any privacy at boarding schools, and there was little space for personal belongings or expressions of individual taste. The children's lifestyle was much more communal than individualistic, requiring the students to share a very limited space with many other pupils. Boys and girls were supervised constantly, and the sexes were kept apart most of the time. The girls' dormitory was on one side of the campus, the boys' dormitory on the other. The buildings were separated by a large expanse of lawn that had a sidewalk and a bandstand in the middle, which students called the "demarcation line," since boys and girls were only allowed to cross it on Sunday afternoons when they were allowed to socialize.[74]

Haskell's efforts to keep boys and girls apart posed serious safety problems. Because the school feared that the boys would pay nightly visits to the girls, the girls often slept in buildings with nailed-down windows and locked fire escapes, exposing the children to great dangers in the case of fire, as Haskell's annual inspection reports reveal. The 1902 report, for instance, strongly criticized the school's lack of safety features. Citing Supervisor Charles's report, the Office of Indian Affairs wrote to Superintendent Peairs: "Referring to the girls' home, he says that the building is occupied by 263 girls, three-fifth of whom sleep in the attic, the remainder being accommodated on 3rd floor; that two narrow stairways (38 inches wide in clear) extend from basement to attic; that there are no fire escapes above the second floor, and should a fire occur it would be found impossible to save the pupils on the upper floors."[75]

In addition to being unsafe, the dormitories had no adequate sanitary facilities. In Haskell's early days, toilets were located in the cold basements, and due to a lack of funds, their maintenance was poor. There were no night toilets, and leaky faucets and clogged drains were commonplace. Especially the boys' bathrooms were in very bad condition, with toilets that had flushing devices that required considerable strength to operate.[76] The sewage disposal system was inadequate, and toilet paper and soap were notoriously absent. Students generally washed their faces and hands communally in troughs, while sharing toothbrushes and a few dirty towels. These conditions substantially contributed to the spread of diseases such as trachoma that were common at boarding schools. Even though conditions improved over the years, changes came about slowly, and Haskell only introduced an individual towel system in 1914.

In the wintertime, Haskell's dormitories lacked sufficient heating, and many buildings were in bad repair, with rotting plastering and floors, narrow staircases, and a lack of light and ventilation. Haskell's students worked constantly to maintain and improve the buildings, but the sheer quantity of things to be done left the school in a chronic state of disrepair. Esther Burnett recalled sharing her dormitory with more than just her fellow students:

> There were rats at Haskell. At night, particularly, we'd hear them running up and down the stairs. They were rather large—you could hear them looping from one stair to the next—and they were heavy! I don't remember anyone being bitten by a rat, but they gave us the creeps nonetheless. There was a lot of joking about the rats. We'd say they must be carrying little shovels on their backs as they worked in the yard. Or we'd joke about them sweeping and mopping the stairs, saving us from work the next day.[77]

For many years, Haskell fell short in providing its students with the most basic elements of care: adequate food, shelter, clothing, and medical attention. The children were subject to strict discipline, hard labor, and inferior living conditions. Over the years, the conditions at Haskell improved, but even by the 1920s, the school did not cater to all the children's physical and emotional needs. Despite these shortcomings, many youth were eager to attend, and many students recall their years at Haskell as a positive experience. The children adapted to the circumstances and compensated for the institution's deficiencies with their great sense of community, friendship, humor, and compassion.

Even though students had to relinquish much of what they had known before coming to Haskell, they quickly became part of a new culture. But this new culture differed markedly from the Anglo-American ideal propagated by the school's administrators. The children entered a world that had its own rules largely hidden from the watchful eyes of the school's staff. It was a culture that was neither distinctly tribal nor mainstream American: It was a boarding school culture that helped to break down traditional barriers to an intertribal consciousness. At Haskell, the students created their own language and rituals. Esther Burnett recalled that while at school, she learned a whole new vocabulary:

There was a "slanguage" common to Haskell, the usage of which made us feel like we were a bonded part of the group. Old students would try to trip new students up by giving them the wrong definition of a word. One of the slang terms common to Haskell was KALE, which meant money, but someone might tell you that KALE meant toilet or orchard or bakery. We also used "uncle" to mean a girl's boyfriend and "aunt" to mean a boy's girlfriend. "Chape" meant "shape," like "What a great 'chape'!" You might embarrass yourself by using a word in the wrong context, which was a hilarious thing to do, but you learned not to be ashamed about it. You tried to take the ribbing with grace. If you didn't, your life could become unbearable, but if you did, you were in.[78]

The children had their own ways of determining who was "in" and who was not. As at other boarding schools, Haskell's students became friends with children their own age and with kids who came from the same location or the same tribal background. They formed lifelong friendships with the children they learned with, worked with, played sports with, and shared rooms, beds, and secrets with. Although Haskell was strict about keeping boys and girls apart, discipline could only accomplish so much, and the students' vocabularies, as well as their memories, bear testimony to numerous romantic encounters. Esther Burnett married her Haskell sweetheart, one of many intertribal marriages inspired by the boarding school experience. In her memoirs, Burnett praised the positive atmosphere that prevailed among children from completely different tribal backgrounds. She did not recall any tribal hostilities but emphasized the great joy students felt in sharing their tribal cultures with their friends:

> We'd discuss the kind of dances or ceremonies that each tribe had and learn about each other's traditions. We would also compare notes as to how students would say common items such as sugar, salt or bread in their language. Again, one might play the trickster and relate the wrong meaning of a word.[79]

Burnett remembered how surprised she was when, while passing by a group of Comanche boys on campus, she realized that Comanche was related to her own language, Shoshone, and that she was able to understand the boys' teasing remarks.

Jesse Rowlodge recalled, in a similar vein, how he and his fellow Cheyenne and Arapaho students shared information about their tribal cultures and ways of life:

> Every tribe wanted to know how we lived compared to how the Northern Cheyennes lived in Montana, and the northern Arapaho in Wyoming. Of course we were much better off than they were. Nice open range, you know, irrigation. . . . Well, we have better lands down there than they have. Course they got lot of wild game there—deer and antelope and elk and moose, and bears.[80]

Asked whether the northern students had a feeling that the southern students were better off, Rowlodge replied:

> Well, they didn't pay much attention. They know that we wore good clothes. I know Oklahoma boys and girls, especially, wore all good clothes.[81]

Like Burnett, Rowlodge emphasized the amicable relationship among students from different tribes—even tribes that used to be historic enemies:

> We were traditional enemies of the Northern Utes. And this boy by the name of George Howe, he and I got talking. We was on friendly terms. I said, "Boy," I said, "if we were out west where they used to fight," I said, "I'd done had your scalp on my belt." "No," he said, "I'd sneak up and get you before you'd got me," he said. Anyhow, that's all there was to it.[82]

When asked whether the children had preferences when selecting friends, Rowlodge explained:

> Well, naturally our Oklahoma Indians associated with the Plains Indians, like the Blackfeet, and the Sioux, and northern Cheyennes and northern Arapahoes. We all had the same ways. Oh we associated with those that had good music knowledge, like those Wisconsins—those Oneidas and Chipewas from Wisconsin. And from Michigan and Minnesota. They were all good musicians. They were mostly part French. . . . Of course the athletes—whatever tribe they were, we associated with them. I had a lot of

good friends from Montana and Oregon and State of Washington. Some from Nevada and California.[83]

One way students from Plains tribes could communicate with each other was through sign language. According to Rowlodge, students used it frequently, especially if they were not able to express themselves in English or when they wanted to avoid the teachers' supervision. Sign language was universal among the Plains Indians, and it served as a neat way of communicating traditionally, without breaking the school's "English-only" rule.

Burnett's and Rowlodge's memories are consistent with the many stories K. Tsianina Lomawaima collected about the Chilocco Indian School in Oklahoma. Ethnicity could be a determining factor in the selection of friends, but the importance of tribal affiliation diminished as students grew older. At Chilocco, younger boys formed gangs that were based on tribal affiliation and degree of Indian blood, but when the children got older, they selected friends according to social factors such as class attendance, mutual work details, athletic or band membership, and individual personality traits. This pattern was more pronounced among boys than among girls. Students speaking the same tribal language tended to stick together, a factor that was certainly of greater importance in the boarding schools' early days, because English was not as widely spoken in the 1880s and 1890s as in the 1920s and 1930s.[84] These findings from Oklahoma are echoed in the recollections of Haskell's students, many of whom remember forming lifelong friendships with children from a variety of tribal backgrounds.

Otis Russell, a full-blood Osage who entered Haskell in 1903, recalled his friendship with Jesse Rowlodge. In 1970, the almost ninety-year-old Russell remembered that it took him a long time to get acquainted with other students when he arrived at the school, but that over time, he became friends with boys from many different tribes, including Sac and Fox, Kansa, Sioux, Cheyenne, Pawnee, Ponca, Chippewa, and Menominee students. Russell said that he used to take his friends out to a little restaurant:

I had money, I take them down. . . . Used to call it eatmobile. Made out of car, big room in it. Had wheels on it and they had—used to make egg sandwiches and coffee. That's all they make. And pie, round pies. And I go down there and give them coffee, pie, egg sandwich. I got acquainted with pretty soon a whole bunch of 'em in there. Used to go down there and see 'em. Them guys, I got acquainted with bunch Kaw Indians and I got acquainted with Sioux Indians. They talk pretty much like Eskimos. I talk to 'em, and they ask—everybody ask what do you call this and I'll tell them. Just them dirty words first."[85]

Otis Russell also recalled his friendship with Jesse Rowlodge, saying that after more than six decades, he would like to see him once more: "I been wanting to see Jesse Rowlodge, but I ain't got no way of going. I'd like to see him. Go to him while I'm living. I think he graduated commercial. Business college. That's what he had come up there for."[86] Many boarding school students kept in touch with their Haskell friends, nurturing bonds formed during a crucial period in their lives. Whether children "fit in" and felt comfortable among their fellow students depended on many factors, such as age, family background, personality, English language skills, and time spent at Haskell. Many students recall that their introduction to the school was tough. Mary Red Eagle, a Quapaw who attended Haskell during the early 1900s, recalled in a 1969 interview that when she was sent to Lawrence, "That's when I cried my eyes out" [laughter]. She added that she spent three years at Haskell and learned to love the place: "I never will regret of going to school in Lawrence, Kansas. That was my—one of my happiest places that I spent."[87]

Some students did not stay long enough to feel at home in their new surroundings. Lottie High Whitefox, a Kiowa-Apache from Oklahoma, told her interview partner in 1967 that although she attended Haskell from 1909 to 1911, she did not have many friends: "Well, I wasn't much acquainted with all the girls. I had one friend I always with. You know chum with. I didn't care much about other girls. Ella Petty. But she pass away about three years ago. She was about my age. She was Otoe."[88] Lottie High Whitefox's recollections of Haskell are less positive and detailed than those of Esther Burnett or Jesse Rowlodge. She explained that she did not learn much and that she spent most of her time in the sewing room. She did not tell the interviewer why she only stayed for a term of two years, but it appears from her description that she did not consider her stay at Haskell as a formative or memorable period in her life. Nevertheless, Lottie had one close friend, Ella, who became her substitute family while at Haskell and who she kept track of until very old age.

Friends did not always make life at Haskell fun or easy, but they did make it a whole lot better. Esther Burnett recalled that when she and her siblings arrived at Haskell, meeting girls from her own tribe made the transition much easier: "A couple of older Shoshone girls from Wind River sought us out soon after we got there; they were kind of like big sisters to us, and we felt a little better. Knowing there were other kids from our reservation there made us feel more at home, even though we didn't know them personally."[89] Students supported each other in an unfamiliar environment far away from their families. They helped each other to adapt to life at school, and to survive in the white man's world.

In 1968, Jesse Rowlodge shared a personal story about a boy whom he befriended:

Then there was a boy from Arizona—his name was Carl Menana. I had a picture of that fellow. He was a Hopi, I think. . . . And his face was just full of blackheads. And he hadn't had his haircut so I said, "Carl, I'm gonna take you to town with me. We're gonna eat up town. So change your clothes." Well, he came back there, and had a shirt on and it wasn't ironed. I said, "Take that thing off." I took my shirt off and give it to him. . . . I took him to a barbershop and had his haircut. And I asked the barber if he could do anything about those blackheads. "You go a half a block north and a half a block west, on the south side of the street, and there's a lady that does that kinda work." So I took him over to that lady. "I think I'll take care of him," she said. So I said, "I'll be back." So I left and about three quarters of an hour later I started back and he was standing outside in front of the store by the door, in front of the shop. I looked at him and he was all cleaned and he looked like a different boy. He always liked me for it.[90]

Students took on the role of surrogate parents and helped their friends endure an environment designed to strip them of their Indian identities. From the students' recollections it becomes clear, though, that through their friendships, the children were able not only to adjust to "civilized" life but also to cling to their tribal identities and to teach one another about their respective cultures. When they came to Lawrence, Indian students learned a lot about the white world, but they also learned much about the different cultural backgrounds of their fellow students. The development of a shared Indian identity that transcended tribal boundaries was one of the most important legacies of the boarding schools. English as a common language enabled students to share their experiences and to gain a wider perspective on their own identity, and new pan-Indian ideas and beliefs, such as the Native American Church, spread across tribal boundaries and wide geographic distances. The irony of the boarding school experience lies in the fact that the very institutions designed to destroy Indian culture and identity also helped to strengthen them. Esther Burnett's memoirs provide evidence of this:

> I also am still carrying around an eagle feather that was given to me when I was a sophomore, by a Ponca friend from Oklahoma. She was leaving and said, "Always carry it with you. It will protect you." I have it still. I feel the spiritual strength of that feather. To me it's the manifestation of the Great Spirit—a link to the Creator. We had a lot of respect for each other's culture and talked about our customs and traditions. We students nurtured a sense of community among ourselves, and we learned so much from one another. Traditional values, such as sharing and cooperation, helped us to survive culturally at Haskell, even though the schools were designed to erase our Indian culture, values, and identities.[91]

From the students' recollections it becomes clear that the children managed to create a sense of community that transformed Haskell from a government school for Indians into an Indian school. Through their friendships and mutual support, Haskell's students made the institution their home, a place where they could survive as Indians, in spite of strong assimilationist pressures, the lack of care, and the harsh military routine. What the school could not provide for them, they successfully provided for each other: emotional warmth and mutual care. Haskell could only survive because the children appropriated the school for their own needs. They transformed it into their own world, a truly Indian school that meant more to them than educators had ever envisioned.

CHAPTER FOUR

The Curriculum

The days of Haskell's students were planned out by the minute and were usually divided between academic instruction and various work details, not leaving much room for play or idleness. The children spent either the morning or the afternoon in the classroom and devoted the rest of the day to gender-specific industrial training. The 1919–1920 school calendar provides an insight into the children's regimented schedule:

DAILY PROGRAM—WEEK DAYS

Forenoon
Rising bell and reveille   5:30
Gymnasium and military drill   6:00
Bugle call; morning roll call   6:25
Breakfast   6:30
Band practice, first band
(morning academic boys)   7:00–8:00
Care of quarters   7:00
Warning whistle for Industrial Department (two blasts)   7:15
Second whistle (one blast). Instruction In Industrial Departments
     7:30–8:00
Productive work begins in Industrial Departments   8:00
School bell, academic   7:55
Academic Department begins sessions   8:00
Midday whistle (one blast). All Departments close   11:30
Mess call; midday roll call   11:55

Dinner   12:00
Afternoon
Warning whistle for Industrial Departments (two blasts)   12:55
School bell   1:05
Whistle (one blast). Industrial and Academic Departments begin sessions   1:10
Academic Department closes   4:10
Band practice, second band (afternoon academic boys)   4:10
Athletics for boys   4:20–5:20
Gymnasium classes and bathing for girls   4:00–5:30
Whistle (one blast). Industrial Departments Close   5:10
Mess call; roll call   5:50
Supper   6:00–6:30
Evening sessions   7:30–8:30
Tattoo   8:45
Call to quarters   9:00
Taps   9:15

On Saturdays, the children worked a half day. In the afternoons, girls and boys were allowed to visit town on alternate weekends, keeping the sexes apart. Sundays were devoted to religious activities as well as to a dress parade and a band concert.[1]

Until the early 1920s, Haskell's academic curriculum only provided training at the grammar school level. After the eighth grade, successful graduates could either attend the business, normal (until 1903), or nursing course or continue their education at a public school. Many students never finished their course of study, however, and left Haskell without a diploma once their term of three, four, or five years had expired. Haskell's academic and industrial departments changed over the years, reflecting the school's dramatic increase in size as well as national trends in Indian policy. The curriculum was more structured and systematized in the early 1900s than it had been twenty years earlier.

From the time when Indian Commissioner Thomas J. Morgan introduced his first course of study for Indian schools in 1890, Haskell's superintendents had worked on their own standardized curriculum. In 1901, Superintendent of Indian Schools Estelle Reel introduced a new "Course of Study for Indian Schools," which led to a shift in pedagogic emphasis away from academic training toward vocational work. In a 1901 letter to Superintendent Peairs, Reel explained that the "chief end in view should be the attainment of practical knowledge by the pupil . . . emphasizing the dignity and nobility of labor."[2] Reel, a strong believer in social evolution, promoted an education that focused primarily on practical training. Her new "realism" assumed that most Indian children would return to an environment at the periphery of American society, where they would not need extensive academic training. In Reel's view, Indian education was supposed to make the students productive and self-sufficient members of society, who would no longer require the government's support. It was not her vision, though, to fully assimilate them into the American middle class.

Haskell's leadership took Reel's philosophy to heart, and in 1911 Haskell finally published its own course of study. The academic subjects included arithmetic, English, agriculture, reading, U.S. history, geography, physiology, spelling, civil government, vocal music, drawing, and writing. According to the 1911 pamphlet, Haskell would only accept students who were over the age of fourteen and who had already completed the second grade. The keynote of Haskell's course of study emphasized the practical orientation of the school's curriculum and reflected Estelle Reel's point of view:

> Our pupils should be educated in the things they will need most—character, followed by and coupled with the ability to earn an honorable living in the environment which will probably surround them. The purpose of this institution is to give definite vocational training. This cannot be too strongly emphasized. Every day, every lesson, should contribute something to this end.[3]

By the turn of the century, most Indian schools had adopted curricula centered on vocational training, teaching their students to become carpenters, agricultural workers, domestic servants, and farmhands. Modern educators did not see Indian education as a means for Indian children to become assimilated into mainstream culture—that is, the culture of the white middle class. Rather, they would be educated in order to find their "proper place" in society, a place among other marginalized groups as obedient members of the rural and later urban working class at the bottom of the capitalist hierarchy.[4] The notion that Indian children were not fit for white-collar work and that it would serve them, as well as the nation, better if they were prepared for a life as manual laborers is apparent in the policies promoted by the Office of Indian Affairs. In September 1902, Commissioner of Indian Affairs W. A. Jones wrote to Superintendent Peairs:

> The instruction in Indian schools must be limited to what would correspond with the eighth grade in common schools of the country. Commercial courses, normal courses, etc., have no place in the function of an Indian school. The money thus expended and the time thus given, in my judgment, can be more profitably expended in improving the industrial training of these schools. You are therefore directed, immediately upon receipt of this letter, to discontinue your commercial course, and the teachers of this course.[5]

The message sent by the government was clear: Indian students should not be educated beyond the eighth grade, and the money and effort invested in their further training would be a waste of resources. Peairs did not agree with this view and asked the commissioner for an extension of the business course. Unlike his superiors in Washington, Peairs was of the opinion that Indian youth should be trained in vocational lines other than manual labor. He and his staff were proud of Haskell's business course, which had been introduced in 1897 and which enabled Indian students to take the civil service examination in order to become clerks, typists, and stenographers. Peairs's request was denied, though, and Haskell had to abide by the ruling. The business department was closed in 1903 and was only reopened under Commissioner of Indian Affairs Francis E. Leupp in 1906. The normal department, which had enjoyed great popularity and success during its first nine years of existence, stayed closed for much longer and was not reestablished until 1921, when Superintendent Peairs was once more in charge of Haskell.

As a true assimilationist in the humanist tradition, Peairs appears to have been less prejudiced regarding Indian students' intellectual abilities than many of his colleagues and superiors. As Haskell's superintendent, Peairs followed the path of General Richard Pratt and Indian Commissioner Thomas J. Morgan. Peairs believed in native students' ability to excel and to succeed in positions other than manual laborers. From Haskell's records, the picture arises that Peairs was more interested in expanding the school's curriculum than any other superintendent. During Superintendent Wise's tenure from 1911 to 1917, Peairs, acting as general supervisor of all Indian schools, suggested to Indian Commissioner Cato Sells that several girls at Haskell wished to continue their studies at the city high school. From the correspondence it is clear that Peairs as well as Sells supported this idea. Wise, however, objected. In a 1916 statement, Haskell's leadership explained that students should stay at Haskell until they had taken full advantage of all the courses offered. According to Haskell's administration, the school's business course was equivalent to many courses taught at local high schools, and students would be able to enter Kansas and Oklahoma agricultural and normal colleges based on the credits earned during the two years of business training. Their confidence in the high quality of Haskell's business and academic training could be judged in a positive light. Haskell's records, however, do not show how many students actually continued their education at the universities and colleges mentioned above, and it is doubtful that more than a handful ever did. It appears that Haskell's administrators objected to the transfer of their students to the local high school not just because they believed in the superiority of their own school but because they did not want to lose the children's labor force and per capita appropriations.[6]

Three years later, Superintendent Peairs, who had been reinstated to his old post in 1917, took a different stance. He very much supported the establishment of the Esther Home for Indian Girls, a boarding house run by the Woman's Home Missionary Society of the Methodist Episcopal Church, where Indian girls attending high school in town could lodge for $5 per month. Peairs assured the director of the home, "You and your Board are providing a means for the more complete education of a few Indian girls which may mean a very great deal to the future of the Indian people, because the time has certainly come when there should be a larger number of Indian young people who can have, and must have, much more thorough education than the government offers."[7] Peairs had always argued for the expansion of Haskell's curriculum to include business, nursing, and normal training as well as more advanced academic classes. Finally, in September 1921, the eleventh and twelfth grade were added, and Haskell became the first and, for several years, the only Indian boarding school to offer a full four-year high school course. The first high school class graduated from Haskell in 1923, and in 1925 the Bureau of Indian Affairs finally authorized high school classes for all off-reservation boarding schools. During the academic year 1927–1928, Haskell's high school curriculum was accredited by the Kansas State Department of Education.

Until the introduction of the high school course, the pedagogic emphasis lay heavily on vocational training. During the early 1900s, Haskell's teachers and administrators worked relentlessly to correlate the curriculum of the academic department with the work of the industrial departments, making the academic work as practical as possible. Superintendent Peairs believed that object lessons were the best way to teach Indian children, since "they are keen observers and learn lessons through the various senses more quickly than in any other way."[8]

In 1910, the course of study used in the Kansas public school system was adopted at Haskell in an attempt to bring the school up to par with public school education. In February 1916, once again a new course of study was introduced in all U.S. Indian schools; it was based on teaching materials drawn from Indian and public schools as well as agricultural, home economics, and trade schools across the country. Like Estelle Reel's 1901 plan, it centered on vocational training rather than academic work and was divided into three divisions: primary (three years), pre-vocational (three years), and vocational training (four years). During the vocational training years, students would receive four hours of industrial work training per day for three years, and the fourth year would be entirely devoted to applied practical work. The academic work during these years included subjects such as English (reading, composition, grammar, and spelling), vocational arithmetic, industrial geography, agricultural botany, farm and household accounts, history, soil and soil fertility, farm and household physics and chemistry, rural economics, insects and insecticides, field crops, and plant disease.[9] The academic work was closely correlated with Haskell's industrial departments, and courses were offered in agriculture, carpentry, blacksmithing, engineering, painting, masonry, and printing for the boys as well as nursing and home economics for the girls. In 1918, Haskell offered twenty-three industrial subjects as well as seventeen academic subjects, including band, vocal music, drawing, physical education, and manners. All students had to participate in certain activities outlined in the course of study, including a twenty-five minute period of general exercises (assembly, current events, music, civics, and penmanship) during the first two years of the vocational period and miscellaneous activities during the last two years that consisted of physical training (including competitive athletics) and military and gymnastic drills as well as daily breathing exercises. Especially in the lower grades, teaching English was the priority. Besides English language instruction, arithmetic, geography, history, and civil government were considered of great importance; other important topics were physiology, which included temperance and anti-tobacco instruction, as well as teachings on the human body, health, personal hygiene, and nutrition.

In Haskell's 1911 course of study, third grade teachers were reminded of the goals of English instruction: "To lead the pupil to form correct habits of using the language. In this (and all of the successive grades) teachers should keep vigilantly in mind the great necessity for teaching English, which is to most of our pupils a foreign language, and particularly the need for oral practice."[10] In 1914, Haskell's principal, C. E. Birch, published a book called *Methods of Teaching English,* which provided teachers in the Indian Service with information concerning the special needs and problems of Indian students as well as actual lesson plans for successful English instruction. In his discussion, Birch pointed out the peculiar difficulties under which "these children labor in their attempts to master the intricacies of the English language."[11] He believed that Indian children had a big disadvantage over immigrant children, since "a foreign child has at least the advantage of a fair command of some language having a rich vocabulary when he begins the study of English." According to Birch's understanding of linguistics, "the Indian child, on the contrary, has spoken a language which depends quite largely upon signs and the inflections of the voice—a language meager in descriptive powers if robbed of these two aids to expression."[12] Birch recognized neither the enormous linguistic variety present on the North American continent nor the extreme richness of native languages or the indigenous oral tradition. He regarded his students' native tongues not just as different from but as inferior to English.

Birch was right, however, to point out the large linguistic gap that separated the students' native languages from English. Unlike immigrant students from European countries, Indian students had to master a language whose linguistic pattern was outside their native morphological and syntactical frame of reference. Many indigenous languages place little emphasis on verb tense; others do not differentiate between verbs, nouns, or distinct linguistic units; still others convey meaning in one word that in English can only be expressed in an entire sentence.[13] In addition to the completely different makeup of Indian languages, one needs to consider the cultural dimension of language use. Learning English did not simply mean learning a new language but also understanding, and sometimes even adopting, a different way of thinking and a new worldview.

Haskell's principal admitted that "the children of different tribes have their different peculiarities," but he continued his discussion by emphasizing that all native children shared a similar linguistic background, which led to a number of common problems in their English language acquisition. In order to demonstrate "typical mistakes" prominent among indigenous children, Birch selected the following example from the written work of Haskell's students: "When I did went to school I saw old man lived in log cabin. He use to go hunting and kill wild animals. When he kill wild animal he get meat for food. He makes a clothing out of the fur or sometime he sell hide and buy the ammunition and go hunting again." In his analysis of the children's writings, Birch points out that besides the frequent omission or misuse of articles, verb forms posed the greatest problem for the pupils.[14] According to Birch, Indian children in general had not been exposed to enough "good" English in their lives, and even after coming to Haskell, they continued to listen to the mistakes made by their fellow students. Therefore, it was imperative to provide them with as much exposure to correct English as possible. He believed that more time should be spent on building vocabulary, and he warned teachers not to overestimate the level of reading and listening comprehension. Often, the students did not understand what the teacher was saying, and it was crucial to always make sure to explain words exhaustively with as many illustrations as possible. In order to remedy these problems, Birch emphasized the importance of extensive oral exercises. He also stressed that the language taught in the classroom should be correlated with that of the playground and the children's outdoor activities: "Perhaps we teachers are too ready to condemn the language our boys use. What would a story of a baseball game amount to shorn of all the delightful lingo, slang if you will, of the game? Why not regard some of these as the 'technical terms' of the trade."[15] Birch argued for language lessons devoid of rigid grammar drills that were unconnected to the daily necessities of speech.

Despite his negative attitude toward his students' native languages, Birch's teaching philosophy and pedagogical methods were modern for his time. He wanted the children to become fluent and comfortable in their use of English, and he opposed lessons based on mere recitation. The preferred teaching method of Haskell's English teachers was called "objective" method of instruction. Under this method, students were shown objects such as shoes, books, tables, hats, and pencils, then given the proper English word for the object, and finally drilled in the proper pronunciation. This way, their vocabulary was built up. It could take months, though, until the children were able to read a whole text or speak in complete sentences.[16] According to one teacher, "the timidity of the Indian child is something that every teacher has to baffle with. The child must know and know that he knows a thing before you can get him to tell it. They are far readier to write on a topic than to talk about it but in life we talk a thousand times to writing once, so that it is another reason why we should have them do much oral work and get them to feeling at home with the English language."[17] Along similar lines, another female teacher wrote: "When called upon to recite orally they fear they will make mistakes and be ridiculed by their classmates. The Indians are naturally very sensitive, so rather than face this ordeal they invariably say they do not know the answer to the question."[18]

Although the teachers' interpretations of Indian children's behavior reflect their Eurocentric attitudes, they also reveal some of the practical problems Anglo teachers faced in their daily work with their indigenous students. There were real cultural differences to overcome, since learning styles in one society did not always correspond to the ones used in another. Indigenous methods of teaching were often based on observation, listening, and hands-on experiences. According to their Anglo teachers, Indian children were good at observing and imitating. They were shy, though, when it came to expressing their views in front of the whole class in a new language. In many Indian societies, ridicule was used as a method of social regulation and punishment, and it makes sense that Indian youth were eager to avoid this kind of negative attention. In many native cultures it was considered important for the individual to be modest and noncompetitive. The value placed on excelling and individualism so prominent in Western classrooms was therefore contrary to what many students regarded as appropriate social behavior. Whereas Anglo-American children generally found their families' values upheld and reassured in the classroom, the opposite held true for many indigenous children.

How successful was Haskell at teaching English? It appears that many students attained a reasonable degree of proficiency after only two or three years. The intertribal character of Haskell and the enforcement of an "English-only" rule added to the children's need to communicate in the new language. Haskell's location in Lawrence, far away from any reservation, as well as the school's summer outing program increased the imperative and the students' opportunities to use English. Their success, of course, depended very much on their prior schooling and exposure to the English language. Over the years, many Indian students overcame cultural and language difficulties and adjusted to Anglo teaching styles and expectations. Nevertheless, the differences were real and made the children's educational experience much more challenging than for their white counterparts.

Haskell's academic curriculum was designed not only to teach the children English but also to introduce them to the knowledge of "civilization" and to the privileges and duties of patriotic citizenship. Each subject was taught with these goals in mind, preparing future citizen-farmers and workers to function in the dominant culture. In arithmetic, for instance, students learned how to count bushels of wheat, how to calculate their worth, how to build buildings with mathematical precision, how to manage financial obligations, and how to avoid being cheated by the local trader.[19] Each subject opened new and sometimes disturbing doors for the children and changed their view of the world forever. This was particularly true for geography and history lessons. In geography many children heard for the first time that the earth was round, that the stars were larger than the earth, and that the universe was infinite. What they learned conflicted in many ways with the stories they had heard from their elders, but it also fascinated the children. This was particularly true for Haskell's early period. Equally as important as the specific content of Haskell's scientific curriculum was the deeper message it transmitted: Haskell's curriculum emphasized human domination over nature, as well as an objectifying, scientific approach to the environment. In the Anglo world, nature had to be controlled, subjected, and exploited.

Patriotism and education for citizenship were important aspects of the academic curriculum. Students attended classes in history and civil government, concentrating on major historical figures and events as well as the government's institution and the meaning of democracy and citizenship. According to Indian Commissioner Thomas J. Morgan, Indian students should "hear little or nothing of the 'wrongs of the Indians,' and of the injustice of the white race." On the contrary, "The new era that has come to the red man through the munificent scheme of education devised for and offered to them, should be the means of awakening loyalty to the Government, gratitude to the nation, and hopefulness for themselves."[20]

Haskell's 1911 course of study entailed a general outline for the history course. In the fourth and fifth grade, students learned about historical figures, events, and places through stories and biographies. From the sixth grade on, teachers used textbooks such as *Short History of the United States* by Horace E. Scudder. Like most history books of the time, Horace Scudder's work has little mention of America's indigenous population, but it also does not entirely avoid the question of white responsibility. In the few pages that the author allows for the subject, he alludes to broken treaties, Spanish cruelty, and the harsh treatment Indians received at the hands of the Puritans. His portrayal of native peoples is fairly (stereo-)typical in describing Indians both as noble and as savage:

> While the tribes differed from one another, all the Indians were in points alike. They were brave, but they were treacherous. They never forgave an injury. They could bear hunger and torture in silence, but they were cruel to the treatment of their captives. They were a silent race, but often in their councils some of their number would be very eloquent.[21]

The way Indian-white relations were portrayed in the country's history books made the task of teaching U.S. history a difficult one. On the one hand, teachers could not be too honest about the cruelties and dishonesty of whites, since their ultimate goal was to convince Indian students that white civilization was superior to their own and that they should embrace the values of the dominant culture. On the other hand, it would have been difficult to tell students whose parents or grandparents had fought at the Little Big Horn and died at Wounded Knee or Sand Creek that these events had never happened and that Indians had no history. The Indian Office recommended that Haskell's teachers:

> Always seek to create a spirit of love and brotherhood in the minds of the children toward the white people, and in telling them the history of the Indians dwell on those things which have showed nobility of character on the part of either race in their dealings with the other. Whenever acts of injustice must be related, show to the pupils that the guilt of the persons committing them does not attach to the whole race, for in every people, no matter how virtuous, there are always a large number of the unconscientious and the cruel.[22]

The eighth grade was entirely devoted to the larger topic of progress and explored in detail changes that had occurred in the fields of production, transportation, trade and commerce, communication, architecture, religion, education, manners, and beliefs. Subheadings included titles such as "from loghouse to mansion" and "changes in ideas of punishment." The purpose of this yearlong celebration of progress was certainly to impress on the students' minds the story of human progression from savagery through barbarism to civilization. The children had to understand their own cultures' position in this grand scheme of human development and had to believe in the inevitability of history. Once they had accepted the Anglo definition of progress, they would be more willing and eager to embrace the assimilationist message propagated by Haskell's leadership. The children had to internalize the belief that there was no turning back to the old ways and that everything they learned at school would be for their own good as well as that of their people. Through Haskell's teachings, students learned the meaning of civilization and the humiliating "truth" of their own "savagery." But they also learned that there was hope for them, since the path to civilization was open to anyone willing to reject his savage past for a brighter future of Christian citizenship.

Haskell's crusade for civilization was reflected in the school's literary practices: the literary texts the students read and the essays they wrote in the classroom as well as their writings outside of the curriculum. In the view of Haskell's administrators, reading and writing played a crucial part in the overall goal to civilize and assimilate Indian children. Literature, if carefully selected, provided an opportunity for students to learn civic and patriotic duty. Indian Commissioner Morgan believed that Indian children "should be taught to look upon America as their home, and upon the United States Government as their friend and benefactor. They should be made familiar with the lives of great and good men and women in American history, and be taught to feel pride in all their great achievements."[23] In keeping with these goals, Haskell's superintendents made sure that the school library held books and magazines promoting Anglo values and culture. According to the course of study, all grades were to be involved in literary societies, which met semimonthly. Teachers were to act as the students' critics and had to report the students' progress for the children's monthly report cards. By 1900, a debating club for the boys was active; there were also four literary societies—the Athenian and Marvin Societies for the young men and the Searchlight and Philomathean Societies for the young women. Reading was encouraged as a great civilizing force, as Superintendent Peairs's letter to his staff illustrates:

> Few Indian homes possess books and few Indians purchase books. The average Indian home possesses few magazines. It seems very certain

therefore that a large portion of the reading at home, if done at all, will be of newspapers, though a few may read magazines. It is the duty of the school to cultivate proper and profitable habits of reading magazines and books as well as newspapers. . . .The pupil should be trained not only to read but also to report on items read.[24]

In 1901, Superintendent Peairs ordered hundreds of new books for the school library.[25] Many of the texts were adventure stories for boys, promoting all the values and character traits considered positive in boys of the time. Through these books, Indian boys were introduced to what was considered appropriate male behavior—the American man as provider, protector, explorer, and conqueror. The books ordered for Haskell's girls strongly reflected the values and expectations associated with the Victorian ideal of true womanhood. Books such as Louisa M. Alcott's *Little Women* introduced Indian girls to the culturally accepted role for women, to the customs and etiquette of white America, and to their future role as civilized mothers and wives. Even though Indian girls would never belong to the white middle class, the values taught in these stories—modesty, compassion, chastity, and piety—were regarded as essential to the process of assimilation.

Of a list of several hundred books ordered in 1901, only a handful had some aspect of Indian history and culture as their topic. At the turn of the century, reading about their own people's history was not regarded as a priority for Haskell's students. Peairs's 1906 book order contained many more Indian titles, however. Among the books listed were works such as Longfellow's poem *Hiawatha,* Charles Eastman's autobiography *Indian Boyhood,* and Helen Hunt Jackson's novel *Ramona,* an all-time favorite among Indian students.[26] In addition to books, Peairs ordered subscriptions to seventeen regional and national newspapers and magazines. In 1897, Haskell's own newspaper, the *Indian Leader,* was first published, giving the students' the opportunity to learn about journalism and the art of printing firsthand. The paper was first published on a monthly basis, but in later years it came out every week. The *Indian Leader* published announcements, information about the students' activities, news about former students, and excerpts from the students' academic writings as well as a section entitled "Current Events." Although the paper served more as a tool for assimilation than as a platform for critical writing, it was very popular among students, and especially Haskell alumni.

As part of their academic training, Haskell's students produced texts on a large variety of subjects. The students' writings illustrate how Indian children rhetorically negotiated whether to affirm, question, and sometimes object to the educational goals of Haskell. The students' essays reflect a broad range of attitudes toward social and political issues connected to their identities as indigenous students. In 1915, for instance, the Indian Office organized an essay contest on the subject of temperance. As this excerpt from the *Indian Leader* suggests, students responded emphatically to the subject:

> We once had a nice home but after alcohol entered it kept on going down and down until we had no home. Papa drank up everything. He caused mother to sell her land and now mother has no home at all. She works. If I had the power, I would crush every saloon to pieces. Fight well, hard and forever until this great enemy is banished from our Nation. I pray God to give us strength to fight this enemy.[27]

Many of Haskell's students could identify with the crusade against alcohol since they had seen the havoc it could wreak on Indian families and communities. Writing gave Indian youth an opportunity to express their feelings and take a position on a variety of issues affecting their lives. As early as 1887, Haskell's students wrote and delivered speeches on topics pertinent to the school's assimilation policy. The students' discussions of topics such as success, self-help, and mental discipline strongly reflect Haskell's educational philosophy. It is difficult to judge to what extent Indian students actually believed in their own oratory, but there is no reason to doubt that at least some aspects of the Protestant work ethic found acceptance among the children. Haskell's intensive education for patriotism and Christian citizenship did not lead the majority of students to reject their Indian identity, but it certainly influenced their perceptions of themselves and the world they lived in.

Haskell's leadership was clear about its assimilationist policy: traditional Indian values, religious beliefs, and lifestyles had no place at Haskell or anywhere else in the United States. Some aspects of Indian culture, though, were regarded as worth preserving. As apolitical and therefore nonthreatening expressions of indigenous cultures, crafts such as weaving, basket making, silver work, and pottery were acceptable expressions of the students' creativity. Haskell's annual exhibits included sections devoted to Indian designs, customs, crafts, games, festivals, and legends.[28] The school also encouraged the children to collect traditional Indian stories, which were published in 1914 under the title *Indian Legends and Superstitions*. The school treated Indian cultural expressions as interesting anthropological artifacts of a vanishing race but not as living cultures. The stories Indian students collected were worth preserving for their entertaining and historical value, but they were clearly "superstitions" of a primitive people. If students were encouraged to pursue traditional arts and crafts, they were at the same time reminded that the worldview that went along with these activities was not acceptable.

As in every school, some students took their academic training seriously, whereas others struggled or found their calling on the gridiron, as a member of the band, in the sewing room, or in the carpentry shop. In 1968, former Arapaho student Jesse Rowlodge was asked whether he ever got discouraged when he was in school and whether he ever thought about giving it up. Rowlodge replied:

> I don't think I ever did. There was a lot of us—friends, stayed four years—three girls, and two of us boys. One was from Wisconsin—his name was Henry LeCroie. And there was three girls—one from Ottawa, Kansas, and one's from Joplin, Missouri and one was from Oklahoma, I believe. And we always studied—tried to overdo ourselves in our rating every month. They had monthly tests you know, and when it come for a final examination—I never had to take no final examination. I was exempt.

When the interviewer asked him whether his grades were high enough Rowlodge said:

> Oh yes. I was—well there was five or six of us—eventually there was a girl, I think, Minnesota—she married an Osage boy. She was there—stayed right with us. We all had good grades—right around a hundred all the time.[29]

Jesse Rowlodge and his friends studied together, supported each other, and competed for the highest grades. These students took their academic work seriously and were trying to impress each other with their achievements. When Jay Black was interviewed in 1967, the ninety-year-old

Cheyenne shared some impressions from Haskell's academic life in the 1890s:

> They got big blackboards, you know, that's where you keep your handwriting. It's a piece of wood, you know, they give you. Then they write it down. It's the only way we start to learn it. After we got used to it, we took . . . wrote the number. Then you start from there and take a book, and second, third, fourth, fifth, and sixth, seventh, eighth, ninth, and after you finish the ninth, you have to go to high school. There was no high school at that time. . . . I believe in the third grade is shorthand writing. You can learn that too you know—short hand.[30]

Jay Black's recollections are sketchy and fragmented, but they are an important testimony from a tribal elder who, after his education at Haskell, became the keeper of the Cheyenne's sacred arrows, a certain sign of how deeply rooted he still was in the traditions of his Cheyenne culture.

Some students were frustrated by the pace of their academic advancement and asked the school for permission to accelerate their studies. During the summer of 1919, eighteen-year-old Ojibwe student Alice Vivia wrote to Principal C. E. Birch:

> I would like to know if I could pass the sixth grade and take seventh and eighth grades next school term when I return. My reason for wanting to advance so rapidly is that I feel too old to linger along like that, so Mr. Birch if you think I am capable of doing the work in one year I would like very much to hear from you.[31]

Before making his decision, Birch asked Alice's teacher, Mrs. Smoot, about the girl's abilities. Smoot supported Alice's request:

> I am quite sure she is capable of doing seventh grade work if she really wants to; whether she could make the eighth this year or not, of course would depend entirely on how well she did seventh, I should think. But she is quiet, studious, well behaved and anxious to advance, so I think she should be allowed to at least try.[32]

In writing to Principal Birch, Alice utilized what she had been taught in the classroom: letter-writing skills. Indian students were required to write home every month in order to inform their parents about their progress and activities at school. Even though Haskell's matron and disciplinarian inspected the mail frequently, many students used their newly acquired writing skills to lodge complaints about their treatment. As Alice's and many other letters indicate, students also voiced their wishes and concerns to Haskell's leadership, frequently breaking the school's letter writing rules, which denied the children the right to write anything negative about the school.

Alice's critique is rather subtle, but it attests to the slow rate of progress characteristic of Indian schools. The students' records prove that many children lingered on for years without advancing in their studies. There were certainly several reasons for this, including unqualified teachers, students' lack of motivation, language problems, homesickness, diseases that hampered the students' ability to study, culturally insensitive teaching methods, and so on. From an economic perspective, and economics played an important role at Haskell, one could also argue that the school did not necessarily have an interest in encouraging the children's rapid advancement. The longer a child remained in school, the more manual labor he or she could perform for the benefit of the institution. And since annual appropriations were based on average attendance figures, every child in school increased the dollar amount available for the upcoming school year.

For multiple reasons, a large number of students did not care much about their academic studies. Some rejected the school altogether, and others were more interested in the practical instruction offered by Haskell's industrial departments. When interviewed in 1967, Kiowa-Apache Lottie High Whitefox was asked what she had learned at Haskell during the 1910s. The old lady replied: "Oh, I didn't learn nothing much. I didn't stay there long." The interviewer asked her what she did while at school, and Lottie High Whitefox explained: "Oh, go to the sewing room, work, sew. We just went to school a half a day. The rest of the time we worked. Sometimes I worked in the mornings, and went to school in the afternoons. I worked in the sewing room. And now I can't even sew."[33] Apart from the rigorous work details, the education at Haskell did not leave lasting impressions on High Whitefox. Esther Burnett, on the other hand, remembered the academic training she received during the early 1920s in a positive light:

> Our classrooms were typical, with desks and blackboards and with a mixture of boys and girls in the same class. The standard high school curriculum included the same kinds of subjects that one would have had in the

public schools.... Our instruction was very intense; the teachers' missionary zeal stemmed from their purpose, which was to take the Indianness out of the Indian in preparation for life in the dominant society. The textbooks seemed to be up-to-date; there was a good library; there were study halls, and we had an abundance of homework. Nine o'clock meant lights off and into bed. In order for us to keep up with our homework, we would often tack a towel over the glass transom of the door so that the night matron would not see that we were burning the midnight oil.[34]

Burnett evaluated her education at Haskell as being equal, if not superior, to the public school system. Even though she acknowledged the school's assimilationist policy, she did not feel victimized by it. For Indian youth such as Esther Burnett and Jesse Rowlodge, Haskell provided a valuable education that they might not have gotten anywhere else during the early twentieth century.

Many students came to Haskell for its well-known commercial course and never attended any other classes. The department opened its doors in 1897, when a class of seven students, taught by the school's stenographer and regular academic teachers, began the country's first business training for Indian youth. In a 1925 memorial edition, the *Indian Leader* recognized Superintendent Peairs's crucial role in the history of the department: "Mr. Peairs, to whom credit must be given for establishing business instruction in Indian schools, was justified in his faith that Indian young men and women could be trained to do what other young men and women can do."[35] In 1899, C. E. Birch became head of the rapidly growing program. When the Office of Indian Affairs ordered its closing in 1903, the commercial course had already attracted sixty students. The *Indian Leader* recalled how:

The class of 1903 was cut short in the midst of a promising career. Approximately twenty young people were denied the opportunity of completing their course.... A number of the members of the class persevered and prepared themselves for office work, either by attending business colleges, night schools, or by private study. As a matter of strict justice these should be accorded the honors of being graduates of Haskell.[36]

According to C. E. Birch,

In 1906, the scarcity of clerical help in the Indian service, and the recognition of the efficient work being rendered in various superintendencies and in the Indian Bureau in Washington by the graduates of the Haskell Business Department, led to the reestablishment of this course at Haskell.[37]

In Commissioner Frances E. Leupp's view, Haskell's location near a large market for clerical workers in Lawrence and Kansas City warranted the school's special emphasis on commercial training. The two-year course taught classes in commercial geography, business arithmetic, business English, penmanship, shorthand, bookkeeping, typewriting, spelling, business law, parliamentary law and debating, rapid calculation, and civics. Students were eligible to enter the course once they had successfully completed the eight-year grammar school course. The graduating class of 1908, the first to complete the commercial course after the department had been reestablished, was the first to take the U.S. Civil Service examinations for positions as typists, stenographers, and clerks. According to the *Indian Leader*, "every graduate qualified for some position and practically all of them entered the service of Uncle Sam in various Government departments—some in the Forestry Service, some in the Army, and some in the Indian Service. Others went into business houses outside the Government employ."[38] In 1915, the course was expanded to three years of study in order to match the practices of other business high schools and colleges in the area.

Until 1915, commercial students did not have to engage in the school's industrial training, but they were detailed to do some janitorial work in the mornings and evenings as well as on Saturdays. As Superintendent Peairs explained to a prospective student, there was also the option to take "a part of the business course, leaving out stenography and typewriting, and one half day take trade work."[39] In order to compensate for the business students' lack of manual labor, the school insisted that the students stay in school over the summer. From 1915 on, sophomore and junior commercial students were also required to spend half the day with industrial training, whereas senior students continued to be in class all day. The business course was so popular that Haskell had to reject many applicants, telling students from the eastern United States to attend Carlisle instead. In 1912, the department had seventy-five students and two teachers. In addition, Assistant Superintendent C. E. Birch taught one hour of shorthand per day, still leaving the department in urgent need of an additional teacher. In 1918, there were already 129 business students, fifty of whom were boys, seventy-nine girls.[40] During these years, Superintendent Wise repeatedly received letters from the commissioner of Indian affairs, criticizing the department's graduation rate and Civil Service examination results. In his replies, Superintendent Wise explained that the department was in need of additional teachers and that English language skills proved to be the major obstacle to the students' success. At the same time he pointed out the high level of difficulty on the Civil Service exams; according to him, considering the general rates of failure, Haskell's students were not doing any worse than other candidates.[41]

From their recollections and letters it appears that most of the business students genuinely valued and enjoyed their time at Haskell. In 1920, Tuscarora student Lillian Henry wrote: "I came to Haskell in 1918 and have been specializing in the commercial course since that time. I have enjoyed my stay here and think it is a wonderful school, offering many opportunities for those who grasp them."[42] As part of their commercial training, students worked as bookkeepers, bank tellers, or typists in one of Haskell's training offices. The main room of the commercial quarters, which were equipped in 1908, accommodated eighty students and contained practice business offices, wholesale houses, banks, real estate offices, and commission houses. Every junior in the program took on the role of a merchant, every senior the role of bookkeeper or manager in one of the offices.[43]

After finishing his grammar school course at Haskell, Jesse Rowlodge decided to continue his studies in the business department. Rowlodge recalled how astonished his relatives were when they visited him at Haskell: "They were surprised I was in the Banking Department. We had a regular bank there at the school. You'd be teller, and cashier, and all that. I was in the Cashier's Department. They walked in and I told them this is where I worked—class work." At the end of the two-year course, Rowlodge passed the Civil Service exam and later attended law school in Minnesota.[44]

For the hundreds of students in Haskell's grammar school course, daily work details and intensive industrial training overshadowed the three or four hours spent in the classroom. Physical labor was a central part of the early boarding school experience, teaching the children work skills and instilling the values and beliefs of rugged individualism. The school's emphasis on individualism stood in opposition to the very notion of tribalism, the force holding Indian families and societies together. The goal of Haskell's leadership was to transform the children into law-abiding, patriotic, and economically self-sufficient citizens who would willfully reject their ancestors' lifestyle. Indian educators believed that they had to teach native children the concepts of habit, regularity, and time. In their view, indigenous peoples had no proper sense of industriousness and were prejudiced against manual labor. Haskell's leadership was under the presumption that Indian societies lacked a commitment or purpose to work and believed that rigorous work details would undo these cultural teachings. Apparently, though, not all Indian children took to the industrial training idea with the same vigor. Time and again, Haskell's leadership lamented the unwillingness of students from the Five Civilized Tribes (the Cherokee, Choctaw, Creek, Seminole, and Chickasaw) to apply themselves in the industrial departments. According to Superintendent Peairs, Cherokee students especially complained about being required to work half of the day, since these children were accustomed to an educational system mainly focused on academic instruction: "Owing to their past environment and treatment it seems next to impossible to make them realize the value of the industrial training."[45] By the late 1800s, the Cherokee nation had already had a long educational history, which included the establishment of public schools and academic institutions such as the Cherokee Female Seminary and the Male Cherokee Academy, which had successfully prepared students for further training at eastern universities.[46]

The ideology underlying Haskell's curriculum was not unique to Indian schools but part of a larger pedagogical movement. Around the turn of the century, vocational training became more and more popular as a form of education for all of America's youth and especially for students living in the country's rural areas. According to longtime Haskell employee C. E. Birch, who over the years acted as head of the business department, principal, and assistant superintendent, vocational training tended "to better fit the pupils of our rural public schools for the actual working problems of life."[47] In his view,

> A rapid change of sentiment toward vocational training is now apparent and greater things are in store. Where one school gave such instruction a quarter of a century ago, a hundred may now be counted giving much more thorough and extended instruction. With the building of many township and county high schools in rural communities has come a new

ideal in education and these schools are coming nearer to the realization of the old saying that "the high school is the people's college" than ever before in the history of our system of free public education.[48]

Birch argued that in the past, country schools had catered to the academic needs of elites, to the few students who intended to go on to college or become teachers. The large majority of students came "because they wished to obtain more schooling before settling down to life on the farm. The school was not as popular as it should have been for the reason that the courses were planned for the minority."[49] The introduction of domestic arts and science, agriculture, and business classes in addition to classical and normal training allowed farm children to learn applicable skills that had actual meaning for their future life.[50] Just as rural students were likely to become farmers and housewives, most Indian students were expected to return to their reservations, spending their lives in the field, in the kitchen, or as laborers in some kind of trade. Consequently, Haskell's leadership considered industrial training as the essence of the school's curriculum.

But Haskell's industrial training program was of "the most practical character" for an additional reason: the students maintained the school and decreased its operational costs.[51] They supplied nearly all the labor necessary to keep the school running and contributed to Haskell's self-sufficiency from the very beginning. According to a local newspaper, Indian children were "tireless once firmly disciplined" and made excellent farm hands and laborers.[52] The paper further reported: "At first some of the boys objected to doing certain kinds of work, saying that they had been taught that it was beneath their dignity. The Governor [Robinson] told them at once that if that was so, he himself would do that work. This settled it and now they take their turn at work of all kinds without murmur."[53] In 1888, Superintendent Robinson praised the children's labor in his report to the Commissioner of Indian Affairs:

> No white or colored labor is employed in any department, except for mason-work. All the buildings have been completed in the year . . . by the pupils, under the supervision of white employees. . . . The work on the farm and garden has all been done by the pupils, under the supervision of a farmer and gardener. Meals have been provided for 360 pupils three times a day, with but one white employee in the dining-room and kitchen.

House-work in the dormitory buildings is done with but one white person in charge of each building. Laundry work has but one white person to supervise it. All assistants and workers are Indian pupils. The same is true for the hospital, sewing, tailoring, and mending room; each have but one white employee.[54]

Haskell's students produced enormous quantities of food and goods. In 1904 the bakery was making an average of 800 loaves of bread per day; in 1914, Haskell's girls produced fifty pounds of butter per week. In 1909, the carpentry department manufactured fifty wagons per year, and the tailoring shop made all the student officer and band uniforms. In 1912, the sewing department finished 718 cotton dresses, 403 petticoats, 300 nightgowns, 226 uniform skirts, 1,260 towels, and 1,034 pillow cases.[55] Besides keeping maintenance and construction costs low, Haskell's students produced many surplus items that were sold at local markets, including wagons, harnesses, suits, and various agricultural products as well as milk and butter from the dairy herd.[56]

At times, students received pay for their work, especially during the summer months. In 1899, for instance, Indian Commissioner Jones approved $400 for the "employment of irregular pupil labor at not to exceed 50 cents per day to perform work about the school, on the farm, and in the garden," but in general, the Indian Office took a clear stance against paid student labor.[57] Haskell's girls sometimes worked in the homes of Haskell employees, spending certain hours of the week with various domestic chores. Because this work took place off campus, the individual employers paid the girls, and their labor was regarded as part of the outing system.[58] During the early 1900s, Iroquois student Lucille Winnie worked for a teacher on Saturday mornings. "The dollar she paid me was a small fortune," she recalled, "and I would make it stretch to at least four trips to The Shack [an off-campus eating place]."[59] In general, however, the children's oftentimes heavy manual labor was not compensated and fell under the category of industrial training. The push for institutional self-sufficiency placed a heavy burden on Haskell's students, boys and girls alike, contradicting the principle that industrial education be genuinely instructive.

Occasionally, Indian educators worried about this reality and imposed special rules to ensure the training value of the work performed. In 1916, Superintendent Wise informed the commissioner that "all the instructors in our various industrial departments are fully advised as to the requirement regarding thirty minutes of definite instruction to the pupils on their details."[60] From Haskell's records it is apparent that many employees in the industrial department were good tradesmen but were neither qualified nor interested or patient enough to teach the boys their trade. This problem led to frequent criticism in the school's annual inspection reports and the repeated replacement of vocational employees.

Indian girls worked arduously in the kitchen, dining room, sewing room, and laundry. Much of their work was repetitive and lacked educational value. Haskell's leadership was aware of this problem and tried to reduce the time students spent on each chore. In 1917, Superintendent Peairs explained that it was

> not advisable at all to keep pupils in the kitchen, laundry or in the sewing room for too great a length of time. The work is too hard on many of the young girls and . . . oftentimes pupils do not remain in school to complete the prevocational work, therefore it is very essential that they have opportunities to learn something of the elementary principles of the work of all the departments. Because of this fact, we change our details here every ten weeks and I believe that the plan works out advantageously to all of the prevocational girls.[61]

Peairs further explained that the boys stayed in each department for the entire number of weeks required to finish their pre-vocational courses. Students working on the farm remained with their detail for the whole year, taking shop courses during the winter months. In 1917, the boys could choose vocational courses in agriculture, carpentry, blacksmithing, engineering, painting, masonry, and printing. The boys' academic work matched the vocational courses and included English, arithmetic, history, and subjects such as farm and household accounts, rural economics, agricultural botany, soil and soil fertility, and industrial geography. Beginning in the late 1800s, Haskell occasionally accepted full-blood students for vocational training only who wanted to learn a trade and felt too old to attend regular classes. After 1907, boys who were anxious to complete their trades were allowed to work full-time, taking academic classes at night.[62]

The instruction Indian children received at Haskell strictly followed white gender roles of the time: agriculture and the various trades for the boys; cooking, cleaning, sewing, nursing, childcare, and teaching for the girls. Haskell's boys and girls lived on a gendered campus and learned according to a gendered curriculum, which generally did not promote professions for the girls. Rather, Indian girls were expected to become mothers, housewives, seamstresses, or domestic servants working for white families. Haskell's popular business, nursing, and normal courses were the exception to this rule, providing some girls with the opportunity to prepare for a life outside of the female sphere of hearth and home. The Victorian gender roles propagated by Indian educators were markedly different from those in many indigenous societies, and the effort to train Indian girls as "good housewives" rested on a number of ideological assumptions.[63]

On the one hand, Anglo ethnocentrism had led to a vision of Indian women as drudges and slaves, toiling for their idle husbands and fathers in an environment of humiliation, immorality, and sexual exploitation.[64] According to the Anglo-American perception, indigenous girls had to be saved from a life in savagery, and their social standing as well as sexual role needed to be changed. On the other hand, the dominant society recognized and exploited the important role of Indian women as culture brokers, who exercised great influence on their partners as well as their children. In Victorian America, the Protestant cult of "true womanhood" had led to an idealized vision of the role of women as the cradle of civilization: pure, pious, obedient, clean, humble, and selfless. In order to Americanize indigenous peoples, Indian girls, the mothers of future generations, had to be "domesticated" according to these European-American standards. Haskell's academic and industrial curriculum, the outing system, and the social and religious activities of the Young Women's Christian Association (YWCA) all worked together to achieve this goal.[65]

Haskell's educators insulted not only the value of work in indigenous nations but also their traditional divisions of labor. In many horticultural tribes women performed all agricultural tasks and owned the land, the livestock, and the houses, whereas men were responsible for hunting, fishing, and warfare. Not all indigenous cultures were matrilineal, but even in patrilineal societies, women often played a prominent role in community life and shared equally with men in social, economic, religious, and sometimes even political roles.[66] European intrusion and colonization undermined much of the autonomy and equality of indigenous women. The imposition of a Christian ethic of patriarchy—a patrilineal kinship system and a male god—led to destructive changes in many Indian societies. The breakdown of male roles (particularly as warriors and hunters) and the decreasing valuation of Indian women had long-lasting, demoralizing effects on Indian communities.[67] Indian education, and especially federal off-reservation boarding schools, played a major role in the indoctrination of American Indians with a paternalistic cultural framework. Indian girls in their role as cultural change agents were expected to carry the merits of civilization into their native communities and to direct their own children away from the "savage" ways of their ancestors. In this way, boarding and missionary schools contributed to the destruction of indigenous kinship systems and the breakdown of Indian families.

Haskell's educational program ensured that Indian girls were trained in all the arts of homemaking.[68] In addition, domestic education was designed to train Indian girls in subservience and submission to authority, either to their future husbands or to their future employers. Even though Americans at the turn of the century saw a white woman's place in the home, the service ethic instilled into Indian girls was more geared toward domestic service than toward their own homes. Racist ideology was responsible for the different experience of Indian women, whose educational opportunities lagged several decades behind those for white women. Whereas the Victorian "cult of domesticity" enshrined white middle-class women's invalidism and fragility, Indian women were regarded as strong and enduring and therefore especially well suited for the drudgeries of domestic service.[69] Even though the rhetoric of Haskell's superintendents placed special emphasis on the civilizing and moralizing component of the girls' education, in reality much of the work the girls performed was strenuous physical labor, which assured the economic survival of the school. The work they performed offered little reprieve from the rigors of physical labor criticized by educators concerned with their tribal home environment.

Indian educators deeply believed in the transforming capabilities of female education and the notion: "Educate a man, you educate an individual; educate a woman, you educate a race."[70] In their view, the boarding school community could successfully replace the girls' real families while molding them to meet white standards of civilized life. Matrons fulfilled a crucial role in this scheme, providing the girls with nurturing care and moral guidance, replacing the girls' "darker and immoral natural mothers."[71] According to Indian Commissioner Jones, the mostly Anglo matron was "to the Indian girl what the white mother is to her child. She should love her girls and be willing to spend most of her hours out of school with them directing their housework and play, giving them heart talks, social purity, [and] the value of service."[72] In his annual inspection report, Special Agent Dorchester noted: "Often all that an Indian girl needs to keep her pure and true is to know that near her is a kind-hearted white woman ready with sympathy, advice, and help."[73] Whether all matrons lived up to this ideal is questionable. Some women did; others failed. Some were popular among the girls and others were not. Considering the large number of girls at Haskell, it must have been impossible for the matron to have a close relationship with all the students. The thought that a single person, even if she was an extremely affectionate woman, could substitute for the children's real mothers is naive, at best. Homesickness, so prevalent among boarding school students, attests to this disturbing truth.

At Haskell's founding, vocational training for girls consisted of domestic arts (sewing) and domestic science (cooking). In 1917, the pre-vocational and vocational course of study still reflected this early emphasis. In the six-year-long pre-vocational divisions, the girls spent their days with home training (ten weeks), cooking (forty weeks), poultry raising (five weeks), sewing (thirty weeks), laundering (fifteen weeks), nursing (five weeks), and "unassigned" work (fifteen weeks). Every work detail lasted for ten weeks at a time, and the girls were working together in groups of sixteen to twenty.[74] After the normal department closed in 1903, girls only had two vocational courses left to choose from: home economics (formerly called domestic arts and science) and nursing. The four-year vocational course in home economics very much resembled the girls' pre-vocational training, centering on domestic life. In addition to English, vocational arithmetic, music, physical training, and history, the girls received instruction in cooking, sewing, child study, rural economics, insects and insecticides, soils and soil fertility, home architecture, decoration and sanitation, household accounts, and household management.[75] After finishing the vocational course, the most promising students were encouraged to take the Civil Service exam for matron and seamstress. Girls passing the exam usually found employment as assistant seamstresses or matrons at Indian schools and agencies across the country.

Nursing was taught as a separate subject, giving some girls the opportunity to continue their education at training hospitals in places such as Kansas City, Chicago, or New York. In 1911, Superintendent Wise informed Commissioner Robert G. Valentine about the state of Haskell's program in practical nursing:

> At Haskell, a detail of eight girls is at present employed in the hospital as assistant nurses. One, during each half day, is in charge of the male wards and one of the female wards. One has both wards during the first half of the night and another during the second half. Two are in the dispensary and assist the physician at the morning sick call, doing minor dressings and handing out medicine as prescribed. All these are under the supervision of a trained nurse. These pupils are expected to give enemas, ice baths and warm baths as well as to apply cold and hot treatments, massages and the like. They are taught to take temperature, pulse and respiration and to record the same. They are also taught to make complete bedside notes. They are given practical work in principles of hygiene, also in dealing with contagion and infection. . . . Every effort will be made to give our girls practical instruction, especially in the matter of the care of trachoma and tubercular cases.[76]

The school's nursing students found ample opportunity to practice their art, as many of Haskell's students suffered from poor health and visited the hospital frequently. The girls were especially needed during recurrent epidemics of influenza and other infectious diseases that raged among the student population and took many children's lives.

By the 1910s, Haskell's curriculum had become more diversified than in earlier years, but the emphasis of the children's education had not changed. Except for the students attending the business course and the few girls taking nursing, boys were still expected to become rural farmers, tradesmen, or laborers, and girls were trained to become housewives or domestic servants. Even though some of the trades taught to the boys, such as harness making and blacksmithing, were beginning to be antiquated by the early 1900s, they persisted at Haskell for years to come. Indian boarding schools were generally slow in adapting to changing social conditions, as their decade-long emphasis on agriculture and nineteenth-century trades implies.

Two programs that figured prominently in female Indian education were the outing system and the domestic science cottage. The outing system was originally designed to provide Indian girls with the opportunity of living among white families during the summer months, where they were expected to learn domestic skills in a truly "civilized" environment. The domestic science cottage was designed to allow female students to live in a model home environment, practicing the Anglo ideal of family home life. Haskell's practice cottage was equipped in 1915 and was designed to "fit the girls for practical and efficient housekeepers and home-makers."[77] According to the *Indian Leader*,

> Haskell's Domestic Science Cottage is a modern three-story house containing three bedrooms and bathroom for the girls; also housemother's room, hall vestibule, living room, dining room, pantry, kitchen, one screened-in back porch and an open porch on the south side.... Eight girls are detailed to the cottage for a ten weeks' term. They are the more advanced girls, third or fourth year vocational, for naturally they could best appreciate the opportunity and the meaning of the plan. The girls and their teacher live here as one family.... The eight girls are in attendance at academic work as usual, so one-half of their time is given to their home.[78]

It is easy to imagine that the girls enjoyed their ten-week stay in the practice cottage, which provided a diversion from the usual work routine and dormitory life. For many of the girls, the cottage was the closest they would ever come to a white middle-class lifestyle. But exactly this truth was a point of criticism. The cottage was a modern home with electric lights, running water, and a furnace—conditions that only few girls would actually find upon their return home. At the minimum, the experience in the practice cottage could be of advantage when girls obtained positions as maids in white middle-class homes.

Many girls enjoyed their domestic training, as the recollections of several former students reveal. Mary Red Eagle, a Quapaw from Oklahoma who attended Haskell in the early 1900s, remembered that "we had all the chance to learn, you know, sewing—like—whatever you wanted to learn you were taught there. So 'course I took sewing—I love to sew and then I didn't know very much about cooking, however. But I tried to study that too. And so I was there three years until, finally I came home."[79] Mildred Richmond, a Menominee student from Wisconsin who attended the school from 1914 to 1918, wrote: "Ever since I can remember I have wanted to learn to sew and to do it well. Since I have been here the opportunity has been given to me and I have tried my best to become accomplished in domestic art. If I could, some day, be a domestic art teacher, one of the best I mean, it would surely mean much to me."[80] In 1916, Chippewa student Jewel Wells wrote to her sister: "We get no marks in the 'girls' industries' this month, because the details were changed only a short time ago, and the matrons have made no reports. I've been put in Domestic Art and like it real well, you know I always liked sewing."[81]

While the girls were being taught to be good homemakers the boys were spending a lot of their time working in the fields. Not all of them enjoyed their farming detail; on the contrary, most of them would have preferred to learn any other trade. In 1907, Superintendent Peairs wrote:

> We have a 1000-acre farm in connection with the school. All of the small children in the school have their individual garden beds, and are given instruction in the spring in vegetable gardening. Of course the farming is done on a large scale, and boys who are taking farming work in large fields rather than in garden plots. As a rule, Indian boys do not seem to like agricultural work very well. Of course, some of them do, and not want to take up any other kind of work at all; but a majority of them prefer the trades.[82]

Over the years, Haskell recognized the boys' need and interest in a wider variety of trade instruction. In 1912, the school reorganized and expanded its industrial department, offering the boys more alternatives to farming:

> The trades that are especially deemed desirable to emphasize are those of carpentry, masonry (covering brick laying, plastering, and concrete work), steam fitting, plumbing, electrical wiring and bell work, and painting. Experience has fully demonstrated that the Indian boys like all these trades, take naturally to them, and they are of a kind specially suited to their physical requirements, enabling them to work largely out of doors.[83]

Since Haskell strove for self-sufficiency, however, agriculture would remain the school's focus for many years to come. Many boys had clear ideas as to what kind of trade they wanted to learn at the school and asked for transfers from one department to another. The school was not always willing to accommodate their wishes, but in general they let the boys choose according to their interests and talents. In 1970, former Arapaho student Arthur Sutton remembered:

> When I moved to Haskell [during the early 1920s], they put me into the Engineer department, which I didn't like because they were using oil in the big boilers. But I was just used to shoveling coal! So I asked for my

transfer to another department. . . . So they asked me, "What kind of a trade you like to follow?" I told them, "auto mechanics." So they placed me there the second year. I was next to the foreman. They give me the key to look after the shop. And when he's gone I took over.[84]

Nineteen-year-old Paiute student Robert Johnson from Nevada wrote in 1920:

Then I heard of Haskell and my hunger for more education made me come to this fine institution. My ambition is to try to work my way up into university and take up drafting as that goes along with my work in carpentry.[85]

Otis Russell (Osage), who attended Haskell in the early 1900s, learned the trade of harness making and was eager to become more proficient in his craft:

I started in a harness shop out there. I made harnesses. . . . The superintendent wanted me . . . to go up there and work in Denver. . . . Wanted to know what I think about it. I told him, I said, I don't believe I'm quite finished yet. I know I didn't cause there's lots of things I needed to learn. . . . Really come down to the fine points of harness making I couldn't do that. So I tried, I told the superintendent I said I don't know whether I can do it or not, but I would like to go one more year in harness making.

When Russell went home to talk to his father about his further study plans, his whole life changed in an instant:

So, I come home. First thing you know, want to marry me off, marry me off. I didn't get to go. . . . He didn't want me to go no more. So he married me off before I knew it. I was sorry I didn't get to go back up there. I wanted to go back up there. That's where I lost everything. From then on everything I try to do I do wrong.[86]

Russell's story contains several interesting elements. It shows the students' initiative when it came to determining their personal course of study and their willingness to assert their views before Haskell's leadership. The story also shows the great influence parents had on their children's education and how, in Russell's perception, his father's opposition to his return to Haskell destroyed his professional future. In Russell's view, Haskell would have provided him with the education needed to succeed in life. He believed that his premature departure from the school prevented him from becoming a successful tradesman.

The children's industrial training did not stop at the end of the school year. Many students stayed at Haskell over the summer months, and the boys especially were expected to work on the school farm to bring in the harvest and to do construction and maintenance work around the school. A number of students participated in Haskell's outing program, working for a variety of employers in Kansas and surrounding states, including Missouri, Oklahoma, and Colorado. The program, which Superintendent Robinson had introduced in 1888, grew over the years to include several hundred students. Until 1911, outings took place during the summer only and were administered by the school's matron and disciplinarian. In the 1910s, Haskell employed full-time outing agents who arranged the children's stays, selected employers, and visited the students once a month during the program. Boys were able to secure employment on farms and ranches or with railroad companies, working as carpenters, laborers, and field hands. Haskell's girls were placed in white middle-class homes to help with housework and take care of the families' children. Over the years, the school established close ties with a number of patrons—in Osage City, Ottawa, Emporia, and Wichita, Kansas, as well as in Kansas City—who repeatedly hired Indian girls for the summer.[87]

Haskell's leadership insisted on the great educational value of the outing program, emphasizing its teaching aspect over the economic side of the arrangement. Superintendents Peairs and Wise believed that outing work would teach the children industry and thrift as well as the ways of "civilized" society. The latter aspect of the program was especially important for Indian girls, who were supposed to profit from the positive influence of a "cultivated" home environment and the association with "respectable" white families.[88] For the students, outing meant the opportunity to save spending money for the upcoming school year, to experience life outside of Haskell, and sometimes to attend public schools in places such as Emporia or Wichita.

Students, as well as their employers, signed an outing contract that laid out the rules of the program. The children agreed to be industrious, honest, and helpful to their employers, to "bathe at least once a week and be neat and clean in personal appearance," and to attend church regularly, take care of their clothing, save money, refrain from alcohol and tobacco use, and not leave their employer without his knowledge and the approval of the school. Patrons also were expected to follow certain rules, which mostly involved keeping a watchful eye over the children.[89] Employers and students agreed to a specified rate of pay that depended on the students' prior experience and the amount of work involved. Employers were required to send two-thirds of the students' wages to the school for safekeeping, since "experience has taught us that most Indian boys will spend money as fast as they earn it and even faster," as Superintendent Peairs put it.[90] The same rule applied to the girls, who were also constantly reminded to "spend judiciously." In the early 1900s, girls earned between two and three dollars per week; by 1918, this rate had gone up to between five and eight dollars. Those students attending public schools while outing only received an allowance of fifty cents per week as well as their board. In exchange they were required to work in the mornings and at night as well as on Saturdays. The boys' wages were notably higher, but the school's records do not allow much insight into their actual experiences. Whereas Haskell's records abound with letters and testimonies from the girls' patrons, the boys' outing program seems to have been much less personal and more a matter of business.

Indian parents frequently supported their children's summer outing as an opportunity to earn wages, asking the school to find good positions for them. In March 1921, Mrs. Rose Anderson from Fort Hall, Idaho, wrote to Superintendent Peairs: "Would it be possible to place my daughter Louise Sosseur on the outing list this summer. . . . It will save me the expense of sending for her. I'd like to have her placed in a good Catholic home where she would be treated kindly and not be allowed to go out alone nights or to the movies or dances."[91]

Peairs promised to find a good outing home for the girl where she would have careful supervision. That same spring, Mrs. Jamison Schanadore asked for her daughter Mamie to come home to Wisconsin during the summer. She was anxious to see her daughter, who had been at Haskell for three years without a vacation. In case the school would not approve the request, she wished to send Mamie on an outing.[92] As could be expected, Superintendent Peairs promised her to find a good outing home for the girl, ignoring the mother's initial plea to have her daughter visit during the summer. It appears that parents and their children had a rather realistic view of the outing program, considering the wage-earning opportunities far more important than the "civilizing" aspect praised by Indian educators. In her autobiography, Esther Burnett remembered her 1928 outing experience in Kansas City:

> I worked for a doctor and his wife as their downstairs maid, and I lived in my own private maid's quarters. I received thirty dollars a month wages. Half of that money was mine to spend as I saw fit, and the other half was sent back to school to be put in my account for spending during the school year. It was a wonderful and rewarding experience to have my own money to spend.[93]

Indian girls and boys were eager to work over the summer, but they were not willing to do any kind of work for any kind of pay. Haskell's boys had greater bargaining power than the girls, since farm hands were desperately needed during the summer months. In the early 1900s, one employer from Baldwin City, Kansas, complained to the school:

> The boys that I hired from the Institute quit me this morning. They asked what they were getting and I told them what you said but they told me they wouldn't work for less than $1.50 per day. They are green hands at the work, to me they weren't worth a dollar a day but I would give them a dollar and a quarter if they would stay with me as I am head over heals [sic] in work and need a man. But they wouldn't work for less. Gave them the best of treatment but for some cause they wouldn't stay.[94]

Obviously the boys did not consider $1.25 enough compensation for the work they were expected to do. Employers did not always make good on the promises made in the outing contracts and often expected more from the children than agreed upon at the beginning of the summer. Haskell's records contain many stories of outing students who felt exploited and were discontent with their positions, and the boys in particular changed employers frequently. The school's outing matron praised herself for her ability to find the right home for each girl,[95] but despite careful selection, the match between students and patrons was not always successful.

Outing girls worked at a variety of tasks such as cleaning, washing, ironing, cooking, serving food, and in many cases, childcare. The transition from

Haskell to life in an outing home was not always easy, and sometimes students complained about being homesick for Haskell or of feeling lonely. For this reason, the school tried to place several outing girls in the same town, but never in the vicinity of Haskell's boys, since "no steps should be taken that could possibly in any way affect the safety and welfare of our girls, or that might in any way work to the disadvantage of their outings."[96] When girls voiced their dissatisfaction, their homesickness, or any problems with their employers, Haskell's superintendents usually encouraged them to stay in their positions, try harder, and avoid becoming an "outing failure." At the same time, the students' patrons were expected to help the girls overcome their difficulties and to be patient with them. From the many letters Superintendents Peairs, Fiske, and Wise wrote to their students, it is clear that in most cases the school favored the interests and opinions of the employers over those of the children. The students were not forced to stay with a family if they really did not want to, however, and every year students returned from their outing earlier than planned. The majority of employers, however, were very happy with the students' performance and sent letters of praise back to the school. The following excerpt reflects this positive experience:

> The time is drawing near for your girls to return to Haskell and I surely dread losing Elizabeth. We are so fond of her it seems we cannot let her go. I give a willing consent only upon knowing that she can get better the work she wishes at school. I cannot praise too much your Haskell girls. . . . I saw a little group of them together the other day and they looked so pretty and fresh. Their modesty and desire not to attract attention was refreshing. It is one of the traits I have noticed and admire most. Elizabeth is a most exceptional girl in every way.[97]

The *Indian Leader* published equally positive reports from the girls, praising their employers, and especially their public school work. In 1915, Oneida student Frances Wheelock wrote of her patron and school experience in Dunlap, Kansas:

> Mrs. Vickers is very good to me and I am doing everything the best I can to please her. I have been doing some embroidery for her and she is real proud of it. . . . I haven't missed one day of school since I came here. I like going to school among white children fine. My favorite studies are Kansas

history and civil government. . . . Mrs. Vickers and Miss Calkins help me with my studies. I like going to school here so well that I have made up my mind to go to high school here this fall.[98]

After visiting Haskell's girls in their Wichita outing homes in 1920, the school's outing matron wrote to Superintendent Peairs:

I wished you could see each girl in her home, all girls have fine airy rooms. Wichita people certainly treat our girls fine and take a parental interest in them.

Concerning the girls' high school experience, she reported:

In Domestic Art the teacher said that the girls were doing better practical work than the white girls. . . . The teacher reported that the white girls were very nice to our girls and went more than half way to treat them well. . . . All the teacher and the office force reported their conduct excellent, appearance neat, do not look overworked, that patrons are interested and require passes if pupils are detained after school. They use no paint or powder and dress hair in very plain style.[99]

But not all students were content with their life in Wichita or lived up to the expectations of the school. The report mentions one girl who decided to come back to Haskell because she did not like to go to school with white children, another girl who had repeatedly stolen things from her employer, and a third one who was taken back to Haskell after "slipping out" with a boy she met at high school. Likewise, some employers were disappointed in the abilities of their new Indian maids and complained that they were not worth their money and needed to be taught everything. Outing girls could be very spirited domestic servants, time after time breaking the rules of their contracts and testing the patience of their employers. Some girls found their employers' constant supervision stifling, and their heavy work duties conflicted with their school attendance. It appears though that many families were happy with "their" girls, and many girls liked their patrons so much that they requested permission to spend the following summer with the same family.

Even though Haskell's outing program was criticized over the years for not living up to its promises, outing continued to constitute an important element in the children's education until the 1930s. The 1928 Meriam Report criticized the outing program for its lack of real vocational training, calling it "mainly a plan for hiring out boys for odd jobs and girls for domestic service."[100] Haskell's records support this interpretation, even though many students viewed their outing experience in a positive light, valuing the opportunity to earn extra spending money. Compared with other boarding schools, Haskell's outing program provided a larger number of girls with the opportunity to visit public schools and to live with families who took a genuine interest in them, a fact that can be attributed to the school's location far from Indian reservations.[101]

Haskell's curriculum was designed to transform indigenous students into industrious and obedient workers who would live their lives as patriotic Christian citizens. Although the training offered at Haskell prepared most students for a work life as laborers and domestic servants, some features of Haskell's curriculum, such as the business course, the nursing and normal programs, and, finally, the introduction of a high school course in 1921, gave Indian students the opportunity to advance beyond the low expectations of white society. The children's testimony proves their genuine interest and frequent success in taking up these opportunities. Haskell's popularity and growth can be attributed to the fact that despite its shortcomings, the school offered more to indigenous students than most Indian boarding schools at the time.

CHAPTER FIVE

Rituals and Recreation

At Haskell, Indian students entered a world that was in many ways different from the one they had known before. The transformation Indian educators had in mind transcended the mere modification of looks and behavior. Their ultimate goal was to create students who not only adapted the knowledge and skills associated with "civilized" life but also deeply believed in the values, religion, work ethic, and patriotism propagated by white society. Indian children had to internalize these teachings in order to become assimilated American citizens. Changes in appearance and lifestyle supported this mental transformation, but they had to be completed by moral, religious, and patriotic training.

From the very beginning, Haskell's administrators placed special emphasis on the ideological dimension of their work, which manifested itself in numerous rituals inside as well as outside the classroom. The Protestant ideology, expressed through religious instruction and the teaching of American patriotism, formed the core of this endeavor. Haskell's curriculum provided for extensive training in these fields, and no student was able to escape the Christianizing and Americanizing influences of the school. Christianity was to supplant all traditional religions, leading Indian children into the light of Christian civilization. As Haskell's first superintendent, James Marvin (1884–1885), put it, "the moral forces that transform men from barbarism to enlightened communities . . . must begin and continue in that 'fear of the Lord,' which is the beginning of wisdom."[1] According to Superintendent Peairs, "a really civilized people cannot be found in the world except where the Bible has been sent and the gospel taught."[2] Haskell's administrators believed that Christianity would reconstitute the children's moral character, bestow on them a love for flag and country, strengthen the nuclear family, and promote the process of individualization and hence detribalization.

Haskell's students came from diverse religious backgrounds. Many of them were practicing Christians; others came from Indian homes deeply rooted in native religions. By the late nineteenth century, many tribes had blended elements of the Christian faith into their traditional religions, and new religious expressions such as the Ghost Dance of the Plains and the peyote religion of the Native American Church had influenced indigenous cultures as well as the beliefs of Indian youth. The fusion of Christian ethics and values and the blending of Christian and traditional rituals and practices that occurred in Indian communities persisted in the boarding school setting. Many students held a syncretic worldview, absorbing some elements of the new teachings while holding on to the essence of their tribal religious system.[3] Other students were devout Christians but at the same time adhered to their tribally specific worldviews. Christianity could serve as a tool to mediate changing cultural circumstances in favor of indigenous values and ideals, ultimately affirming ethnic identity. Like other areas of school life, the realm of religion reflects the complex cultural encounters taking place at Haskell and the complicated cultural decisions that students made every day.

Especially in Haskell's early years, many students entered the school at a very young age with only a partial understanding of their tribal ceremonial cycle and belief system. Living at a boarding school cut the children off from the yearly ceremonial cycle at home. They missed ceremonies taking place during the fall, winter, and spring, and they were not present to receive the religious teachings of their elders and spiritual leaders. By taking the children out of the religious life of their tribes, boarding schools disrupted the knowledge transfer from one generation to the other and contributed to the loss of complex belief systems.

It was in this context of removal from the children's native religious environment that boarding school superintendents waged their campaign of Christianization. Even though Haskell was a government school, religious instruction and on-campus chapel services were mandatory, and students were encouraged to attend a weekly church service in town. Upon arrival, the school asked the children for their denominational preferences and church membership. Many children already belonged to an organized Christian church and maintained their membership at Haskell. Others chose a denomination while at school. If the students were under the age of eighteen, Haskell consulted their parents concerning their choice. Due to the different missionary efforts across the country and the reservations, students belonged to a variety of churches: Catholic, Presbyterian, Baptist, Methodist, Lutheran, Episcopal, and many others. In 1911, for instance, 153 students were Catholic, 114 Methodist, 130 Baptist, 62 Presbyterian, 44 Episcopalian, and 165 Lutheran. A few students belonged to other denominations such as the Congregational Church, the Quakers, or the Mennonites.[4]

Haskell's first superintendent, Dr. James Marvin, exemplified the missionary idealism of many Indian educators of his time. Under his leadership, the school focused on imparting Christian morality as the key to knowledge and understanding of American civilization. He introduced compulsory nondenominational services on Sunday mornings, as well as Bible school classes in the afternoons. Haskell's subsequent superintendents continued the religious routine established under Marvin,[5] and during the 1891–1892 school year, students formed a chapter of the Young Men's Christian Association on campus, which was soon followed by a chapter of the Young Women's Christian Association. By the 1910s, the system of religious education at government boarding schools had become more elaborate and formalized. In accordance with the "General Regulations for Religious Worship and Instruction of Pupils in Government Indian Schools" published by the Office of Indian Affairs, Haskell held Bible school classes every Sunday morning that were divided up according to the different denominations. On Sunday afternoon, the school conducted general chapel exercises, which were nondenominational and compulsory for all students. During these school assemblies, Haskell's superintendents would lecture on topics ranging from Christian ethics and morals to patriotism and Christian citizenship.[6] The Sunday afternoon meeting served also as a general school assembly during which announcements concerning the events of the upcoming week were made. In order to provide students with the opportunity to be taught in their particular faith, the school allowed two hours per week in which representatives of each church could provide religious instruction at the school. It was against the school's rules for employees to try to convert students, and any missionary efforts by the personnel were strictly forbidden.[7]

Haskell's religious program was designed as a perfect tool for assimilation, indoctrinating the children with the wisdoms and values of the Anglo-American world. The transformation of the children's bodies, the rigors of military discipline, the lessons of industrial training, and the effects of academic teachings could only be successful if complemented by a comprehensive religious program that transformed the children's minds. Indian children had to learn the importance of chastity, monogamy, charity, temperance, honesty, and self-sacrifice as well as pure thoughts and language. Superintendent Peairs considered the work of the YMCA and the YWCA extremely valuable with regard to character formation and the children's education for Christian citizenship.[8] It was Peairs's goal to get as many students involved as possible, and both organizations played an important part in the students' social and religious life.

How well did the school succeed in its mission? Did the children change their worldview and become devout Christians? Did they joyfully participate in Haskell's religious activities, or was religious instruction an area of contestation? As with other areas of school life, the records can only provide some of the answers to these questions. It appears that many students were actively involved in YMCA and YWCA activities and that, in general, the children enjoyed the change in the weekly routine that Sundays and especially holidays provided. Younger children enjoyed the biblical stories they learned in Sunday school, which were reminiscent of stories they had heard at home. According to one teacher's account: "As soon as an Indian understands enough English to follow the simple stories, he can never get enough of them. Some of the friskiest boys will sit like graven images through a whole evening."[9] Considering the importance of storytelling in native cultures, it is not surprising that the children enjoyed this aspect of religious instruction. The same would be true for songs, music, rituals, and prayers—concepts that were not new to children used to elaborate tribal ceremonies. Haskell's records indicate that a substantial number of students had at least a temporary interest in, and devotion to, a Christian lifestyle. One should keep in mind, though, that many students already came from Christian homes and that the willingness to participate in Haskell's religious activities could stem from a variety of factors other than a belief in the Christian faith. Christian associations such as the YMCA and the YWCA offered the opportunity to take on leadership roles, to socialize in a "morally" acceptable way, and to engage in charitable and communal activities only open to active members. Traveling to student conferences and attending summer camps were welcomed diversions from the monotonous school routine. Former students recall the excitement surrounding Christian holidays and the short-term freedom that a YMCA lawn social or a Sunday church excursion into town could provide. Jesse Rowlodge recalled Haskell's Sunday routine during the early 1900s:

> In the mornings, Sunday mornings—there was a register there and we'd file in—some of them were Catholics and some were Presbyterians. I belonged to the Congregational Church at that time. After breakfast we'd fix up and go on to town, about a mile and a half. Go up there in bunches, girls and boys, and go to respective churches. Some of us came out in cabs—team-drawn cabs. Eat dinner in a restaurant till about two o'clock. Then church services were held in the big chapel there. Different denomination ministers come out.[10]

Arthur Sutton, an Arapaho who attended Haskell during the early 1920s, remembered that Haskell was the place where he "got started with" his Bible work. According to Sutton, the different denominations collected money during the year to help Indian children attend summer camp:

> I was the one picked out in the whole school to take over charge of the boys that's going to that camp. Well, while we were there, we were taught leatherwork and different things. In the evenings we'd go to study the Bible. Then we went back—we done the best work among all the children participating there in the camp—we took everything—athletics—the way we carry on, the way we took care of our barracks, and we had to do our dishwashing, too! So they give us a plaque to take back to the school, showing that we representatives showed outstanding work among our other races of people that attended.[11]

Although Haskell's strict discipline prepared the boys for camp life, their involvement in religious activities made the trip possible. For Arthur Sutton, his religious training at Haskell laid the foundation for his adult life in Oklahoma. In a later part of the interview he explained:

> So that's where I got in contact with the church movement. And when I came back home I started working with my people down at Geary. And we moved up—I got married and we moved up here. And got my church transferred into Mennonite movement by letter. So I been working ever since.[12]

Like many other students, Sutton internalized the teachings he received at Haskell and devoted his life to the gospel.

For many children, though, going to church and joining Christian associations was mainly a social affair, and they went along because their friends did it. Esther Burnett admitted that she enrolled in a Bible history class taught by a professor from Kansas University because "Bob Horne, a California Hoopa student of whom I was quite fond, was signed up for it, and that was a way I could socialize with him more."[13] Otis Russell's story about how he came to join a Christian Church likewise reflects a social motivation:

> One time we was playing ball Sunday morning, Easter Sunday. I was playing with bunch of boys in front of the chapel. . . . They said come go with us. Where are you going? We're going to church. . . . I said wait then I'll get my cap. . . . I followed them and we went to the Methodist church. . . . So we went in there. . . . That minister he said the children place get way down front. Show me where to sit. When they did I was last one, but when we got to the aisle, I was the first one. . . . He talked to the congregation. He told 'em what he was going to do. Got some boys we want to baptize. So, it's Easter Sunday morning. When I got baptize they pour water on my head. Told 'em all to pray. He done 'em all that way . . . [laughter].[14]

From Otis Russell's recollection it is not exactly clear whether the other Indian boys knew that they were about to be baptized. Russell certainly did not. He went along because his friends asked him to, and he might not have understood the full implication of his actions until later. Whether the Methodist minister baptized the boys without their consent is unclear, but considering the strong missionary spirit prevailing around the turn of the century, it is certainly possible. In the remainder of Russell's interview, he does not mention any church-related activities on his part. On the contrary, he talks about the danger of losing the old ceremonial songs of the Osage tribe, about traditional dances such as the Pipe Dance and the Hun Kah Dance, about racehorses and the Hominy Drum. To Otis Russell, the story of his baptism was only one among many amusing episodes in his long life.

On the other hand, there were many deeply religious youth among Haskell's students. A number of students had visited mission schools and had been actively involved in religious activities before coming to Lawrence. Students such as Arthur Sutton deepened their Christian faith while at

Haskell and became avid Christian spokespeople and missionaries in their home communities. A good example of the deep convictions held by some Haskell students is the resolution adopted by Haskell's delegates who attended the 1919 YMCA Rocky Mountain Student Conference, an annual event that was held in Estes Park, Colorado. Excerpts from this resolution read:

> That we as delegates . . . recommend that steps be taken at once to insure that every student attending government Indian schools be given instruction in the principles of Jesus Christ through an adequate religious education program; That we urgently appeal to the churches to increase their endeavors in religious education for our people. . . . That deeply realizing the great and increasing menace of peyote to the very existence of many Indian tribes of our country, we declare ourselves unalterably opposed to its use.[15]

Whether the students formulated their criticism of peyotism and their support for the eradication of native religions independently or with the support of Haskell's staff or local ministers can only be guessed. The last section of the resolution, however, seems to bear the students' signature:

> That at the earliest possible moment, the rights, privileges and immunities of full citizenship be granted to the Indians of the United States. . . . Whereas we want for the Indian race, self-expression, self-control and self-determination. Be it resolved: That we recognize in the Society of American Indians an organization where these attributes can find realization and that we will support this movement in order to bring about such worthy ends.[16]

Without doubt, the authors of this resolution were devout Christians. But they were also American Indians. The students believed in their peoples' right to become independent American citizens determining their own fate. They believed in an educated Christian Indian: acculturated, but still recognizable as an indigenous person. The students pleaded for acceptance by white society, and they believed that this acceptance could be earned through strict adherence to Christian values and beliefs. They did not see a contradiction in striving to become better Christians as well as better Indians.

Haskell's records reveal many stories about students' religious ambitions, their hopes and desires, underlining the fact that many children were practicing Christians before, while, and after attending Haskell, a reality that is not surprising considering how many children came from mixed-blood families and had at least one parent raised in the Christian tradition. Others, however, resisted the school's conversion efforts, or blended their traditional beliefs with the teachings they received at school—most notably by becoming active members in the Native American Church. The forces shaping students' religious attitudes were complex and included their home environment, their prior exposure to Christianity, their age, and their personality.

At Haskell, the teaching of American patriotism complemented the teaching of Christianity. The school expected the children to become not only obedient Christians but also patriotic American citizens. As the topics outlined in Haskell's religious work program indicate, Christianity and citizenship went hand in hand, and success in one was thought to be dependent on success in the other. Patriotic indoctrination pervaded every aspect of school life: inside the classroom in history and civil government lessons, in church, and on the school grounds. In 1889, Commissioner of Indian Affairs Thomas J. Morgan advised that "Indian youth should be instructed in their rights, privileges, and duties as American citizens; should be taught to love the American flag; should be imbued with a genuine patriotism, and made to feel that the United States, and not some paltry reservation, is their home."[17] Morgan instructed all Indian schools to raise the American flag on campus and to teach the children "to reverence the flag as a symbol of their nation's power and protection." Haskell's boys took the message to heart and even decorated the columns of their dormitory assembly hall with red, white, and blue bunting.[18] In 1920, the flag pledge used in public schools, "I pledge allegiance to my flag and to the Republic for which it stands—one nation, indivisible, with liberty and justice for all," was introduced at Indian schools across the country.[19]

Indian schools were ordered to conduct "appropriate exercises" in observance of all major national holidays. Haskell's superintendents introduced patriotic celebrations for Decoration Day (now known as Memorial Day), Washington's Birthday, the Fourth of July, Arbor Day, Thanksgiving, Christmas, and New Year's Day. In addition to these national holidays, Indian schools began to celebrate February 8 as their special holiday, Franchise Day, in commemoration of the passage of the 1887 Dawes Act, which instigated the allotment of Indian land. The holiday was supposed to remind Indian youth of the great opportunities and new obligations that followed from this law. But recognition of the flag and the celebration of American holidays was just a first step in the patriotic training that was to prepare the children for the duties and privileges of American citizenship. Indian educators believed that indigenous children required more than subjection to the trappings of patriotism. If they were to really understand and appreciate American democracy, the training had to go much deeper and pervade all of the students' curricular as well as extracurricular activities.

Whether patriotic iconography and indoctrination had a lasting effect on the feelings of Haskell's students is hard to tell, but there are indications that at least some students internalized the lessons. In 1917, for instance, eighteen-year-old Pomo Josephine Smith wrote to her sister: "The boys salute the flag every evening before supper. The girls never do but did last year. I think they ought to let them because we should be loyal to our flag and our country too."[20] World War I was certainly a time when waves of patriotism swept through the country, and many Indian students asserted their identity as Americans and their belief in the nation's principles. More than 300 of Haskell's boys served in the American Expeditionary Force, most of them as volunteers, and the students were active in every aspect of the relief effort. When the United States entered the war in April 1917, Native Americans who were American citizens got drafted just like other Americans, and more than 6,500 Indians answered the government's call to arms. In addition, more than 6,000 Native Americans volunteered, fighting "the war to end all wars" in the trenches of eastern France and Belgium. The Bureau of Indian Affairs strongly encouraged Native American participation in the war, hoping that military service would further advance the federal Indian policy of assimilation.[21] Likewise, Haskell's administration supported students in their decision to volunteer for military service.

Like other young Americans, Indian youths had many different reasons to enlist: Many were eager to serve their country, to flee poverty and isolation on the reservations, to seek adventure and see the world, to learn new skills or find economic opportunities. Some wanted to escape the boarding school routine; others who came from tribes with a strong martial tradition were hoping to gain status as warriors. Partly due to white perceptions and stereotypes of Indians as being particularly brave, "instinctive," and fierce fighters, Indian men were often assigned dangerous duties as scouts, messengers, or snipers. Consequently, the number of Indian casualties was five times higher than among non-Indians.²² Native American soldiers displayed great courage and dedication during the war, and many non-Indians were surprised by the patriotism and loyalty these young men showed. The same held true for Indian civilians, Native American women in particular, who supported the country's relief effort by buying large amounts of Liberty bonds and war saving stamps, joining the Red Cross, and expanding their farming and stock raising endeavors. In addition, hundreds of Indians, many of them skilled graduates of Indian boarding schools, found wartime jobs in the nation's shipyards, automobile, and aircraft industry.²³

Indian boarding schools were an important source of Native American recruits during the war, and many students and alumni were eager to serve. Already used to military routine and strict discipline and possessing various vocational skills, many Indian school students adapted well to military life and were often able to gain better paying positions within the service owing to their training as clerks, carpenters, blacksmiths, or electricians. One negative aspect that the war had on Haskell and other Indian schools was a reduction in government funds for Indian education and health services and a loss in per capita appropriations due to the large number of boys enlisting. By the summer of 1918, almost 300 of Haskell's male students had left school for the military. Their departure posed a logistic problem for Haskell's administration: "I fear we will have great difficulty in getting enough boys next fall, but there is such demand for enrollment of girls that if we don't get the boys we will fill up with girls."²⁴ In addition, several of Haskell's employees had left for war service, among them the school physician, as well as a number of teachers, leaving Haskell in a difficult position. Although supporting the war effort, Superintendent Peairs also had reservations about the departure of so many young Indian men:

> Taking out of the Indian communities so many thousands of the educated and trained young men, keeps Indian progress back for the time being, at least, many years. I am proud to see the Indian young men go into the Army in such large numbers and especially proud because practically all go as volunteers, but, nevertheless, it is a serious blow and sets back general progress of Indian communities.²⁵

In the fall of 1918, Peairs had anticipated that several hundred boys would leave for the front and had therefore accepted many more students than in previous years. As a result, when the war was suddenly over in November, instead of facing a shortage of pupils, Haskell once more experienced overcrowding.

During the war years, Haskell not only produced hundreds of Indian soldiers but also increased its agricultural production and sent many students to work on local farms during the summer months to help the relief effort. Many of those who attended school during the war years intensely supported the war and their fellow students and relatives at the front.[26] While searching for a religious director, Superintendent Peairs explained to one candidate that if he were a pacifist, he might not fit in at Haskell: "I mention this matter because the Indian students are almost, if not entirely, without exception loyal and aggressively so in the prosecution of the present war."[27] Haskell's students supported the United States in a war to defend freedom and democracy, even though many of them were not yet citizens in their own country. World War I had important effects on Native Americans, their perception of themselves, and the way American society viewed them. Several aspects of traditional Indian cultures and values experienced a renaissance during the war years, such as ceremonies and dances related to warfare, including going away rituals, giveaways, war songs, victory dances, and elaborate death rituals. Among many tribes, young people witnessed and participated in these revived and frequently modified aspects of their culture for the first time.[28] For many veterans, including Haskell's students, the war was a life-changing experience, leaving deep physical and emotional scars. At the same time, though, it broadened their horizons and equipped them with new attitudes, skills, and views of the world, helping them to survive and sometimes succeed in the postwar period. Many of the young men who fought in Europe questioned their place in American society, and a not insignificant number became active in tribal politics and Indian reform organizations. Through their military service and home-front sacrifices, Native Americans showed the country that they were equal and patriotic comrades and neighbors, and their contributions during the war influenced the passage of the Indian Citizenship Act in 1924.[29]

During the first two decades of the twentieth century, Haskell offered more to its students than academics, work details, and religious training. The school was famous for its successful athletic teams as well as for its excellent band

and orchestra. Extracurricular activities helped to positively motivate students who were otherwise critical of the school, making life at Haskell much more bearable and at times enjoyable.[30] The children became members of the choir, wrote for the school newspaper, learned to play musical instruments, attended lawn socials, took art instruction, played theater, and joined debating societies, glee clubs, or athletic teams. Students looked forward to holidays such as Thanksgiving and Christmas and enjoyed such special events as commencement exercises and homecomings. Haskell's extracurricular activities reflected white middle-class values and introduced indigenous students to Victorian norms and notions of leisure. Many of the children's social activities were ritualized and did not leave the children much personal freedom. The girls' free time especially was carefully monitored and chaperoned.

Over the years, Haskell's social life became more varied and included regular activities as well as special entertainments. Every school year, Haskell's superintendents invited a variety of lecturers and artists to the school, provided their messages and performances were in line with the school's ideology and strict moral standards. During the first two decades of the twentieth century, Haskell's entertainments included lectures from local ministers and Kansas University professors who addressed a wide variety of topics ranging from religion and moral welfare to temperance, public speaking, and hygiene.[31] Outside speakers traveling the country, some famous, some less so, were also invited to lecture on morally uplifting issues. Among the 1909 and 1910 entertainments were a visit from African American advocate Booker T. Washington and a dinner with the Indian actors participating in Buffalo Bill's Wild West Show.[32] Beginning in 1917, Haskell owned its own motion picture machine and showed films every other week. In the early years of film, the choice of pictures was quite limited, and Superintendent Peairs complained to a colleague about his difficulties in procuring films that did not "contain objectionable features, such as drinking and smoking."[33] Special events during the 1918–1919 school year included visits from the Minneapolis Operatic Company and the Little Playhouse Company as well as a performance of *Huckleberry Finn*.[34]

The school's 1919–1920 calendar allows an insight into activities scheduled on a weekly basis as well as events taking place irregularly. The students' weekly schedule provided time for band practice, athletic training, literary societies, denominational religious meetings, and library work. On the second and fourth Friday night of the month, a moving picture was shown. On the first Saturday night of the month, the school held a social, which took place on the lawn during the summer time and in the gymnasium during the colder season. Every second Saturday night, there was a band concert, and on the third and fourth Saturdays, parties and athletic events were scheduled.

Cultural entertainments provided students with insights and inspirations unattainable during regular school days, giving the children access to experiences that most of them would not have had on the reservations or in their hometowns. Sometimes, students were so impressed by the visiting entertainers that they were tempted to leave with them, as was the case when Buffalo Bill's Wild West Show appeared in Lawrence in 1909.[35] Compared to the regimen of boarding school life, the idea of traveling across the country with a Wild West show must have been appealing to adolescent boys yearning for adventure, freedom, and economic opportunities.

Haskell's students were not only enthusiastic consumers of Victorian high and popular culture but also gifted producers of their own entertainments. Music was an integral part of Haskell's social and religious life from the very beginning and was performed at chapel services, entertainments given by the literary societies, and commencement exercises and during many concerts and special musical programs throughout the year. By the early 1900s, Haskell prided itself on several musical organizations, including its famous band, a concert orchestra, a mixed chorus, a mixed choir, and a mandolin club. Vocal music was taught in all grades, and students showing special talent received extra lessons. The school even performed operettas, which were highly esteemed by Lawrence's citizens.[36]

Haskell's band gave frequent concerts in and around Lawrence and performed regularly at school entertainments. Over the years its reputation grew, and by the early 1900s, Haskell's band had itself become a cultural commodity "traded" through the Slayton Lyceum Bureau in Chicago. At the zenith of their popularity, Haskell's thirty-two musicians, who came from fifteen tribes, performed two daily concerts at the 1904 World's Fair in St. Louis. This engagement was followed by a tour of Ohio, Pennsylvania, Colorado, and other faraway states. The band's rise to stardom was closely linked to its Oneida bandleader, Dennison Wheelock, a former Carlisle student and gifted composer. Talking about future projects for the band, Wheelock explained:

> The original Indian music is a strange thing. It is devoid of harmony, but the melody and time are there, and it is easily harmonized. Some great

critics say that our aboriginal music is the same as played by all primitive people the world over.... I am planning now a composition called the evolution of music. I hope to show the growth of harmony. First, some of our musicians will come out in Indian costume, playing some primitive melody. Others will follow playing something more advanced, and so on until the whole band is on the stage and we are rendering a grand opera.[37]

Wheelock's words illustrate the strong assimilationist dimension of the school's musical instruction: indigenous musical elements were included in the band's program to demonstrate the remarkable evolution from primitivism to high culture that could be observed within the music as well as among its Indian performers. While on tour in Colorado during the summer of 1904, the band received nothing but praise from the local press. The *Denver Times* wrote about its performance in Pueblo: "The crowds that have been going to hear the band have been unprecedented even for City park. The band is most proficient and discourses music that would do credit to bands whose fame is greater.... The Indians are naturally a music loving people, and under the able leadership which they have the band is a most excellent one."[38]

As members of the band, students enjoyed more time off from the regular work details than their fellow students. Touring the country during the summer time was a special privilege and a more interesting way to earn money than to work long hours on a local farm. Many Indian parents were interested in their children's artistic pursuits and wrote to the school in order to arrange for lessons. In 1908, Osie Vieux's mother requested that her daughter be allowed to take piano lessons. In his reply, Superintendent Pears explained:

> I have to advise you that there is not a question of so much of music teacher giving Osie lessons, as it is to get an instrument to practice on. We have only a limited number of pianos and therefore are compelled to limit the number of pupils who can take lessons. As Osie had lessons last year it seems but fair that somebody else be given a chance this term. I wish that more pupils might have the opportunity but unless we can have more instruments it is impossible to give all who want lessons.[39]

That same year, Commissioner Leupp informed Pears that at the close of the fiscal year, the position of music teacher would be abolished. Leupp apparently regarded piano and vocal lessons as too refined for Indian pupils, and he did not share the public's enchantment with Haskell's band.⁴⁰ Despite Leupp's stance against musical training, music continued to play a crucial role in many students' lives. Former Arapaho student Jesse Rowlodge was a tenor in Haskell's choir and played the cornet. He remembered taking classical music lessons from an old, German-born music teacher and recalled being friends with other musically inclined students:

> Oh we associated with those that had good music knowledge, like those Wisconsins—those Oneidas and Chippewas from Wisconsin. . . . They were naturally good musicians. . . . White music. Some were good violinists, and some were good piano players, guitar and mandolin and banjos and all such as that. They'd studied in their homes.⁴¹

Haskell's musicians performed on stages across the country as participants in the popular circuit Chautauqua system. By the late 1910s, Chautauquas had become favorite summer entertainments in rural America, providing small towns with three to six days of diverse artistic performances, including concerts and educational lectures. Circuit Chautauquas were prearranged "entertainment packages" that could be booked through the Standard Chautauqua System in Lincoln, Nebraska. Unlike single performances booked through a lyceum bureau, Chautauquas were traveling shows with multiple performers, whose purpose was to "render service to the community by means of wholesome entertainment, providing an opportunity for people of the town and community to see and hear talent in their own town at little expense, which without the chautauqua many would be entirely unable ever to hear," as the 1919 brochure of the Community Chautauqua System explained.⁴² The Haskell Indian Orchestra Band signed a thirteen-week contract for the 1919 season, agreeing to perform two-and-a-half hours per day in "native Indian costumes" as well as in uniforms. The tour took the students throughout the New England States and into Canada, providing the children with an extraordinary educational and travel experience.⁴³ Independently from the orchestra, eighteen-year-old Oneida student Pearl Archiquette toured the country as part of a female trio performing Indian music for the Community Chautauqua's Midwestern circuit.

As ethnic entertainers, indigenous musicians were expected to perform in accordance with popular American stereotypes about "primitive people," albeit culturally enlightened through a Christian education. Their performance had to be devoid of any offensive or controversial elements, "safe" for predominantly Anglo Chautauqua audiences to hear and see.[44] A romantic image of Native Americans as a reminder of the country's frontier past was infused with the assurance that Haskell's students were civilized savages, an image that was both alluring and tame. The students' performance clearly made the point that Anglo-cultural enlightenment was instrumental for the improvement of primitive people. The school's leadership insisted on the civilized dimension of the children's appearance on stage. Before signing the 1919 contract, Superintendent Peairs wrote to the organizers about the use of traditional Indian costumes: "I would not be willing to have them use them only under certain conditions, namely, that they should be used for the purpose of contrasting the old with the new." Peairs, who was well aware of the romanticizing tendencies of ethnic Chautauqua entertainments, was eager to present Haskell's students not simply as trained savages but as living proof of the government's successful assimilation program. The great success of Haskell's orchestra proves that Chautauqua audiences, curious about other cultures but not wanting to feel threatened by the "other," could relate comfortably to the "civilized savage" metaphor propagated by the tour's organizers.[45]

Over the years, Haskell's musicians performed at a variety of events ranging from local fairs and church services to official government functions in the nation's capital. Whether on the local or national level, audiences across the United States and Canada were impressed by the students' abilities.[46] Haskell's students acted as ambassadors of the school, promoting a new "civilized" age for America's indigenous population. They took on the role of culture brokers and were proud to show to the nation what modern Indians could do.

Even though Haskell regarded classical music as an important component in the process of civilization, it considered other elements of Victorian social etiquette as even more significant. The Victorianization of male-female relations was not just at the core of Haskell's curriculum but was also supported by ritualized social activities. Whether in the dining room, in the classroom, at cultural events or social gatherings, Haskell's leadership deemed appropriate gendered behavior a priority. In the 1890s, the Indian Office recommended that boys and girls share a common dining table as well as common classrooms. The carefully monitored integration of the sexes taught the girls "ease and grace in company" and the boys a respect for women thought to be lacking in indigenous societies.[47] It is not clear whether Haskell followed this recommendation throughout its early period. During the 1920s, though, boys ate on one side of the dining room and the girls on the other. Seats were assigned by company. The dining ritual followed Victorian gender rules, and it was the girls' responsibility to serve the food, clear the tables, and wash the dishes.[48] Outside the classroom and the dining hall, Haskell's employees kept contact between boys and girls to a minimum, limiting it to carefully planned and chaperoned social occasions.[49] Saturday night and Sunday afternoon socials were among the few occasions when boys and girls were allowed to spend their free time together. Lucille Winnie, who attended Haskell during the early 1900s, remembered the school's socials as "the biggest event of the week, as that was the only time we could visit with the opposite sex." Matrons and disciplinarians were "eying us from the sidelines" while the students ate lunch together, sat side by side talking, and listened to the band's concert. Boys and girls with a "bad case" (who were romantically involved) were eventually "driven into the fold by the matrons."[50]

Esther Burnett's recollections from the mid-1920s paint a similar picture. She described the lawn between the girls' and the boys' dormitories as an effective demarcation line separating the sexes during the week:

> The lawn was no-man's land except for Sunday afternoons when we could visit with our boyfriends and listen to a band concert, or have a watermelon social. We all really looked forward to those afternoons, which were one of the few times that the girls and boys were allowed to be together. . . . We'd walk around and around the bandstand in the center of campus, just visiting with each other. When the weather was bad and in the winter we stayed inside or had club get-togethers. We rode to town on the streetcar on some Saturdays, accompanied by chaperones. If we had money, we could go to the movies.

Burnett added: "I think that the school feared that a girl might get pregnant without constant supervision, which did sometimes happen."[51] Indian educators believed that indigenous children lacked any inclinations toward morality and chastity and saw constant surveillance as the key to regulating relations between the sexes.

Supervising hundreds of adolescent youth, however, was a difficult task, and romance was certainly a more important aspect of the students' experience than Haskell's administrators would have liked to admit. Students found ways to meet secretly, wrote each other love notes, and sometimes even eloped. Unwanted pregnancies did occur, and some of these delicate and at times tragic stories have survived in Haskell's records. Most of the relationships formed in boarding schools were within the boundaries of Victorian propriety, however, and some even ended in marriage, as in the case of Esther Burnett, who married her former Haskell sweetheart. Not all students were interested in romance, and many youth were rather shy when it came to associating with the opposite sex. Eli Stover, a Creek student who attended the school during the 1910s, recalled how awkward he felt when a friend encouraged him to meet with a girl during one of the socials:

> He told me "Girls was talking about you. You making good record in athletics." Said, "Girls want to get acquainted with you." He said, "We got a girl for you, you clean up and dress up and we come and get you." I went to my room, and I got ready and clean up and went out on the social ground. We walked around there and finally we find a girl. Her name was Beatrice Kye. We got acquainted and said, "Well you ought to walk around now." And we walked around and talked, but I didn't talk much. Let her do all the talking. I never have been associated with no girls.[52]

In general, the school supervised the girls more closely than the boys. According to Esther Burnett, boys enjoyed greater freedoms than the girls, who spent a lot of time indoors, reading, writing letters, and playing board games:

> There were no phonographs or radios in our dorm rooms at Haskell. Some of the girls knew how to do the Charleston, but we usually just danced in our rooms. We'd spend what little spare time we had visiting and singing together. "Janine" was a favorite song. There were never boy-girl dances at Haskell while I was there, but different departments like the Normal Training Department or the Officers Club had parties, and we could invite our boyfriends or girlfriends.[53]

Superintendent Peairs's 1909 description of the children's' games supports Burnett's recollections. According to the superintendent, Indian boys at Haskell played:

the usual out-door games such as are played by all school boys namely, baseball, football, basketball, track work and shinny. When there is ice they skate. About the only indoor game they have is basketball. . . . The girls play very few games. It seems extremely difficult to get the girls to enter in games of any kind. The most of their outdoor exercise consists of walking, running and romping over the campus. Occasionally they play basketball and pitch quoits. We have tried to get them to play tennis and croquet and have succeeded to some extent but they seem to tire of these games very soon. The little girls have swings and seem to enjoy them.[54]

Peairs commented on what he perceived as the distinctive social behavior of Indian children as compared to white youth:

One thing noticeable among Indian boys and girls in all athletic sports is the absence of noise that is so characteristic among white boys and girls. They are very quiet at their games. They are also very kind to each other and it is very seldom there is any quarreling resulting from disputes in athletic games. They do not take the initiative in athletics as other children do but need leaders. Many of the boys and girls themselves become excellent leaders after they have had some training. A great many boys have wonderful athletic ability when it is developed.[55]

In April 1916, Superintendent Wise wrote a report to Indian Commissioner Cato Sells, discussing Haskell's social life in detail. He reported that the school held regular Saturday "sociables" and that games and sports were generally encouraged and enjoyed. Wise pointed out to the commissioner that Haskell's students, "though far from perfect, are at this time on the whole as courteous and polite as any lot of young people with whom I have come in contact. Due allowance should be made for some of our young people, considering the homes and the environment from which they come."[56]

Unlike other Indian schools, including Carlisle and Chilocco, Haskell had banned dancing for most of its history, since it considered the contact between dance partners as too intimate and detrimental to the school's discipline. In 1916, Superintendent Wise reported to the commissioner of Indian affairs that "the present feeling on the part of the large majority of our young people, including the older and more prominent ones, is decidedly averse to dancing. One of the employees, a few days ago in discussing the matter, made the remark that the pupils themselves had 'ridiculed it to death.'"⁵⁷ Although dancing was banned, the school actively supported other art forms. Haskell's students created works of art ranging from drawings to fancy needlework, which were often exhibited during fairs and government exhibitions around the country. According to the Office of Indian Affairs, these activities were of special interest to a large number of people since they ran "the entire gamut of human endeavor and comprise all intelligent processes for the development of a dependent race into an independent position in the body politic of our nation."⁵⁸

This same philosophy had motivated Haskell's participation in the 1893 World's Fair in Chicago and the 1904 World's Fair in Saint Louis. In Chicago, Haskell participated in a demonstration school and an exhibit in the Chicago fair's Indian Village. For three weeks, fifteen boys and fifteen girls became part of the demonstration group, joined by sixteen Haskell band members. Twice a day the students gave band concerts and received lessons in the demonstration school. In between, they performed songs, recitations, and other popular features. Each grade exhibited its schoolwork, and representatives of the industrial department demonstrated their trades, including harness making, tailoring, and carpentry. Public interest in the school's work was substantial, and the smallest attendance registered for any one day was 2,000, whereas the largest was 25,540. Altogether, 262,000 people visited Haskell's exhibit.⁵⁹ To those promoting Indian education as the solution to the "Indian problem," this enormous interest came as a positive surprise and reassurance. To the fair's visitors, seeing "real Indians" going to school and working at various trades was a great excitement at a time when the memories of the Plains wars, the Little Big Horn, and Wounded Knee were still fresh in the public's mind. The "civilized savages" wearing school uniforms intrigued Americans, who were amazed by the peaceful transformation displayed before their eyes. There could not have been any better advertisement for the educational work of the government.

The great success of the Chicago World's Fair was repeated at the 1904 World's Fair in St. Louis. During the so-called Louisiana Purchase Exposition, Haskell's boys engaged in the construction of the Indian Exhibit building, making the structure itself part of the exhibit. As in 1893, diverse samples of the students' classroom work were displayed, and for the three-months duration of the fair Haskell employees conducted demonstration classes in sewing, manual training, wagon making, and blacksmithing.⁶⁰

During the World's Fairs, Americans learned that the "frontier" was gone forever. Indian cultures were portrayed as a relict of the past, as beautiful but backward and soon to be extinct. The exhibits demonstrated the organizers' deeply held belief in assimilation, Western civilization, and a white definition of progress. Visitors admired traditional Indian cultures, including arts and crafts, but the exhibits never presented them as equal to white cultural expressions. Indians could only be part of the modern world if they internalized the "book knowledge as well as the hand skills" of the white race. Indian schools were the living proof of the feasibility and rationality of this argument. In the eyes of the fairs' visitors, Haskell's students validated the government's claim for a peaceful solution to the "Indian problem." This official portrayal of Indian history did not leave any room for cultural survival, conflicting identities, resistance, or negotiation. The progression from "savagery" to "civilization" was depicted as linear and conflict free. According to Washington's view of history, Indians as a distinct cultural group belonged to the past. Their future as assimilated members of American society, however, was painted in bright colors.

A similar spirit pervaded cultural activities taking place at the school itself. Haskell's theater productions and commencement exercises clearly illustrate the savagery-civilization paradigm so prevalent in the school's early history. Every year, Haskell's teachers encouraged senior theater productions of ideologically and morally acceptable plays such as *Hiawatha, A Midsummer Night's Dream,* or *Wa-Ya-Wa-Ble* (I Am Going to School). The latter play was performed during Haskell's twenty-fourth Commencement Exercises in 1908 as part of the "Commercial Class Day" program. The performance included songs as well as dramatizations. The play exemplifies the tenor of many of Haskell's theater productions as well as the department's motto, "Onward Ever, Backward Never." In the play, the younger generation convinces the older generation through its mastery of a typewriter to let them attend Haskell's business department. Although the typewriter's utilization lies beyond the reach of the older people, its importance is obvious even to the tribe's greatest skeptics. According to the play, progress moves in one direction only: Western culture and technology must win over native traditions and nature.

The following year, during Haskell's quarter-centennial celebration, students staged Henry Wadsworth Longfellow's epic poem, *The Song of Hiawatha,* for an audience of more than a thousand people. The play about the noble Indian prince Hiawatha was such a success that the production received an engagement to give two performances in Denver in June 1909. *Hiawatha* had been staged in earlier years and had been so popular that in 1905 the actors received a two-months contract to perform at the popular summer resort of North Port, Michigan. One can imagine that for the students these engagements were a "delightful" outing experience, as Superintendent Peairs explained to the father of a Laguna actress.[61]

Through Longfellow's poem, Indian themes had for the first time gained white recognition as sources of imagination, power, and originality in American literature. With his epic life-story of an Indian prince, Longfellow gave a mythic dimension to the country's historical imagination. The verse narrative, which ends with the coming of the white man and Hiawatha's death, appealed to Anglo audiences' romanticized image of the doomed but noble savage. Letting Haskell's students perform *Hiawatha* was a safe way of allowing them to "be Indian." By playing in *Hiawatha,* indigenous students portrayed the Anglo interpretation of their own history, an act that could be interpreted as the ultimate proof of their assimilation. At the same time, though, the play allowed students to celebrate their indigenous cultures and to assert their Indian identity in front of a white audience.

According to the press, the 1909 Denver performances of *Hiawatha* were well received, and the forty students traveling to Colorado that summer enjoyed their stay. Arapaho student Jesse Rowlodge was part of the group. In 1968, he remembered that summer in great detail:

> In 1909 we organized the Hiawatha play. We put that on in Kansas City. We were big headlines all over the papers all over the country. We were putting it on in Lawrence, Kansas, and Denver invited us in July. Before that I had come on home to get some buckskin clothes for men and women—moccasins, war bonnets, and a cradle—a beaded cradle. . . . A Cheyenne woman owned that. It was her cradle. She grew up in it. . . . And we rehearsed once or twice a week. Forty-three of us went to Denver, including three of our teachers that help us work out that play.

The students were eager to portray their ancestors' cultures as meticulously as possible, recreating a stage environment that was distinctly Indian:

> I got that regular tobacco—Indian pipe tobacco. We'd make that stage smell like Indian, you know. Sitting around and smoking their pipes in

buckskin costumes. I played the part of Gitchee Manitou, the Priest. And Mendawin—the one that wrestled with Hiawatha. . . . When I played Gitchee Manitou I was dressed all in white. Had my tobacco bag and I even had a bald eagle war bonnet—white.

To the question of whether he liked being in the play, Rowlodge answered:

Oh yeah. I loved it. . . . The more we put it on, the bigger crowd there was. Then we moved to Colorado Springs. We stopped there at the Antlers Hotel, the swank hotel there, and we put that on that night. It just made a big hit. Well, we were doing at that time was make enough money to save at least five thousand dollars for band uniforms. For school. And we made it. We made beyond that. Made about fourteen thousand.[62]

Being part of Haskell's successful theater productions meant a lot to the students, and it provided them with the opportunity to socialize, to express themselves artistically, and to enjoy their personal moment of fame. In the 1920s, Esther Burnett starred as Hermia in Shakespeare's *A Midsummer Night's Dream*. In her autobiography, she recalled how excited she and her fellow students were to participate in the play:

The boys and girls who auditioned for the play worked hard to be chosen, because it was a chance to socialize with each other and to be on-stage. Interpretive dance was integral to this 1927 Haskell production. I was awkward in the regular physical education activities but loved interpretive dance because of the opportunity for self-expression. . . . I starred as Hermia and will always remember the thrill of that acting experience, as well as being presented a dozen long-stemmed roses by Ruth and Ella [her Indian teachers Ruth Muskrat Bronson and Ella Deloria] for my efforts. Movie stars and prima donnas were the only people who I believed could be the recipients of this honor; it was as though I was being recognized as a real star.[63]

During the course of the school year, Haskell's students participated in various holiday celebrations, observed in order to teach the children to identify with the myths and rituals of white society. The purpose of these celebrations was to reaffirm the children's place in American society by showing them that the benefits they received from contact with Anglo society, meaning from cultural domination, were greater than any injustices their ancestors had endured. Even though the meaning of all these celebrations was not always clear to the students, they quickly learned to appreciate the break in the usual routine associated with these festivities. Events such as Halloween and Christmas created a pleasant atmosphere at Haskell. Christmas was an exciting time for the children, many of whom experienced the holiday for the first time while at Haskell. Like their white counterparts, Indian children soon came to identify the day with Santa Claus and gift giving. Many parents sent small amounts of money or gifts to the school, so that their sons and daughters could join the gift-giving ritual. If the parents sent money, Haskell's staff saw to it that small gifts such as a pair of gloves, a shawl, or a book were purchased for the students. Among the gifts that parents sent to their children in 1901 were dolls, plates, napkin rings, handkerchiefs, watches, ribbons, albums, and neckties.[64] Special programs on Christmas included church services and the singing of carols as well as a special holiday dinner.

Even though there was a short break between the fall and the spring term, in general, Haskell required its students to stay in school. Sometimes the administration made exceptions and let students travel home for a short period of time, and sometimes the children were allowed to go on a visit or receive visitors themselves. In 1908, Superintendent Peairs wrote to Chilocco's superintendent, J. R. Wise (who would become Haskell's superintendent in 1912):

> Two or three of the girls, formerly students at your school, who are now students here, have asked to be allowed to spend a few days during the Christmas holidays visiting students and employees at your school. I write to ask whether it will be convenient for them to do so. I know sometime so many visitors come in that it is difficult to take care of them. Do not hesitate to let me know just what the situation is and I will be governed thereby.[65]

Superintendent Wise replied that he would be happy to accommodate his former students for a visit. This episode illustrates the strong bonds that existed between students, their school friends, and their former schools. Esther Burnett recalled the importance of friendships and social interaction around Christmas time:

We decorated our rooms and there was competition between the boys' and girls' dormitories. The boy officers judged the girl's room and vice versa. . . . There was a big tree in the assembly room that the students would decorate. Christmas was a joyous time of anticipation for us. Haskell was our home away from home, and everybody stayed on campus during the holidays. There were kids from all over the United States, including Alaska. There would have been a great number of unhappy kids if some had gone home while others who couldn't afford to leave had had to stay. We were with our "school family" of friends. We missed our biological families but created our own holiday atmosphere. There were special events that replaced the academic routine for the holiday week—intramural games, club parties and movies, special assemblies, and Santa Claus with his special treats like candy and nuts, apples and oranges.[66]

Holidays such as Christmas were times outside of the ordinary; times to socialize and to cross boundaries that otherwise were strictly drawn. These special occasions allowed students to escape the routine, the discipline, and the regimentation of regular boarding school life. Other holidays such as Washington's Birthday or Franchise Day might not have provided students with quite as much entertainment, but they were nevertheless "instructional" and a welcome diversion. An important patriotic holiday was Decoration Day (now called Memorial Day), the country's occasion for honoring all soldiers who had fallen in battle as well as the deceased in general. At Haskell, the presence of a school cemetery gave the ritual a special meaning. On Memorial Day, the school honored all the students who had died while at school with processions, flower bouquets, and prayers as well as religious and patriotic hymns. Rituals such as Memorial Day celebrations played an important role in the larger scheme of assimilation. Through patriotic celebrations, the school hoped to explain to indigenous students who they were, where they fit into the story of America, and what they were expected to become in the future. As manifestations of the dominant ideology, rituals guided the "right" path for the children to follow. No celebration made this clearer than the school's annual graduation exercises, rites of passage overflowing with patriotic imagery and instructions. During these celebrations the school staged plays, invited motivational speakers, organized athletic events, and hosted parents, alumni, and other interested visitors. Students gave speeches and demonstrations of their work, and in some years the commencement exercises included distinctly Indian entertainments such as indigenous dances or music.

In 1909, Haskell held its quarter-centennial celebration. The *Indian Leader* reported on the great success of the program, including the inspiring speeches given by Superintendent of Indian Schools Estelle Reel, Superintendent Peairs, and former superintendent Charles Meserve as well as the enthusiasm, pride, and loyalty displayed by the school's alumni. According to the paper, Superintendent Peairs "welcomed the old students and gave them the privileges they desired so much in their school days—the right to go to meals without falling in line; to stay up after taps, and assured them if the disciplinarian should attempt to make them 'walk the circle' he would protect them!"[67] Haskell's leadership accorded great importance to the school's annual graduation exercises, regarding them as reflections of successful government policy. Even though the number of students graduating was small (from the 5,315 boys and girls who had attended the school until 1909, fewer than 400 had graduated), the events were planned with great care and all decorum. According to Lawrence newspaper reports, local citizens showed great interest in the school's work and regularly attended the ceremonies.

Perhaps the biggest event in Haskell's boarding school history was the widely publicized 1926 homecoming celebration, which had been organized for the dedication of Haskell's new athletic stadium from October 27 to 30, 1926. Motivated in part by the great national success of Haskell's football team, American Indians from across the country had participated in a massive fund-raising campaign to construct the new, 10,500-seat stadium. Indigenous donors had provided almost $250,000 for the project; Haskell students, alumni, and friends had provided most of the manual labor; and on the Halloween weekend of 1926, more than 1,600 Native Americans from more than seventy tribes gathered in Lawrence to celebrate and to dedicate the new athletic venue. The event blended white and American Indian festive traditions and provided a formidable opportunity to Native Americans to assert their ethnic identities and to express their resistance to white civilization in a ritualistic and symbolic way.[68] The three-day festivities were planned around the stadium dedication and a Haskell–Bucknell College football game, which Haskell won 36–0. The event included an intertribal powwow, a big Indian encampment with canvas tepees, Indian dances, drumming and campfires, native foods such as "jerked" buffalo and fry bread (ironically, some Indian guests tried buffalo for the first time), theater performances by Haskell's students, a baby contest (won by a 1918 Haskell alumna and her child), and a parade through downtown Lawrence. More than 20,000 whites enjoyed the homecoming, and the event received extensive local, national, and even international newspaper coverage.

But although Haskell's students, relatives, teachers, and administrators celebrated the new stadium as a great achievement, the 1928 Meriam Report was much more critical in its assessment, pointing out the pretentiousness of the huge stadium: "A vast amount of money was put into it, so that it presents a marked contrast with the living and working quarters provided for the children. A far more splendid memorial and contribution could have been made to this school if the same amount of money had been used to reconstruct the living quarters."[69]

Even though the school's leadership and the national press promoted the festivities as an expression of Indian progress, the display of traditional cultures was far more complex than Superintendent Peairs and his followers would admit. For both whites and Native Americans the event held multiple and in many ways contradictory symbolic and ritual meanings.[70] From the Euro-American perspective, Peairs argued that the festivities fit well into the progressive narratives that guided federal Indian policy. The school was careful to emphasize the differences between Haskell's students, allegedly belonging to a modern generation, and their parents and relatives who were framed as traditional, vanishing Indians, even though many of them were boarding school alumni themselves. To highlight this contrast, Haskell organized separate activities for the students, including the football game, gymnastic performances by the girls, band concerts, drills, and a performance of the famous play *Hiawatha* in the school's new stadium. During the homecoming parade, Haskell's students proudly displayed twenty floats representing the school's different departments, visually contrasting their modernity with the "primitive" habits of their ancestors. To this end, some students appeared in headdresses and traditional clothes while the majority dressed as office workers, nurses, teachers, or soldiers. Outside the parade and the stage, Haskell's students wore their uniforms, and newspapers commented very positively on the children's civilized attire, contrasting their appearance with the "characteristic colorful holiday dress" of the Indian visitors.[71] Peairs did not see the activities organized for the Indian visitors in terms of cultural preservation. This attitude was also reflected in the speech of Secretary of the Interior Hubert Work, who attended the dedication ceremony as the official U.S. government representative:

This is an occasion, unique in the annals of world history. Marvelous have been the changes wrought among American Indians in the last half century. . . . The wonderful success of the educational method of dealing with the Indians may be appreciated in a slight degree by contrasts of this occasion. The camp, its occupants in the dress of bygone days, the buffalo, the barbecue, the dance—all of these forming the background of this picture. The school, its students in the modern dress of times, the classrooms, the shops, the dairy, the gardens and farm, the tennis courts, the baseball field, the gridiron and the stadium we are about to dedicate in the foreground. A wonderful picture representing the progress of a half century, through education.

The secretary's speech continued with his interpretation of the indigenous population's motivation for funding the stadium as well as the significance of this act:

This magnificent stadium is the gift of Indians and Indians only. It is an expression of the gratitude of representatives of 50 tribes of Indians for what has been done for them during the past 50 years in providing educational facilities for Native Americans.[72]

Clearly, the secretary of the Interior saw the stadium dedication as a sign of assimilation. In a similar fashion, many newspapers reported the event in the government-backed narrative of progress, employing the image of the "noble savage" transformed into a "civilized" citizen. Some papers, however, were more ambiguous in their portrayal, expressing doubts about the "tameness" of the cultural performances taking place. The *Kansas City Times* described the dances as exciting, but also as dangerous and threatening:

The animals and birds, squaws and children, sweep over the shadowy field in an inter-tribal dance, the combined tom-toms thundering, the grandstands echoing. It is Custer's last stand, the Halloween of beasts and birds. There is madness in the air. It would not be weird in the sunlight, but in the strip of dim light on a dark night and the air clouded with fogs of a thousand cigarettes, it was diabolism.[73]

Descriptions like this one depicted Indians as uncontrolled savages who still needed to be tamed. Their identities as Indians were not seen as a thing of the past but as something that was threateningly alive in the present.[74]

Although Native Americans funded the stadium, thereby participating in a certain aspect of mainstream culture, the terms of this participation were hardly as clear cut as the dominant hegemonic interpretation presumed. According to a contemporary *New York Times* article, Haskell alumni were especially eager to donate funds to the cause, citing "race loyalty and school allegiance, as well as an inborn love for outdoor sports" as major reasons as well as the hope that Haskell would rise to the same prominence in Indian sports as Carlisle had before its closing in 1917.[75]

Native Americans used elements of the dominant culture both to oppose white society and to assert and negotiate their own identities. To the Indian visitors, the celebration of their traditional cultures was not only an entertainment show for whites but an expression of their cultural survival and persistent ethnic identities in a complex era of their history. During the 1920s, the nature of newly gained Indian citizenship was contested territory and the terms were still being negotiated (and still are).[76] The 1926 homecoming helped to affirm and strengthen a common Indian identity that transcended tribal boundaries, provided an extraordinary opportunity for Native Americans to experiment with a wide range of different identities, and allowed them to show their opposition to white society and culture in a dramatized fashion.[77] Dancing was at the heart of the event. For several decades, the American government had opposed Native American dance—on the reservations as well as in Indian communities and government schools. During the 1920s, however, opposition to Indian dancing was slowly waning. From a white perspective, Native Americans could claim Indian cultural traits in their performances and in the production of arts and crafts as long as they did not return to their tribal ways.[78] During this time, powwows were gaining great popularity among the southern Plains tribes and also among Native Americans in other parts of the country. Powwow culture was developing into a powerful source of ethnic pride and intertribal identity, and the Haskell homecoming provided an unprecedented opportunity to celebrate this newly developing cultural form. The Haskell powwow allowed Native Americans from more than seventy tribes to display their ethnic identity and cultural autonomy while promoting powwow culture in front of more than 10,000 white and Indian spectators—an opportunity that Haskell's white administrators certainly did not grasp in its complexity and multiple meanings.[79]

Another major source of Indian pride was the Haskell Fighting Indians' 36–0 win over Pennsylvania's Bucknell College Bison. For more than two decades, Haskell's successful intertribal football team and star athletes such as John Levi had sparked great ethnic pride among Haskell's students and across Indian communities. To Haskell's athletes, the football field was a place where they felt they could fight their white opponents on equal terms, proving their intelligence and physical skills. To them, Indian-white football was not just a game. It was about crossing and defending boundaries, history and myth, the frontier, Crazy Horse, and Custer.[80] The important emotional and symbolic role Indian football played in the hearts and minds of native communities explains the great generosity with which the natural resources–rich Oklahoma tribes especially contributed to the Haskell stadium building project. To them, the new stadium was a great expression of ethnic pride, a place where Indians could symbolically challenge and beat white society.[81] The same held true for the other features of the homecoming, which provided a unique opportunity for Native Americans to revisit and celebrate many of their traditional cultural forms. At the same time, they found a safe environment in which to affirm and create new cultural forms such as Indian football and the intertribal powwow. In many ways, the 1926 homecoming reflected the complexities and multilayered identities of Haskell's students and the school itself—neither traditional nor mainstream American but something new and at the same time distinctly Native American.

During the 1926 homecoming, Haskell's officials celebrated the students' success and patriotism, seeking to prove to white spectators and Indian visitors that the school produced truly American citizens.[82] The new athletic stadium and its formidable World War I memorial arch bore testimony to the children's successful Americanization on and off the playing field. Indian educators regarded athletics as an important symbol of assimilation and a sign of successful participation in mainstream society. Indians who mastered the gridiron, the baseball field, or the basketball court were capable of mastering modern life, of playing by its rules, and of casting off their native cultures. Football in particular was thought to teach young men teamwork and the value of precision, order, discipline, technical efficiency, and obedience. It was a game propagating core American values such as self-reliance, hard work, and self-control as well as the concept of "winning." Most of all, football gave ritualistic expression to one of America's prominent ideologies of the time: survival of the fittest.[83] Indian educators believed that football could help to change native students' public image, convincing whites that Indians could become fully integrated members of American society. The huge success of Carlisle's and a little later Haskell's football teams and the extremely positive reception Indian football players received from their mostly white observers seemed to prove their point. In 1903, Haskell's athletic director explained the school's ideology and rituals surrounding athletic events to a local newspaper:

> We have no college or school song. Our institution is strictly a government institution and because of that we recognize the song of "America" as our school song. We are training youths for American citizenship. The tune "America" and the flag, symbols of true Americanism, give us inspiration in such training. Our college yell is: *Sizzle Crackers! Fire Crackers! Sis Boom Bah! Haskell Indians! Rah! Rah! Rah!* (emphasis added)[84]

Indian schools were never able, however, to fully control the meaning that spectators, journalists, and the students themselves attached to athletics and especially football.[85] To the students, the game certainly held multiple meanings. For the players, athletic excellence, intertribal team spirit, the pride and admiration of their fellow students and families, the chance to travel the country and get special treatment while in school, and the great public attention and the opportunity to show white society what they could do provided plenty of motivation and meaning to their sport. At the same time, the gridiron served as a modern-day battleground, as a place of symbolic Indian resistance to white society. Public representations of Indian boarding school sports immediately picked up on this dramatized battle between the races. The struggle for control of territory taking place on the football field inspired press accounts filled with allusions to the frontier conflict and Indian-white wars. No doubt, to the journalists and spectators, Indian-white football was war, a dramatic reenactment of the frontier conflict during which two races invaded and defended each other's territory. The gridiron became a mystic space where Native Americans and whites were reliving their turbulent history and where old scores were settled. But unlike their fathers, grandfathers, and ancestors, Indian students at the end of the nineteenth century had the sympathy of the crowd. White football fans loved to cheer for Indian teams and did so for several reasons: appreciation for the achievements of the Indian students, a belief in their equal capabilities and a growing acceptance that America's indigenous population had been terribly wronged in the past as well as nostalgia and a longing for a time and frontier bygone.[86] The notion of a ritualistic battle between the dominated and their oppressors is just as vivid in the students' own language. In 1914, one of Haskell's football players explained:

> Our football men are busy each day putting in hard practice for the coming war. We have been mobilizing our troops since the first of September and they are now trained and equipped for the coming campaign. They have done considerable skirmishing and I was wounded on the right shoulder.[87]

That same year, Haskell's students cheered for their football team singing "Old Haskell Will Be There," to the tune of "Marching through Georgia":

Gather round me, Haskellites, and join me while I sing,
Telling of the glories that our players help to bring.
Telling how our fears have flown and hope is on the wing,
While we go marching to vict'ry. Chorus

CHORUS:
Hurrah, hurrah, Old Haskell will be there,
Hurrah, hurrah, with touchdowns and to spare,
All the paleface players seem afraid they'll lose their hair
While we go plunging to vic'try.

Haskell's line is holding well, for Haskell boys are strong,
Yielding not a moment, tho' the fight is fierce and long,
And Haskell girls are joining in this good old Haskell song
While we go marching to vict'ry. Chorus

Every Haskell heart today is beating stout and true,
Haskell lads keep fighting on and Haskell lassies too,
For Haskell players always find a way of getting through,
While we go marching to vict'ry. Chorus [88]

Like the newspaper reports of the time, the song employed frontier images to express the special character of the students' athletic prowess. Its reference to the athletes' Indianness stands in contrast to the "all-American" message communicated by the school's athletic director only a decade before. The students were cheering for their heroes as Indians and not as American citizens—ethnic pride and symbolic revenge were clearly among the multiple meanings that Haskell's students attached to the game.

In the early 1900s, sports at Haskell served several functions. On the one hand, they were part of the school's comprehensive physical education curriculum designed to provide recreational activities to the students and to remodel the children's Indian bodies. In 1901, Estelle Reel, superintendent of Indian schools, expressed this thought in her universal *Course of Study:* "In order to get the best out of life, it is necessary to look into the physical condition of pupils and give them training that will counteract the influences of unfortunate heredity and strengthen the physique, in order that they may be able to bear the strain that competition in business and earning a living will impose."[89] According to Reel, sports would help Indian children to overcome their assumed biological inferiority. Therefore, physical education should benefit all children, boys and girls alike, and not just elite star athletes. On the other hand, athletics served as an important vehicle for public relations. Through Haskell's great success on the gridiron, the school proved to the American public that Indians were capable of beating whites at their own game—on and off the playing field. Not to mention that the game generated tens of thousands of dollars in revenue for the school, a fact that could hardly have been overlooked by school administrators constantly struggling with insufficient funds.

Throughout the history of Indian boarding schools, sport's different functions caused controversy. Haskell's superintendents were concerned about the possible negative effects of semiprofessional athletics on the larger student community. Even though they actively recruited prospective players, hired professional coaches, and spent much time on the organization of the annual game schedule, the superintendents repeatedly emphasized the importance of physical education for all. To an applicant for the position of coach, Superintendent Peairs explained the particularities of coaching Indian students:

> Indian young men and boys are somewhat different from other boys, and experience has taught us that any one starting to coach any of the athletic teams must be very sure of his ability to succeed in the line of athletics which he has taken up, at the beginning, in other words it is very neces-

sary that he gain the confidence of the Indian boys at the very start, otherwise it is next to impossible to get their confidence at all. Once having their confidence, the coach can do almost anything he wants with them.[90]

Judging from Haskell's victories, the school's mostly white coaches established successful relations with their players. Superintendent Peairs advertised Haskell's 1904 football program to a prospective student by pointing out the quality of the team as well as the exciting game schedule:

Haskell Institute has had one of the best teams in the west for four years. The team has defeated all of the Universities in the Missouri valley with the exception of Nebraska. We are making a great effort to get a team together this year that can defeat Nebraska. Would you like to come to Haskell and play with the team this year? We have a very interesting schedule. We play Kansas University, Missouri University, Nebraska University, and Washington University at St. Louis on the World's Fair grounds.[91]

That fall, Haskell finally succeeded in its efforts to beat Nebraska and went on to win the Missouri Valley Championship. Despite the team's great success, Haskell's leadership insisted that even the school's star athletes participate in the regular work details and course of study. It is reasonable to assume that the players enjoyed some advantages, but they were by no means freed of academic or industrial training.

Esther Burnett remembered how Haskell's athletes struggled to live up to the school's demands, on and off the football field, and how the other students supported their athletes:

In an effort to keep the football players in good academic standing, especially when they had to be off campus, some of us girls volunteered to help them with their assignments. It was a combination of hero worship, supporting the team, and resistance to the non-cooperative boarding school system. They were expected to maintain excellence in their schoolwork in addition to excellence on the playing field.[92]

Almost twenty years earlier, in 1908, Superintendent Peairs had written a letter highly critical of Carlisle's leadership, particularly its management of the school's famous football team. Peairs accused Carlisle of recruiting ineligible students for the team (for instance, students who had deserted or been kicked out of other schools), of paying the players illegal wages, of offering money to players if they made a touchdown, of luring students away from other schools in order to join the Carlisle team, and of enrolling students for football only, without requiring them to attend school. Peairs emphasized the bad influence that professionalism had had on other Indian schools and asked Carlisle to consider reforming its practices:

> I might say in closing that three or four years ago we had a little taste of Professional Foot-Ball here but did not go to any such extent as Carlisle has but with as little as we had here, results in the school were very bad indeed and it has taken several years to get athletics on a good healthy basis.[93]

The controversy over "big time football," which was resolved in the 1930s by Indian Commissioner Collier's ban of interscholastic competition, did not prevent Haskell's students from feeling a deep pride in their team's successes. Esther Burnett remembered that

> During football season, and even throughout the rest of the year, football was an event of top priority for the students. We were a winning team and were enthusiastic supporters of the team's efforts. A home game brought many visitors from the surrounding area and as far away as Oklahoma. Most of the student body attended and got carried away in the excitement of the game. A "gridgraph" was used to watch the progress of the game played away from home. . . . The crowd went wild! We yelled feverishly and got just as excited as when we were watching our team play at home.[94]

Similarly, Lucille Winnie, who went to the school during the 1910s, described the pride she felt in the achievements of Haskell's athletic teams—football, track, baseball, and basketball.[95] Eli Stover, a Creek student who attended Haskell from 1910 to 1916, became one of Haskell's star athletes. Interviewed in 1970, he recalled his athletic career in Lawrence:

> I went to Haskell in early fall of 1910. And when I was at Vivian, I run fast among them rocks and stumps and bushes and chase them squirrel. And

when I went up there at Haskell, I did never see football in my life. They practice. I didn't go out for the school team; I went playing with dairy barn team. And I was fast. I got so good down there, they want me to try out on school team. And I went out in the fall of 1912 and football wasn't nothing to me because I had been used to running in the rock mountains and I was fast. I made the team and I played football, I played basketball, I played baseball and I took track. I broke a school record in broad jump and I took part in high jump and 100 yard dash. I organized a little ball team. Little bitty boys big enough to play. I organized two teams. I let 'em play each other. They sure played a good game.

To Stover, athletics became a natural extension of his prior physical activities. His memories resemble those of many other boarding school alumni who attributed their athletic success to their culture's emphasis on physical training. Navajo and Pueblo students, for instance, believed that their tribes' tradition of running made them especially suitable for the track team. Students associated sports not only with successful assimilation but also with cultural memory and ethnic pride. Although Eli Stover excelled at a variety of sports, it was his success on the football field that brought him recognition beyond Haskell:

I played football on the regular Haskell team and in 1914, I was selected captain. In 1914, I made all Missouri Valley, in 1915, I got All American mention. I played fullback. We played some big colleges, like Notre Dame, Wisconsin, Illinois, Texas A&M, Texas University and LSU. I left school in 1916. When school out I had to go to war. I went to war, went across the water, stayed over there two years and played football on the Divisional team. I never had no idea I make the team. A lot of good college players there, but I beat 'em out when I played football over there in France and Germany.

Over the years, Stover's athletic achievements, like those of so many Native American athletes, have largely been forgotten. When asked whether he had any clippings or certificates left from his athletic career, he replied: "I've lost all of them. I used to have them. They said I was second in the U.S. next to Jim Thorpe. There is a picture of me in the 1915 rulebook. I was second to Jim Thorpe."[96]

But athletics also had a darker side. Students suffered from overexertion, got injured, and even died from their athletic pursuits. Lucille Winnie lost her brothers to sports: "Those 'Fast Winnie Brothers' whose speed and prowess on the athletic field was proclaimed far and wide are now buried on the family plot in Oklahoma," she wrote, "great Haskell athletes, whose hearts were not equal to the demand."[97] Likewise, Arthur Sutton, an Arapaho who attended Haskell during the 1920s, remembered Haskell as the place where he ruined his health:

> Running on the track. We run a hundred and ten yards for the man—the best man they had in history. Hard running. And that very evening I had to be rushed to the hospital. Overworked my heart. And after I got well the doctor told me, "You have to be very careful. When you get old you're going to have heart attack." Sure enough it hit me. I've had three of them already. So that's where I advised my young boy here not to be a hero in athletics.[98]

For the most part, Haskell's students fondly remembered their athletic careers. Far from being the straight ally to assimilation envisioned by Indian educators, boarding school sports were a complex cultural practice that served to express resistance against the regimentations of school life, provided a space to symbolically contest white society, and offered opportunities to feel and openly display ethnic pride. Victories on the athletic field thrilled many indigenous students, and the fame of Haskell athletes such as Eli Stover, John Levi, Louis Weller, Buster Charles, and Pete Hauser motivated Native Americans across the country. Their successes were victories won by Indians for Indians. Boarding school sports were truly pan-Indian, unifying students from diverse tribal, cultural, and social backgrounds.

Sports were also an important agent of socialization, allowing students to have fun and excitement. In an otherwise sexually regimented environment, athletic events provided boys and girls with the opportunity to socialize and to express their emotions as spectators. Especially for Indian women, athletic events were opportunities to enjoy the pleasures of public spaces so often denied to them within the boarding school routine. Whereas Victorian ideals did not allow girls to participate in athletics outside of physical education classes, being part of the passionate crowd furnished some compensation. Haskell's girls played an important role as loyal Indian fans, cheering on their team and displaying great ethnic pride in their songs and chants. Athletic events provided Indian students with the enjoyment of public life as well as a public setting for the expression of their ethnic identity.[99]

The role of recreational activities in boarding schools is complex and contains hegemonic, as well as counterhegemonic, dimensions. Athletics, theater, music, and other extracurricular activities of boarding school life were just as assimilationist, conservative, and colonizing as they were liberating and oppositional. Although sports such as football promoted school spirit and American patriotism, they also allowed students to feel ethnic pride, develop intertribal identities, and symbolically contest white society.[100] The same holds true for many of the other activities that provided students with an opportunity to simultaneously resist and adapt. Extracurricular activities let the children explore their talents, gain self-confidence, take pride in their abilities, experience pleasure, and form close friendships outside of work details or the classroom. Through their participation in athletics and other extracurricular activities, Haskell's students made sense of a rapidly changing world and found alternative ways of forging their identities as indigenous people.

Haskell's business course was very popular with Native American students, shown here in a shorthand class, ca. 1910. The business department's motto was "Onward Ever, Backward Never."

Haskell was famous for its football team, pictured here in 1914. The school played and beat many large universities, and football was a source of great ethnic pride for the students.

Primary students in the early 1900s. These students, sometimes as young as five, six, or seven years old, received academic lessons but were also taught Victorian etiquette.

Many Indian students, such as these shown in the early 1900s, joined the YMCA for its educational and social activities. The school very much encouraged the work of Christian associations because of their "civilizing" influence.

Haskell's chapel and school building, ca. 1900.

View of the Haskell campus from the school's farmlands, 1903.

Haskell's band, pictured in the early 1900s, played an important role in the school's social life and was highly acclaimed throughout the country.

The Reading Room of the Haskell library in the early 1900s. The school encouraged reading as a civilizing force, and Haskell's girls were especially likely to spend a lot of time in the library.

Haskell's commercial department, ca. 1910, is where students learned typewriting, shorthand, business arithmetic, business English, and many other subjects. These classes qualified them to enter the Indian Service or the business world as clerks, secretaries, or accountants.

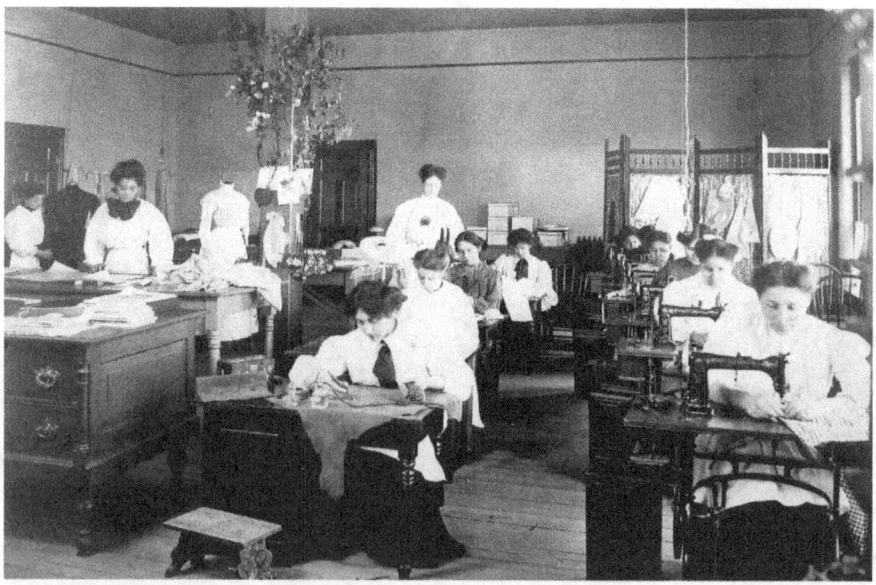

In their domestic arts classes, Native American girls learned sewing and tailoring, as shown here in this early 1900s photograph. Many girls valued their industrial training, but others found it difficult to apply their skills back on the reservations.

These students are in Bible class, which all Haskell students attended, in the early 1900s. As in so many aspects of their boarding school lives, these classes were taught separately for boys and girls, creating gender-specific spheres.

A domestic arts class in the early 1900s. During these classes, Indian girls produced many of the clothes, towels, and pillowcases for their fellow students. The school relied heavily on the girls' work to keep the children dressed.

During their vocational training, Haskell students learned how to make wagons and wheels, as shown in this early 1900s photograph.

A blacksmithing class in the early 1900s. For many decades, blacksmithing was one of the trades taught at Haskell. Critics observed that Indian students were still trained in this art when the era of horse and buggy was already over.

Haskell's Small Boys Building, early 1900s.

The girls' dormitory, early 1900s.

These girls are shown making butter in the early 1900s. Although Haskell's students produced most of the food for the school themselves, butter was a delicacy that the children themselves did not get to enjoy often.

Haskell's successful football team, 1896.

Haskell's hospital, early 1900s. At Haskell, infectious diseases such as tuberculosis and trachoma were widespread, and sadly, many children died while at school. The construction of Haskell's hospital improved the care the students received, but due to the harsh living conditions, the students' health only improved gradually.

Haskell's gymnasium in the early 1900s. Haskell's boys played basketball, football, and baseball as well as other sports such as track and field.

As this early 1900s photograph shows, Haskell's girls received gymnastics lessons as part of the school's mission to change the students' bodies and minds. Victorian gender roles, however, did not allow female students to compete in sports.

The girls at Haskell spent the little free time they had playing board games and reading in the school's YWCA room, shown here in the early 1900s. Haskell's boys, however, frequently played outside, roaming the campus and the adjacent farm and wetlands.

The YWCA provided a "morally acceptable" way of socializing for Haskell's younger girls, pictured here in the early 1900s.

These young men, shown in early 1900, were trained to build stairs as part of their industrial training. Haskell's students learned all the skills necessary to maintain the school grounds and buildings.

Many Indian boys learned to become carpenters, constructing cabinets and other furniture for the school and for sale to external customers, as shown in this early 1900s photograph.

CHAPTER SIX

Health and the Body

Haskell Institute, Lawrence, Kansas

Dec. 4, 1899
Miss Reel:

    I am write a few lines to you this evening and I am going to tell you that I am been sick about two weeks on my back, may be consumption, and I don't think that I never get well again, and so will you please kindly help me? I want going home soon as possible before I get very worse. I like this school but I cannot help it that I am sick. Hoping to hear from you as soon as you can, I am Jack White, one of the Wyoming boys.

    Jack White[1]

Jack White was one of many indigenous students suffering from tuberculosis, a deadly disease very common in Indian boarding schools. Boarding school life was difficult under the best of circumstances, but it could become unbearable once a child's health was failing. Parents constantly worried about their children's well-being, and their fears were often justified. Boarding schools were in many respects unhealthy environments that exposed Indian students to a whole range of communicable diseases and health hazards. The 1928 Meriam Report gives a detailed and graphic account of the deplorable health conditions at federal boarding schools, emphasizing that the lack of funds, as well as the lack of trained medical personnel, was to blame for the many inadequacies discovered. According to the report, medical services at boarding schools were substandard, and the health of Indian children was generally below the normal health status of white children.² According to the Meriam team, boarding schools were not taking good care of their students: the food was insufficient even for healthy children and much more so for children with low general health, the dormitories were overcrowded, the work was too hard, and the prevention of diseases was neglected. The Meriam Report pointed out tuberculosis and trachoma as the two greatest health problems in Indian boarding schools and emphasized the need for more physical exercise for all children as well as the need to improve the quality and frequency of physical examinations in general. All the conditions described by the report were evident at Haskell—the inferior diet, the overcrowding, the hard physical labor, and the insufficient medical attention given to the individual student.

As discussed in the previous chapters, Haskell's ideology aimed at the complete transformation of the children's bodies and minds. The students' outer appearance, demeanor, posture, and personal hygiene were as much targets of the assimilation campaign as were their language, religion, way of thinking, and view of the world. Haskell's administrators believed in their mission to help Indian children to overcome the limitations and disadvantages imposed upon them by their racial background. In their view, Indian children were part of a weakened race in need of physical and mental improvement. Indian educators believed, however, that the cultural, historical, and biological disadvantages faced by Indian students could be cured through hard work, a Christian education, and strict discipline. Haskell's curriculum included the subject of physiology, which was supposed to teach Indian children *the* correct way of taking care of their bodies. Indian educators might have believed in bodily practices as valid expressions of culture, but only as long as these practices were part of their own, dominant culture. During the assimilationist campaign of the late nineteenth and early twentieth centuries, the body became a contested territory similar to the Indian's soul, which had endured centuries of missionary encroachment. Domination, resistance, and transformation were all played out in bodily practices, representations, and beliefs.³ In Indian boarding schools, the children's bodies were the conscious objects of the government's assimilation policy. Indian educators imposed hegemonic conceptions of the body, involving the central practice of discipline.

Discipline was manifested not only in the school's military organization and training but also in Haskell's concern for the bodily state of its students.

The bodily transformation of the children was central to the educators' efforts, since physical well-being and appearance were regarded as symbols of the children's spiritual state. Disease, dirt, and sexual license were seen as symbols of "paganism" and racial inferiority. The relationship between the body and salvation was central and explicit. Indigenous bodily practices had to be replaced with Christian notions and rituals of hygiene, which included the children's clothing, hairstyle, demeanor, physical activities, and cleaning rites. Only a clean, healthy body could eventually become Christianized, civilized, and assimilated. Bodily discipline was the cornerstone of Indian education, controlling the children's productive labor as well as their sexuality and social relationships and practices. The school indoctrinated the students' minds with Western concepts of health, inspected their bodies frequently, and especially monitored the girls' bodily functions carefully. In order to deter sexual promiscuity among students, matrons even kept detailed records of the menstrual cycles of the girls.[4] Despite all efforts to deny and control the students' sexuality, Indian educators knew that total control of 700 adolescent children was impossible. Sexual activities did take place at Haskell, and the school's medical records give some indications of the way the school dealt with this reality. Annual reports list several cases of syphilis and gonorrhea as well as abortions performed. It appears that sexually transmitted diseases, which mostly affected Haskell's boys, were not always treated at the school, but that students thus afflicted were sent home for treatment. In Haskell's records, references to the students' sexuality and sexually transmitted diseases are generally brief and at times evasive, reflecting Victorian beliefs and customs in dealing with "delicate matters." This was especially true when Haskell's female students were involved. Although boys were not always punished for their sexual adventures, infractions committed by the girls usually led to expulsion.

When Cherokee student Susie Mars (pseudonym) entered Haskell in September 1911, the girl was already one month pregnant. When her condition became apparent during the winter months, Susie was expelled from Haskell.[5] Although the girl had gotten into trouble during the summer months, other girls experienced sexual encounters while at school. In 1911, Allison Goodwin (pseudonym), an Ojibwe student, and Colin Nevitt (pseudonym), assistant property clerk and a former student himself, were found "in such a compromising position . . . that it was necessary to summarily dismiss the employee and expel the girl."[6] Superintendent Fiske explained to the reservation agent that the young people had been attached to one another for a long time and had intentions to get married:

> Upon being discovered as they were Saturday, they both wished to be married immediately, but to this course of procedure, I could not give my consent for the reason that it would be a very bad principle to establish to permit any young man and girl of this Institution to believe that because they were found in a compromising situation, that it will be sufficient reason for them to be permitted to leave the Institution and be married immediately. It would undoubtedly lead to many similar occurrences where boys and girls become infatuated.[7]

Superintendent Fiske added, however, that in principle he agreed to the marriage and thought it would be "the best and logical outcome of the whole affair."[8] Although the couple was in love and eager to spend their lives together, the case of Crow students Edgar Cain (pseudonym) and Connie Peterson (pseudonym) involved sadder circumstances. According to Fiske's report, the girl was raped by Edgar Cain during the winter of 1909–1910 and was pregnant as a result of this crime:

> The girl at the time of the occurrence was simply fulfilling her duties on the dining-room detail, and had carried some slops to the back porch to empty them. She did not know of Cain's presence there at the time, according to her friend's statement. He took hold of her, and she resisted vigorously at first, but after a time yielded. I am advised that he now tells her it was all her fault for being out there. In that, however, it will be seen that she was simply accomplishing her duties.[9]

The superintendent suggested either forcing Cain to marry the girl, should she and her parents wish it, or, if not, bringing him to trial on a charge of seduction. According to Fiske, "Putting this boy through will have more salutary effect than anything else I know toward putting a quietus on this sort of thing in the future, and primarily for the girl's sake I feel that we should get him at once and make him come to time."[10] In August 1910, Fiske received a telegram from the Crow Agency in Montana, stating that Connie Peterson objected to marriage. A second telegram three weeks later reversed that decision. On September 22, 1910, Fiske wrote to the Indian Office in

Washington: "Connie Peterson unable to travel—she and parents want Cain to marry her—County Attorney is willing. Will leave with him for Crow Agency tomorrow unless otherwise directed. Believe incarceration in county jail sufficient object lesson."[11]

This episode clearly indicates that in Haskell's Victorian moral climate, a girl's reputation was regarded as more important than the punishment of a severe crime and the prospect of an unhappy and potentially abusive marriage. Rape did happen at Haskell, but authorities were inclined to downplay sexual crimes. By doing so, the school to some extent blamed the victims for the rape and, instead of protecting the girl, protected the moral reputation of the school. The following February, Barbara Deer (pseudonym) gave birth to a baby boy at Haskell. Superintendent Fiske reported the unusual circumstances of the case to the commissioner of Indian affairs:

> The only extraordinary feature of this case is that it should have been possible for a woman to give birth to a child without having shown the slightest evidence of her condition to anyone, even her roommates. The Matron never suspicioned the case at all. The girl in question being one of her trusted and thoroughly reliable officers. The Seamstress who measured the girl for dresses on a number of occasions noticed nothing whatever which would indicate the approach of such an event. I saw the girl a few days before the occurance and such a possibility never occurred to me.[12]

Fiske reported that the girl had become pregnant while visiting relatives in Oklahoma and that the father of the child could not be prosecuted since he had gotten married to another woman. Barbara Deer and her baby boy were expelled from the school. These stories reveal that all attempts to control the students' sexuality had their limits. Even though cases such as these were the exception rather than the rule, they happened frequently enough to indicate the young people's resistance to the strict Victorian codes of conduct imposed on them. Whereas Haskell tried to discipline the children's bodies, minds, and sexual behavior, the stories reveal how even a "total institution" could never exercise total control.

The overlapping of racial ideology, religion, and bodily practices manifested itself in Haskell's curriculum as well as in the school's extracurricular activities. In 1901, Dr. James Naismith, inventor of basketball and physical director of Kansas University, addressed Haskell's boys on the "physical advantages of being a Christian," showing how closely linked these issues were in the perception of the dominant culture. Haskell's physiology curriculum addressed not just medical issues but also morally charged topics such as temperance. The 1911 course of study instructed the teachers to be "familiar with home conditions among the Indians and be prepared to intelligently direct the pupils in the proper methods of correcting evils which menace their health and welfare." According to the bulletin, talks and observation lessons should lead to "an appreciation of the necessity for temperance and cleanliness of person, clothing, grounds and living rooms."[13] Topics taught included "The Skin and Bathing," "Clothing and How to Use It," "Effects of Tobacco and Alcohol on the Body, Particularly the Growing Body," "Tuberculosis; Its Treatment and Prevention," "Importance of Hygiene," and "Caring for the Health." As part of their physiology training, students frequently listened to lectures and wrote essays on health-related topics. In 1913, for instance, the children discussed "What Is Being Done to Prevent Tuberculosis." Their essays reflect the many rules they were taught in order to prevent the disease. Naomi Russell, a student from the Oglalla nation, wrote:

> It is said that in the whole United States nearly nine tenth of the people die this disease. Mostly all the people are Indians. To prevent it we should eat wholesome food, drink pure water, use our own towels, do not wear others clothes, sleep alone, and do not cover our head with the blankets. If there is one person in the family that has the tuberculosis, the rest of the family should be examined, this one person should use his or her own towels, dishes, etc. the dishes should be boiled daily, towels washed frequently.... In our own school we are helping to prevent tuberculosis germs by studying physiology and writing compositions on certain subjects. And in our industrial work learning how to keep clean and work clean. When I go home I will teach my people how to avoid tuberculosis. There is one thing that I always did and will do is to try and keep the flies out of the house and the food.[14]

Two years after writing this essay, Naomi Russell was sent home to Pine Ridge owing to a massive loss of weight, from 150 to 117 pounds during the school year, and active tuberculosis.

At least in theory, personal hygiene, cleanliness, order, and discipline were fundamental concepts of the school's mission. In many ways, though, the realities of boarding school life made it impossible to achieve these ideals. Both

Haskell's annual health reports and the Meriam Report reveal conditions that severely affected the children's ability to stay "clean" and "healthy" and to follow the many rules they were taught in their physiology lessons. According to the reports, Haskell's dormitories lacked light and ventilation, and the children frequently had to share beds and towels. A 1914 health report, for instance, described how the towel system used at the school contributed to the spread of tuberculosis and trachoma:

> From a hygienic and sanitary standpoint, the present towel system is very unsatisfactory. Towel racks are used in the girl's dormitory but from one to three towels are often seen on one hook. On an average, the towel hooks are about 4 1/2 inches apart, and the towels being hung by the middle overlap each other. To prevent stealing and exchanging the towels when on the racks, most of the boys keep their towels hid around their beds, and you can find them stuffed in the bedding, between the mattresses and the springs, within the pillow case, amongst old clothes, in their suitcases or dressers—in fact, any old place that offers a handy hiding place.[15]

There were not enough toothbrushes for all the students, and the sanitary facilities were insufficient: toilets did not function properly, soap was not available, and bathrooms were dark, damp, and cold. The children were only allowed to bathe once a week, the floors were constantly dusty, and there were no spitting cups, which would have prevented the boys from regularly spitting on the floor. The children were overworked, and their diet lacked essential nutrients. Under these conditions, it was very difficult to fulfill the school's expectations when it came to personal health and hygiene. Outside health inspectors repeatedly noted the lack of preventive health measures at Haskell, a situation that, in their view, made it impossible for the students to live up to the Office of Indian Affairs' strict health standards.

Concerning the negative impact of "overactivity," the Meriam Report notes that boarding schools in general did not adjust the assigned work details to the actual strength and health condition of the individual child. Neither did the work performed serve educational purposes:

> The laundries are perhaps open to the most criticism. As has been pointed out, the amount of labor spent is far greater than necessary, a waste due to the old, inefficient equipment. Practically all the work requires the child to

stand. The monotonous ironing of simple dresses and shirts for hours is frankly production work and not necessary to teach the child the simple processes involved.[16]

The report emphasizes that the amount and nature of work performed by the students was an important factor in explaining the low general health conditions at the school. Parents were very concerned about the amount of work their children were expected to do and sometimes even wrote to Haskell's superintendent to make sure their sons or daughters were spared from the heaviest details. In 1917, Martha Wright appealed to Superintendent Peairs:

> My daughter, Marie Wright, informs me that she suffers with a wound quite severely where she was operated on last May. She had a complication of troubles, appendicitis being one of things the matter with her. The Doctor told her she must not do any heavy work for at least one year. She tells me that she is working in the laundry which is quite heavy for her, therefore since she has been at Haskell she has been suffering severely, although she will never tell the Matron, as she will work as long as she can. . . . She is all the child I have and I hope you will realize what her health means to me. Mr. Peairs please look into this matter at once, as I am quite uneasy about Marie.[17]

In 1908, Haskell became the target of a month-long health investigation, designed to find out why the school had such a large number of tubercular cases. In his final report, Special U.S. Indian Agent McConihe described the harsh working conditions at Haskell:

> Another pernicious system which prevails here and which I consider has baneful results, is the detailing of boys from fourteen years of age and under, to sweep and scrub the halls and . . . the detail made at the beginning of the school year continues until next June and unlike other details, is not changed from time to time, or about every ten weeks. One of the boys named Fernandez was on the detail the whole last year and is back on it this year again. There is not one boy in this detail strong enough to carry water up two and four flights of stairs, which they have to do, without taxing his strength to its utmost. These youngsters sweep the assembly halls

and the other halls without first sprinkling the floors with water to keep down the dust. The result is they are enveloped in a cloud of dust perhaps reeking with all sorts of microbes and this dust must certainly be a serious cause of irritation to a healthy pair of lungs to say nothing of those that are in a weakened condition. No discrimination between the healthy and the unhealthy has been made in the selection of this little detail.[18]

McConihe's report shows the carelessness with which the children were assigned to their work chores, and the school's irresponsible approach to preventive health. Another health risk identified by the Meriam Report was the children's diet, which lacked even minimal amounts of fruits, vegetables, and milk products. A majority of children were underfed as well as malnourished, owing to the low quality, quantity, and variety of foods served. A 1914 health inspection at Haskell revealed that the school needed to pay more attention to the diet of students who were losing weight or were frail and delicate: "It is the break in the monotony of the routine diet that increases the appetite at the diet table, and with the addition of milk, butter, eggs and fruit, etc. to the diet, these pupils soon make great gains in weight and improve in color, strength and general condition."[19]

In addition to a healthy diet, physical exercise was an important health factor. The same inspection revealed that Haskell's female students were in much worse shape than the boys. Forty percent of the girls had lost weight over the period of investigation as opposed to 20 percent of the male students. Health inspector Dr. Van Cleave explained: "Since the girls have been given no physical training and have but little opportunity to get out in the open air other than in going to and from various departments, the reason for this difference in weight is very apparent to me.... The girls need regular and systematic physical training."[20]

The shortcomings in material and living conditions resulted in a student population that was highly susceptible to certain diseases, suffering from weakened immune systems. What aggravated the situation was Haskell's apparent failure to control communicable diseases as well as the school's inability to provide the children with adequate medical care. During the school's first three decades, the health staff consisted of a trained nurse, who was assisted by some of the female students detailed to the school's hospital. Until 1911, Haskell employed neither a resident physician nor an athletic director. Instead, the school relied on the disciplinarian to direct the students' physical training, and contracted with a Lawrence doctor who visited the school one hour each morning. For a boarding school with more than 700 students, these arrangements meant that little time could be devoted to the individual child and that the students' physical fitness suffered. The school remedied some shortcomings over the years, but others persisted for decades.

The 1908 health inspection led to the discharge of 57 students with active forms of tuberculosis, increasing the number of children sent home because of the disease since January 1908 to 104. In addition, Dr. Joseph A. Murphy identified 76 cases of tubercular infection, but to a less dangerous extent. Of the 133 pupils diagnosed, 84 were boys and 49 girls, almost twice as many boys as girls. Seventeen percent of Haskell's student population was found to be tubercular that fall, posing a grave risk to the school's other 663 students. According to the report, many affected children had entered Haskell without sufficient health certifications or careful physical examinations and had probably arrived at the school already infected with tuberculosis. Many others, though, contracted the disease at the school. Haskell did not exercise precaution to prevent the spread of tuberculosis, neither segregating infected from healthy pupils nor providing living conditions that would have helped to contain the disease. It appears that the preventive measures did not go beyond the activities mentioned in the students' essays: physiology lessons, lectures, and essay writing.

The special agent's report described the overcrowded conditions in Haskell's dormitories that particular fall. Since the girl's dormitory was under renovation, all the girls were moved into the Small Boys' Building, whose residents, in the meantime, were housed in tents on the school grounds. Every single bed in the girls' temporary home was shared by two girls, and the airspace was "consequently cut down to one half of what was barely sufficient for one."[21] Dr. Joseph A. Murphy, the inspecting physician, added: "In most of the rooms there were no closets, wardrobes or other facilities for hanging clothes, so that at night clothes hung in windows blocking out the air, over the head or foot of the beds or in few cases on chairs. Frequently windows were all closed so that with no artificial system of ventilation the air in these rooms could not be other than foul."[22] When the weather turned cold, the small boys were moved from their tents to the basement of the school building and chapel. According to the inspectors, ninety-nine boys were crowded into forty-nine single beds in one large room containing six windows, while eighty-nine boys had to share sixty-three single beds "placed in the gymnasium room, the windows of which were generally kept closed, the only fresh air being admitted through a few broken panes of glass."[23]

The reason for Superintendent Peairs's negligence was simple. Haskell's leadership was trying to keep attendance at full strength. Sending home a large number of children after the beginning of the school year owing to a lack of space would have meant a drop in attendance and consequently a drop in appropriations. Peairs argued that the school simply could not afford to lose part of its already meager funds. In order to keep the school operating, Peairs would rather risk jeopardizing the well-being of his students.

The inspectors found other conditions that favored the spread of tuberculosis. For instance, clothing and bedding used by students sent home due to tuberculosis had been assigned to other children without being disinfected, and musical wind instruments were passed from child to child without disinfections. Some students were sent home because of the disease just to be readmitted the next term; others spent their vacations at home with tubercular families and were never reexamined upon their return to school. Students diagnosed with the disease were allowed to go back to the dormitories to spread the infection, and other students did not report their conditions to the hospital or matron, concealing their symptoms from the school authorities for as long as possible.[24]

Haskell's nurse at the time, Lucretia Ross, supported the inspectors' findings, voicing strong criticism of Superintendent Peairs's attitude. In her report, she mentions several students the doctor had declared unfit to remain in school. Despite the physician's advice, the children stayed at Haskell for several more months and were even required to participate in the school's regular activities. Nurse Ross told the shocking story of a boy who had been admitted to the hospital with pneumonia and tuberculosis in February of 1908:

> He remained in the hospital three weeks and then was sent back to the quarters to make room in the hospital for sicker boys. He was sent to school and work, although he coughed a great deal and spit blood every time he coughed. He remained at the school until May 15, 1908, when he was sent home. During all that time Dr. Anderson asked Mr. Peairs almost every week to send [him] home, as he was a menace to the other pupils. The boy went personally to the superintendent and asked repeatedly that he be allowed to go home. When he was finally sent home he was so weak from the loss of blood that he could scarcely walk.[25]

In June 1908, Nurse Ross asked Superintendent Peairs for authority to examine a number of students for tuberculosis, to segregate the infected ones, and to fumigate the children's quarters. Ross described Peairs's reaction to her requests: "Mr. Peairs appeared skeptical in regard to the health of the pupils and seemed to think my fears for their health a mere fancy. He told me there had never before been so many cases of tuberculosis in the school and thought it strange that so many were thus diagnosed."[26] Peairs granted the examinations but was reluctant to send infected children home. In several cases he made them stay till after commencement or even over the summer—a clear indication that attendance figures were on his mind.[27]

The strained relationship between Ross and Peairs did nothing to improve the children's situation. According to Dr. Murphy, Nurse Ross was a highly competent professional, "a woman of strong sympathy," who was "deeply interested in the welfare and health of the children" and whose "efforts have been unceasing in attempting to stamp out the tuberculosis at this school."[28] Superintendent Peairs, on the other hand, not only had the well-being of the individual child in mind but also felt responsible for maintaining the school's funding and consequently the attendance figures. These differing priorities led to Peairs's perception of Nurse Ross as being "over zealous . . . doing everything in her power to force the diagnosis and cause almost the disruption of the school."[29] According to Dr. Murphy, "This lack of harmony between the Superintendent and the nurse has made it seem as if all the trouble which the school was encountering had been caused by the nurse, whereas the fact is that all cases returned to their homes have been by the written recommendation of the physician stating his diagnosis to be tuberculosis."[30] This episode demonstrates that Haskell's students not only faced harsh living conditions and a lack of responsible care but that they were also at the mercy of their superiors' personal quarrels and diverging priorities.

The commissioner of Indian affairs, Francis E. Leupp, quickly responded to the 1908 inspection reports and asked Superintendent Peairs to take immediate action to remedy all the shortcomings identified. In his reply, Peairs admitted having been too lax when it came to examining the children in the past, but he denied any conscious wrongdoing. Rather, he blamed the alarming health conditions at Haskell on the scarcity of funds, which prevented him from making all the necessary improvements in the students living conditions. Peairs promised to put Dr. Murphy's recommendations into effect as quickly as possible, emphasizing that in order to make the necessary changes, he would require additional appropriations from Washington. He referred to his earlier order of 150 single beds, which in the end could not be purchased owing to a lack of funds. Also, he expressed the need to bring in fifty more boys, since the departure of seventy tubercular children had reduced the attendance to only 700. To Peairs, the students' weak health was disturbing not because the conditions leading to their suffering were unethical or inhumane but mainly because the high infection numbers caused a disruption in the smooth operation of the school. Nevertheless, Peairs obeyed his superior's orders. In February 1909, Dr. Murphy and Special Agent McConihe arrived at Haskell for an unannounced follow-up visit, finding most of their recommendations on tuberculosis prevention in effect.[31]

Health inspections revealed the deplorable living conditions at Haskell and the health risks indigenous children faced at federal Indian boarding schools. Haskell's superintendents, however, were quick to assure anxious parents that their children were absolutely safe in their care. Superintendent Peairs's words, "Your daughters are as safe from disease as if they were with you," ring hollow considering the poor general health of Haskell's student population. No doubt, parents would have been terribly worried if they had known the actual conditions at the school. Their notions of good care certainly did not include their daughters having to share beds with tubercular children, their little boys having to scrub germ-infected floors, or their seriously ill children not being returned home as soon as their condition became known. In many instances, a lack of communication between the school and the parents caused unnecessary anxieties. In some cases, parents were only informed when their children were already seriously ill, and sometimes only after they had passed away. Haskell's superintendents claimed that they did not want to upset parents if their children's illness was minor and could be cured easily. It appears, however, that the school used a much broader definition of minor illness than the parents would have agreed upon. Parents were frequently distressed because they only learned of their son or daughter's illness through other members of their community and not from the school or the children themselves.[32] Haskell received many letters from anxious parents who were worried about their children's state of health. In 1909, Susan Sears Clark from Porcupine, South Dakota, inquired about her son's health:

> I have been informed that my son William Sears' health is very poor. If such is the case, please for a pleading mother's sake, send him home

before it is too late. I think it was so heartless of his Father to send him back there to school. When he knew the boy's health was failing. What good will an education do him when his health is gone. All he needs now is a good home and a loving mother's care.[33]

As so often, Superintendent Peairs assured the concerned mother that even though her son was not in the best of health, there was no reason to worry. The boy would be observed carefully, and if his condition should demand it, he would be sent home right away. Indian parents shared information about the care their children were receiving, and negative experiences could influence the attitudes of whole indigenous communities. Replying to Haskell's request to send a group of pupils from the Navajo reservation, the local Indian agent told Superintendent Peairs that he feared the children's parents would not give their consent. He explained that "these Indians are a little afraid of Haskell on account of the children getting sick there."[34] Likewise, Agent Nellis from the Pawnee Agency in Oklahoma informed Superintendent Wise in 1911:

Roam Chief has just come to the office and arranged for placing his son Harry Richards in school for another term. In talking over the matter he stated to me that he had been told that sick children in Haskell were not always given necessary attention. He asks that you give this matter personal attention. . . . He is one of the head chiefs of the tribe and wields considerable influence.[35]

For Haskell's enrollment, it could be detrimental if an influential tribal leader had any doubts about the children's safety. Since the school depended on the parents' cooperation and consent to fill its ranks, it was in Haskell's best interest to keep negative health reports from finding their way into indigenous communities. This was certainly one of the main reasons why the school did not inform parents about what it considered "minor ailments," trying to uphold the impression that Haskell was a safe and healthy place to be. In many cases, of course, the children themselves informed their parents and triggered angry responses. In 1913, an upset parent wrote to the commissioner of Indian affairs:

Dear Sir: I have five children at Haskell Institute of Lawrence, Kansas, and my daughter Mabel tells me that 3/4 of the 600 pupils there have "Trachoma" or granulated "sore eyes." A government eye specialist now here (Mr. Harrison, I believe) tells me that three years ago he examined these Haskell pupils for the Indian Department and found 147 pupils with Trachoma.... I sent my children to this school under the impression that it was progressive and sanitary. Would you like your children to be thus exposed?[36]

As this letter indicates, parents could react quite strongly if they felt that their children's health was in danger. This parent took his/her complaint to the highest instance, appealing directly to the commissioner of Indian affairs and his sense of justice. By invoking the opinion of an expert and referring to progressivism and hygiene, the author's line of argumentation directly counters stereotypes about Indian ignorance and "savagery."

When children wrote to their parents about being ill and feeling neglected, their families naturally blamed the school for their son's or daughter's suffering. Usually, the school did not take any responsibility for the child's poor health but argued that the student had arrived at Haskell already infected. Although that was true in many instances, the boarding school environment aggravated the children's condition. Once infection had occurred, malnutrition, hard labor, and unhealthy living conditions weakened the children's immune systems and increased their risk of developing active tuberculosis.

Sometimes, sick children remained at the school because they had no one to care for them in their communities. After Ruth Peacock (pseudonym) had been diagnosed with tuberculosis, her guardian asked Superintendent Fiske to keep the girl in school since "her mother is dead and her reputed father, John Peacock (pseudonym), is absolutely no good, and has no home for her."[37] Just as Haskell became a home for many orphaned and neglected children, it became a place of recovery, and sometimes death, for children who had no one else to take care of them. Even though the health conditions at the school were far from ideal, they were not necessarily worse than on many of the reservations. At the least, Haskell provided the children access to a hospital, a nurse, a doctor, and medications. What the school could not provide, however, were true emotional support and the kind of loving care that sick children needed the most.

Haskell's medical system was part of a Western culture of medicine, which objectifies the patient. In this biomedical system, the hospital becomes the privileged space of disease and thus of medical control.[38] It is difficult to assess how indigenous children reacted to what were in many cases unfamiliar medical techniques and the scientific approach to disease prevalent at the school. Considering the children's cultural backgrounds, it is likely that many of them felt alienated by the dominant society's biomedical concepts and by the kind of care they received. The objectification typical of Western medical care went against the children's prior experiences, which had placed the sick child in the larger context of family, community, and tribal culture. What the children would have needed in addition to an accurate biomedical diagnosis or a successful chemical treatment was a holistic approach to their illness, paying attention to their individuality, psychological needs, and cultural background.

A subtle rebellion against medical authority could be read into the observation that many afflicted children concealed their tubercular condition as long as possible from school authorities. Lying isolated in a sterile hospital ward might have been even more frightening than to feel ill while participating in dormitory and schoolroom life among friends. At times, students did complain about neglect on the part of their doctor, but their protests were rarely taken serious. When Grace Stanup complained to her guardian about the doctor's ignoring the lumps on her neck and her back pain, Superintendent Fiske defended the physician:

> These children are not very appreciative of the requirements of medicine, and if the Doctor treats them and the treatment does not give immediate relief they consider that he is neglectful or that he does not know what he is doing. I have a very excellent Physician at the school who has a very large outside practice and is fully up-to-date in his knowledge and methods of treating disease, and the girl can have no grounds whatever for her complaint.[39]

Because the doctor was "up-to-date" in his scientific medical practices, Superintendent Fiske assumed that the girl received all the necessary care. Considering the high number of children suffering from serious diseases, it is questionable whether a single contract physician and one nurse would have been able to give adequate attention to all their patients. According to the Meriam Report and the school's inspection reports, medical exams were often conducted in a superficial manner, and many diseases remained undetected or untreated for an extended period of time.

Although students sometimes hid their diseases from school authorities, on other occasions they might have used illness as an escape from the daily routine and as a means of resistance to the pressures of school life. In 1900, the school physician discussed Delia Miller's (pseudonym) case with Superintendent Peairs:

> I have to say that after several weeks of observation, I fail to find anything seriously wrong with the girl. . . . She has a good appetite; she has the appearance of good general health; she usually seems well enough if there is frolic or entertainment in sight; but I am impressed with the conviction that work has rather a depressing effect on her mind. . . . It is very evident to my mind, speaking in all sympathy and kindness, Delia would find herself practically well if she would bring her mind to the condition of thinking so.[40]

Delia Miller might not have suffered from a serious physical condition, but obviously her psychological state was not "healthy." The girl might have been homesick or depressed or might have suffered from another psychosomatic illness. The doctor clearly associated her symptoms with her state of mind, implying that Delia only imagined her illness. In his view, disease was purely a biomedical concept with no room for psychological or social dimensions. If health refers to the maintenance of homeostasis, the balance of body and mind, Delia, and with her many other children, were certainly suffering from subjectively experienced illnesses. The absence of physical disease does not automatically imply a state of health. Considering the difficult living conditions at Haskell, the separation from their families, and the cultural pressures weighing on the children, it is likely that many of the students suffered from psychological problems. In Delia's case, she might have consciously or unconsciously used her illness as a means of escaping from Haskell's hard work details or as a way of receiving extra care and attention in a school environment that did not provide much emotional support for the individual student. As Cora Folsom, director of Hampton Institute's Indian program, confessed in her memoirs, "homesickness with them became a disease; boys and girls actually suffered in the flesh as well as in spirit; could not eat, would not sleep, and so prepared the way for serious trouble." She described their pain and desperation: "An Indian throws himself flat upon the bosom of mother earth and, scorning the weakness of tears, lies there in dumb misery for hours together, oblivious to dampness, to cold or heat."[41]

In 1903, Superintendent Peairs pointed out the limitations the school faced in providing medical care for its students:

> During the autumn and winter months we have our greatest number of cases of sickness, growing out of exposure to cold about which the Indian persists in being careless or thoughtless. These always fill up our wards; not necessarily with seriously sick people, but with boys and girls who in civilized homes would be kept in by their mother and in a day or two, with her nursing, turned out cured. In the absence of home and mother, the hospital and nurse become the substitutes. Their temporary ailments are overcome, they are dismissed and others take their place to be taken through similar processes.[42]

Peairs emphasized the strain that these cases of minor illnesses posed on the school's resources, especially in the event of recurring epidemics, which hit Haskell almost every winter. Since the hospital was not spacious enough to accommodate all patients, the school frequently converted dormitory rooms into temporary sick wards, thereby disrupting school life and unnecessarily exposing healthy students to the disease. The situation improved after the construction of a larger hospital building in 1905, which provided more space to separate children suffering from contagious diseases from the rest of the student population. As was revealed in Haskell's inspection reports, however, the separation of sick students from healthy ones did not always take priority, and especially in the case of tuberculosis, preventive measures seemed to have been almost nonexistent.

At Haskell, students suffered from the disease's most life-threatening form, pulmonary tuberculosis, as well as from the less dangerous but also debilitating form, scrofula. Pulmonary consumption resulted in massive weight loss, coughing, spitting up blood, and hemorrhaging, which in many cases led to the child's death. Scrofula attacked the lymph glands, causing eruptions or running sores in the area of the lower face and the neck. Both forms of the disease were highly contagious.[43] Once a child hemorrhaged, there was not much that could be done, and neither encouraging words nor medical treatments could conceal the truth. The psychological burden of seeing friends and fellow students suffer and eventually die must have been great. Even though the school was reluctant to send students home if they were still able to work and attend classes, once all hope for the child's improvement had vanished, Haskell's leadership was quite eager to dismiss the pupil. Although the family home was correctly considered the more appropriate environment for the care of a terminally ill child, this measure also helped to keep down the school's death rate as well as to avoid the trauma associated with the passing away of a student. The children were certainly aware of Haskell's practices and the health risks they were exposed to while at school. Esther Burnett remembered:

> Throughout my years at Haskell, several students came down with tuberculosis. In my dorm, two girls were diagnosed as being in the last stages of TB. They were not hospitalized but rather were sent back to their cots in our room until arrangements could be made to send them to the Sioux Sanatorium in Rapid City. I have often wondered why they were not isolated in the hospital. They were our friends, and we felt sorry for them because we didn't know if they would get well or not. Later in my life I had exploratory surgery to ascertain the nature of two large masses, one in my lungs and one in my throat. It was discovered that they were not cancerous but rather were healed tubercular areas. It's quite possible that I was contaminated while rooming with these two tubercular-infected students.[44]

Sometimes, the school waited too long, and the child's condition had worsened to a point where traveling home was no longer an option. In 1900, the school physician informed Superintendent Peairs:

> Charles Adams, a Pawnee, suffered last evening at about 6 o'clock, a very severe hemorrhage of the lungs, and at 3 o'clock this morning there was a reoccurrence of the same, but not quite so extensive. The immediate final result is uncertain. It does mean, however, that for several days the boy will be absolutely confined to his bed with the hope that plugging and healing of the blood vessel may occur. My judgment is that it is the result of tuberculosis, and that it is very doubtful whether healing will occur. In any case it is out of the question for the present, to consider his going home. Everything will be done for him that can be with the hope that we may be able to put him on his feet.[45]

For Charles Adams, hope was not enough. Charles was sixteen years old when he died from tuberculosis. The inscription on his grave at Haskell's school cemetery reads: Charles Adams, Pawnee, 1884–1900.

During the first two decades of the twentieth century, the Office of Indian Affairs established a number of school sanatoriums for tubercular students, where the children did not have to work and were given special care. Haskell's superintendents frequently suggested sending afflicted students to these institutions, a decision that had to be made by the child's parents. When the Fort Lapwai Indian Sanatorium School opened its gates in 1912, Haskell received an invitation to send students with incipient tuberculosis to Idaho. Advanced cases were not admitted since there was nothing that could be done to save them.[46] Due to its proximity to Haskell, however, the Sac and Fox Sanatorium in Toledo, Iowa, was the hospital used most frequently by the school's administrators.

Once their ailing children arrived at home, parents were sometimes shocked by the condition their son or daughter was in. Annie Valley, mother of two daughters who attended Haskell during the early 1900s, was distressed when her daughter Mamie arrived back in Nevada with a severe case of tuberculosis. In the ensuing correspondence, the mother, through letters written by her Anglo-American friend Cora Tabor, requested the return of her second daughter, Maud, since she feared for her safety at Haskell. Apparently Mamie was in such bad condition during the trip, that even "the conductor on the train in which Mamie traveled was so alarmed at her appearance that he himself called the doctor for her when they arrived."[47] Mamie was so ill that the doctor feared she might die during the coach trip from Elko to the reservation. The girl therefore remained at the local clinic for treatment. Superintendent Peairs's response to Mrs. Valley's concerns was rather cold. He claimed that Mamie had already arrived at Haskell infected with tuberculosis, blaming the agency physician for the girl's troubles. Concerning her agonizing trip home, he noted:

> When we did send her, we knew that she was in a very weak condition, and that it was somewhat risky to send her the long distance alone, and yet the school physician felt that she could make the trip. Under those circumstances, I felt sure that her mother would rather have her come home than to stay here and die. My experience has been that parents almost invariably prefer to have their children sent home when their health fails.[48]

Peairs emphasized that there was no reason to send Maud home since there was absolutely no danger for her to contract the same disease as her sister, an interesting assessment of the situation considering that at the time almost 20 percent of Haskell's student population was infected with tuberculosis.[49] In her reply, Cora Tabor told Peairs that even though Mamie might have contracted the disease before her departure, she had been a picture of health when she had left home the previous fall. The blame, however, was

> in the fact that Mamie was kept at the school for so long after you saw what was the trouble. You said that the disease appeared very shortly after she arrived there last fall, seven or eight months ago; she was not sent home until it had reached the last stages and she had very little chance for her life. As you say, parents almost invariably prefer to have their children sent home when their health fails, and I certainly think that you should have obeyed her mother's requests (she tells me that she wrote twice asking for Mamie's return) and sent her home at the outset.

Referring to the mother's request to have her other daughter, Maud, return home, Mrs. Tabor expressed the anxieties and frustrations felt by many Indian parents:

> It seems to me that it is not a question for you and me to decide as to whether it is best for Maud to come. Her mother wants her and she keeps asking me to write for her. It is a small comfort to her that Mamie may have had the disease before she left here. She only knows that she is apparently beyond help, that many others have died at the school, and she wants the other girl to come home; and she is certainly the one who should have the say in the matter.[50]

It was exactly the parents' right to choose what was best for their own children that was constantly violated by Indian educators. Once parents had agreed to send their sons and daughters to boarding school, they had given up their rights as parents. School authorities treated them as incapable of making rational decisions, implying that Indian parents were merely children themselves. This perception of the Indian's racial childhood formed the basis for Indian educators' paternalistic attitude toward indigenous people. In the case of Maud Valley, Superintendent Peairs finally agreed to let the girl go home, as long as the family would provide the money for transportation.

Besides tuberculosis, many other diseases ravaged the student population. Typhoid fever, meningitis, smallpox, whooping cough, mumps, measles, respiratory infections, malaria, influenza, and pneumonia were frequently reported, with typhoid and pneumonia claiming the highest death rate among the children. Students also suffered from gastritis, sexually transmitted infections, rheumatism, impetigo, conjunctivitis, and appendicitis. Pneumonia frequently developed as a complication from influenza, keeping the children confined to their beds for several weeks. In 1903, Haskell's contract physician summarized his experience with pneumonia:

> I note that in ten years we have recorded 125 cases of Pneumonia. In a large majority of the cases the attack was directly [traceable] to some individual indiscretion, such as lying on the cold ground, leaving a warm building for the open air without sufficient extra wraps, sitting before an open window in a cold draught when heated, or failing to seek dry clothing when for any cause those worn had gotten wet. The greater numbers of these cases have occurred during the winter months of January and February. Nine of the cases have proven fatal.[51]

In 1910 and in 1916, Haskell reported epidemics of measles and mumps, which affected more than fifty students at a time. Perhaps the most serious epidemic occurred in 1918, when Haskell fell victim to an epidemic of Spanish Influenza that was sweeping the whole country at the time. The first wave of the flu hit in the middle of March; within days, more than 100 students became sick, running temperatures as high as 106° F. U.S. Public Health inspector Major Chas. E. Banks attributed the rapid spread of the disease not to any local conditions but to the climatic conditions prevalent at the time: "A long dry spell followed by high winds, creating dust storms. This resulted in infection of the respiratory membrane and affected all classes of pupils alike, irrespective of age, residence or occupation."[52] A similar epidemic had recently struck army camps in the vicinity, affecting 1,000 army personnel at Camp Funston, Kansas. Like the soldiers, the children complained about headache, sore throat, nausea, vomiting, chills, pains in the glands of the neck, and general lassitude.

Haskell's medical staff was completely overwhelmed by the large number of patients, and over the course of the epidemic, the school had to hire extra help from outside. Dr. Van Cleave, special physician in the Indian Service, Major Banks of the U.S. Public Health Service, two Lawrence doctors, five physicians from the Kansas State Board of Health, as well as the Kansas University Bacteriology Department, rendered their services and supported school physician Dr. Charles Ensign during this trying period. Also, "three additional trained nurses were secured and with Miss Cunningham and Miss Anderson, five nurses were in constant attendance, besides six to eight school nurse apprentices, insuring that the patients received every attention possible."[53]

Over the course of the two-week epidemic, 500 students (out of 750) were afflicted, and 207 of them were cared for in the school's hospital. The other children remained in the dormitories and occupied the sleeping porches. The school's regular work came to a complete stop while teachers and fellow students helped to care for the sick. Most children recovered after a few days of bed rest, but others had to stay in the hospital for up to three weeks. Several cases were serious, and twenty students developed streptococci pulmonitis, a severe illness similar to pneumonia. By early April, five students had died from the complications of this disease. Among them were fourteen-year-old Carrie Rice from the Sac and Fox Agency in Oklahoma and fifteen-year-old Mary Marshno, a Potawatomie student from Mayetta, Kansas. Mary's mother had come to Haskell and had cared for her daughter for a number of days preceding the girl's death, a circumstance that must have provided comfort to mother and child. Despite these losses, Superintendent Peairs felt that the epidemic had spared them the worst. He explained to Carlisle's superintendent, John Francis:

> It seemed hard to lose five children in such a short time, but considering the large number who were ill and also considering the results in Army camps and elsewhere, we feel that we have been very fortunate. Dr. Banks who was in very intimate touch with the epidemic at Camp Funston, gave us a splendid report. He said that the epidemic here was handled with care and skill and very satisfactory results; that the death rate in the camp was four or five times as great as here. In fact, we had only one death which seemed to be the direct result of the epidemic and three were indirectly, due to former illness. Some of them were from families where there had been Tuberculosis and some had weak hearts. One strong, hearty athletic boy, after a hard fight for life, succumbed.[54]

In October 1918, a second influenza epidemic hit the school, confining more than 200 children to their beds. As in the spring, there was a general shortage of medical personnel, and the school was forced to employ teachers, as well as female students from the University of Kansas, as nurses. Once again, several children developed serious cases of pneumonia, which claimed at least one student's life. The 1918 influenza epidemics did not just affect Indian schools and military camps but were ravaging across the United States, claiming lives in cities as well as on the reservations. Superintendent Peairs's letter to U.S. Indian Service inspector W. S. Coleman sheds a light on the horrible impact the epidemics could have on individual Indian families:

> No doubt you will remember Mr. Eastman whose boy died here. He came for his daughter today, who had been quite ill but who has almost entirely recovered now, and he told me that one of his married daughters and her three children died with the influenza and pneumonia and the child of another died from the same cause. His family has certainly been greatly afflicted.[55]

In December, a partial quarantine was declared at Haskell on account of the prevalence of Spanish Influenza in the vicinity. The school's leadership did not want to risk another epidemic at the school, and informed parents that their children would not be allowed to return home during the Christmas holidays nor would their parents or the students' friends be permitted to visit during that time. In the wake of another influenza epidemic in January 1920, which confined more than fifty students and several employees to the hospital, Haskell finally vaccinated the children with an influenza-pneumonia vaccine.[56]

Although epidemics like these were dramatic and put a great strain on the school's human, as well as financial resources, the chronic and constantly present diseases such as tuberculosis and trachoma posed the greatest risk to the children's health. Trachoma, an eye infection that was painful and difficult to cure, could lead to blindness; it afflicted large numbers of children in boarding schools across the country. Apart from being extremely painful, trachoma led to a fuzzy, blurred vision, which impacted the children's ability to read and consequently to follow their classroom lessons. Trachoma, or "sore eyes," was highly contagious, but all that doctors knew at the time was that a specific microorganism caused it. At first irritating and painful, characterized by secretion, granules on the inner eyelid, and ulcers and scarification on the cornea, trachoma leads to a partial loss of sight and, if untreated, can result in complete blindness.[57]

The level of infection among Haskell's student population was shockingly high. Like tuberculosis, trachoma spread rapidly in unsanitary and overcrowded conditions, and at times, almost half of Haskell's students suffered from the disease. During the 1900s, 1910s, and 1920s, the methods of treating trachoma were at best primitive. The method most often used was very painful and consisted of scraping or pinching the inflamed inner eyelid with small tongs, rinsing the eye with a solution of boric acid, and prolonged follow-up treatments, rubbing the eyelids with a copper sulfate stick.[58] Follow-up treatments were regarded as essential in the management of the disease. In order to guarantee the necessary aftercare, health officials encouraged boarding schools to retain their infected students as long as possible. Haskell's physician expressed this belief in his report to Superintendent Peairs: "With reference to Lena Bearskin; her general health is very good. She has granulated eyelids for which she is being treated and is slightly improving. She will need to be under treatment constantly for several months to get them in good condition. Unless her mother is located near some specialist or someone who can look after her eyes she had better leave her here."[59]

Despite the school's claim that trachoma could and would be treated effectively, inspection reports reveal that treatments were sporadic and that the success rate was low. During the 1910–1911 school year, Inspector Dr. Murphy recorded 148 cases of trachoma at Haskell, out of which only eight had been treated at all. This neglect was explained by the fact that the Indian Service relied on the work of a few field specialists to treat the disease and that during that particular year, this specialist had not been able to come to Haskell. To remedy the situation, Dr. Murphy recommended that "the trachoma work should be actively taken up by the physician at Haskell without waiting for further visits from the field specialists."[60] Two years later, the situation had not improved, though, and Superintendent Wise had to inform a worried South Dakota parent:

Dear Madam:

I have your letter of the 24th instant in regard to your daughter Elaine having trachoma. In reply you are advised that just now we have no school physician, our last one having been transferred to another branch of the Service. We expect a new physician here very soon and then we will find out whether he is able to treat the trachoma cases. . . . If Elaine has trachoma there is no occasion for either her or you being unduly anxious about it. Of course it is a serious trouble but all the authorities agree that it can be cured, although it takes prolonged and faithful treatment.[61]

During the summer of 1913, a special examination of the children revealed that the disease afflicted 43 percent of Haskell's students. Visiting physician W. E. Van Cleave observed: "Among the boys there were many chronic cases of long standing but very little visual damage was noted among these. Trachoma among the girls seemed much milder and of more recent origin."[62] Haskell made no effort to separate infected children from healthy ones. In fact, the school did not even hesitate to enroll students known to be afflicted with the disease. Superintendent Peairs explained to a Montana Indian agent that he was willing to enroll two girls with trachoma since "they have it only in a mild form."[63] When Dr. Van Cleave returned eighteen months later, he was finally able to report some improvements. Even though he still found 258 out of 704 students infected with the disease, in his view, this reduction from 43 percent to 36.6 percent signified a remarkable improvement. A 1917 health report revealed a further improvement of the situation, finding about 20 percent of the children affected with trachoma. According to the report, "the school physician and nurse are very energetic in their efforts to reduce this disease to a minimum, and are ably assisted by the pupil nurses. The girls present a lower incidence and are more faithful than the boys in coming for treatment."[64] Dr. Culp suggested that treatments should no longer be given on alternate days but every day except Sundays, since especially the boys tended to skip their Saturday treatments.

Even though over time trachoma treatments became more effective and the percentage of children infected declined, the disease continued to be a serious problem at Haskell for years to come, and Indian students were still being treated for trachoma in the 1940s.[65] Although trachoma was certainly the most serious and most painful eye disease affecting Haskell's students, other vision impairments also hindered the children's efforts to learn. A large number of Haskell's students had defective vision and were in need of glasses. If the children were not able to afford glasses, the government helped them pay the $3–5 for the exam, the frame, and the lenses.[66] Nevertheless, many children disliked wearing glasses and preferred to get by without them, a tendency that seriously impacted their classroom work. Sometimes, language problems could make it more difficult to determine whether a child actually needed glasses. In 1910, Superintendent Fiske reported on behalf of Shawnee student Frank Puckskino:

The doctor reports that Frank is totally blind in one eye. He is going to do everything that he can to save the other eye but he finds it very difficult to make an examination of Frank since Frank is unable to speak English intelligibly. Of course an occultist in making an examination has to go very largely by the test of letter reading and as Frank sometimes does not know how to say the letters the occultist cannot tell whether it is because he does not know how to say the letters or whether he cannot see them. I sent an interpreter with Frank today and shall do so at every future examination. This ought to facilitate the matter somewhat.[67]

Another health problem which affected the children's well-being was the serious condition of their teeth. When health inspector Dr. Van Cleave examined the school's 696 students in 1914, he found 2,660 simple cavities, 274 compound cavities requiring bridges or crowns, 109 pupils in need of extractions, 236 students who needed their teeth cleaned, and only 48 children without any dental problems. According to Dr. Van Cleave, the previous year only 5 percent of all necessary dental work had been performed:

> The dental work at Haskell has sadly been neglected. Mr. Wise takes the position that dental work is a personal matter and has allowed the pupils to use their own initiatives in the matter. He also thinks that for the Government to pay for any pupil's dental work would be establishing a serious precedent. To my mind, it would be just as criminal to allow a pupil to suffer from the stomachache because he had no funds as to make them go without dental relief for the same cause.[68]

In his report, Dr. Van Cleave criticized the suffering Superintendent Wise's policy caused for the students: "During the past four months I have seen several children come to the hospital from time to time suffering from dental caries, but who, on account of lack of funds were denied dental attention."[69] Dr. Van Cleave suggested "a general crusade for better dental conditions" and emphasized the need for a change in funding policy. In early 1917, Haskell was once again target of a government health inspection and Special Physician Dr. Culp criticized the students' lack of dental hygiene:

> It was reported to me that no toothbrushes have been furnished this school this year. Many pupils have supplied themselves. Perhaps 50% have no brushes. At any rate, those who have no brushes have very

unclean teeth, and in one school room in particular which is sort of clearing-house for miss-fits, in one class of 32 boys examined, 30 presented no evidence of ever having seen a tooth brush.[70]

As the discussion of tuberculosis, trachoma, dental work, and Haskell's general health conditions reveals, changes in the prevention and administration of health problems were slow to come about. Even though the school's leadership was aware of many of its own shortcomings, limited funds, inflexible bureaucratic procedures, carelessness, and apathy prevented Haskell from providing its students with the health care they deserved. The school's inability to take care of the children caused unnecessary suffering for Indian students and their families. In the end, Indian children paid a high price for their education: while at Haskell, many of them ruined their health and some even lost their lives. Haskell's school cemetery is a sad reminder of this truth. Until the 1920s, 102 children were buried at the east edge of the Haskell campus, their names, dates of birth and death, and their tribe engraved on four rows of identical markers. Haskell's intertribal character is reflected in the school's cemetery: children from thirty-seven tribes lie buried in the same earth. Ironically, despite the school's efforts to destroy the children's cultural heritage, the tombstones acknowledge the children's tribal identity.

During Haskell's first harsh winter in 1884–1885, ten children passed away, all due to pneumonia and lung ailments. The first child to die at the school was not a student, though, but six-month-old Harry White Wolf, a Cheyenne baby who was part of the Cheyenne and Arapaho party accompanying their children to school. The next five years proved to be disastrous. Conditions went from bad to worse, and by 1890, the population of the cemetery had grown to forty-nine. Short on funding, Haskell's first years were marked by terrible living conditions. In the 1890s, the situation slowly improved, and the death rate went down. Nevertheless, death continued to be an unsettling part of boarding school life.

Why were the children buried at Haskell? Some students died unexpectedly before their families could be notified, becoming the victims of inclement weather, bad communication systems, and inadequate transportation. Others were orphans without anyone to care about their death or their burial. Communication problems seemed to have been a major reason for the children's burial at the school. The usual route of communication was from the school's superintendent to the reservation agent, who was responsible for passing on messages to the children's families. This system did not always work as intended, however. There were delays and miscommunications, and Haskell's records show that there were tragic instances when messages were not delivered at all. The school's records contain handwritten notes from families who, weeks after death and burial, pleaded for news or asked for the body of the child to be returned. It must have been every parent's most terrible nightmare to receive these belated news:

Dear Sir:

I am very sorry to have to report to you that your son Arleigh passed away today at about half after 1 o'clock. He had been sick two weeks altogether. He did not report to me the first day of his sickness. He was taken with a chill and thought it was a light matter, but after 24 hours found it more serious and came to the hospital when I found that he had a well-developed attack of pneumonia. The case, while severe, ran its regular course. The fever finally left him about three days ago, and I had strong hope that he would recover. It seems, however, that the damage to the lung and to his constitution generally, was so great that he had not sufficient strength to tide over and throw off the fluid in the lungs. He was restless last evening, but quite hopeful. This morning however, the case was looking more serious and about the middle of forenoon it became certainty that he could not last very long as he was unable to raise the secretions as they accumulated in the air passage. I wired you this morning by way of South McAllister, care of Frank Arnold. Unless we receive notice from you differently, we shall pursue our usual custom and bury him here some time tomorrow. Lizzie [the boy's sister] has been by him throughout his sickness and he has had every attention that could be given to a sick boy, and in his latter sickness has talked about his faith that reached beyond the grave and took hold of a living Savior.[71]

Arleigh Perry was nineteen years old when he died at Haskell. The boy was buried at the school cemetery, depriving his family of any opportunity to observe Ojibwe funeral customs. According to Ojibwe historian Brenda Child, to have children buried long distances from home was greatly distressing to Ojibwe families, since they "held wakes and burials for children and adults that involved the ceremonies of preparing food and new clothing for the deceased, and of burning fires for many nights near a new grave. Ojibwes built grave houses where they offered wild rice, maple sugar, or other traditional foods throughout the year."[72] Boarding schools not only separated children from their families and cultures while they were alive; they sometimes even kept them apart in death.

At Haskell, children died from tuberculosis and pneumonia; from malaria, meningitis, typhoid fever; and from all kinds of accidents. The latter were common at the school, bearing testimony to the children's dangerous work environment. In 1903, Oneida student Sophie Webster seriously injured her hand in the laundry, by having it "caught and mashed in a Mangle, by which she lost all the fingers of that hand leaving but a mere stump of the body of the hand."[73] Similarly, in 1910, Navajo student Pahhe Yazza lost his left hand in the carpenter shop, when it was drawn into the planer and crushed "so that it was impossible to save any part of it."[74] While these accidents were debilitating, others were deadly. In 1902, nineteen-year-old Wyandotte student Charles Quain died of a sunstroke while working in the fields. That same summer, Lomo Congwhio from Keams Canyon, Arizona, died from a heart rupture he experienced while carrying lumber. In 1908, ten-year-old Lakota student Tom Little Wolf died by coming in contact with a live electric wire on the roof of one of the lavatory buildings, and in 1909, nineteen-year-old Roy Spybuck died during a football accident. In 1911, a runaway team killed Minnesota student James Reece in a farm accident.[75] That same year, two boys from southeastern Oklahoma, Christian Tehee, Cherokee, and Callis Peter, Choctaw, ran away from Haskell. The boys were apparently headed south toward home, when sixteen-year-old Christian was severely injured by a freight train. The boy died shortly after at St. Margaret's Hospital in Kansas City, Kansas.[76]

The fear of accidents was one of the reasons why school administrators and parents alike were deeply concerned about deserting students. Distances were far, and the children were exposed to many dangers. Boys jumped trains as a means of transportation, and there were stories about children freezing to death during the winter months. It appears that boys were much more prone to be the victims of serious accidents than girls, a circumstance that can be attributed to the nature of the boys' daily work details and the greater freedom they enjoyed. Of the 102 children buried at Haskell, more than 70 percent were boys. Although accidents happened frequently and were especially tragic, the main causes for the children's deaths were diseases such as tuberculosis and pneumonia, which were in many cases directly related to the students' unhealthy living conditions. The youngest students buried in Haskell's cemetery were six and seven years of age. Most students, however, died in their teenage years; the average age of the children buried at the school was sixteen.

To the school community, the death of a student was a traumatic experience, especially when the child was popular and socially active. Children and teachers mourned for their deceased friends and pupils. When eighteen-year-old Cherokee Peter Tanner died in 1915, the *Indian Leader* ran the following obituary:

> Peter Tanner smiled for 18 1/2 years. Then one day he passed to the place prepared for him by his Master. And all Haskell sorrowed. For Pete was the cheeriest boy to be found anywhere. Everybody was his friend; he was a friend to everybody. He was always happy, and ought to have been. Young, strong, clean; a true Christian. Yes; a true Christian. A conscientious student, his teachers say. A willing worker, the carpenters tell us—for Pete was learning to be a carpenter. And a good playmate; the very best. When the big football teams sent an avalanche of interference around his end he dumped 'em with his short, muscular body, and crawled from beneath the pile smiling. He was a good brother to his one sister, Nancy; they were orphans together. He joined the church a year ago, and he always had his shoulder under the Y.M.C.A. Pete was a full-blood Cherokee, born July 3, 1897, at Vinita, Oklahoma. He came to Haskell in 1913. It was his first year on the varsity. For two weeks he played very little, because his ear, which had hurt him for a long time, grew worse. Meningitis developed Sunday, November 7, and the next morning he was unconscious. Forty-eight hours later he died without regaining his consciousness, without knowing his intense suffering.[77]

Peter was remembered as an exceptional boy, whose unexpected death deeply saddened the school community. Peter's obituary pays homage to an all-American boy whose death was considered especially tragic because he "played by the rules." Peter personified the ideal propagated by Indian educators: an Indian who lived, played, and worked like a white boy.

Life at Haskell was by no means easy. The boarding school environment was neither healthy nor safe, and Indian families experienced great anxieties while their children attended the school. Haskell's administrators alienated parents by failing to maintain open communications about their children's health and repeatedly broke the trust that Indian families and communities had put into them by leaving their children in the school's care. In the early 1920s, Commissioner of Indian Affairs Charles Burke initiated an investigation of Indian health conditions, which was conducted by Florence Patterson, an experienced public health nurse. Her report revealed the saddening truth of boarding school life:

> This program, combined with the strain of bells, bugles, and horns, forming in line five or six times each day, and the mental struggle to combat physical fatigue, could not fail to be exhausting, and the effects were apparent in every group of boarding school pupils and in marked contrast to the freedom and alertness of the pupils in the day schools. One gained the impression that the boarding school child must endure real torture by being continually "bottled up" and that he somehow never enjoyed the freedom of being a perfectly natural child. One longed to sweep aside his repressions and to find the child. As a small child he had undergone a terrific shock in adjusting himself to the school life and routine so difficult from any previous experience in his life. Again, after several years of non-reservation boarding school life, he would have to face a similar shock in returning to reservation life, from which every effort had been made to wean him.[78]

Although Patterson criticized the schools' harsh living conditions, her description of the boarding school experience goes far beyond an indictment of unhealthy physical circumstances. Rather, her critique identified an environment in which Indian children suffered great emotional stress while trying to survive the government's assault on their bodies as well as on their cultural identities.

CHAPTER SEVEN

Accommodation and Resistance

Wapanucka, Ok, December 17, 1918

Dear Sir:

    I am very sorry of what I done. I can see the great opportunity I am missing. I think I have two more years there, if you will accept me back. I hope you will forgive, and give me another chance. I have made up my mind to get down to business. I would be very glad if you would let me know whether I can come to school or not, I am ready to come any time.

    Yours truly, Edward Whale[1]

Superintendent Peairs granted the boy's wish, and Edward Whale (pseudonym) returned to Haskell with the promise to "do better." Half a year later, however, the Choctaw boy deserted for a second time.[2] Edward Whale's story exemplifies the internal struggles thousands of Indian students faced in their attempt to cope with the harsh realities of boarding school life, during which they were torn between the urge to resist and the desire to accommodate. Like hundreds of other children, the boy resisted Haskell's regimentation by running away, but later came to regret his actions. He returned to the school voluntarily, showing his willingness to adapt to Haskell's routine and "play by the rules."

    The relationship between superiors and subordinates is frequently characterized by an institutionalized system to expropriate labor, services, and goods from the subordinate group. Ideologies justifying domination emphasize the inferiority of the subordinate group and generate rituals and practices of insult, denigration, and assaults on the body that take away from the dignity and autonomy of the dominated individuals and infuse the relationship with an element of personal terror. Etiquette or certain rituals that support the superiority of the dominant group regulate public contact between the groups, that is, the *public transcript*. Control over the subordinate group is never total, however, and subordinates have at least a limited social existence outside the immediate control of their superiors that allows a shared critique of domination, the *hidden transcript,* to develop.[3]

This pattern also holds true for boarding school students, who recall nightly gatherings in the dormitories when they spoke their native languages, told Indian stories, ate stolen food, and shared their experiences concerning teachers, matrons, and boarding school life in general. The school grounds provided another location where students could at least temporarily exchange ideas freely, without intrusion from their superiors. At Haskell, students found multiple ways to escape from the watchful eyes of their superiors. Esther Burnett recalled how students "were given demerits for sloppy detail work, loitering in the halls on our way to class, crawling out on top of the dormitory to sun, sneaking around to meet the boys in the orchard or bakery, going to the Shack [a little off-campus store closely supervised by school personnel] without permission, or swearing. Boys and girls would sometimes meet in the apple orchard for visiting and socializing."[4]

The school's orchard figures prominently in countless communications about the students' wrongdoings, and several students were expelled for sneaking out there at night. Haskell's boys enjoyed more freedom than the girls and regularly roamed the school's farm and the nearby wetlands. Areas near the Wakarusa River were out of the direct reach of the school's disciplinarians, providing a playground for the children as well as a meeting place for family reunions. According to Haskell professor Chuck Haines, the wetlands served an important spiritual function:

> As the children grew up at Haskell, they identified with the Wakarusa River and the flooding, which occurred yearly. From the basis of many remarks of elders about Haskell and the children who survived the early years, the symbol which most typified their spirit and identity was the Wakarusa River and its yearly flooding that the government was unable to stop or control. The river humbled the staff. The river and floodwaters stood as a symbolic representation of the children's spiritual power. The river was

also the place where Mother Earth could listen to their silent prayers and teach their identity as Indian people. The river and the children are forever linked in an embrace of spiritual connections, a connection that the boarding school and the brutal treatment could not break or sever.[5]

In 1908, several local farmers complained to the school that Haskell boys trespassed on their property while hunting and that they were guilty of disturbing livestock and stealing fruit from the farmers' orchards. According to Special U.S. Indian Agent McConihe, "Saturday and Sunday after dinner they are allowed to roam at will. . . . I find that but few of the boys possess a gun and I have suggested to the Superintendent that he take away from the boys their guns and allow them to hunt only when they go to the disciplinarian and register and say where they are going." During the summer, the boys used a cornfield north of the school grounds "for smoking purposes and I have seen them day after day climbing fences and returning. The school authorities are fully cognizant of this state of affairs but have not taken active measures to suppress them this year."[6] The described hunting and smoking excursion allowed Indian boys to escape from the school's constant surveillance and to create a space outside of the realm of the school's domination.

The school took a clear stance against tobacco and alcohol, even though the use of these substances was almost impossible to control. Superintendent Peairs lamented: "Indian boys, or at least a great many of them, learn to use tobacco when they are mere children; therefore, when they come to school, it is a very hard matter for them to break away from the habit."[7] Smoking and the use of snuff were common among the male students, and Haskell's medical personnel vehemently objected to the harmful effects of these substances. To many boys, though, the use of tobacco might have had cultural significance, serving as a means of indigenous cultural preservation as well as an expression of personal choice and freedom. In the eyes of the school, the consumption of alcohol constituted a much more serious breach of the rules. If caught intoxicated or in the possession of alcoholic beverages, Indian students faced serious consequences, including expulsion from the school. Haskell's records provide ample evidence that the boys smuggled alcohol onto the school grounds and that many students drank when they were out on the town. Despite laws prohibiting the sale of alcohol, it appears to have been easy for the boys to buy liquor.[8] Haskell's administrators were worried not only about the students' substance abuse but also about their use of profane language and gambling. When a seventeen-year-old Choctaw student ran away from the school in September 1917, he justified his action on the grounds that Haskell was an "immoral" environment, harmful to his business education. In his affidavit, Clarence Thomas stated:

> I considered the influence of the school detrimental to me. Between classes there was continual gambling among the students and cursing going on on the grounds and in the rooms among the boys and continual playing of cards and craps and boasting of secret drinking among the students. And the use of Copenhagen snuff among the boys was very obnoxious to me and I felt that I could not do good work because of the habits of my associates.[9]

Superintendent Peairs dismissed these words as the "exaggerated statement of a deserter who is trying to make an excuse for leaving the school without permission."[10] At the same time, though, Peairs admitted that under the previous administration of Superintendent Wise, discipline had been lax, and the use of rough language, as well as occasional gambling, had been reported. A similar critique came from Lucille Abert, who attended Carlisle before coming to Haskell in 1918: "Haskell would be a nice school if we only had some nice employees that would make the girls mind.... The discipline here is terrible. The children almost run the employees instead of them running us. Some of them are just like wild animals."[11] Although Lucille Abert's letter was motivated by her homesickness for Carlisle, her perception of Haskell's girls as lacking discipline suggests that the school's control over the children was far from total. Peairs's crusade against temptations lurking in the town of Lawrence supports this impression: "Another evil, which needs attention, is the pool hall situation. Our boys flock to the pool halls when they go to town on Saturday afternoons and I am convinced that the influences, in some of them at least, are the worst in Lawrence. I wish something could be done to, at least, control such places."[12]

It is clear that Indian boys engaged in behaviors that were not tolerated by Haskell's administrators and went against the Christian behavior and morality taught at the school. At the same time, though, the school failed to control these activities. The boys sneaked out at night to meet with girls, hunted, roamed the surrounding farms, smoked, drank, used profane language, gambled, and visited "immoral" establishments in town. All these activities gave boys an opportunity to bond with each other and to develop their own boarding school culture away from their superiors' supervision. This freedom, however limited, allowed them to develop a shared critique of their domination and a shared identity as indigenous people in a federal Indian boarding school. Although the boys' behavior contained strong elements of resistance, it can also be interpreted as a way to accommodate: by creating a space of their own, the boys formed an environment for themselves, which made the boarding school experience bearable and at times even enjoyable.

For girls, the opportunities to escape from the watchful eyes of the matrons were more limited. Some girls did sneak out at night or left the school grounds without permission, but most girls' private space was limited to their dormitories and the greens and playgrounds adjacent to the school buildings. Once unsupervised, however, students would use their native languages, tell each other tribal stories, teach their friends about their tribal customs, and eat food they had smuggled from the bakery or the kitchen. Esther Burnett recalled that when she first came to Haskell, she considered herself a follower: "I racked up my share of demerits by getting into a great deal of mischief. I was really seeking to belong to a group, and one way of doing that was through resisting the structure imposed on us there."[13] Belonging to a group was extremely important in an environment devoid of traditional family, tribal, and community structures. Boarding school students formed close relationships and subcultures on the basis of age group, gender, tribal affiliation, and social activities; doing so allowed the children to survive boarding school as part of protective and nurturing support groups.[14] Communal resistance deepened those bonds and strengthened the children's identities as Indians in an environment dominated by whites. Burnett's interpretation of her own resistance reinforces the argument that subordinate groups create a hidden transcript, a shared critique of their domination, that stands in sharp opposition to the school's "public transcript."

One girl recalled that being at Haskell actually helped her to preserve the Ojibwe language: "Well, it was not encouraged but we did talk Indian when we were in the dormitory or at physical culture class. My sisters who stayed at home and didn't go to Indian school actually lost their language, because my mother didn't use it around them. I never did lose my language, and I use it to this day."[15] For many students who came from mixed-blood families and had not grown up on a reservation, Haskell provided an environment more "Indian" than anything they had previously experienced. The school exposed them to a multitude of tribal cultures, which, rather than destroying their sense of being Indian, helped to increase their ethnic awareness. Although boarding schools contributed to the destruction of Indian cultures in several ways, they also provided an environment for the rise of a larger Indian identity that transcended tribal boundaries. Friendships and supratribalism fed and in turn were fed by resistance, which was a reaction to the foreign, regimented, and confining lifestyle at boarding school.[16] Arapaho student Jesse Rowlodge recalled that during the early 1900s, students shared information about their respective tribal cultures and that the school failed in controlling their use of native languages. Osage student Otis Russell, a school friend of Rowlodge, remembered bonding with students from other tribes: "I stayed with them boys all the time. Arapaho Indian, bunch of them . . . [and] Cheyennes from down near Arapaho. So, I slept with them too. And they had a gourd, they'd sing peyote songs. That's where I learn peyote songs. I know 'em all. . . . That's how I learned to sing Arapaho and Cheyenne songs."[17]

Otis Russell's recollections demonstrate that students secretly performed Indian rituals at Haskell and that they continued to practice at least some aspects of their indigenous religions while at school. Acts of cultural preservation and cultural construction can be observed in the girls' language practice as well as in the boys' nightly meetings. Starting in the 1880s, the peyote religion attracted thousands of followers in Oklahoma, the Great Plains, the Great Lakes region, and the Southwest. Peyote meetings were characterized by a blend of indigenous and Christian spirituality, the endorsement of community and family values, and a strong sense of intertribal unity. Many Indian leaders at the time endorsed the new religion owing to its positive influence on Indian families and communities and its counterbalancing force against the widespread use of alcohol. According to ethnologist Omer C. Stewart, "peyotism has been a unifying influence in American Indian life, providing the basis for Indian friendships, rituals, social gatherings, travel, marriage, and more. It has been a source of comfort and healing and a means of expression for a troubled people. And it has resulted in one of the strongest pan-Indian movements in the United States."[18] As expressions of supratribal beliefs and spirituality, peyotism and the Native American Church found many adherents among Haskell's diverse student population. Peyote meetings were a unique and innovative form of gatherings that reflected the new social and cultural realities the children faced. The Native American Church, which was incorporated in Oklahoma in 1918, offered students models for behavior and beliefs that fit into their changing world view and reflected the fusion of cultures the children experienced at school and on the reservations. Many students embraced peyotism because it offered them a form of spirituality that was deeply rooted in Indian traditions while at the same time helping them to find answers to the complexities of modern life. At the same time, participating in peyote ceremonies or becoming a member in the Native American Church did not rule out being active in a Christian denomination or attending tribal ceremonies back home. Rather, peyotism allowed an educated, English-speaking boarding school generation to combine the old and the new, native traditions and Christian teachings, tribal identity and pan-Indian ideas. It provided a ceremony where the Christian ideals learned at school could be celebrated in a setting that was familiar and indigenous.[19] Peyote ceremonies had a strong spiritual, mental, and physical healing dimension, and participants gained emotional strength from prayers, songs, and the use of peyote.[20]

By the time Haskell was founded, peyote ceremonies already played an important role in the life of many Oklahoma tribes and the religion quickly spread across the Plains and the western United States. As Otis Russell's recollections show, Cheyenne and Arapaho students from Oklahoma shared their knowledge of peyote songs with students from other parts of the country. Being able to converse among each other in English and sharing similar religious experiences at school certainly facilitated the adoption of peyote rituals into the students' lives. Whether students held actual peyote ceremonies using the plant on campus or along the nearby Wakarusa River is difficult to say. It is certain, though, that they talked about the new religion, shared their knowledge, practiced peyote songs, and used gourd rattles to accompany their singing.[21] It is also reasonable to assume that peyote found its way onto Haskell's campus as the students' individual protective fetish, since this was a common use of the plant.[22]

Whether they learned about the use of peyote at school or at home, hundreds of former students eventually adopted the new religion. Many of Haskell's alumni became leading figures in the Native American Church, determining the course of peyotism for decades to come.[23] Jesse Rowlodge, for instance, became an active peyotist and took part in meetings of the newly chartered Native American Church of the United States in the early 1950s.[24] At Haskell, indigenous cultures were not only destroyed or forgotten but also learned, changed, and transmitted.

Patterns of resistance displayed by subordinate populations have certain characteristics in common. The dominated usually do not dare to question their subordination in public. Among themselves, however, they create a social space in which offstage dissent to the official transcript of power relations may be voiced.[25] Domination creates a hegemonic public conduct that stands in opposition to the discourses among subordinates but that tends to be reinforced by the dominated. Out of mere self-protection, powerless groups have a strong interest in reinforcing hegemonic appearances.[26] This display of public consent should, however, not be interpreted as a proof of the subordinates' acceptance of the social arrangements that reproduce their subordination.[27]

For many Indian students that certainly held true, since on a daily basis, strict discipline and the mere threat of punishment kept the children in line. The avoidance of punishment led to creative ways of coping with an extremely restrictive lifestyle while it drew the students closer together, creating subcultures within the boarding school system. If students were caught breaking the rules, however, penalties were swift and harsh. Students recall being beaten, locked up in the school's jail, or detailed to humiliating and exhausting work details, such as working on the rock pile or scrubbing floors. When their violations were less serious, they were denied the right to participate in the school's social activities and other special privileges. Esther Burnett recalled being punished rather harshly for a minor prank:

> My chum, Rose LaFromboise, and I had decided to pose as flappers with rolled-down hose and hiked up hickories. We rolled up white papers to look like cigarettes and stuck them in the corner of our mouths so that we would appear to be worldly, and then we got a friend to photograph us in this pose. Not only did the matron, Miss Ritter, confiscate our treasured pictures, but we were also made to march around the flagpole for a couple of hours with a broomstick over our shoulders. That was our punishment to work off the demerits that we received for the prank.[28]

Esther Burnett's recollection shows how a small breach of the rules could result in a demeaning punishment that inflicted physical pain as well as embarrassment. Parents and students alike resisted the school's harsh punishments and frequently denounced them. Although some students accepted their punishment as deserved, others complained that they were treated unjustly. As one Ojibwe girl recalled:

Well, I was always being punished, and I think the matron just looked at me first and thought I was somebody else. Ever hear somebody say, "All Indians look alike to me, I can't tell them apart"? Well, we did all have the same clothes and the same haircuts and the same glasses. I was always scrubbing stairs and floors as punishment, and finally I made an appointment to talk to the superintendent, and I told him that if that's all I was going to be doing at school, I would just as soon go home and do that for my mother, because she could use my help.[29]

Walking around the flagpole, scrubbing floors, and being excluded from town visits were unpleasant experiences, but more serious offenses such as sneaking out at night or getting into arguments with the staff could result in the most severe punishments, such as whippings, lengthy confinement, or expulsion from the school.

Parents frequently complained to the school about their children's maltreatment. In 1907, William Smith, father of two children at Haskell, received a letter from his daughter Amelia, telling him that she was having a very nice time at Haskell and that she very much liked her new teacher. She added, however, that her "brother does not like Haskell anymore because they whip him too much . . . and they always punished him for nothing . . . so that is what is making my brother lonesome."[30] The worried father wrote to Superintendent Peairs: "I thought I would write to you to let you know that my boy get so much whipping and I want to know if you can stop it. If you cannot stop it sent him home."[31] In reply, William Smith received the following lines: "Dear Sir: I wish to acknowledge the receipt of your letter of the 5th instant, and assure you that your boy will not be mistreated."[32]

It seems unlikely that such a general statement would have sufficed to appease parents worried about their child's possible maltreatment. Many parents were shocked to learn that their children had been victims of corporal punishment or solitary confinement. Obviously, the standards as to what constituted acceptable punishment differed between the school and the parents as well as across cultures. Although some parents supported the school in their disciplinary measures, many others asked the staff to be more lenient and to try to reason with the children instead of locking them up or beating them. The school, however, insisted that strict discipline could only be maintained if the threat of severe punishment was credible.

To prove this point, Haskell operated a guardhouse or jail, which was still in operation in 1928, when the Meriam Report condemned the use of jail punishment at boarding schools across the nation. During his 1908 health inspection of Haskell, Dr. Joseph Murphy noted: "The jail is a small poorly lighted, old converted ice house, and unless kept well aired and clean soon becomes a dangerous place for pupils to be confined. There were on one occasion seven prisoners confined there, groups of two chained together, one of the seven a pupil in Class Three [tubercular]."[33] Asked by the commissioner of Indian affairs to clarify Dr. Murphy's report, Haskell's disciplinarian, J. O. Milligan, explained:

> I had confined seven boys November 18, for drunkenness and defying authority. They made an attempt to break out, and were chained together by twos until repairs could be made for safe keeping. A guard was also placed over them. Concerning the boy in Class Three, will say that he had not been examined until after he was released. . . . The guard house is used only in the most serious cases of discipline.[34]

In his report to the commissioner, Superintendent Peairs added:

> Mr. Milligan is generally very careful in matters of discipline and I feel confident that it was only to meet the emergency that such strenuous measures were adopted. As soon as I learned of the fact I had the chains removed.[35]

Ten years later, however, Peairs denied any knowledge of students being put in chains. In 1917, he wrote to Commissioner Cato Sells:

> I cannot remember personally about a ball and chain ever having been used during those years. I do remember that in the early years of the institution, probably back in the 90's, such punishment was resorted to occasionally, but only in the most extreme cases. . . . I certainly do not believe in harsh or brutal methods of discipline.[36]

This last statement seems ironic, considering the overbearing evidence that corporal punishment was exercised regularly and that Peairs himself had been involved in a serious case of physical maltreatment. Before becoming superintendent, Peairs had been employed as Haskell's disciplinarian. In the early summer of 1887, Peairs was accused of breaking the leg of student John Yellow Bear. When an investigation revealed that the "break" was in reality "just" a sprain, the commissioner of Indian affairs decided that Peairs's employment did not have to be terminated as originally requested, and Peairs remained closely associated with Haskell for another four decades.[37]

In 1910, a new three-room guardhouse was constructed. According to Superintendent Wise, "the structure is of brick, stone and concrete, with concrete floors, and is perfectly sanitary and fire proof. It is about twenty feet square, one story, and is well lighted and ventilated."[38] The new jail was used frequently, especially during the spring months, when desertions became an even greater problem than during the remainder of the school year. According to Superintendent Wise, with the advent of warm weather, the boys showed "signs of becoming unsettled, a sort of spring fever," making it necessary to confine offenders "from ten to thirty days."[39] Girls were usually not locked up in the school's guardhouse but in confinement rooms located in their dormitories. Sometimes they had to stay in solitary confinement for several days; in other cases they were allowed to go to school and their work details during the day but were locked up at night to make sure that they would not sneak out. While in confinement, the students received reduced meal rations, consisting of bread (hardtack) and water.

In 1922, Montana student Anna McKiver was severely punished for running away as well as for being disobedient and "climbing out of windows, leading other girls to do the same, in order to meet boys."[40] Anna, who was eventually expelled from Haskell, complained bitterly about her treatment. According to a friend,

> She was put in the dungeon for 8 days. She was only fed twice a day, she had only her nightgown on, the place is very small; without a ray of light, and the only air was what comes in around cracks of the door. Anna says the hot water pipes made it so hot she had to lay on the floor with her mouth as near the crack of the door for breath of air. The whole time she was in there she was given no water in which to wash and her slop jar was emptied only once a day.[41]

Ironically, while denying Anna's charges of maltreatment as "very greatly exaggerated," Peairs's explanation of the case bears testimony to the abusive methods Haskell used to control its students:

She was never punished in any way that would endanger her health or injure her and her story about the dungeon is very greatly exaggerated. The room which was used to confine her so that she could not see or have any communication with other pupils is a dark room made so purposely because, as long as such students as Anna can have communication with other students, confining them does no good but when the confinement is solitary confinement and they cannot have any communication whatever, we have found that it has a wonderful effect and within a very short time any girl, or any girl for whom there is any hope of reformation, finds herself and is made to realize that she has brought punishment upon herself.[42]

Peairs stated the school's philosophy very clearly: to conquer in order to save. Although many students gave up their resistance in face of such overwhelming force, eight days in solitary confinement did not suffice to break Anna's will. The girl resisted throughout her ordeal and finally left Haskell. But cases like Anna McKiver's were the exception rather than the rule, and in general students obeyed the school regulations and tried to avoid harsh punishment.

The hidden transcript can also be examined without direct access to the discourse of subordinate groups, since it is expressed, albeit in disguised form, through folktales, songs, gestures, rumors, gossip, jokes, theater, and the like. The following poem by Navajo boarding school students gives us a rare insight into the weapons of the weak:

> If I do not believe you
> The things you say,
> Maybe I will not tell you
> That is my way.
> Maybe you think I believe you
> That thing you say,
> But always my thoughts stay with me
> My own way.[43]

At Haskell, for many years students used the daily prayer at mealtime as an opportunity to subvert the school's authority. Whenever the children were expected to chant a blessing, it led to "more or less disturbance, because in some of the farther corners of the room pupils were likely to make a joke of the chant rather than to do it in earnest." Eventually, the blessing was changed to a silent blessing, during which the children had to bow their heads for a minute or two before eating.[44] The poem, as well as the children's appropriation of Haskell's prayer routine, exemplifies patterns of ideological insubordination that went along with expressions of material insubordination through everyday forms of resistance such as poaching, evasion, foot-dragging, pilfering, and flight. It is in the realm of the hidden transcript that we find the origins of new political forces and demands that might germinate into more open, elaborate, and institutional forms of political life. It would be a mistake to discard the hidden political terrain of subordinate groups as "apolitical." The political environment of the weak lies between motionlessness and revolt, in the low-profile, disguised, and undeclared resistance that is confined to informal networks such as family, friends, neighborhood, and community that provide the cover as well as the structure for it.[45]

Nevertheless, the described forms of insubordination are "real politics" in the face of repression and persecution through which powerless groups can gain or lose real political ground. They create subcultures of resistance that give back to the powerless a sense of dignity and hope. Indian boarding school students developed many ways of resisting their victimization, strategies that allowed them to retain their dignity, some degree of freedom, and a positive sense of themselves in a system that they felt they could not substantially change. The forms of resistance described above made boarding school life psychologically bearable and in some instances even agreeable, as many positive recollections of boarding school alumni illustrate. The children certainly derived emotional gratification from subverting the order imposed on them, even if only in petty ways.[46] It is within the students' hidden transcript that counterhegemonic discourses and dreams were being formulated, always threatening to become a reality.[47] To counter this possibility, the school tried to create the appearance of consent and unanimity among staff and students, minimizing the students' opportunities for unauthorized collective action. The unsupervised or "idle" times, for instance, were kept to a minimum. The free association of students of different ages and different sexes was limited as much as possible and usually restricted to formal occasions such as school celebrations and supervised social dances. Haskell's parades and public celebrations are examples of authorized gatherings that convey unity and discipline under a single authority and that banish any evidence of divisions, disorder, lack of discipline, and informality from the public platform. In reality, however, this idealized state of total domination was rarely encountered by school authorities and was compromised by the very forms of resistance under discussion.

Students often went to the limits of the permissible, testing out how far they could go without facing severe punishment. They resisted through pranks and acts of cultural preservation and through their refusal to participate in school lessons and work details as well as through the act of running away. Sometimes, students even committed crimes such as arson, selling alcohol, forging checks, and stealing from fellow students or from stores and citizens in town. Although the records do not indicate any known case of arson at Haskell, the threat of such an act loomed large in Indian educators' minds. "Mysterious" fires were common throughout the school service, and reports of actual student involvement from schools such as Carlisle increased that fear. The Indian Service prosecuted offenders with full force. In 1905, two Menominee girls who had burned down their reservation boarding school were sentenced to life in prison at the penitentiary in Leavenworth, Kansas. The story was widely circulated in school newspapers as a warning to those children who might have contemplated similar acts.[48] The *Indian Leader* frequently ran stories intended to convey the message to Haskell's students that arsonists would pay a heavy price for their crimes.

When a portion of a Haskell school building burned down in 1907, the school started a thorough investigation into the possible causes of the fire, and Superintendent Peairs voiced his suspicion that arson might be involved:

> A few days after the fire . . . a boy, who was on duty, at night with the watchman, at the time of the fire, deserted. I have been trying to locate him and I have just within a few days gotten hold of a letter which indicates that he may be at Chilocco. . . . The fact that he deserted a few days after the fire and that he was on night duty and that he has assumed a different name, makes one rather suspicious.[49]

Although there is no evidence that the boy had actually committed arson, the story illustrates that Haskell's leadership was very much aware of the possibility and eager to follow up any leads that might uncover a dangerous crime.

Most crimes students committed, however, were of a less serious nature. Boys got into trouble more frequently than girls and were often caught fighting among each other. Girls were more often reprimanded for minor offenses such as "immoral behavior," staying out late, taking things from their fellow students, or being rude to the matrons or teachers. In 1920, "as a matter of discipline," Pawnee student Sara Baxter (pseudonym) was denied the privilege of going home in the summer. According to Superintendent Peairs, "Sara had trouble with Mrs. Daly, one of the domestic science teachers during my absence recently. I have not learned all of the circumstances, but I know that she was very much wrong, because she struck Mrs. Daly which is, of course, a very serious offense for any student. She has been punished since the incident occurred, and it was thought that she was really sorry for her conduct." When the girl returned late from a picnic a few days later, however, she further jeopardized her standing and forfeited the privilege of spending the summer at home. Peairs noted: "Sara is not a bad girl, but she has gotten to the point where she needs to be straightened up, and I want to keep her here just a little while to have an opportunity to allow her to prove to me that she intends to be a good girl."[50]

Attacking a teacher was a rare occurrence though. More commonly, children showed their dissatisfaction through a lack of interest in their chores or schoolwork and through general disobedience. In 1923, Shoshone student Vina Cleveland was dropped from Haskell's roll owing to her lack of interest and her disobedience. Vina, who had been an exceptionally well-adjusted student back at the Shoshone Boarding School in Wyoming, did not adapt to life in her new surroundings and failed to obey Haskell's rules. The girl showed up late to formations, took a box of face powder from another girl without permission, and eventually ran away from the school. Vina's case is interesting since the correspondence between Haskell and the agency reveals that the girl was "one of the best girls" in her Wyoming school, "never making . . . any trouble and doing all she could to obey all the rules and regulations."[51] Obviously, Vina did not enjoy being at Haskell and resisted her new school in every way possible. Even though she seems to have liked being in school on the Shoshone reservation, it appears that the girl was not willing or able to make the same adjustments in her new environment.

When Margaret Tarbell was expelled in 1920, Superintendent Peairs informed the girl's father:

> I am very sorry to have to report to you the reason for sending your daughter, Margaret home. Ever since she has been enrolled at this school she has shown a disposition to be disloyal, insubordinate and unappreciative

of what the government is doing in the way of offering an opportunity to get an education.[52]

Margaret, who was upset by Peairs's letter to her father, replied to the superintendent:

> I am herby returning your kind letter about me in this return mail, I sincerely hope it will help you along in your business at Haskell. You could not have done anything better for me than to allow me come home. There's no regret whatever about me returning to my home. I can easily get along without a Diploma. This letter which you wrote did no good for anyone so I think maybe it will for you.[53]

In her letter, Margaret took the opportunity to express her deep resentment toward Superintendent Peairs and his actions. Having been expelled already, the girl no longer had to abide by the protocol of power relations or hide her true feelings behind the hidden transcript. Once away from the school, Margaret felt comfortable denouncing Haskell and its leadership.

Indian children frequently expressed their dissatisfaction to their parents as well as to teachers, school administrators, and Indian Service employees in Washington. They complained about their treatment in oral as well as in written form, utilizing the very form of communication taught to them at school. In general, students' complaints were not taken very seriously by school officials, and in most cases, they were simply dismissed as unreasonable and unfounded. Parents, on the other hand, took their children's criticism of Haskell much more seriously and frequently wrote to the school in order to find out whether the complaints were justified. Since the school was eager to uphold its dominance over students and parents alike, parents were often treated in a condescending and paternalistic manner, which in turn infuriated a number of parents, leading to angry exchanges of letters. In 1888, a dissatisfied student, writing home to complain about a lack of shoes and her heavy work in the laundry, asked her parents for permission to leave Haskell. The girl's angry father wrote to Superintendent Robinson:

> She is My Own Flesh and Blood, now think if you had in like conditions, what would you do. Intended to go today after her, but have not. I did not send Her there to be an Irish washerwoman. She is Indian Blood, the more the pity. The Indians have been kicked from east to West, and North

to South and penned up in this little place, and now it seems that the wish is to kick them into Ether world. . . . I shall try your School a short time longer hoping that by so doing that things will change. I cannot stand [hearing] anymore "Dear papa come and get me."[54]

While the records do not contain Robertson's reply to this letter, similar incidents indicate that the school took a nonconciliatory stance toward parents who expressed their opposition to the school's policies. Not all parents were opposed to the school's practices, though, and many showed a cooperative spirit when dealing with the school's leadership.[55]

Haskell's leadership was reluctant to admit any wrongdoings on the school's part. In order to keep up the existing power structure, the school went to great lengths to justify its actions before students, parents, and the Office of Indian Affairs in Washington. Maintaining discipline and order were among the school's main objectives. Sometimes, the school even dismissed employees for their failure to discipline the students. In 1909, Assistant Disciplinarian Wilson B. Charles was fired because of his "easy-going way of handling the boys."[56] In 1917, Haskell's head matron, Mary J. Freeman, faced similar accusations and was replaced due to her "inability to govern" and to maintain strict discipline.[57] More frequently, however, it was the teachers in the industrial departments who were criticized for being too lax with the students.[58] In rare cases, however, employees were dismissed or reprimanded for being too strict with the children. In 1920, Mrs. Douglas, the girls' matron, was encouraged to resign after giving the order to have one of the girls whipped for disobedience. By instructing the disciplinarian in this manner, the matron had knowingly acted against Superintendent Peairs's will and falsified his orders. Mrs. Douglas was fired owing to her "ugly disposition, the latter causing so much friction among the girls and matrons . . . and her unwillingness to listen to instructions of superior officials in the school."[59] Haskell's leadership required nothing less than total obedience from students and employees alike. Three years earlier, Haskell's head matron, Katherine Keck, had also come under pressure for mistreating the girls. The following student petition to the commissioner of Indian affairs triggered the discussion:

Dear Sir:
    The girls of Haskell are being mistreated by the head matron, Miss Keck, and we wish you would look into the matter as soon as you can. There has been more trouble with the girls this year than ever and we all

dislike the matron very much. Girls have run away because of her meanness and strict rules. This is vacation time and we want a vacation and not feel as if we were in prison. We await your reply with the wish that Miss Keck would resign.

Sincerely yours, Girls of Haskell[60]

Although Superintendent Peairs informed the commissioner that the letter was written by a single girl who had been under punishment and was, therefore, not the work of the "Girls of Haskell," he at the same time admitted that it expressed the sentiment of many of the school's female students. Peairs told the commissioner that there had been considerable dissatisfaction since Keck had taken charge as matron. According to Peairs, Keck lacked the "mother instinct" as well as sympathy and understanding for young people.[61] Peairs added, however, that he was reluctant to suggest her transfer. Although he was sympathetic to some of the girls' complaints, he placed a higher value on the school's discipline and power to dictate the rules than on the students' rightful criticism of their treatment. Obviously, Keck's case differed from Douglas's situation with respect to the source of criticism. Although both matrons were criticized for their bad disposition, Douglas was fired because she disobeyed the superintendent's orders. Keck, on the other hand, was allowed to stay at Haskell because she had not broken any of the school's regulations. Apparently, maltreating students was in itself not a sufficient reason for discharge. As these cases prove, the students' criticism, even if justified, usually did not carry enough weight to lead to an employee's dismissal.

The girls' petition to oust Keck was one of several petitions drafted by Haskell's students over the years. Explicitly political in nature, petitions were important instruments for voicing resistance against school policies, causing strong reactions from school officials. Unlike more individual forms of resistance, petitions required a certain level of political organization and united several students in their goal of bringing about changes in their treatment or living conditions. Therefore, Haskell's leadership considered petitions as especially threatening to the school's authority. During Haskell's early years, several petitions provide evidence of organized resistance to the school environment. During the 1887–1888 school year, for instance, students asked for rule amendments, such as disposing of the daily reveille sounded in the boy's dormitory, and for permission to dance.[62] A more serious petition addressed the school's deplorable health conditions and the high number of fatalities. After an epidemic of scrofula (a tubercular affliction) and pneumonia struck in the spring of 1888, claiming the lives of sixteen children, the students were determined to learn "what is the cause of so many deaths amongst us. There has been no such case known to us before. Surely there must be something wrong somewhere, either in the medicine or care that is taken of them."[63] The nineteen students who signed the petition took the school's rhetoric on care seriously and openly questioned Haskell's commitment to their health. The children were very much aware of the dangers that the Haskell environment posed to their health and chose an organized political approach to express their grievances. Unfortunately, the records do not indicate whether Haskell's leadership took students' concerns and recommendations to heart. Evidence from other cases, though, suggests that the students' pleas probably remained unanswered. But even if the petitions proved inconsequential, they doubtless provided satisfaction to their authors, who, if nothing more, created a stir among the school's administrators and the Office of Indian Affairs. In 1916, students once more requested permission to dance. In their petition, the boys were supported by the school's Catholic priest, Father Gordon, who "vehemently urged the right of pupils to dance, and also the right to petition."[64] Haskell's leadership was determined to play down the incident and to counteract Father Gordon's influence as much as possible. The fact that an employee of the school was supporting the students posed an even greater threat to the school's authority than if the children had acted on their own.

The most dramatic communal act of resistance during Haskell's early years occurred one night in October 1919. That evening, Haskell's unpopular matron, Mrs. Douglas, had issued an order forbidding boys and girls to sit together during the nightly entertainment held at the school's chapel. While the girls marched in, most of the boys protested the new rule and refused to join them. As punishment for their disobedience, Mr. Shields, the school's disciplinarian, sent them to their rooms for a study period. Inside the chapel, the invited speaker was ready to begin his lecture, when suddenly the whole school went dark and all electrical lights went out. While the school's assistant superintendent, C. E. Birch, was quieting the girls and few boys inside the chapel, he was called over to the girls' dormitory. In his report to Superintendent Peairs, who was out of town on a business trip to Washington, D.C., Birch described the following events:

> Hurrying to the girls' dormitory, I found the boys lined up in the road. Mr. Shields and I drove them away. . . . In the meantime I had sent for the engineers to look for the difficulty with the lights. . . . Some of the more

criminally and viciously inclined boys had obtained a ladder and gone to the pole where the lights entered the grounds, near the café, and torn the connection loose. After considerable damage and commotion of a pretty disgraceful character had gone on, I succeeded in getting hold of the boys and persuaded the most of them to go to bed. Soon after this the lights came on, and we had no difficulty in quieting everything down without much trouble.[65]

According to the report, some light bulbs were smashed, and the boys broke into the apple orchard and rang the school bell. They were yelling to the girls: "Are you with us?" and "Let's have a social" as well as "Let's string him up!"—the latter yell being aimed at the school's assistant superintendent. Although no serious harm was done, Birch acted quickly:

I began quiet investigation immediately to find the ringleaders, and have located the most of them. I have dismissed the following from the school, sending them out quickly and quietly. Have also tried to prevent newspaper and other notoriety, although it will, of course be known pretty generally in town.[66]

Four boys were immediately expelled from the school; five girls were also sent home on charges of "general insubordination." While the school's leadership continued its search for more offenders, the entire student population was denied town and church privileges the following weekend. According to Birch, the expulsion of the ringleaders had helped to restore discipline and order at the school, and the employees were "in good spirits, not discouraged, and ready to fight it out."[67] Although the report played down the gravity of the situation, assuring Superintendent Peairs that things at home were under control, it is clear that the event caused considerable anxiety among the school's staff. Considering the unpredictable dynamics of large groups, the boys' communal rebellion could easily have caused more harm than it did. The school was especially worried about the expected publicity and long-term effects of the event, fearing that it might have a lasting negative impact on Haskell's ability to control its student population. Therefore, the actions taken were swift, and the guilty parties were expelled and sent home immediately. All other students were taken aside for a "heart to heart talk," in the hope that the "better element of the school" would listen and learn from the incident.[68]

Most forms of domination can accommodate resistance, as long as the resistance is not made public, thereby threatening the public transcript. If the symbolic status quo has been harmed, however, symbolic restoration of power relations becomes necessary. Public apologies, remorse, and confessions can, therefore, be considered more important elements in processes of domination than punishment itself. Subordinates' admission of their wrongdoings reaffirms the legitimacy of their domination and contributes to the conception that its most disadvantaged members willingly accept the hegemonic order.[69] Symbolic restoration of power relations was omnipresent in the boarding school setting. Haskell's leadership insisted on students' public apologies and even published repentant letters in the school's newspaper. If students showed remorse for their infractions, punishments were usually less severe, and the school's leadership was more willing to forgive their offenses. As the events surrounding Haskell's 1919 "rebellion" illustrate, the school feared any negative publicity and was afraid of newspaper articles making the incident publicly known. The students' communal action presented a real threat to the school's public transcript, and power relations had to be restored immediately. There are many examples of individual students showing remorse for their actions. Although some of their letters might have been written in order to avoid further penalties, others appear to have been genuinely felt. In either case, the students' repentance helped to uphold Haskell's public transcript and thereby the persisting hegemonic order.

While at school, Indian students constantly had to negotiate between their desire to resist and their longing to fit in and succeed. Accommodation and resistance went hand in hand, and frequently small acts of resistance made the adjustment to school life bearable and in the long term even more successful. Many children only rejected certain aspects of the boarding school experience while embracing others. When students requested a change in the grade level they were in, their work detail, their diet, or their clothing allocation, they did not automatically object to the very notion of being at Haskell. They only asked for small concessions that would help to make their adjustment to boarding school life easier. Even students who ran away often did so for reasons unrelated to their experience at the school. Although many children ran away owing to homesickness or because they genuinely disliked being in boarding school, others left for very pragmatic reasons, usually related to the student's family situation. Many chronic deserters were at the same time successful students—a sign that through simultaneously adapting and resisting they were able to claim personal victories in both worlds.

Most children experienced some homesickness upon their arrival at

Haskell. Even though the majority eventually got used to their new environment, others wrote desperate letters to their parents, asking to be allowed to return home. In 1911, Superintendent Fiske explained to the Creek Indian agent that it was very bad for the school's reputation if these negative letters were circulated among the children's families. According to Fiske, the best method to counteract such reports was to bring the parents themselves to Haskell, so that they would see that their children's complaints were simply the result of homesickness.[70] In some cases, however, parental visits to Haskell led to the opposite result. When a group of Cherokee parents from Tahlequah, Oklahoma, expressed their wish to find out why their sons and daughters were so dissatisfied at Haskell, Superintendent Fiske was happy to take them on a tour of the facilities. But unlike some parents, the Cherokee visitors were appalled by what they saw and, as a consequence, became determined to take their children out of school.[71] Apparently, upon signing their children's contracts, a number of Cherokee parents had been misinformed by their Indian agent about the nature of Haskell's educational program and the terms of enrollment. They had expected that their children would receive mainly an academic education and did not at all agree with industrial training. But as the Cherokee Indian agent saw it, "Their real objection is largely their aversion to manual labor. Their ideas of education have been along seminary lines, with the idea that their education was to prepare one to live without work."[72] According to Superintendent Fiske, it had been impossible to convince the parents of the value of the work in the shops, and they insisted on taking their children home with them.[73]

Parental support made a crucial difference in the students' adjustment to Haskell. If parents were in favor of their children's schooling, the chances were much better that the students would come to accept or even like their new environment. Many parents wrote encouraging letters to their children, asking them to make the best of their time at Haskell. In 1911, an Oklahoma father wrote to his daughter Maggie: "How are you getting along? We are all well. I hope that you are getting along nicely in school and in your work. I would like to see you too, but don't think about home all the time like you said you did, study hard and be good."[74] Although pro-Haskell parents did not always generate docile, well-adjusted students, their positive attitude prevented many children from running away. If, on the other hand, parents supported their children's desertion, there was almost no way the school could prevent it.

In general, though, parents' visits were the exception rather than the rule, and the school did little to foster close family ties, which ran counter to Haskell's ideology of separating the children from their indigenous environments. The presence of a family member served as a reminder of home and all that was precious and familiar and would direct the children's attention away from all they were supposed to be learning (and forgetting) at boarding school. Esther Burnett recalled that she and her siblings longed for more contact with home and that, unlike herself, her sister could not bear boarding school life:

We didn't hear from home very often; sometimes it would be months at a time. My mother had not gone to a government boarding school, so she didn't seem to realize how important letters and packages were. . . . So, when I did receive a letter from her, I really treasured it. Bernice and Gordon and I would read it over and over. Of course, Gordon was on the opposite side of the campus, and it was hard to get used to not being able to talk to your brother whenever you wanted. It was good at least that Bernice and I were together. Bernice did not stay at Haskell for more than a couple of years. She couldn't adjust to the school. She was so homesick that she was physically ill much of the time, and they finally sent her home. My mother did come to see us one time during my high school years.[75]

Many depressed and homesick new students threatened to desert if not allowed to return home. In 1910, one desperate student wrote to his guardian:

Write to my uncle and tell him that I want to come home and he don't come after me I am coming in I guess. I can walk it in in about two weeks and if one of you all don't come after me I will come in myself. . . . I can't stay any longer here. . . . I can't learn nothing here but some of the Boys gets drunk here. I guess I will come some days no telling when I will come in home. I can't help but to think about home this is first time that I have been this far from home. I know my uncle will be sorry to hear that I can't stay here where he sent me. But I can't help it I am sorry myself.[76]

The author of this letter had apparently come to Haskell with his family's support but found it impossible to live up to his uncle's expectation. It is not clear whether this boy actually ran away, but many others did. In 1899, the commissioner of Indian affairs asked Peairs to give a full report with regard to student deserters from the Standing Rock reservation in South Dakota. The commissioner pointed out that out of fifteen recently transferred boys at Haskell, thirteen had run away and that the children's parents were worried about their safety. Although most students had reached their Dakota homes safely, others were still en route. One student had died in his attempt to travel home, and the commissioner expressed his sympathy with the worrying parents, since "endeavoring to travel across the country in that section in winter is extremely dangerous even when provided with the proper necessities for travel, and of course it is very hazardous for an Indian boy to attempt such a trip on foot, therefore it is no wonder that these parents are very anxious about their children."[77]

During Haskell's early years, the number of desertions was especially high. In 1885 alone, 45 students ran away. In some years, the numbers were even higher. In 1910, for instance, 53 students ran away in September, 35 in October, and 21 in November. Some of them returned to Haskell voluntarily; others were captured by the police and brought back by Haskell's staff. Many students deserted repeatedly, earning themselves the title of "chronic deserters." In order to encourage the capture of runaways, the school paid a three-dollar bounty (termed "expenses") to anyone assisting school administrators in locating fugitives and sometimes even placed search notices in local newspapers such as the *Kansas City Star*. Haskell's superintendents insisted on the return of the pupils for disciplinary reasons and also because they could not afford to see attendance figures drop throughout the year. As one student remembered, desertions played a major role in lowering student numbers: "We would start school in September with around a thousand students, but by the middle of the year so many of them would be gone. They would leave, some got sick, some just left, ran away, so that at the end of the year it looked to me like almost half of them were gone."[78]

Although boys were much more likely to run away than girls, a number of female students also deserted each year. Superintendent Fiske explained to the commissioner of Indian affairs that the main reason for girls to leave the school was homesickness: "They naturally irk under the unaccustomed restraint and magnify into personal grievances many purely disciplinary measures."[79] Some girls, however, had "led immoral lives before coming here" and exercised a harmful influence on other students. Therefore, the school was not hesitant when it came to expelling girls who had run away repeatedly or who had behaved in an "immoral" manner.[80] Sometimes, boys and girls ran away together, living out their romances away from the school. In 1914, two Pawnee students ran off together to Kansas City, where they remained for two days before returning to the school. The two young people had fallen in love during the previous summer vacation in Oklahoma. In his report to the commissioner of Indian affairs, Superintendent Wise pointed out that their case was just another example "of the bad results so often resulting from permitting pupils to spend their vacations at home" and added that especially the girl's influence on other girls had been considered "more or less unwholesome."[81] Therefore, the school expelled both students immediately. In another case, two Creek students eloped and got married while on the run. Despite their changed marital status, the school insisted on their return to Haskell for disciplinary reasons, followed by their expulsion from the school.[82]

When students deserted, staff— including the superintendent himself, teachers, assistants, and disciplinarians—traveled the country to accompany truant students back to Haskell. Since most children were homeward bound, it was usually easy to track them down. Sometimes, school officials greeted the runaways at their parents' doorsteps. In many cases, the parents had already been notified by the school and were determined to send their children back. In other instances, however, parents only learned about their children's desertion weeks after the event and were angered by the school's failure to keep them informed. Most parents were extremely concerned about their children's safety and warned them not to run away. When Esther Burnett left for Haskell, her mother had told her: "If you run away from school, you'll go *back* faster than you came home."[83] The dangers of traveling across great distances were real, and students did get hurt and sometimes even killed in their attempt to reach home. Burnett took her mother's warning seriously and never tried to run away. Many of her fellow students took the chance, however, and faced harsh punishments in return:

> There *were* those kids who just could not cope with boarding school life, and in an effort to escape, would run away, hoping to reach home. We called this going AWOL. . . . I used to hear stories of AWOL kids getting locked up in cells prior to my time at Haskell, but that did not happen while I was there [mid-1920s]. The belt line was a more common punish-

ment for going AWOL, and it was a serious disciplinary measure. A company would be lined up in two long lines facing each other. The students would remove their belt and strap clothed offenders on the rear as they dashed through the line. Some were such good runners and such good dodgers that they defeated the purpose of the punishment.[84]

Burnett's recollections attest to the severity of the punishments experienced by runaway students. The children were beaten, they were deprived of town and other privileges, and they had to spend days or even weeks in the school's jail. Students were required to physically punish their fellow students, a custom that was certainly difficult to bear for many children since they could identify with their friends' reasons for running away. The school had a great interest in returning deserters, since the children's successful departure and adventures during the escape were causing excitement among the other students. When two Oklahoma boys were apprehended after thirty-seven days of flight, Superintendent Wise complained to their Indian agent:

> I can hardly tell you how much the escapade of this boy and his companion has cost Haskell in the matter of reputation and discipline. The matter has been on the lips of nearly all the students here for weeks. These boys have been going up and down the lengths and breadth of three different states and have been cutting up in a way that certainly has done the reputation of Haskell no good.[85]

Desertions were particularly numerous at the beginning of the school year, when new students suffered from homesickness, and also during the spring and summer months, when the children became restless, wishing to spend time with their families. Once the school had denied their or their parents' request for a summer vacation, running away offered an alternative to homesick and unhappy students, eager to go back to their communities. Parents longed to see their children after long months or even years of absence and in many cases counted on their offspring's help during the agricultural season. Another important reason for parents and children wanting to reunite were cases of severe illness in the students' families. Naturally, children wanted to visit their parents, siblings, or grandparents if their relatives' health was failing. Haskell's administrators, however, were less than cooperative and sympathetic when it came to these requests. Once their families' requests for their return had been denied, many students chose to leave without permission. In his 1908 letter to the Lapwai Indian agent, Idaho student Caleb Carter explained his reasons for considering desertion:

> The next step I want to take is going home. I must and did ask the superintendent yesterday. Why what will my mother do without a boy like me. We've got plowing to do pretty soon, and hay to put up next summer. And besides the wood has to be cut and other chores. There is no question that I must come home. If I don't go one way there is some other ways a fellow like me can go. I just got to go that's all there is to it. . . . You know that I tried to come home on account of my little brother's death but still it was the same old supt. that stood in between and we could not agree. The first year I was here not three months after my arrival I was notified of my oldest sister being awful sick again it was Mr. Peairs that was Johnny on the spot. This is my third attempt and I must succeed or else desert just the same.[86]

Caleb's letter expresses the frustrations experienced by students and parents alike when dealing with the school's uncompromising leadership. The inflexibility of boarding school policies left many children with no choice than to leave Haskell without permission.

Although students deserted for a variety of reasons, it was especially Haskell's rigid vacation and leave of absence policy that created dissatisfaction and compelled students to leave the school without permission. Haskell's administrative leadership insisted that about 250 students remain at the school each summer to keep the institution running, do repair work, and bring in the harvest. Of the other students, those with "good homes" were allowed to travel home, if their parents could pay for their fare and if they deposited the money for the return trip in advance. First-year students were the last to be allowed to go home, since they had only been at the school for nine months.[87] Indian educators feared that during the summer time, children would fall back into their traditional customs and behaviors, get into trouble, behave immorally, or succumb to the native "habit" of idleness. The school's fears were not completely unfounded, since the summer was an important time for the children to reconnect with their families and culture and to enjoy the freedom they were deprived of during the school year.

Jesse Rowlodge recalled how he spent his summers in Oklahoma: "I usually get my pony and saddle and go to visit Canton, maybe Colony and just live it the way I want to. I didn't have to go to no bathroom, barbershop, something like that. Oh, I went to the barber shop for hair trim. I'd go down to the river and swim—a bunch of us guys—whoever I'd be with. Go out fishing, and go out to Indian doin's and just have good time all summer. Just forget about civilized life."[88] For Rowlodge, his summers in Oklahoma meant complete freedom from the rigors of "civilized" life. He enjoyed his pony, the company of his friends, as well as Indian celebrations and ceremonies. To him, spending the vacations the way he liked did not mean that he rejected everything he had learned and done at Haskell. But it meant that he was ready and able to take a break from being a "white" boy and to enjoy the way of life customary among the Arapaho people. Like so many other children, Jesse Rowlodge had no trouble readjusting to life on the reservation once summer came along. In September, however, he just as willingly returned to Haskell to begin one more year of boarding school life.

Vacation requests were often a reason for conflicts between Indian families and the school, and many parents objected to Haskell's patronizing attitude. In 1917, one Wisconsin parent angrily wrote to the school:

> I write to ask you about Mildred Richmond, why she has not started for home, I think I have done all that was required. I do not see any reason why she should be barred from coming home, of course I signed the agreement for her to attend your school but that was not to release all claims of her. I think I have the right to have her during vacation, then I am willing for her to return and finish her term.[89]

Every September, the school's leadership had difficulties motivating students to return and spent much time and energy in the process of bringing them back. The administration sent out letters reminding parents and children that it was time to depart for Haskell, organized train tickets to be placed at stations across the country, and sometimes even provided escorts for groups of children traveling from the same communities. If students failed to return on time, the consequences could be severe and sometimes even resulted in expulsion, especially if the offender was considered a less than "desirable" student or if the school was already overcrowded. Once a student had been expelled from one government school, he or she was no longer eligible to attend any other Indian school. If a child was not able to continue his education at a public school, expulsion could mean the end of the student's formal education.

Despite the high costs of travel and the school's lack of cooperation, parents pleaded for their children to come home, frequently pointing out their old age or ailing health as pressing reasons to see their sons and daughters. Some children did not see their parents for years and became alienated from their families and their communities. A Yakima father from Washington State expressed the ever present fear of estrangement in his note to the school: "If Julia don't want to come home, don't make her to come. It may be that she don't like my ways of living the Indian ways."[90] As it turned out, his fears were unwarranted, and Julia chose to visit her family for two months. Nevertheless, the father's concerns were justified, and many children indeed lost close contact with their families, especially if they had come to Haskell at a very young age, if their parents were too poor to pay for their trips home, or if they came from places as far away as California, Washington, Idaho, or Arizona. Parents were aware that their children's extended absence could lead to alienation from home and family. In 1907, a father from Idaho sought the school's approval to take his children home:

> They eagerly insist on coming home and I do not feel like compelling them to stay there, as they do not know much about home or home ties. They have been continually away at school, ever since Lillian was seven years old. Lillian has passed two vacations at home and Althea three during all this time. They can go to public school here as we live only a half mile from the school and less than half a mile from the Fort Hall Indian School. It is better perhaps that they should come as I may become better known to them.[91]

Like many other boarding school students, Lillian and Althea had spent most of their childhood and youth at Haskell and had not been able to form close bonds with their families at home. One can only imagine the difficulties this lack of intimacy must have created between children and their communities upon their return home and how trying the readjustment period must have been. No doubt, the boarding school experience transformed Indian children and the way they viewed the world, especially if they had come from homes adhering to a way of life deeply rooted in indigenous traditions. The cultural rift between the early boarding school generations and their communities could be severe, and children had to learn to function socially in two very different environments. The extent of the cultural gap between Haskell and home influenced a child's ability to cope and to adjust to boarding school life. For children who came from more westernized families, as was frequently the case with students from the Midwest and Oklahoma, and students with mixed Indian-white ancestry, the adjustment to Haskell's teachings and regimen was easier than for children who had grown up in more traditional environments. The students' age, lengths of stay at the school, family background, relationship with teachers and staff, ability to form friendships with fellow students, and personal motivation to get an education all played an important role in their ability and willingness to adjust to the boarding school environment.

Although for many children life at Haskell was difficult and at times even unbearable and traumatic, for many others it was agreeable and satisfying. Whereas over the years, hundreds of students ran away from school and refused to return after their summer vacation, hundreds more were looking forward to school life and were excited to come back to Haskell. At the end of the summer, Haskell's superintendents received many letters from students such as Joseph Comer, expressing their positive attitude toward the school:

> Dear Friend:
>
> I am now going to drop you a line, and let you know that I am working hard, helping my folks making hay. My step-father raised some potatoes that were fine, I think he is the only one that raised such good potatoes. I wish you were here that you might take a look at our crop. I am all through with my work, and so I want to come back to dear old H.I. again. I feel lonesome ever since I came back to this reservation. So I think if you will send me a ticket I am going to sign up for some more years. He said I can too; this is why I am writing to you ("father").
>
> I am your friend Joseph Comer.[92]

Joseph was one among many students who had a positive relationship with Haskell's leadership. They regarded Superintendent Peairs as their friend, as a father figure who guided them in their educational endeavors and who took an interest in their life beyond Haskell. No doubt, during years of absence from home, younger children in particular developed strong attachments for kind and warmhearted employees, and teachers and superintendents could become the children's most important mentors and role models.

The children's letters also bear testimony to the great importance of friendships and social ties formed at Haskell. The children's peers and closest friends were at school, and over the summer they missed their company. Reservation life could be lonesome once a child had become accustomed to the company of hundreds of fellow students. Especially during adolescence, friends played a crucial role in the students' development, and parents and younger siblings could not always substitute for the absence of a best friend, a boyfriend, or a girlfriend. Former boarding school students mention lifelong friendships as the most important aspect, as well as legacy, of their boarding school experience. Sharing the challenges, trials, and joys of life at Haskell created a sense of community among the children that defied authority as well as many of the negative experiences associated with boarding school life. Friends listened to each other, shared their culture and experiences, comforted, supported, nurtured, and understood each other. They cried together, laughed together, and cheered each other up when homesickness and punishment made life hard to bear. The strong sense of community that existed among boarding school students explains why, despite all the school's shortcomings, students generally showed a fierce loyalty to Haskell, promoted the school among their families and friends back home, and stayed in touch with schoolmates, and sometimes even employees, for years after leaving Haskell.

Students had different reasons and motivations for adjusting to the boarding school routine. Many children liked going to school and were eager to get the best education they could. Even though not all of these students internalized the ideological underpinnings of Haskell's program, a significant number probably did. Their belief in the dominant ideology was expressed in letters, speeches at various school functions, and articles written for the school's newspaper. Although some students saw Haskell as their gate to civilization, many others shared a more pragmatic approach to education, accepting certain aspects of the school's teachings while rejecting others. The majority of children saw education as a means to an end. What they learned at Haskell would help them to earn a living, to understand the white man's world better, and to adjust to life as twentieth-century citizens of the United States. By the 1910s and 1920s, many Native Americans had come to agree with U.S. policymakers that in a world dominated by white society, education had become the only way to ensure racial survival. Indian youth had to learn the ways of the dominant society in order to succeed in the modern world. That did not necessarily mean giving up everything that was Indian. Rather, it meant utilizing education to find a place as an indigenous person in a changing world and to employ one's skills as a weapon to defend tribal interests. Many boarding school alumni used the knowledge they had gained at boarding school to advance their people's situation and became avid spokespeople and leaders of their tribes.

A less political, but just as pragmatic response to boarding school life can be seen in those students who came to Haskell as a temporary escape from difficult conditions at home. An unhappy family situation, extreme poverty, alcoholism, and the diminished prospects of reservation life as well as the sometimes restrictive nature of tribal traditions could entice children to long for school. Life at Haskell was not always easy, but for many children it was better than anything they had experienced at home. Esther Burnett emphasizes this reality:

> The boarding school provided a safe environment for me. The reason it was such a positive experience was that I had security there. You see, I had security in my home until my father died, but after that we were never sure of where our next meal would come from. . . . My mother was grieving, and there wasn't much security in our house. She wasn't home much, and we were left to pretty much fend for ourselves.[93]

And finally, many children adapted to Haskell because they genuinely came to enjoy the social aspect of school life. Extracurricular activities, including athletics, literary societies, religious organizations, music, and theater, offered students opportunities to excel and to socialize that were unavailable at their homes. In 1916, Ojibwe student Jewel Wells wrote to her sister about the school's nice Christmas celebration, about her intensive studies, and about the fun she had: "I don't mind having to go to school, in fact I am beginning to like it once more. Just think of us going skating here, don't it surprise you? We may go after school this afternoon, if we are real good."[94] Seventeen-year-old Pomo student Josephine Smith frequently wrote to her sister in California, telling her about band concerts, the boys' parades, football and basketball games, her debating society, the school's Thanksgiving program, her work in the dining room, the things she studied in her academic classes, and how she learned to cook a good meal and make coffee. To Josephine, being at Haskell was a positive experience, and she emphasized repeatedly how glad she was to have come to the school.[95] Students such as Jewel Wells, Josephine Smith, Jesse Rowlodge, and Esther Burnett became involved in a variety of extracurricular activities that allowed them to have fun, develop their creativity, and feel a sense of personal pride and achievement. Success in the classroom, on the shop floor, in the sewing room, or on the athletic field certainly influenced the students' perception of themselves and of Haskell as the agent of their fulfillment.

In her autobiography, Esther Burnett describes how she came to develop inner poise and decided that accommodation was the right path for her. She emphasizes the importance of role models in her decision to adapt to boarding school life and recounts how two teachers in particular, Ella Deloria and Ruth Muskrat Bronson, had a profound impact on her life. Both ladies taught at Haskell during the 1920s and belonged to a small group of Native American professionals who had found their way into the federal Indian education system. Ella Deloria, Standing Rock Sioux and a graduate of Columbia University, taught girls physical education and drama. Ruth Muskrat Bronson, Cherokee and a graduate of Mount Holyoke College, taught English. Burnett emphasizes the women's wonderful sense of humor and very strong respect for Indian culture, which they successfully integrated into Haskell's Anglo curriculum. According to Burnett,

> They taught their students to have a healthy respect for themselves as individuals and a pride in their heritage. They taught us about Indian values and kept them alive in us. . . . They taught us that we could accomplish anything we set our minds to. . . . They taught us how to defend ourselves, as Indian people, without getting angry or defensive. This lesson has been valuable to me throughout my life. . . . Ella and Ruth taught us about generosity and about sharing. . . . We Indians have been criticized for our giveaways, but there is so much joy and satisfaction in giving. . . . Students at Haskell had a great deal of respect for these two, probably because they came from the same background as us. They were Indian, and so we knew that they understood us, just as they understood where we came from and what our needs and beliefs encompassed. They were both well-educated Indian women whose desire to help Indian youth led them to commit and dedicate their lives to us.[96]

Teachers such as Ella Deloria and Ruth Muskrat Bronson were rare in the Indian school service, especially during Haskell's early days. Most teachers were Anglo-American and had neither the knowledge nor the inclination to engage in culturally sensitive teachings. In general, former boarding school students remembered Indian staff more fondly than non-Indian employees, pointing out their greater kindness and patience in dealing with the students. Staff working on the farm and teachers who taught in the industrial departments often left a more positive and longer-lasting impression on Indian students than academic teachers, probably because the children spent longer hours working than being in the classroom.[97] But many children also developed affections for white teachers and matrons who, through their care, made the students' daily school life a little bit brighter and the separation from home a little bit easier. One former student remembered:

> The matron liked us, so when my little brother got lonesome at night sometimes she'd send for me, and I'd be shaking in my shoes thinking I had done something wrong, and I'd be reviewing all my activities for the day, and when I'd get there she'd say "your brother's in the living room, so if you take off your shoes you can play" and I'd turn the radio on and read to him for an hour or so. But we were the only ones that did this, and the matron used to say, "Now be very quiet, and don't say anything about it" and so if one of the girls asked me what I was sent for I'd say, "Oh, she just wanted to talk, lecture me."[98]

Expressing similarly positive feelings, another girl wrote home,

> We had no school last week and I was wishing to go to school all the time. Oh Papa, you do not know how much I love my teacher.[99]

When Gertrude Golden took a teaching position at a different Indian school, she received a very sentimental letter from one of her former Haskell students:

> How are you getting along these days? Every morning we sing gypsies' song and Concha and Lillie and I always cry. The school room is lonesome without your sweet smiles. I wish I could see you but I cannot get my wish. It is so lonesome over here without your sweet face I just only wish I could see you once more and then I won't wish for anything else.[100]

The departure of a beloved teacher could mean a serious loss to a child who had forged strong ties with his or her "surrogate" parent. The wish to live up to the expectations of their favorite teachers certainly enticed some students to choose the path of accommodation rather than resistance. Although some teachers had more empathy for their students than others, Esther Burnett recalled that "by and large they were a dedicated lot. I have the fondest memories of my Haskell teachers. They seemed to care about me and the other students there; they knew that they were our family, as well as our role models."[101] Her decision to become a teacher herself was influenced by her Haskell role models: "I aspired to work with Indian youth, giving them the same nurturing and consideration that Ruth and Ella had given me."[102]

In the 1920s, the school was in many ways a less restrictive environment than in the previous decades. Students had more academic and vocational choices; the dress code had been liberalized (fashionable dresses, make-up, and contemporary hairstyles were all permitted), and some progressive indigenous teachers had been able to gain employment. These developments made the children's adaptation to boarding school life easier. In addition, many of the students attending Haskell during the 1910s and 1920s were already second-generation boarding school students or even Haskellites. Students whose parents had gone through the same experience were much better informed and consequently prepared for the difficulties associated with boarding school life. When Lucille Winnie graduated in the 1920s, she had made her father's dream come true: to see his daughter graduate from the same school he had attended a generation before.[103]

Ironically, in the early twentieth century, going to boarding school had become part of the Indian experience, a rite of passage equal in some ways to former cultural milestones such as waging war on the enemy. At Haskell, students fought a different battle against the white man than their forefathers had, but in many ways, it was still a battle. Through the successful completion of their boarding school education, Indian children transformed themselves into full members of their communities while proving that they could survive and in many cases even thrive among the "enemy." By the time the children left Haskell, they were transformed in a multiplicity of ways. Nevertheless, very few became completely acculturated to white ways of living and thinking. Throughout their boarding school years, most students remained in touch with their Indian past and identity and were willing to rediscover parts of their indigenous cultures upon their departure from Haskell.

As this chapter has shown, exploring the students' hidden transcript can help us to make sense of their resistance to as well as their accommodation with forced education. The boarding school experience in many cases created conflicting identities, composed both of dominant and subordinate values and practices. The fact that the educational assault on Indian students did not succeed on a larger scale can at least partially be attributed to the limited time that most students spent in school as well as to the discrimination and marginalization they faced after leaving the institution. Ironically, through their marginalization, American Indians were able to preserve many elements of their indigenous cultures.[104] In order to truly understand student responses to the boarding school experience, one has to look beyond the years of school attendance. Haskell's administrators clearly understood that the ultimate test of the boarding school concept was whether Haskell's alumni would live up to policymakers' expectations or whether they would go "back to the blanket."

CHAPTER EIGHT

Life after Haskell

Lodge Pole, Montana
April 11, 1917
My dear Mr. Peairs—

    I have seen by the Leader that you are again at Haskell as Supt. and although I am not there yet I feel as tho I too am affected. I do not really know which deserves the most congratulation you or the school but I think the school does. . . . Dear old H.I. how I too love her. We were always so anxious to leave school and go out for our selves little thinking what a world of trouble there were and that the happiest days we knew were our school days, now we are scattered all over but I am sure that all those who have been at H.I. feel as I do that those days were the happiest and always keep a warm spot in our hearts for her. I am
    One of you
    Mrs Nellie (Toombs) Helgeson[1]

Nellie Helgeson's letter is one of many positive letters written by former students congratulating Superintendent Peairs upon his return to Haskell in 1917. Like hundreds of other alumni, Nellie Helgeson eagerly read Haskell's newspaper to keep informed about her alma mater, her former teachers, and especially her fellow students. Through Haskell's newspaper, former students could pick up news of old friends, relive the school's athletic events, and read the superintendent's views on the Indian issues of the day. But nothing could boost alumni's spirits like personal letters. Haskell rightfully prided itself on keeping in touch with its alumni, and letter exchanges between Haskell's administrators and former students were part of the school routine. Many alumni expressed sentimental feelings as well as nostalgia for their alma mater, praising the good that their education had done for them while frequently lamenting that they had not taken advantage of all their opportunities while at school. In 1919, Clara Toombs wrote from Montana: "Enclosed is a letter to one of my old schoolmates I wish you would see that he gets it. If he isn't at Haskell and you know his whereabouts please forward the letter. I am really lonesome for my old school days and I often wish I had it all to do over. I certainly would have stayed in school but a person never realizes what there doing until it is too late."[2]

The school published many of these letters in the *Indian Leader* and frequently added information on "successful" former students to motivate those still in school. The school's superintendents took time to respond to the students' letters, giving them advice, praise, and encouragement, but also strong criticism if they felt that their former charges did not "do good." Many former students returned to Haskell for a visit at some point in their lives, mostly at graduation time, or on special occasions such as the 1909 quarter centennial or the 1926 homecoming and stadium dedication. The school also held summer institutes and conferences, which reunited alumni with their alma mater. Visits to Haskell offered former students the opportunity to renew school ties and listen to pep talks from their friends and the school's employees. By inviting alumni to return to Lawrence, Haskell's leadership hoped to guide the direction former students were taking in life.

Some alumni were so proud of Haskell that they wanted their own children to share in the experience. In 1919, Dennisson Wheelock, Oneida attorney, former Carlisle student, and ex-leader of Haskell's band, wrote to the school:

> Mrs. Wheelock and I have decided that it would be very desirable for many reasons to entrust the education of our daughter Louise, who was born at Haskell, to your supervision. . . . So far as I remember no child born at the school as Louise was, has ever applied to be admitted as a student to secure her education. Louise was born at Haskell sixteen years ago and is now in the ninth grade. I am particularly anxious to have her where she can learn domestic science and art, in addition to her academic education. . . . I may say that I have searched all over the country for a school where the training could be given her exactly the way you give your stu-

dents, but without success, and for this reason I am asking to have her admitted.³

Louise was only one among many "grandchildren," as the school liked to call their former students' children. That Haskell alumni chose to send their own children back to Lawrence speaks against a predominantly negative reading of the boarding school experience. Many indigenous returnees felt that Haskell had been a positive influence in their lives, which they wanted to pass on to their own children. Although the alumni's nostalgia and positive feelings for Haskell were certainly honest and shared by many Haskellites, it would be wrong to assume that everybody felt that way. Obviously, students who had had largely negative experiences at Haskell did not care to stay in touch with the school's leadership or to send their own children to Haskell. Their doubts and their pain have not been preserved as part of the school's "official transcript" but were shared with families, friends, and fellow alumni back home. Although many positive letters reached the school, many critical ones remained unwritten.

Graduation time was a joyous time at Haskell, but it also meant the beginning of a period in students' lives filled with uncertainties and conflicting choices. According to Esther Burnett's recollections,

> leaving Haskell was very traumatic, particularly because I was leaving security. The notion existed that Indian students went to boarding school and became so secure in their environment that they didn't want to be pushed out of the nest. I don't really think that was true for the majority of the enrollees. It certainly wasn't true for me. Like anyone leaving security, we were ambivalent and apprehensive about the unknown, but part of our training had been to meet and welcome challenges.⁴

When it was time to leave Haskell, students had to decide whether to return home, continue their education, get married, or seek employment either at home or in the "white" world. Although a substantial number of graduates found jobs with the Indian Service throughout the country, most indigenous students returned home to their communities and reservations, facing the complex task of readjusting to families and lifestyles they had left behind years before. Homecomings could be just as disappointing and difficult as the children's first arrival at Haskell. Especially during Haskell's early years, many students returned to tribal environments that stood in stark contrast to what they had learned and experienced at boarding school.

Initially, most students suffered from reverse culture shock, realizing that they no longer saw and understood their indigenous world in the same ways as their friends and relatives. Haskell had not turned them into white people, but it most certainly had transformed them. Many children suffered from a loss of their native language ability and had difficulties communicating with their families. They felt torn between their parents' lifestyle and all they had been taught at school about being "civilized." Their education made them feel superior in some ways, but their loss of tribal languages and customs could also make them feel inferior, unaccepted, and even ridiculed. Students who tried to live according to Haskell's teachings were frequently met with resentment by their tribe, facing ostracism and strong pressures to return to their indigenous ways. Many students experienced culture clashes between the white ideology of rugged individualism they had been taught at school and their communities' emphasis on communalism and sharing. In addition, their adoption of Christian beliefs could generate tribal resistance, creating pressures to once more conform to their families' beliefs and religious practices. Even though strong kinship ties and loving families helped many students to readjust to tribal life, many others felt alienated from their communities and chose to leave home once more. Just as the boarding school experience differed from child to child, so too did their experiences upon returning home.

The story of Irene Stewart, who spent her childhood in the Canyon de Chelly area of the Diné (Navajo) reservation, shows the conflicts and inner struggles faced by many boarding school students. As a small child, Irene Stewart lived with her father and grandmother in a traditional Navajo hogan, herding sheep and learning the ways of the Diné people. During the following decade, she attended the government boarding schools in Fort Defiance, Arizona, and Haskell Institute. Although adjustment to school life was painful at first, Irene eventually got used to her new environment: "I had begun to like Haskell.... Before I knew, the four years were up. I was anxious to go home, and at the same time reluctant to leave Haskell."[5] When she arrived in Arizona, nothing was as she had expected: "I felt out of place again. How these sudden changes make a Navajo student feel is only to be understood by one who has experienced them.... The school regimen was hard to break away from; it had left me with problems unsolved." Stewart did not return home with her father right away but decided to spend the summer in Fort Defiance, working for the Indian agent as a housemaid. When she finally returned to the Canyon de Chelly region, her fears were confirmed: "When I left the Navajo country years before, I felt heartbreak; now I was disappointed in it. I could not make up my mind to stay on the reservation. Hogan life—once a great pleasure to me, and in later years so satisfying—was not for me."[6]

Although her negative response did not last for the remainder of her life, initially Irene Stewart decided that traditional Navajo life was unacceptable and registered at Albuquerque Indian School to finish her education. Even though she did not like Albuquerque as much as Lawrence, she stayed and graduated in 1929. For a time, she became a Christian missionary in California, preaching mostly to white children. She eventually returned to the Navajo reservation as a missionary worker and later became active in tribal politics. According to Stewart, her "attempt to live the traditional Navajo way of life was chopped up with school life."[7] As Indian educators had hoped, years in the boarding school environment had alienated her from her people and their lives. Stewart had grown accustomed to modern comforts: "Having gotten used to living where there are hygienic facilities, it is very hard to live again in the old Hogan life."[8] She wanted an income and the opportunity to better herself. But even though her years in boarding school had transformed her, Irene Stewart remained in touch with her Navajo heritage and identity and eventually found her place within a changing Diné society, participating in her nation's political life.

There were also former students who chose to live predominantly by the values and beliefs they had acquired at Haskell and who found that their families were following an equally "progressive" path. In 1917, former Winnebago student Evangeline Johnson-Gover, an alumna of Haskell's business department, shared with Superintendent Peairs her joy over her and her mother's life choices:

> I am so happy in my present mode of living that I find it necessary to write someone the facts.... Christianity has done everything for my dear mother, Mrs. Louisa J. Bear, and I.... Mother was converted in the year 1908 and from that time has been an earnest Christian worker among her tribesmen.... We, her four children, were not acquainted with our own relatives until we were quite old enough to choose proper companions.

Mother practically educated herself by reading good books and periodicals and associating with the missionaries and agency force. In 1915, she became a member of the Society of American Indians and has been an active and interested member.

Johnson-Gover continued her letter by talking about her brother, who was in the U.S. Navy, and about her mother's fundraising tour through the eastern states to raise scholarship money for the Winnebago Indian Mission School. She told Peairs that she herself was about to enter a nurse training program:

> This war is demanding nurses for the Red Cross and since I am so well blessed with health and strength I almost feel like a "slacker" if I do not grasp this chance. It is a big thing, but I am going to put forth every effort that's in me to "make good." . . . I shall need the prayers of all you Christian people there.[9]

Due to her family's embrace of dominant values and beliefs, Evangeline certainly faced fewer difficulties readjusting to home life than other returned students. From Haskell's perspective, she was the ideal returned student, living up to reformers' expectations and continuing the school's work both on the reservation and in her own family. Returnee stories like Irene Stewart's and Evangeline Johnson-Gover's could be told hundreds of times from reservations and indigenous communities across the United States. Although there were exceptions, in general readjustment to home life was not easy and created cultural as well as intergenerational conflicts in American Indian families and communities. Nevertheless, many Haskell alumni used their schooling to advance their position within their tribe's social and political life and put their newly acquired skills to work for the betterment of their communities.

The "returned student problem," as the Office of Indian Affairs liked to call it, created considerable controversy inside and outside of native communities and occupied the minds of parents, alumni, white reformers, missionaries, and government educators alike. From the point of view of boarding school officials, it was crucial to prove the success of their assimilation scheme. Only if students would lead "civilized" lives upon returning home could the great expenditure on behalf of Indian children be justified to Congress and the American people. For a long time, schools such as Haskell, Carlisle, and Hampton insisted that about 75 percent of their graduates succeeded in "doing good," living productive and assimilated lives, and thereby positively influencing the "traditional elements" in their communities. The fears that this estimation did not correspond to reality ran deep, however, and consumed much of Indian educators' thinking. Boarding school officials were dismayed by the public's tendency to lump together all returned students into one group and insisted on the separation between actual graduates and those returnees who had attended boarding school but had not finished the course of study. According to Indian educators, the success rate among actual graduates was very satisfying, whereas the rate of "regression" was much higher among returnees who had only spent a few years in school. By 1909, for instance, only about 20 percent of Haskell's 2000 alumni were certified graduates, which to Indian educators partly explained the "returned student problem."

Over the years, schools such as Haskell conducted surveys among their returned students to find out whether their alumni were carriers of progress and civilization or whether they had "returned to the blanket." The surveys contained questions about the former students' activities since their departure from Haskell, their salaries, whether they owned a home or land, whether Haskell had been helpful to them, and whether they would promise to keep in touch with their alma mater.[10] Haskell's 1919 survey, for instance, included information on occupation and yearly income. The report focused on graduates of Haskell's commercial and normal departments as well as on students who had learned a trade or completed the course in home economics. The report emphasized that 63 graduates had died during World War I and the influenza epidemic of 1918 and that at least 450 of Haskell's students and ex-students had at some point served in the army or navy. At the time of the survey, several graduates of the course in home economics were taking courses in nursing, and a number of students were attending various schools offering higher training.

The survey reviewed the activities of 720 graduates, of whom 448 were found to be self-supporting. Of these, 345 were considered as successful, 60 as fairly successful, and only 3 as complete failures. With the exception of 4, all graduates had a good or fair standing in their communities. The range of activities engaged in by Haskell's graduates was very wide, with farming and clerical work the leading occupations. Others reported being homemakers, cashiers in banks, clerks in stores, ministers, postmasters, chicken raisers, railroad men, automobile mechanics, disciplinarians, interpreters, nurses, band directors, sales managers, bookkeepers, laundresses, tailors, printers, plumbers, engineers, teachers, telephone operators, carpenters, matrons, electricians, and many more. Annual salaries ranged from as little as $600 for an Indian Service employee to as much as $7,500 for a sales manager of a milling company.[11] The *Indian Leader* editorial accompanying the survey emphasized the measure of success that these findings signified:

> We believe the showing is creditable, and when it is considered that there are hundreds of highly successful former students, who are not graduates, scattered all over this country, the showing becomes impressive.... In our opinion these facts should most emphatically justify the work our schools have done and are doing.[12]

The article also pointed out that there was still "much to do." Three years earlier the Office of Indian Affairs had conducted an extensive survey questioning nearly 150 reservation and boarding school superintendents about their experiences with former boarding school graduates. The superintendents' letters left little doubt that on every reservation there were a large number of returned students who did not live up to the expectations of white educators and policymakers:

> In the opinion of almost all the superintendents the principal cause of the so-called "failures" of returned students is the Indian reservation; its life and environment; its unattractive, poverty-stricken, unsanitary hovel-like homes; its lack of opportunities to put into practice what is learned at schools; its lack of remunerative employment; its lack of means to acquire farming and industrial implements and tools, live stock and poultry; its old, uneducated Indians with their strong prejudices and conservatism which easily influence the younger Indians.[13]

Many superintendents believed that the deplorable conditions and influences graduates faced upon their return home were intensified by the boarding schools' tendency to destroy the children's ability to be self-sufficient. According to this view, government paternalism had taken away any need for young people to become self-reliant and responsible. Another criticism addressed the uselessness of some of the trades taught at school in the reservation environment, which led to unemployment and idleness. Some superintendents pointed out immoral conditions on the reservations as a reason for the alumni's failures while others lamented the resilience of Indian "nature": "The Indian lacks ambition to rise above a certain standard, this standard being accorded to their own ideas. That there is a deep rooted feeling among our Indians that the white man and his ways are inferior to the Indians."[14] Missionaries were especially concerned about the apparent relapse of former YMCA and YWCA members, who, as soon as they had returned home, gave up on their Christian religion altogether. Despite their negative observations, the interviewees maintained that every returned student was "better in some respects than his uneducated fellow" and that the children of returned students were "more plastic, brighter and quicker to acquire knowledge than were their parents."[15] In their view, however, only a massive improvement of reservation life—morally, as well as materially—could help to solve the "returned student problem."

For Haskell's alumni, finding employment was a tremendous challenge. As the surveyed superintendents had pointed out, many youth returned to communities plagued by unemployment and poverty. Many reservations were dry and barren and did not lend themselves to agricultural pursuits, and many of the trades the students had learned, such as harness and shoe making, plumbing, printing, or tailoring, were simply not in demand on the reservation. Employment opportunities with the local Indian agencies were at best limited, and well-paying jobs in neighboring white communities were equally scarce. In 1888, Robert Dunlap asked Superintendent Robinson to help him find employment and housing after returning to the reservation: "I want to find out if there is any way for the government to help a boy that is willing to make a living & not be idle like the rest of the Indians," Robert wrote. "Now I have little education & I want to make use of it. I don't want to go back to my old way, but I want to stand to what I have learned."[16] Robert Dunlap's letter speaks as much to the knowledge gained at Haskell as to the lack of opportunities to put his newly acquired skills to use.

Whereas male former students faced the difficulties of attaining economic self-sufficiency, female alumnae faced the challenge of applying the lessons they had learned in their domestic arts and science classes to the conditions of reservation life. The difficult realities of daily life destroyed many female aspirations to follow along the lines of Haskell's domestic training.

Indian girls trying to live up to the housekeeping standards taught at boarding school frequently faced opposition from their own families, who were less than enthusiastic about the girls' attempt to do everything according to white customs. When her mother and sister were working at a Chinese restaurant in Green River, Wyoming, Esther Burnett chose to stay home and take care of her younger siblings. She recalled:

> I cleaned the house thoroughly and wanted to keep it that way. I insisted that the children play outside, except for meals and to go to bed. I didn't want them messing up my clean house. My mother had to talk to me about how important it was for our house to be a home. She said to me, "Essie it's their house! They need to live in it." I guess that the rigors of my Haskell training were not always in line with my mother's ideas.[17]

For Indian women, basic role expectations did not differ as much between the white and the Indian world as they did for Indian men, and most of Haskell's girls eventually got married, had children, and became homemakers. Although Haskell's authorities wanted their female graduates to be well educated, they also wanted them to become wives and mothers. Marriage was desired and promoted by Haskell's superintendents if the spousal choice of the girl met with the school's approval. Haskell clearly made a distinction between "good marriages" and "bad marriages," the former referring to liaisons with self-supporting progressive Indian or white men, the latter to "camp Indians" or African Americans. Making a good marriage also included adopting a European-American lifestyle, living in a house, sending one's children to school, and speaking English all the time. Haskell students frequently married each other, either directly out of school or later in life. Partnerships that grew out of common experiences enabled students to share their memories of their boarding school years. Former students tended to have similar expectations and could better understand each other's feelings and thoughts as well as their partner's outlook on life. This might also account for the fact that many returnees married former students from Carlisle or Chilocco, who had had similar educational experiences. Boarding schools were responsible for a notable increase in intertribal marriages, thereby contributing to the rise of a larger Indian identity during the twentieth century. Nevertheless, on an individual basis, interracial and intertribal marriages also created frictions and discussions on the reservations. Stereotypes and intense dislikes existed not only between whites and Indians but also between members of different indigenous nations. Returning students bringing non-Indian spouses or partners from other tribes oftentimes faced negative attitudes and even discrimination from their own communities.

For graduates who were determined to become economically self-sufficient and were willing to leave their home communities, joining the Indian Service seemed like a natural choice. The U.S. Indian Service and its subbranch, the U.S. Indian School Service, were responsible for staffing reservation agencies and schools as well as off-reservation schools. Both services, which existed within the Office of Indian Affairs, distinguished between titled positions such as superintendent, agent, teacher, clerk, matron, and disciplinarian and more vocationally oriented jobs such as laundress, seamstress, baker, cook, laborer, and farmer. Especially during the nineteenth century, most titled positions were held by whites and enjoyed higher pay scales than the latter jobs, which were frequently held by indigenous employees. Although positions such as teacher or clerk were not gendered, female employees only received about half the pay of their male peers.[18] Between 1888 and 1899, the number of Indian School Service employees tripled, and by the late 1890s, 1,160 employees, or 45 percent of the workforce, were American Indian. The majority of these employees were former boarding school students. Most of them filled the lower echelon of Indian Service positions, however, earning their wages as assistant matrons, assistant clerks, laundresses, laborers, and farm workers. In 1899, out of 397 teachers, only 78 were Indian.

In 1905, Commissioner of Indian Affairs Leupp established the Indian Employment Bureau under the leadership of Charles Dagenett. Leupp instructed Dagenett to "gather up all able-bodied Indians who . . . would like to earn some money, and plant them on ranches, on railroads, in mines—wherever in the outer world, in short, there is an opening for a dollar to be gotten for a day's work."[19] Every summer, Haskell's superintendents sent a detailed list of graduates and students leaving Haskell to the Employment Bureau. The information included each student's age, degree of Indian blood, course of study, contact information, and disposition. Charles Dagenett, who headed the office for over a decade, kept in close contact with Haskell's superintendents and approached the school regularly in order to fill positions in his own department. As a Carlisle graduate, Dagenett had a genuine interest in seeing indigenous youth succeed in the Indian Service. He deeply believed in his work and in the Protestant work ethic and was eager to instill these values into boarding school graduates. Haskell's leadership supported the students' search for employment, especially if the young people had proven to be reliable and well-adjusted students. When Anna Bender, a graduate of the business course, expressed her interest in an assistant clerk position at the Indian school in Chemawa, Oregon, Superintendent Peairs enthusiastically endorsed her application:

> If you have a vacancy, I unhesitatingly recommend Miss Bender. She is an unusually capable young woman. She is a graduate of the normal department at Hampton Institute and of the two years' business course here. If you secure her you will be getting one of our very best graduates. I can give her no stronger endorsement than to say that I would gladly employ her here had I a position vacant. I am sure that if you employ her you will find her a very valuable employee.[20]

Deserters and repeated offenders of school rules, on the other hand, rarely received recommendations, since they had been "ungrateful to the Government."[21]

Although many positions were obtained through the Indian Employment Bureau, schools and agencies also directly approached Haskell's leadership in the search for qualified Indian employees. In 1918, for instance, the Mescalero Agency in New Mexico searched for five Haskell graduates to fill the positions of disciplinarians, laborer, electrician, assistant laundress, and assistant cook, for salaries ranging from $300 to $1,000.[22] As was the custom in the Indian Service, the positions of assistant cook and laundress were advertised with female students in mind and paid significantly less than the "male" positions of disciplinarian, laborer, and electrician. Some former students got their first working experience at Haskell, either as clerks and assistants in the school's administration, as assistant teachers, or as workers on the farm or in one of the industrial departments. During the 1890s, Haskell employed an average of ten Indian aides per year, most of them former students. An example was William Pollock, an accomplished Pawnee artist, who worked in Haskell's wagon shop. Pollock's paintings of "civilized" Indians adorning the sides of wagons built at Haskell became a trademark of the school.[23] In the early 1900s, Haskell maintained four positions for Indian assistant teachers, three of which paid $300 per year, with the fourth at $480 per annum, as well as a position for an Indian kindergarten teacher. When the Office of Indian

Affairs announced the discontinuation of three of these positions in 1909, Peairs complained to Washington, pointing out that these positions provided an excellent training opportunity for Indian girls who desired to fit themselves for teaching.[24]

In 1912, nineteen-year-old Ojibwe student Agnes Wright decided to leave her summer outing home in Emporia, Kansas, and applied for a position with the Indian Service. Agnes, a recent graduate of Haskell's commercial department, passed the civil service examination for typewriting, and soon received an offer from Charles Dagenett for a position as assistant clerk at the Indian Employment Office in Washington, D.C., at an annual salary of $600. The girl accepted, explaining to Superintendent Wise that she would "accept any position that is offered me to get experience if nothing else, as I am anxious to put in practice what I have learned at Haskell and promise you that I will do my very best to hold the position."[25] In a letter to Superintendent Wise, Charles Dagenett pointed out his reasoning in selecting Agnes above other recent graduates: "I selected Miss Wright not for her rating but because she was much more Indian than any of the rest and knowing the Reservation conditions in a general way at her home as I do I thought it would be a good thing to give her an immediate start rather than have her return home."[26] Agnes only remained in Washington for three months, after which she was transferred to the Department of Justice at Detroit, Minnesota. The following summer, she was transferred again, this time to the Ft. Lapwai Agency in Idaho, from which she wrote to Haskell:

> I like Idaho very much and I like my work here very much. My work is quite different than the other two I had prior to my coming here. In Detroit I copied records by hand for seven long months, never used my shorthand nor the typewriter so I had to work some to catch up when I came here. This is a very busy office, but I like it. I don't get very much time to get lonesome, don't have time to think about it.[27]

After fifteen months of service for the Nez Perce tribe, Agnes transferred back to Washington, D.C., and then, after another six months, to Pawushka, Oklahoma.

As Agnes Wright's employment record indicates, there was high turnover in Indian Service work, and it was not unusual to find alumni repeatedly changing positions. For many former students, the adjustment to their new and, in many instances, remote surroundings was difficult. After taking a position at Orton, Utah, in 1907, Cordelia Garvie wrote back to the school:

> I am now getting used to my work and like it very much. Reached here safe although I was on the road longer than I had expected. The country and the people all seem rather strange to me, therefore get very lonesome for Haskell and friends. But hope to get used to it all and to do my very best, and live up to your expectations if possible.[28]

The transition to an unknown locale far away from either Haskell or home was at times so demanding that graduates were eager to transfer as soon as possible. During the winter of 1917, Hattie Wright, a graduate of the school's course in home economics, was excited to take her first position as assistant matron at Tongue River School in Montana. The job paid only $480 per year and was located in a very remote area, but Hattie was determined to make the best of it. After two months, however, she wrote to Superintendent Wise:

> I like this place very much but I can not say that I am so well pleased with the pupils they are so backward and so hard to teach anything. It seems to me as if they don't care to learn. But otherwise I like it very well. . . . We have in all about seventy-four students. I have charge of the boys' side of the building. They all have quarters in the same building, I mean boys and girls. The school rooms and everything are in the same building. Mr. Wise I certainly thank you for your assistance all through school and in getting this position. Mr. Wise I would like to ask this one more favor of you and that is should you know of any other place that you think I could successfully fill I should be glad to have you recommend me for it.[29]

On Hattie's letter, the last passage about a possible transfer was marked with a pencil and the telling exclamation "already!" No doubt, Haskell's superintendents were less than delighted when their former charges showed a lack of appreciation for their new positions and signs of dissatisfaction and instability. Superintendent Wise's reply reflects his disappointment:

> I have your letter dated March 7th and was pleased to hear from you and to know that you have been enjoying your work in Montana. I was some-

what disappointed, however, to know that you are already thinking of a change. Don't you think, Hattie, that it would be best for you to stay where you are at least long enough to show that you have "made good"? . . . You say that it seems the pupils there do not seem to care to learn. Of course, the boys and girls there have not had the advantages that many young people have, and perhaps there is much you can do for them, with all your training, in the way of helping them to become interested in their school work and to see the necessity of training themselves for their work in life.[30]

Hattie Wright's first impressions from Montana attest to Haskell's undeniable "civilizing" force. To Hattie, who had spent several years at Haskell, the children at Tongue River School seemed backward and "uncivilized." Her reaction to the school building as well as to its inhabitants reflects a belief in the "savagery-civilization" paradigm propagated by her alma mater. For her, the transition from a "finishing school" such as Haskell to a reservation boarding school was disappointing, and she did not care to prolong the experience.

When former commercial student George Selkirk took a position as assistant clerk at the Sisseton Agency in South Dakota, he was equally surprised by the remoteness of his new home. In 1910, he wrote to Haskell how beautiful but lonely Sisseton was and how difficult it was for him to stick with his assignment:

Often times I have been on the verge of resigning my position at this Agency to go to the Cities or to be back in school, but always I think of my dear old Father whose wish is to have me stick to a place until I have proven my ability to do things without question, or doubt and then again I think of my classmates who, perhaps, are in as lonesome places as I am and who seem to be contented with their surroundings.[31]

George had the luck of working with two other Haskell graduates, Henry E. Roberts and E. J. Price, and the three were well liked by their employer:

I dare say that the Agent here thinks a great deal of his Haskell Employees. By the way, that brings many little incidents and a few big ones to mind and I can truthfully say that all of my success has been due to my training received under your instruction at H.I.

George emphasized that it was the company of his fellow students that made his life at Sisseton bearable and that compelled him to stay:

> We have decided, if everything turns out well, to stick here until spring, when we are going to leave the Service hoping to better ourselves, and we look forward to a more pleasant time and a better place to live.[32]

Six years later, however, George Selkirk still worked at Sisseton, filling the position of acting finance clerk, which paid $1,000 per annum. He had married a former Chilocco student and had become the father of a baby girl, another "grand daughter of Haskell Institute," as he called her in his letter to his former business teacher, C. E. Birch. George had apparently settled down and "made good." He described his life in positive terms and voiced his intention of organizing a Returned Students Association in the region.[33] Associations of former boarding school students had sprung up across the nation as early as 1883, offering Hampton, Carlisle, Chilocco, Haskell, and other alumni practical and moral guidance and a sense of belonging. Indian agents encouraged the formation of chapters on their reservations, in part because they furnished an organizational base for converting traditional Indians to "civilized" ways. More important, however, they provided psychological support to former students tempted by the allure of traditional indigenous culture.[34]

In addition to the remoteness of the assignments, working for the Indian Service had other negative sides. Sometimes, agents resented or felt threatened by the returned students, since boarding school graduates had the self-confidence and education to demand fair treatment and had a better understanding of the system than their less-educated peers. To prevent the graduates from having too much influence in their respective posts, the Indian School Service made it a rule not to employ Indians in their home communities. The temptation to speak in the tribal language or the inability to escape local factionalism was usually given as a reason. In reality, though, the rule served to remove the Indian staff most likely to protest illegal or arbitrary behavior.[35] Over the years, the percentage of Indian employees in the Service decreased as racism, resistance from white staff, and indifference in the Office of Indian Affairs mounted. After the turn of the century, salaries and titles for Indian employees were cut more frequently, and by 1905, differences along racial lines in both salaries and quality of position had intensified.[36] Despite these developments, Indian Service work offered one of the few professional avenues open to Haskell's graduates. When Haskell alumni chose to work for the Indian Service, either in schools or on the reservations, they at least temporarily agreed to embrace the federal agenda of assimilation. Whether it was their intention or not, as employees of Indian schools and agencies, Haskell's graduates helped to perpetuate the system that had created them in the first place.

Not surprisingly, Haskell's business graduates had the best chances to find their place in the workforce, either inside the Indian Service or outside in the business world. In his 1918 report to the commissioner of Indian affairs, C. E. Birch contended that he could not name a single outright failure among Haskell's more than 250 business graduates. According to Birch:

> Among these graduates will be found several superintendents of Indian schools or agencies, several chief clerks, an accountant in the Indian Office in Washington, scores of clerks, stenographers and other assistants. For example, Superintendent J. W. Balmer, Lac du Flambeau, is a commercial graduate here; also Superintendent L. S. Bonnin of the Kickapoo Agency, Horton, Kansas. Mr. James Plake is one of the accountants in the Indian Bureau in Washington. This list might be continued indefinitely.[37]

Birch added that Haskell's thorough business education enabled graduates to pass the civil service examination, secure employment in the Indian Service or business houses, and transact business for themselves. The business course also served as a preparation for college entrance examinations, and it helped students to earn a living while attending college: "It seems to me this is an answer to the critics who say we do not make it possible for our Indian students to acquire a college education."[38] Even though only a small number of Haskell graduates found their way into the nation's colleges, most who did had mastered Haskell's commercial training.

Many of Haskell's business alumni shared their former teacher's praise for the program. In 1917, sixteen years after graduating from the course, John E. Snake, an Indian Service employee at the Indian Agency in Shawnee, Oklahoma, wrote to Superintendent Peairs:

> I come to your school in early part of September in the year of 1898, and during my three years training there I learned lots of good things and I am glad to say that I still have those good things in my head, as we know

education does not get away from the fellow, like gold mine does and so education is way better than gold mine in some cases. I take great pleasure saying that Haskell Institute is one of the best commercial training schools I know of. Nearly every Indian Agency or Indian School contains Ex-Haskellites employees and doing well and had been leaders and most of them are very capable workers.[39]

Although many business graduates worked in Indian agencies and for the government, others took positions in the business world. In 1909, for instance, the employment department of the Underwood Typewriter Company helped to place several Haskell graduates as typists and stenographers with companies across the country. One graduate was placed with the Phoenix Stone Company in Kansas City, another girl with the Santa Fe Railroad in Wellington, Kansas, and a third with the Pullman Car Company in Kansas City.[40] Several of Haskell's business graduates found employment in nearby Kansas City, where they established "their own little colony," as Superintendent Fiske called it. Even though he was not in support of girls and boys working and living in the same vicinity, fearing immoral behavior, he supported their employment by business houses, since he felt that on the reservations, "the knowledge of the subjects which they have attained . . . will be virtually valueless to them, outside of the domestic arts and science, and . . . they will, of necessity, lose their proficiency in what they have learned."[41] For this reason, Haskell supported the students' quest for employment off the reservation. The school's administration exchanged numerous letters with companies and factories, inquiring about employment opportunities for Haskell's alumni. During the 1910s, schools such as Carlisle, Hampton, and Haskell helped a number of mechanically inclined graduates to secure employment in the automobile factories of Ohio, Michigan, and Indiana. In 1917, Supervisor of Indian Employment Dagenett informed Haskell's administration that the minimum wage for automobile factory work was twenty-eight cents an hour, that the workday was nine hours long, that Indian boys were welcome to room at the local YMCA, and that the boys were expected to save parts of their wages in order to open their own small businesses after leaving the factories.[42] In 1918, Haskell's administrators approached General Electric's plant in Erie, Pennsylvania, inquiring whether students who had just finished their grammar school course or first year of high school would be acceptable in the factory's machine shop.[43] General Electric replied that it would be glad to hire any "intelligent person of proper age and physique," that the work would be on machines without much variation in the tasks performed, and that the company's welfare department and the YMCA would keep careful watch over the boys.[44] Haskell's leadership was concerned about the boys' moral welfare and wanted to make sure that potential employers provided an environment free of "temptations." Once former students took jobs in eastern factories, the school maintained contact with their employers in order to learn how the boys were getting along.

Some Haskell alumni found employment of a different nature, embarking on careers in vaudeville and Wild West shows. These entertainments were especially interested in hiring young, educated Indians who would be willing to present the virtues of "real" Indians dressed in feathers and who at the same time would be able to appear on stage as "civilized" Americans. Haskell graduates were given the jobs because they spoke English, were literate, and were capable of following orders. Employers such as William ("Buffalo Bill") Cody saw their show Indians as culture brokers, serving as interpreters who would tell non-Indians about native cultures and their tribal communities about their experiences in the white world. According to Cody, his Indian employees were contributing to what he called the great task of "harmonizing the races."[45] Haskell's alumni joined the shows for money, travel, and adventure—and received all three in abundance. The show environment was a multiethnic and multicultural environment that allowed young men to travel to faraway places, to experience the big cities of the East, and to earn a very good living—all while being allowed to remain Indian.[46] Haskell's records do not indicate whether the school supported student careers in the entertainment industry, but it is clear that a number of former students followed this attractive route, appearing on stages in the United States and in Europe.

A popular career goal for Indian women was nursing, either with the Indian Service or in one of the nation's hospitals. Haskell's girls received basic training in nursing while at school and later attended nursing courses at larger hospitals. In the late 1910s, Superintendent Peairs contacted several hospitals in Kansas, Missouri, and Minnesota, seeking to establish relationships with a certified nursing program that would accept Haskell girls on a regular basis.[47] Peairs explained that although Haskell's nursing program was designed as a four-year course, the school was not really able to give the girls all the practical experience they needed, especially in the field of surgical nursing. During the spring of 1919, Mary Martin was one of four nursing graduates seeking a hospital for further training. Haskell's nurse supported the girl's ambition: "She desires to choose nursing as her future work and I can recommend her as being faithful, kind, honest, and of excellent character."[48] Superintendent Peairs corresponded with hospitals in the Minneapolis–St. Paul area, securing training positions for all four girls. Together with her peer Eva Flying Earth, Mary Martin entered the nursing training course of Saint Mary's Hospital in Minneapolis for a three-year term. The girls had to pay for their uniforms, books, and personal expenses. Board, room, and laundry expenses were defrayed by the hospital. Apart from teaching and clerical work, nursing was one of the few professions open to Indian girls during the early twentieth century. Over the years, many of Haskell's girls became nurses in health care facilities on and off the reservations, and during World War I, Indian girls serving as nurses for the Red Cross were sent abroad as part of the American Expeditionary Forces (AEF).

While Haskell's female graduates provided clerical and nursing services during World War I, Haskell's boys volunteered for the U.S. military. In addition to the more than 12,500 Indians who served on the battlefields of western Europe, several hundred Native Americans assembled military vehicles in the Ford factories.[49] By late 1917, more than 150 Haskell students had left the school to join the military, most of them on a voluntary basis, with only a few having been subjected to the draft. In a December 1917 report, their tribes and positions were listed, indicating that the boys came from a wide variety of nations and mainly served in the artillery and the infantry. The school estimated that altogether, more than 500 of Haskell's students and alumni served during the war.[50] As mentioned earlier, Indian boarding school students were frequently praised for their adaptability to army camp life, attesting to their familiarity with military process and protocols. No doubt, Haskell had already provided them with the basics of military training. After all, the military was just another institution to be survived. Camp life was not much different from boarding school life: seventeen-hour days, physical exercises, kitchen duty, ground maintenance, target practice, bayonet drills, uncomfortable olive-drab uniforms, and marching exercises. Ironically, former boarding school students mention that they ate better in the camps than at school.[51] Many of Haskell's boys received their military training as part of Battery B, Field Artillery, at Ft. Sill, Oklahoma. One of their superiors reported back to the school: "I might add that all the Haskell boys are doing well in the Battery.

They are making good soldiers and are observing strictly the orders given them."[52]

Haskell insisted on the written consent of the students' parents before agreeing to their enlistment. Boys who left the school without parental and school consent were considered deserters and treated accordingly. Although some boys over the age of eighteen enlisted against their parents' wishes, it appears that most boys followed their families' advice. Orphans were sometimes encouraged to join the military since their Indian agents believed that army service would be more beneficial to them than returning to the reservation without proper supervision.[53] Many parents, and especially mothers, were opposed to their sons' military service, giving as a reason that they had sent their sons to school for an education and not to bear arms and get killed. Some parents emphasized their old age and bad health, which made it necessary for their sons to be able to come home at any time if the need arose. Others rejected the idea of military service for religious reasons, quoting passages from the Bible. One concerned mother from Oklahoma wrote:

> I am opposed to war, the Bible tells us thou shalt not kill. We stand for peace and Sam is hard of hearing and we kneed him at home afful bad his stepfather ant very stout this spring he cant do any vary hard work he has smitherin spells and he is lible to drop dead any time then what would I do the other children is small and he would be my only dependence for help at war.[54]

Many other parents, however, consented to their son's military service, seeing the war as an opportunity for their sons to learn new skills, show their patriotism, and prove their bravery on the battlefield. One father, for instance, wanted his son to join the navy, so that he could get expert training as an electrician, the trade he was learning at Haskell.[55] Another father expressed strong support for his son's enlistment for cultural reasons, referring to the Pawnee's proud warrior tradition:

> He has my full approval, for the government has all these years trained him to be loyal to our country's flag. . . . I hope all Pawnee young men will join the army or navy and show to the world the bravery of Pawnee Indians. . . . Tell Lawrence I shall be proud of him. Knowing that he has shouldered the gun to defend our country's rights, and if he should go to

the front, for him to show no cowardice, but to be brave and keep up his ancestors' courage, for many of them died upon the plains, fighting for the government. Tell him that I say that it is an honor among the Pawnees to die upon the battlefield than to die at home and be buried. This is a serious thing to join the army, but knowing as I do, it is best for my son to go and I only hope and pray that he may make a good soldier and make a good record for himself.[56]

For Indian boys, joining the military was their chance to make a record as warriors—for their country, their tribe, their family, and Haskell. One Cherokee student who deserted from Haskell and joined the army wrote to his mother: "Tell all Haskell students that I am going to do my share in whipping the Kaiser!"[57] Even though the boys substituted the confines of one institution for that of another, the military provided a chance to excel and to show courage and bravery. In addition, serving in the army or navy was an attractive alternative to being unemployed on a reservation and opened up opportunities to see the world and acquire new skills. When the war ended in November 1918, former Haskell students were among the 200,000 American soldiers wounded and the 50,000 who lost their lives on Europe's battlefields. In February 1919, Superintendent Peairs received a letter from Vigil Isidro, a former Navajo student who had just returned from Europe:

> I joined the army in 1916 and I was one of the first Americans to go across. I went with General Pershing's Troops and I had bad luck while I was across I got wounded last October and lost my left leg and they said I was of luck at that all my other of a company of 250 men got kill and I wish I gotten kill myself this is a hard country to live when you are wounded. We lost about 34,000 men of the first Division . . . was in battle the longest time of American troops that went across. I would like to visit the school some time. I like very much to see you. I write to you because my parents are all gone and got no body left. . . . Give my regards to all the boys at the school, I think I am the first Haskell school boy wounded in the great war.[58]

In his reply, Superintendent Peairs invited Vigil Isidro to visit Haskell and promised him help in securing veteran's benefits. No doubt, the war had left a lasting impression on the nation as well as on the thousands of Native Americans who had actively participated in the war effort. When they returned from the training camps and the battlefields, Haskell's veterans once more faced the uncertainties of securing employment and the problem of readjustment to their families, communities, and reservations.

Most boarding school students perceived their years at Haskell as a formative experience, one that had a long-lasting influence on their life. Although time impacts memory by lessening negative recollections and nurturing nostalgic emotions, many students harbored a positive attitude toward their alma mater.

In her memoirs, former Iroquois student Lucille Winnie emphasized that Haskell was more than strict discipline, bad-tempered officers, and intolerant matrons: "Whether we liked them or not, they helped us to become better citizens and adjust to a better way of life when we left Haskell."[59] Winnie, who was a second-generation Haskell student and came from a largely acculturated family, saw her training at Haskell during the 1910s in positive terms: "The academic education we received at Haskell was not slanted to college entrance, but based on the needs of our people at the time. We learned what was essential to our future. No foreign languages were taught, but we got a good basic English foundation and were taught to speak and write English correctly."[60]

Lucille Winnie, who spent most of her life in white society, made good use of her education. After working as a teacher in the Indian Service and at several other jobs, Winnie joined the early flight industry, was employed by magnate Howard Hughes, met Amelia Earhart, and worked in Hawaii. Later on in life, she helped the Cheyenne nation to organize a craft industry on its reservation.[61] Although her life story is not representative for the majority of boarding school students, in some respects it is not unusual. Former Haskell students moved around the country, lived in Native American and non-Indian communities, and worked in a variety of occupations, inside and outside of the Indian Service. The generations of boarding school students who left Haskell in the 1890s, 1900s, 1910s, and 1920s found themselves in multiple locations and with many agendas.

Boarding school alumni, forced to negotiate between cultures and lifestyles, became cultural brokers and spokespeople for their indigenous communities. Numerous Haskell alumni became involved in tribal politics and worked as administrators, translators, teachers, and lawyers for the good of their people. Instead of turning away from their own communities, they eventually returned home and put their education to use for the benefit of their tribes. It is no coincidence that many of today's tribal leaders had parents or grandparents who attended Haskell. Most former students maintained ties with their Indian communities, and many were among the first proponents of formal, intertribal political organizations, such as the Society of American Indians. They formed a national network of friendships based on their boarding school experience. Like Esther Burnett and Lucille Winnie, many Haskell alumni lived partly acculturated lives, setting examples for their own people of how to adapt to the dominant society while at the same time holding on to their tribal identities.

In her memoirs, Esther Burnett described how her two favorite Indian teachers, Ruth Muskrat Bronson and Ella Deloria, taught their students to survive in different environments—Indian as well as non-Indian. The teachers took Burnett and her peers on programs that were presented to schools, churches, and service organizations: "Instrumental and vocal music and talks relating to our Indian heritage were part of the programs we presented."[62] Although the tours provided a welcome opportunity for the students to escape the confines of the boarding school, Bronson and Deloria had a more important function in mind:

> They wanted us to be proud of who we were as Indian people and as boarding school students but also to be comfortable in explaining our identity to the non-Indian world. I suppose one could say that this was a "safe" way of being Indian, that is, according to the expectations of white society. But for us it was not this way. With Ruth and Ella as our Indian mentors, these excursions became expressions of our Indianness that may not otherwise have been possible, given the poverty and discrimination so prevalent on most reservations.[63]

Burnett made an important point: To her, being educated and versed in various aspects of the dominant culture, while at the same time retaining her Shoshone identity, were equally important components of who she was as an indigenous woman during the 1920s. She did not regard her partial assimilation to white society as a sign of "selling out" or losing her Indianness. Rather, Burnett saw her accommodation with dominant values and culture as an expression of changing realities and historical circumstances. Burnett's self-identification is consistent throughout her memoirs. She saw herself as an indigenous person emerging into mainstream culture without a simultaneous loss of her native values. Burnett chose from multiple identities, which differed according to her audience and setting: former boarding school student, Haskell graduate, teacher, Indian Service employee, or member of the Shoshone nation as well as an American Indian woman, daughter, sister, mother, and wife. Even though her family background was racially mixed, her ethnic identity was clearly Indian, as her recollections indicate. Indian teachers such as Esther Burnett perpetuated Native American cultural traditions within institutions originally intended to lead to cultural assimilation. Talking about her first position at Eufaula Boarding School in Oklahoma, a school for Creek girls, Burnett explained:

> I worked very hard to be an outstanding teacher. I was the only Indian teacher, and I was not going to be a failure. I was not going to let my alma mater down; I was not going to let my Indian people down; and I was not going to let my family down. I wanted both sides of my family, both the Indian and non-Indian, to be proud of me. I had a lot of energy and a strong desire to succeed.[64]

Later in her career, Esther Burnett taught at Wahpeton Indian School in North Dakota. Among her students were several boys who would later become prominent leaders in the American Indian Movement: Leonard Peltier, Dennis Banks, and George Mitchell. Burnett's life story very much reflects the complexities of the boarding school experience and the schools' ironic legacy of cultural survival.[65] It appears that many boarding school alumni followed a similar path, living a blended version of indigenous and white cultures, without abandoning their Indian identities.[66] Former Arapaho student Jesse Rowlodge, for instance, became an important political intermediary for his people, assisting the Arapaho tribe of Oklahoma in relations with non-Indians and government officials.[67] Jesse Rowlodge was born in 1884 and as a child and adolescent learned tribal culture and history from his stepfather, Row-of-Lodges, an Arapaho chief. While growing up, he developed a comprehensive knowledge of his tribe's social and political organization, participated in men's age-grade societies, and attended Sun Dances in Oklahoma and Wyoming with his family. At age fifteen, Jesse began to join peyote ceremonies. From age six onward, Jesse attended the Arapaho Boarding school at Darlington, and in 1904 he enrolled at Haskell. As described in the previous chapters, he was among Haskell's more successful and well-adjusted pupils, a member of the band, an athlete, an actor in the school's theater productions, and a good scholar.

After his graduation from the commercial department in 1910, he passed the civil service examination and later studied law in Minnesota. Rowlodge then returned to Oklahoma; farmed his mother's land; married Carrie Lumpmouth, the daughter of an Arapaho chief; and filled various positions in the Indian Service, including those of stenographer, accountant, and finance clerk.[68] Jesse Rowlodge became a member of the Arapaho tribal council at age twenty-six and served his tribe in key political positions for more than fifty years. He became a well-known and highly respected leader among the Arapahos. During the 1920s, 1930s, and 1940s, boarding school alumni, many of them from Haskell and Carlisle, gained prominence in Arapaho and Cheyenne politics and made up a growing part of the tribes' political leaders. The generational change taking place in the tribal council was not conflict free, however, and many traditional leaders resented the growing influence of the boarding school graduates. The fact that many of the younger, educated men were of mixed Indian-white ancestry certainly contributed to this divide. Factionalism ran high in tribal politics, and at times Jesse Rowlodge experienced and withstood strong criticism from tribal elders.[69] In his various capacities as corresponding secretary, council president, chairman of the business committee, and council member, he made more than forty trips to Washington, D.C., helping his people to press claims cases against the government. When Rowlodge became involved with Arapaho land claims, he finally resigned from government work. In a 1968 interview he stated that his legal work for the tribal council made it impossible for him to get any first-rate government jobs and that he "didn't get along too well with the government" after that.[70]

Jesse Rowlodge was well-versed in the traditional culture of his tribe and anxious for it to be preserved. By the late 1960s he was one of only two surviving members of the Star Hawk Society, one of the old age-grade warrior societies, and expressed his hope that the organization would be revived in modern times. He was a member of the Baptist Church but felt that the peyote ceremony gave him the greatest personal fulfillment and inspiration.[71] Although he did not possess Arapaho ceremonial status, his participation in

Sun Dances and peyote ceremonies, as well as his membership in a Christian church, enabled him to relate to Arapahos of various religious orientation. Rowlodge acted as a culture broker on many levels. He was deeply committed to his people and served as their political intermediary. At the same time he communicated his knowledge about Arapaho culture to the larger society, working with famous anthropologists such as A. L. Kroeber, James Mooney, and Fred Eggan.[72]

Jesse Rowlodge's experiences reflect the conflicting realities of being Indian during the twentieth century. He worked for the U.S. government as well as for the Arapaho tribal council; he supported federal policies and also pressed land claims against the government; he was a peyotist as well as a Baptist; he played American football, appeared on Haskell's stage, and studied law while at the same time representing the traditional Arapaho Star Hawk society. His life bears testimony to the complex processes shaping indigenous cultures and identities under assimilationist pressure. When he died in 1974 at the age of ninety, Jesse Rowlodge had lived up to his stepfather's ideal that an Arapaho chief should be a "public hearted and public spirited" leader.[73]

As dynamic products of human agency, ethnic cultures and identities are by no means static but constantly adapting to historical changes and challenges to their survival. During the nineteenth and twentieth centuries, Native American cultures underwent significant changes, some of them voluntary, many forced. Through processes such as preservation, syncretism, innovation, and assimilation, indigenous cultures, like all cultures, have constantly undergone construction and reconstruction. Communities faced with external pressures for assimilation or annihilation often respond to that threat with the creation of new cultural patterns or the revision of existing cultural forms. The history of Indian-white relations suggests that indigenous societies in many instances responded to white encroachment with cultural innovation and revision, since changing their culture was the only way for Indian tribes to protect it. Boarding school students contributed to the revision of their cultures by blending white and native cultural practices and lifestyles. Likewise, they helped to preserve their cultures by secretly carrying on cultural traditions at school and later in life on the reservations and in their families and communities. They also contributed to cultural innovation by participating in newly emerging cultural forms such as peyotism and supratribal political organizations. Jesse Rowlodge's life stands as an example of the multiple ways in which former boarding school students combined the old and the new, the dominant and the traditional, while at the same time maintaining an Indian identity.

Of course, this does not imply that participation in two worlds, as well as the creation of their own "modern" Indian world, was easy or conflict free. Like Rowlodge, Burnett, and Winnie, thousands of boarding school students constantly had to negotiate their desires to be "Indian" versus "white," experiencing severe internal conflicts in the process. Undeniably, the boarding school experience had long-lasting negative effects on native families and communities, and scores of former boarding school students, as well as their descendants, suffered from these consequences. Although boarding schools alone cannot be blamed for the loss of Indian cultural forms and languages, they certainly contributed to linguistic decline and the destruction of indigenous cultures. Linda Grover's study of the effects of boarding schools on Ojibwe families supports this view. All of the interviewees recalled that the boarding school experience had profound and permanent academic, social, cultural, and political effects on both the students who attended the schools and the generations that have followed them.[74] Among the most serious consequences were the loss of native language ability and the attempt to remove Indian children from their tribe's religious traditions. The loss of the Ojibwe language was especially devastating because it meant an irrevocable loss of large portions of the people's traditional culture and oral history. All participants in the study observed a significant loss of native language in their families, declining from the first boarding school generation's fluency in Ojibwe, to the third or fourth generation's inability to understand more than just a few words. Many members of the first boarding school generation stopped using their native language once they had children themselves, fearing that they would be punished if they knew how to speak Ojibwe and hoping to help their children's advancement in white society by teaching them English only. One interviewee recalled:

> When we were kids and used to say Indian words around the house my grandmother would say things like, "Shh, you're not supposed to talk like that." And that was when she was in her fifties and sixties, you know, but I think she still had that fear that she would be punished, or we would be punished if we were talking that way.[75]

A former Haskell student explained:

> "I don't know anyone who speaks it anymore except for my brother, and we can only talk long-distance on the telephone. When I'm by myself, I talk in Indian to myself all the time, so I don't forget."[76]

Boarding school education led to conflicts of values such as individualism versus communalism and instilled a feeling of cultural inferiority and shame. Although many Ojibwe expressed pride in what their elders had done to survive and bring them into the world, they also expressed the feeling that society did not recognize or acknowledge that pride as legitimate. Boarding schools, through their inherently racist ideologies, had a negative effect on Indian students' self-esteem. As one interviewee pointed out, the schools instilled the idea that it was "not ok to be Indian," a notion that leads to social maladies such as alcoholism: "It's having their grandparents and their parents and themselves told it's not ok to be Indian, that if you are Indian there's something wrong with you, you're a drunk, you're lazy, or not as smart."[77]

Another serious, long-term consequence of the boarding school experience is its impact on indigenous attitudes toward education. As one Ojibwe described, "Unfortunately some of the parents and grandparents . . . became very suspicious of the White man's education. It's not that Indians wouldn't like to encourage and help their children, it's just that they don't know how to do it, and some of that is due to their frustrations with education, and that can be traced back to the boarding school."[78] Often, indigenous parents lacked trust in the public school system and had not had the opportunity to experience and develop the ability needed for effective involvement in their children's education outside the Indian community and the boarding school system. According to the study, the children of former boarding school students frequently did not expect school to be a positive experience and fared accordingly.

The most intimate and at the same time devastating effect of the boarding school system was its impact on Indian families. All of the Ojibwe interviewees agreed that boarding schools weakened indigenous family ties and prevented generations from developing necessary parenting skills. A former Haskell student recalled: "In my own family, because I was away at school and I'd come home during the summer months, it was like they resented me coming back. I was learning about home economics, and about culture, and all these new things, and they didn't want me to think I was better than they were."[79] Another interviewee observed, "People usually learn parenting skills from their parents, and if they're not around their parents, how are they going to learn? It almost seems like the parenting skills and a lot of the culture stopped at a certain point because of boarding schools, and has never really caught up again."[80] Children sent to boarding school were cut off from their families, and especially from their elders. Since they were no longer able to learn from their grandparents, one of the traditional means of cultural transmission was severely disturbed and in many cases completely destroyed.[81] The breakdown of native family structures caused by the boarding school experience has affected the ability of indigenous peoples to successfully cope and thrive in modern society.

Despite all the pain and suffering caused by the schools, boarding school alumni and their descendants agree that ultimately, Indian families and communities were stronger than the destructive influences of federal government policies. As Ojibwe historian Brenda Child has pointed out,

> The letters between family members speak for the deepest of bonds, able to survive separation and efforts to undermine American Indian families. This essential communication kept young people from feeling abandoned and sustained children and parents alike. The boarding school agenda did not triumph over Indian families or permanently alienate young members of the tribe from their people. Descendents of boarding school alumni at Red Lake and other Ojibwe communities are still taught to know and value their relatives, as their families always wished.[82]

Linda Grover's sources shared this view and expressed their pride in their families' ability to survive as well as genuine admiration for their elders, who overcame great odds to maintain their families' identities and thus the Ojibwes' identity as a people.[83]

Indian families, communities, and cultures have been altered by the boarding school experience, but they have not been destroyed. Most Indian children survived their years at boarding school and, despite the pain and the loss, often succeeded in turning their experience into something positive.[84] Their descendants have not accepted the destruction of tribal cultures as inevitable and feel a particular obligation to prevent the further erosion of indigenous culture and tradition. They keep their ancestors' memories and experiences alive and pass them on to the next generation. As Ojibwe scholar Linda Grover phrases it: "The boarding school experience has not left us, we have not left that experience." The experience was of such magnitude and depth that it continues to influence indigenous people's lives beyond their educational experience: "We hold on to that boarding school experience and remember it because it is ours. Much of our bondage to the past is by our own choice. Indianishly, the choice empowers us."[85] Even though many indigenous people have negative feelings about boarding schools, they acknowledge the experience as part of their history, taking their identity as a people from it, and drawing strength from their survival. Esther Burnett's positive recollections of Haskell underline this point:

> The sense of community at Haskell was very strong. Among Indian people this is very important. We had a pride in our school and in our teams, and we had such a strong school spirit. We were so proud to be associated with Haskell. Most of us who are alumni of Indian boarding schools feel a great pride and sense of belonging to a unique and special group of people—people who we keep in touch with and who have become part of our extended families. Even though boarding schools took children away from their homes, families, and communities, we created our own community at the school. We were proud of our accomplishments and proud that we had retained so much of our Indianness. Critics dismiss boarding schools as assimilationist institutions whose intent was to destroy native culture. While this may be a true generalization, the students and teachers at Haskell will forever be an integral part of who I am as an American Indian.[86]

There is no single story that captures Haskell. The school meant and continues to mean a thousand different things to a thousand different people. For every story of heartbreak, pain, and failure, there is a story of joy, friendship, and personal success. It is a story that some people remember with pride and about which others refuse to speak. What all the alumni's stories have in common, though, is a search for meaning and a strong will to survive as indigenous people in a rapidly changing world. American Indians have emerged from the boarding school experience changed from the people they were before. The disruption of native cultures created by the schools has not yet waned; the scars are visible throughout indigenous families and communities. Forced cultural change, cultural construction, and reconstruction have become integral parts of the Indian experience. But just as Haskell has survived and become an institution dedicated to cultural survival and the strengthening of ethnic identities, so too indigenous peoples have survived this controversial chapter in their history. Haskell's students and alumni share a collective identity as boarding school students and as members of America's First Nations. Their ethnic narrative includes the past, the present, and the future. It awakens pride and self-confidence as well as anger, fear, and inferiority. By remembering the life stories of boarding school students, indigenous people strengthen their collective identity. Through stories, they make sense of their experiences, and through stories they create themselves as American Indians. Ironically, even after more than 120 years, Haskell's motto, "Onward Ever, Backward Never," rings true. There is no turning back, but the experiences of the past shape the visions for a brighter future, at Haskell and throughout America's indigenous communities.

Notes

Introduction

1. Warren Ondelacy, short autobiography, 1920, HR, RG 75, NADC.

2. K. Tsianina Lomawaima, *They Called It Prairie Light: The Story of Chilocco Indian School* (Lincoln: University of Nebraska Press, 1994).

3. Stephen Cornell, *The Return of the Native: American Indian Political Resurgence* (New York: Oxford University Press, 1988); Joane Nagel, "Constructing Ethnicity: Creating and Recreating Identity and Culture," *Social Problems* 41 (1994): 152–176; Joane Nagel, *American Indian Ethnic Renewal: Red Power and the Resurgence of Identity and Culture* (New York: Oxford University Press, 1996).

4. Thomas G. Andrews, "Turning the Tables on Assimilation: Oglala Lakotas and the Pine Ridge Day Schools, 1889–1920s," *Western Historical Quarterly* 33, 4 (Winter 2002): 407–432; Clyde Ellis, "We Had a Lot of Fun, but of Course That Wasn't the School Part: Life at the Rainy Mountain Boarding School, 1893–1920," in *Boarding School Blues: Revisiting American Indian Educational Experiences*, ed. Clifford E. Trafzer, Jean A. Keller, and Lorene Siquoc, 66–68 (Lincoln: University of Nebraska Press, 2006).

5. As quoted in Cornell, *Return of the Native*, 114.

6. Frederick E. Hoxie, *A Final Promise: The Campaign to Assimilate the Indians, 1880–1920* (Cambridge: Cambridge University Press, 1984); David Wallace Adams, *Education for Extinction: American Indians and the Boarding School Experience, 1875–1928* (Lawrence: University Press of Kansas, 1995).

7. On a theoretical level, James C. Scott has been helpful in understanding the ways in which boarding school students have resisted their victimization. James C. Scott, *Domination and the Arts of Resistance: Hidden Transcripts* (New Haven, CT: Yale University Press, 1990), xii.

8. Haskell's *Vision 2008* and *Academic Vision*, available at www.haskell.edu (accessed January 2, 2008).

9. The records examined for this study, listed under Records of the Bureau of Indian Affairs, RG 75, include, among others, Individual Student Case Files (1884–1980), Enrollment Records (1899–1901), General Correspondence Files (1886–1960), Chronological Correspondence Files (1900–1914), Correspondence with Schools and Agencies (1886–1960), Correspondence with the Commissioners of Indian Affairs (1900–1914), Subject Correspondence Files (1917–1942), Superintendents' Correspon-

dence Files (1915–1942), Annual Reports (1910–1920 and 1939–1951), School Calendars (1920–1925), and Photographs and Related Records (1916–1921).

10. All the files concerning the period under investigation are by now unrestricted.

11. David W. Adams, "Beyond Bleakness: The Brighter Side of Indian Boarding Schools, 1870–1940," in *Boarding School Blues: Revisiting American Indian Educational Experiences,* ed. Clifford E. Trafzer, Jean A. Keller, and Lorene Siquoc, 37 (Lincoln: University of Nebraska Press, 2006).

12. Throughout this study, the students' first names are being used, since in most cases, the students were children and teenagers when they attended Haskell. In no way does this choice reflect any disrespect for the students or their families.

13. Brenda J. Child, *Boarding School Seasons: American Indian Families, 1900–1940* (Lincoln: University of Nebraska Press, 1998); Theresa Milk, *Haskell Institute: 19th Century Stories of Sacrifice and Survival* (Lawrence, KS: Mammoth Publication, 2007). At least seven master's theses have the school's history as their topic. None of them has been published, however, and only a few of them deal with issues transcending the chronological development of the school. The few published materials on Haskell include James Goodner, Richard G. Woods, and Arthur M. Harkins, *Characteristics and Attitudes of 1968 Haskell Institute Students,* National Study of American Indian Education, Series III, No. 6, Final Report (Washington, DC: Office of Education, Bureau of Research, 1970), as well as some booklets on the school's development that were published as part of the 75th and the 100th Anniversary Celebration by the Haskell Institute Press. The seven theses are the following: Eric P. Anderson, "An Imperfect Education: Assimilation and American Indians at Haskell Institute, Lawrence, Kansas, 1884–1894" (M.A. thesis, University of Kansas, 1997); Geneva Goddard, "A Study of the Historical Development and Educational Work at Haskell Institute" (M.A. thesis, Kansas State Teacher's College, 1930); Mary Loretta Granzer, "Education at Haskell Institute, 1884–1937" (M.A. thesis, University of Nebraska, 1937); Robert Hoffmann, "A History of the Commercial Department of Haskell Institute, 1895–1963" (M.A. thesis, Pittsburg State University, 1964); Jack C. Naylor, "A Study of the History of the Vocational Department at Haskell Institute, Lawrence, Kansas" (M.Ed. thesis, University of Kansas, 1969); Charles O'Brien, "The Evolution of Haskell Indian Junior College, 1884–1974" (M.A. thesis, University of Oklahoma, 1975); Martha K. Robinson, "Assimilation, Ambivalence, and Resistance: Students at Haskell Institute, 1920–1930" (M.A. thesis, University of Kansas, 1996).

Chapter One. Beginnings

1. *Indian Rights Association Papers: A Guide to the Microfilm Edition 1864–1973* (Durango, CO: Fort Lewis College, Center of Southwest Studies, 1975), 1.

2. Vine Deloria Jr. and Daniel R. Wildcat, *Power and Place: Indian Education in America* (Golden, CO: Fulcrum Publishing, 2001), 1–6.

3. Linda Legrade Grover, "Effects of Boarding School Education on American In-

dian Families: A Qualitative Study of Perceptions from an American Indian Viewpoint" (Ed.D. diss., University of Minnesota, 1999); Jon Reyhner and Jeanne Eder, *American Indian Education* (Norman: University of Oklahoma Press, 2004), 3–13; Clifford E. Trafzer, Jean A. Keller, and Lorene Sisquoc, "Introduction: Origin and Development of the American Indian Boarding School System," in *Boarding School Blues: Revisiting American Indian Educational Experiences,* ed. Clifford E. Trafzer, Jean A. Keller, and Lorene Sisquoc, 5–6 (Lincoln: University of Nebraska Press, 2006); David Wallace Adams, "Fundamental Considerations: The Deep Meaning of Native American Schooling, 1880–1900," *Harvard Educational Review* 58, 1 (1988): 1–3.

4. Joel Spring, *Deculturalization and the Struggle for Equality: A Brief History of the Education of Dominated Cultures in the United States* (New York: McGraw-Hill, 1994), chap. 1; Reyhner and Eder, *American Indian Education,* 52–58.

5. Francis Paul Prucha, *The Great Father: The United States Government and the American Indians* (Lincoln: University of Nebraska Press, 1984), 1:488–500.

6. Frederick E. Hoxie, *A Final Promise: The Campaign to Assimilate the Indians, 1880–1920* (Cambridge: Cambridge University Press, 1984), 13–19; Prucha, *Great Father,* 2:611–630.

7. Adams, "Fundamental Considerations," 1–27.

8. As historian Frederick Hoxie phrases it in the subtitle of *Final Promise.*

9. Ibid., 54–55; Prucha, *Great Father,* 2:687–715; Reyhner and Eder, *American Indian Education,* 72–73.

10. David Wallace Adams, *Education for Extinction: American Indians and the Boarding School Experience, 1875–1928* (Lawrence: University Press of Kansas, 1995), 52.

11. Reyhner and Eder, *American Indian Education,* 3–13.

12. K. Tsianina Lomawaima, *They Called It Prairie Light: The Story of Chilocco Indian School* (Lincoln: University of Nebraska Press, 1994).

13. Ibid.; Adams, *Education for Extinction;* Hoxie, *Final Promise.*

14. The selection of the land would take place within four years of the enactment of the law, and surplus land would be sold to individual white landowners, leading to a checkerboard pattern on many former reservations. The allotted land was held in trust by the federal government for a period of twenty-five years. After that time, the Indian owners would receive their tracts in fee-simple and would be eligible to sell their property. Reyhner and Eder, *American Indian Education,* 81–111; Prucha, *Great Father,* 2:659–686.

15. Prucha, *Great Father,* 1:501–533; Adams, *Education for Extinction;* Hoxie, *Final Promise.*

16. For an interesting and in-depth discussion of the different philosophies influencing Indian policy, see Adams, "Fundamental Considerations," 1–27, and Jacqueline Fear-Segal, "Nineteenth-Century Indian Education: Universalism versus Evolutionism," *Journal of American Studies* 33 (1999): 22, 323–341.

17. Hoxie, *Final Promise,* 85, 143–144.

18. Examples are the 1903 Lone Wolf case, which asserted the plenary power of

Congress, or the 1906 Burke Act and the 1910 Omnibus Act. Prucha, *Great Father*, 2:775–776.

19. As quoted in Reyhner and Eder, *American Indian Education*, 96–101.

20. Hoxie, *Final Promise*, 197–210.

21. Elliott West, *Growing Up in Twentieth-Century America: A History and Reference Guide* (Westport, CT: Greenwood Press, 1996), 46–48.

22. During the 1920s, Indians were not the only targets of racist minority policies. In 1924, immigration legislation established the National Origins Quota System, which drastically curtailed immigration from nonnorthern and nonwestern European countries, reflecting the xenophobic attitudes prevailing in Washington and across the nation.

23. Lewis Meriam, *The Problem of Indian Administration* (Baltimore, MD: Johns Hopkins Press, 1928), 346–403.

24. Hoxie, *Final Promise*, 243–244.

25. Jorge Noriega, "American Indian Education in the United States: Indoctrination for Subordination to Colonialism," in *Genocide, Colonization and Resistance*, ed. M. Annette Jaimes, 383 (Boston: South End Press, 1992).

26. Eric P. Anderson, "An Imperfect Education: Assimilation and American Indians at Haskell Institute, Lawrence, Kansas, 1884–1894" (M.A. thesis, University of Kansas, 1997), 19.

27. *Douglas County Historical Society Newsletter*, May 1984.

28. *Lawrence Daily Journal*, September 28, 1883.

29. In 1867–1868, land disputes had resulted in the death of more than 200 settlers, and in 1878, a group of Cheyenne led by Little Wolf and Dull Knife had killed more than thirty Kansans during their northward flight from an army troop. Anderson, "Imperfect Education," 21.

30. Charles O'Brien, "The Evolution of Haskell Indian Junior College, 1884–1974" (M.A. thesis, University of Oklahoma, 1975), 10–11.

31. Anderson, "Imperfect Education," 39–40.

32. Ibid., 24; O'Brien, "Evolution of Haskell," 11.

33. *Lawrence Daily Journal*, September 18, 1884.

34. Ibid., August 21, 1884; September 18, 1884.

35. Ibid., September 21, 1884.

36. O'Brien, "Evolution of Haskell," 12; Anderson, "Imperfect Education," 41.

37. John D. C. Atkins, *Report of the Commissioner of Indian Affairs* (Washington, DC: Government Printing Office, 1885), 456.

38. Ibid.

39. Ibid.

40. Ibid.

41. John D.C. Atkins, *Report of the Commissioner of Indian Affairs* (Washington, DC: Government Printing Office, 1887), 320.

42. Anderson, "Imperfect Education," 48–49.

43. Ibid., 60.

44. Robinson, Haskell's third superintendent, is quoted in Rev. William P. Ames, "Highlights of Haskell Institute: A Brief Sketch of the Half Century of Indian Educa-

tion at Haskell Institute, Lawrence, Kansas," 1936, Kansas Collection, Kenneth Spencer Research Library, University of Kansas, 5.

45. John Williams, personal letter, March 11, 1887, CSRC. KSHS.
46. Atkins, *Report of the Commissioner of Indian Affairs*, 1887, 321.
47. Anderson, "Imperfect Education," 91–92.
48. Ibid., 86.
49. Theresa Tucquinn to Superintendent Robinson, May 18, 1888, Student Case Files, HR, RG 75, NACPR.
50. Atkins, *Report of the Commissioner of Indian Affairs*, 1887, 321–322; John D.C. Atkins, *Report of the Commissioner of Indian Affairs* (Washington, DC: Government Printing Office, 1888), 260–261.
51. *Lawrence Daily Journal*, March 16, 1887.
52. Thomas J. Morgan, *Report of the Commissioner of Indian Affairs* (Washington, DC: Government Printing Office, 1889), 320.
53. Ibid., 322.
54. Anderson, "Imperfect Education," 106.
55. Ibid., 116.
56. Daniel M. Browning, *Report of the Commissioner of Indian Affairs* (Washington, DC: Government Printing Office, 1894), 381.
57. Daniel M. Browning, *Report of the Commissioner of Indian Affairs* (Washington, DC: Government Printing Office, 1895), 345–346.
58. O'Brien, "Evolution of Haskell," 16–21; Ames, *Highlights*, 13–22.

Chapter Two. Coming to Haskell

1. Sophia La Pointe to Superintendent Peairs, July 24, 1907, Box 22, SCF, HR, RG 75, NACPR.
2. Michael Coleman, *American Indian Children at School, 1850–1930* (Jackson: University of Mississippi Press, 1993), 69.
3. Brenda J. Child, *Boarding School Seasons: American Indian Families 1900–1940* (Lincoln: University of Nebraska Press, 1998), 11–19.
4. Esther Burnett Horne and Sally McBeth, *Essie's Story: The Life and Legacy of a Shoshone Teacher* (Lincoln: University of Nebraska Press, 1998), 30–31.
5. In *No Turning Back*, for instance, Polingaysi Qoyawayma wrote that during the early 1900s, Hopi grandparents and parents desperately tried to hide the children from white reservation officials and their Navajo policemen. Polingaysi Qoyawayma, *No Turning Back* (Albuquerque: University of New Mexico Press, 1964), 26; David Wallace Adams, *Education for Extinction: American Indians and the Boarding School Experience, 1875–1928* (Lawrence: University Press of Kansas, 1995), 63–64.
6. K. Tsianina Lomawaima, *They Called It Prairie Light: The Story of Chilocco Indian School* (Lincoln: University of Nebraska Press, 1994), 32–35.
7. Adelia Sandoval to Superintendent Peairs, 1909, Box 104, Student Case Files, HR, RG 75, NACPR.

8. Ibid.

9. Superintendent Peairs to Adelia Sandoval, 1909, Box 104, Student Case Files, HF, RG 75, NACPR.

10. Superintendent Peairs to W. R. Johnson, January 26, 1905, Box 148, CCF, HR, RG 75, NACPR.

11. Raymond Bonnin to Superintendent Peairs, January 22, 1908, Box 21, SCF, HR, RG 75, NACPR.

12. Joseph E. Maxwell to Superintendent Wise, February 5, 1914, Box 170, CSA, HR, RG 75, NACPR.

13. Superintendent Wise to Joseph E. Maxwell, February 17, 1914, Box 170, CSA, HR, RG 75, NACPR.

14. Superintendent Peairs to James H. McGregor, July 10, 1917, Box 175, CSA, HR, RG 75, NACPR.

15. Superintendent Peairs to Marion Kidder, August 19, 1907, Box 22, SCF, HR, RG 75, NACPR.

16. Mary Lawrence to Superintendent Peairs, September 10, 1909, Box 22, SCF, HR, RG 75, NACPR.

17. Box 22, SCF, HR, RG 75, NACPR.

18. Superintendent Stinchecum to Superintendent Peairs, July 9, 1917, Box 22, SCF, HR, RG 75, NACPR.

19. Adams, *Education for Extinction*, 62.

20. Morgan is quoted in Eric P. Anderson, "An Imperfect Education: Assimilation and American Indians at Haskell Institute, Lawrence, Kansas, 1884–1894" (M.A. thesis, University of Kansas, 1997), 139.

21. Adams, *Education for Extinction*, 63.

22. Ibid.

23. Ibid., 63–64.

24. Without taking inflation into account, boarding schools were usually funded annually in the amount of $167 per student. Ibid., 65–66.

25. Superintendent Peairs to ?, n.d., Box 3, SCF, HR, RG 75, NACPR.

26. Marion Kidder to Superintendent Peairs, August 12, 1907, Box 22, SCF, HR, RG 75, NACPR.

27. The Commissioner of Indian Affairs to Superintendent Peairs, October 23, 1901, Box 137, Correspondence from the Office of Indian Affairs, HR, RG 75, NACPR.

28. Box 136, Correspondence from the Office of Indian Affairs, HR, RG 75, NACPR.

29. The figure of 141 reservations was quoted in the *Annual Report of the Commissioner of Indian Affairs* in 1880; it changed in the following decades owing to Oklahoma statehood and other historical developments.

30. The Commissioner of Indian Affairs to Superintendent Peairs, March 28, 1902, Box 137, Correspondence from the Office of Indian Affairs, HR, RG 75, NACPR.

31. Ibid.

32. Supervisor Chas. L. Davis, "Report of Enrollment Status at Haskell Institute," December 31, 1909, Box 8, SCF, HR, RG 75, NACPR.

33. Superintendent Wise to the Commissioner of Indian Affairs, November 1, 1912, Box 8, SCF, HR, RG 75, NACPR.

34. Ibid.

35. Box 19, SCF, HR, RG 75, NACPR.

36. Adams, *Education for Extinction*, 65.

37. Commissioner of Indian Affairs Leupp quoted in Scott Riney, *The Rapid City Indian School, 1898–1933* (Norman: University of Oklahoma Press, 1999), 24.

38. Superintendent Peairs to H. L. Tuttle, June 16, 1908, Box 22, SCF, HR, RG 75, NACPR.

39. Flandreau Indian School to Superintendent Peairs, June 8, 1908, Box 168, CSA, HR, RG 75, NACPR.

40. C. E. Birch to Superintendent Peairs, August 19, 1907, Box 22, SCF, HR, RG 75, NACPR.

41. Adams, *Education for Extinction*, 68.

42. Riney, *Rapid City Indian School*, 20.

43. Adams, *Education for Extinction*, 61.

44. Alan Peshkin, *Places of Memory: Whiteman's Schools and Native American Communities* (Mahwah, NJ: Lawrence Erlbaum Associates, 1997), 73.

45. *Lawrence Daily Journal*, February 1, 1888.

46. Ibid., February 11, 1888.

47. Ibid.

48. As quoted in Coleman, *American Indian Children at School*, 65.

49. Ibid., 68.

50. Daniel M. Browning, *Report of the Commissioner of Indian Affairs* (Washington, DC: Government Printing Office, 1893), 420.

51. Box 22, SCF, HR, RG 75, NACPR.

52. Interview with Mary Poafpybitty Neido, July 7, 1967, Doris Duke Oral History Collection.

53. Lizzie Fuller to Superintendent Peairs, November 8, 1909, Box 22, SCF, HR, RG 75, NACPR.

54. Box 22, SCF, HR, RG 75, NACPR.

55. Telegram from W. E. Hudspeth, May 12, 1906, Box 141, Correspondence from the Office of Indian Affairs, HR, RG 75, NACPR.

56. Statement by Myrtle Hudspeth, May 21, 1906, Box 141, Correspondence from the Office of Indian Affairs, HR, RG 75, NACPR.

57. Statement by Fannie Janis, May 24, 1906, Box 141, Correspondence from the Office of Indian Affairs, HR, RG 75, NACPR.

58. Box 141, Correspondence from the Office of Indian Affairs, HR, RG 75, NACPR.

59. Ibid.

60. Herman L. Crow to Superintendent Peairs, August 5, 1907, Box 22, SCF, HR, RG 75, NACPR.

61. Interview with Jesse Rowlodge, Arapaho, April 23, 1968, Doris Duke Collection.

62. Ibid.

63. Charles McGilbery to Superintendent Fiske, May 15, 1910, Box 22, SCF, HR, RG 75, NACPR.

64. Patrick O'Neil to Superintendent Peairs, January 17, 1910, Box 22, SCF, HR, RG 75, NACPR.

65. John Taylor to Superintendent Fiske, February 4, 1910, Student Case Files, HR, RG 75, NACPR.

66. Coleman, *American Indian Children at School*, 61.

67. Child, *Boarding School Seasons*, 24.

68. Horne and McBeth, *Essie's Story*, 31.

69. Joseph E. Maxwell to Superintendent Wise, February 5, 1914, Box 170, CSA, HR, RG 75, NACPR.

70. Horne and McBeth, *Essie's Story*, 31.

Chapter Three. Living by the Bell

1. Esther Burnett Horne and Sally McBeth, *Essie's Story: The Life and Legacy of a Shoshone Teacher* (Lincoln: University of Nebraska Press, 1998), 31.

2. As quoted in Michael Coleman, *American Indian Children at School, 1850–1930* (Jackson: University Press of Mississippi, 1993), 81.

3. David Wallace Adams, *Education for Extinction: American Indians and the Boarding School Experience, 1875–1928* (Lawrence: University Press of Kansas, 1995), 113.

4. Ibid., 123.

5. Eric P. Anderson, "An Imperfect Education: Assimilation and American Indians at Haskell Institute, Lawrence, Kansas, 1884–1894" (M.A. thesis, University of Kansas, 1997), 72–73.

6. Ibid.

7. See Anderson, "Imperfect Education," 72–73. The charges against the students were only specified as "their late misdemeanors," without any further details.

8. Horne and McBeth, *Essie's Story*, 33.

9. Ibid., 34.

10. Starting in 1917, individuals of less than 50 percent Indian ancestry, as well as students over the age of twenty-one who had successfully completed a course at a government Indian school, were declared citizens. In 1919 the same privilege was extended to all Native American veterans of World War I. In 1924, the Curtis Act finally granted citizenship to all American Indians.

11. Linda Legrade Grover, "Effects of Boarding School Education on American Indian Families: A Qualitative Study of Perceptions from an American Indian Viewpoint" (D.Ed. diss., University of Minnesota, 1999), 121.

12. Commissioner of Indian Affairs Thomas J. Morgan, quoted in Adams, *Education for Extinction*, 119.

13. Horne and McBeth, *Essie's Story*, 25.

14. Harry L. Saslow, "Research on Psychological Adjustment of Indian Youth," *American Journal of Psychiatry* 125, 2 (August 1968): 225.

15. Horne and McBeth, *Essie's Story*, 34.

16. Coleman, *American Indian Children at School*, 88.

17. Sally Hyer, *One House, One Voice, One Heart: Native American Education at Santa Fe School* (Santa Fe: Museum of New Mexico Press, 1990).

18. Saslow, "Research on Psychological Adjustment," 225.

19. Wolfgang Lindig, *Navajo: Tradition and Change in the Southwest* (Zurich: U. Baer Verlag, 1991), 140.

20. As quoted in Alan Peshkin, *Places of Memory: Whiteman's Schools and Native American Communities* (Mahwah, NJ: Lawrence Erlbaum, 1997), 89.

21. Coleman, *American Indian Children at School*, 87.

22. As quoted in ibid., 88.

23. Ibid.

24. Horne and McBeth, *Essie's Story*, 36.

25. Ibid., 37.

26. Superintendent Wise to Adjutant General C. I. Martin, June 3, 1914, Box 159, CCF, HR, RG 75, NACPR.

27. Grover, "Effects of Boarding School Education," 105.

28. Ibid., 104.

29. Ibid., 44.

30. Adams, *Education for Extinction*, 101.

31. Coleman, *American Indian Children at School*, 81–82.

32. Brenda J. Child, *Boarding School Seasons: American Indian Families 1900–1940* (Lincoln: University of Nebraska Press, 1998), 30–31.

33. Adams, *Education for Extinction*, 108.

34. Ibid., 103.

35. Anderson, "Imperfect Education," 146.

36. The Commissioner of Indian Affairs to Superintendent Peairs, July 13, 1903, Box 139, Correspondence from the Office of Indian Affairs, HR, RG 75, NACPR.

37. Superintendent Peairs to Frank A. Thackery, Shawnee, Oklahoma, September 4, 1908, Box 176, CSA, HR, RG 75, NACPR.

38. Grover, "Effects of Boarding School Education," 109.

39. Superintendent Wise to ?, n.d., 1914, Box 160, CCF, HR, RG 75, NACPR.

40. Horne and McBeth, *Essie's Story*, 37.

41. Interview with Jesse Rowlodge, April 23, 1968, Doris Duke Oral History Collection.

42. A. S. Wyly to Superintendent Peairs, March 18, 1920, Box 132, Student Case Files, HR, RG 75, NACPR.

43. Superintendent Fiske to the Commissioner of Indian Affairs, July 25, 1910, HR, RG 75, NADC.

44. Interview with Jesse Rowlodge, April 23, 1968.

45. Ibid.

46. Ibid.

47. Coleman, *American Indian Children at School*, 81–83; Child, *Boarding School Seasons*, 28–29; Horne and McBeth, *Essie's Story*, 31–32; Adams, *Education for Extinction*, 97–112.

48. Grover, "Effects of Boarding School Education," 90.

49. Deloria quoted in ibid.

50. Morgan's position is discussed in Anderson, "Imperfect Education," 51.

51. Ibid., 51–52.

52. Interview with Lucy Logan Griggs, May 5, 1969, Doris Duke Oral History Collection.

53. Adams, *Education for Extinction*, 111–112.

54. Interview with Jay Black, July 11, 1967, Doris Duke Oral History Collection.

55. Child, *Boarding School Seasons*, 32–33.

56. Box 176, CSA, HR, RG 75, NACPR.

57. Lucille Jerry Winnie, *Sah-Gan-De-Oh: The Chief's Daughter* (New York: Vantage Press, 1969), 49.

58. Letter exchange between Superintendent Peairs and the Commissioner of Indian Affairs, December 1902, Box 144, Correspondence sent to the Commissioner of Indian Affairs, HR, RG 75, NACPR.

59. Ibid.

60. Child, *Boarding School Seasons*, 34.

61. Interview with Jesse Rowlodge, April 23, 1968.

62. Ibid.

63. HR, RG 75, NADC.

64. Horne and McBeth, *Essie's Story*, 35.

65. Ibid.

66. Ibid.

67. Child, *Boarding School Seasons*, 34.

68. Horne and McBeth, *Essie's Story*, 38.

69. W. H. Sears, "An Evening at Haskell Institute," *Lawrence Daily Gazette*, February 2, 1887.

70. Commissioner of Indian Affairs Leupp to Superintendent Peairs, 1908, Box 143, Correspondence from the Office of Indian Affairs, HR, RG 75, NACPR.

71. "Commencement Exercises of the Training School: A Day with the Indians," *Lawrence Daily Journal*, June 1888.

72. As quoted in Child, *Boarding School Seasons*, 38.

73. Horne and McBeth, *Essie's Story*, 38.

74. Ibid.

75. The Commissioner of Indian Affairs to Superintendent Peairs, 1902, Box 138, Correspondence from the Office of Indian Affairs, HR, RG 75, NACPR.

76. Child, *Boarding School Seasons*, 38.

77. Horne and McBeth, *Essie's Story*, 39.

78. Ibid., 32.

79. Ibid., 33.

80. Interview with Jesse Rowlodge, April 23, 1968.

81. Ibid.
82. Ibid.
83. Ibid.
84. K. Tsianina Lomawaima, *They Called It Prairie Light: The Story of Chilocco Indian School* (Lincoln: University of Nebraska Press, 1994), 157–159.
85. Interview with Otis Russell, May 5, 1970, Doris Duke Oral History Collection.
86. Ibid.
87. Interview with Mary Red Eagle, December 15, 1969, Doris Duke Oral History Collection.
88. Interview with Lottie High Whitefox, June 15, 1967, Doris Duke Oral History Collection.
89. Horne and McBeth, *Essie's Story*, 32.
90. Interview with Jesse Rowlodge, April 23, 1968.
91. Horne and McBeth, *Essie's Story*, 33.

Chapter Four. The Curriculum

1. Haskell School Calendar, 1919–1920, Box 20, HR, RG 75, NACPR.
2. Estelle Reel to Superintendent Peairs, 1901, Box 137, Correspondence from the Office of Indian Affairs, HR, RG 75, NACPR.
3. "An Outline of the Course of Study," 1911, Haskell Institute Records, Kenneth Spencer Research Library, University of Kansas.
4. Alice Littlefield, "The B.I.A. Boarding School: Theories of Resistance and Social Reproduction," *Humanity and Society* 13, 4 (1989): 435.
5. The Commissioner of Indian Affairs to Superintendent Peairs, September 1902, Box 138, Correspondence from the Office of Indian Affairs, HR, RG 75, NACPR.
6. Statement by C. E. Birch, 1916, Box 21, SCF, HR, RG 75, NACPR.
7. Superintendent Peairs to the Esther Home for Indian Girls, 1917, Box 26, SCF, HR, RG 75, NACPR.
8. Superintendent Peairs to W. F. Aven, Principal of H.I., December 15, 1908, Box 23, SCF, HR, RG 75, NACPR.
9. Charles O'Brien, "The Evolution of Haskell Indian Junior College, 1884–1974" (M.A. thesis, University of Oklahoma, 1975), 24–25.
10. "Outline of the Course of Study."
11. Clarence E. Birch, *Methods of Teaching English* (Lawrence, KS: N.p.,1914), 7.
12. Ibid.
13. David Wallace Adams, *Education for Extinction: American Indians and the Boarding School Experience, 1875–1928* (Lawrence: University Press of Kansas, 1995), 139.
14. Birch, *Methods*, 9.
15. Ibid., 10–11.
16. Adams, *Education for Extinction*, 137.
17. "Notes on Teaching," Box 193, HR, RG 75, NACPR.

18. Ibid.

19. Adams, *Education for Extinction*, 143.

20. Thomas J. Morgan, *Report of the Commissioner of Indian Affairs* (Washington, DC: Government Printing Office, 1890), 293.

21. As quoted in Adams, *Education for Extinction*, 147.

22. Ibid.

23. Amy Goodburn, "Literacy Practices at the Genoa Industrial Indian School," *Great Plains Quarterly* 19 (1999): 37.

24. Superintendent Peairs to Haskell's staff, April 4, 1917, Box 13, SCF, HR, RG 75, NACPR.

25. The Commissioner of Indian Affairs to Superintendent Peairs, January 4, 1901, Box 137, Correspondence from the Office of Indian Affairs, HR, RG 75, NACPR.

26. The Commissioner of Indian Affairs to Superintendent Peairs, June 6, 1906, Box 141, Correspondence from the Office of Indian Affairs, HR, RG 75, NACPR.

27. *Indian Leader*, May, 8, 1915, 2–3.

28. Ibid., June 26, 1908, 5.

29. Interview with Jesse Rowlodge, April 23, 1968, Doris Duke Oral History Collection.

30. Interview with Jay Black, August 8, 1967, Doris Duke Oral History Collection.

31. Alice Vivia to C. E. Birch, July 7, 1919, Box 122, Student Case Files, HR, RG 75, NACPR.

32. Mrs. Smoot to C. E. Birch (n.d.), 1919, Box 122, Student Case Files, HR, RG 75, NACPR.

33. Interview with Lottie High Whitefox, 1967, Doris Duke Oral History Collection.

34. Esther Burnett Horne and Sally McBeth, *Essie's Story: The Life and Legacy of a Shoshone Teacher* (Lincoln: University of Nebraska Press, 1998), 39.

35. *Indian Leader*, May 22, 1925, 2.

36. Ibid., 1.

37. C. E. Birch to the Commissioner of Indian Affairs, October 29, 1918, Box 3, SCF, HR, RG 75, NACPR.

38. *Indian Leader*, May 22, 1925, 2.

39. Superintendent Peairs to William S. Jackson, April 26, 1907, Box 22, SCF, HR, RG 75, NACPR.

40. C. E. Birch to the Commissioner of Indian Affairs, October 29, 1918, Box 3, SCF, HR, RG 75, NACPR.

41. Letter exchanges between the Commissioner of Indian Affairs and Superintendent Wise, August 26, 1912, and August 31, 1912, as well as January 15, 1916, and February 5, 1916, HR, RG 75, NADC.

42. Lillian Henry, short essay, 1920, HR, RG 75, NADC.

43. *Indian Leader*, June 26, 1908, 8.

44. Interview with Jesse Rowlodge, April 23, 1968.

45. Superintendent Peairs to Superintendent O. H. Lipps, Chilocco Indian School, June 17, 1918, Box 14, SCF, HR, RG 75, NACPR.

46. Joel Spring, *Deculturalization and the Struggle for Equality: A Brief History of the Education of Dominated Cultures in the United States* (New York: McGraw-Hill, 1994), chap. 1; Margaret Connell Szasz, "Through a Wide-Angle Lens: Acquiring and Maintaining Power, Position, and Knowledge through Boarding Schools," in *Boarding School Blues: Revisiting American Indian Educational Experiences,* ed. Clifford E. Trafzer, Jean A. Keller, and Lorene Siquoc, 187–202 (Lincoln: University of Nebraska Press, 2006).

47. C. E. Birch, "Three Forward Movements" (n.d., ca. 1908), Box 193, Notes on Teaching, HR, RG 75, NACPR, 1–2.

48. Ibid.

49. Ibid., 2.

50. Ibid., 4.

51. John D.C. Atkins, *Report of the Commissioner of Indian Affairs* (Washington, DC: Government Printing Office, 1885), 459.

52. *Lawrence Daily Gazette,* September 8, 1885.

53. Ibid., February 24, 1887.

54. Daniel M. Browning, *Report of the Commissioner of Indian Affairs* (Washington, DC: Government Printing Office, 1894), 382.

55. *Indian Leader,* May 8, 1914, 2.

56. Browning, *Report of the Commissioner of Indian Affairs,* 382.

57. The Commissioner of Indian Affairs to Superintendent Peairs, July 18, 1899, Box 136, HR, RG 75, NACPR.

58. Superintendent Wise to the Commissioner of Indian Affairs, October 1, 1913, Box 146, Correspondence sent to the Commissioner of Indian Affairs, HR, RG 75, NACPR.

59. As quoted in Michael C. Coleman, *American Indian Children at School, 1850–1930* (Jackson: University Press of Mississippi, 1993), 114.

60. Superintendent Wise to the Commissioner of Indian Affairs, February 24, 1916, HR, RG 75, NADC.

61. Superintendent Peairs to Flandreau Indian School, December 15, 1917, Box 168, CSA, HR, RG 75, NACPR.

62. The Commissioner of Indian Affairs to Superintendent Peairs, December 5, 1899, Box 136, HR, RG 75, NACPR. Superintendent Peairs to William S. Jackson, April 26, 1907, Box 22, SCF, HR, RG75, NACPR.

63. Katrina A. Paxton, "Learning Gender: Female Students at Sherman Institute, 1907–1925," in *Boarding School Blues, Revisiting American Indian Educational Experiences,* ed. Clifford E. Trafzer, Jean A. Keller, and Lorene Siquoc, 174–186 (Lincoln: University of Nebraska Press, 2006).

64. Robert A. Trennert, "Educating Indian Girls and Women at Nonreservation Boarding Schools," in *Major Problems in American Indian History,* ed. Albert L. Hurtado and Peter Iverson, 382 (Lexington, MA: D. C. Heath, 1994).

65. Paxton, "Learning Gender," 175.

66. Beatrice Medicine, "North American Indigenous Women and Cultural Domination," *American Indian Culture and Research Journal* 17, 3 (1993): 123; Theresa Amott

and Julie Matthaei, *Race, Gender, and Work: A Multicultural Economic History of Women in the United States* (Boston: South End Press, 1991).

67. Medicine, "North American Indigenous Women," 124.

68. *Lawrence Daily Gazette*, September 9, 1885.

69. K. Tsianina Lomawaima, *They Called It Prairie Light: The Story of Chilocco Indian School* (Lincoln: University of Nebraska Press, 1994), 83.

70. Brenda J. Child, *Boarding School Seasons: American Indian Families 1900–1940* (Lincoln: University of Nebraska Press, 1998), 78.

71. Ibid., 79.

72. As quoted in ibid.

73. Report of Special Agent Merial A. Dorchester, 1892, HR, RG 75, NADC.

74. *Indian Leader*, November 29, 1918, 13, 14, 17, 19.

75. The Commissioner of Indian Affairs to Superintendent Peairs, September 6, 1917, HR, RG 75, NADC.

76. Letter from Superintendent Wise to the Commissioner of Indian Affairs, October 26, 1911, Box 145, Correspondence sent to the Commissioner of Indian Affairs, HR, RG 75, NACPR.

77. *Indian Leader*, November 29, 1918, 6.

78. Ibid.

79. Interview with Mary Red Eagle, Quapaw, May 18, 1969, Doris Duke Oral History Collection.

80. Mildred Richmond, short autobiography, 1918, Box 110, Student Case Files, HR, RG 75, NACPR.

81. Jewel Wells to her sister, December 4, 1916, Box 126, Student Case Files, HR, RG 75, NACPR.

82. Superintendent Peairs to Mr. Bolton Hall, April 23, 1907, Box 19, SCF, HR, RG 75, NACPR.

83. Superintendent Wise to the Commissioner of Indian Affairs, February 7, 1912, Box 145, Correspondence sent to the Commissioner of Indian Affairs, HR, RG 75, NACPR.

84. Interview with Arthur Sutton, Arapaho, November 18, 1970, Doris Duke Oral History Collection.

85. Robert Johnson, short autobiography, 1920, HR, RG 75, NADC.

86. Interview with Otis Russell, Osage, December 26, 1968, Doris Duke Oral History Collection.

87. 1904 Outing Report, Box 139, Correspondence from the Office of Indian Affairs, HR, RG 75, NACPR.

88. Outing Rules, Box 16, SCF, HR, RG 75, NACPR.

89. Ibid.

90. Superintendent Peairs to Mr. Good, Eudora, Kansas, March 5, 1908, Box 110, Student Case Files, HR, RG 75, NACPR.

91. Rose E. Anderson to Superintendent Peairs, March 10, 1921, Box 16, SCF, HR, RG 75, NACPR.

92. Mrs. Jamison Schanadore to Superintendent Peairs, March 30, 1921, Box 16, SCF, HR, RG 75, NACPR.
93. Horne and McBeth, *Essie's Story*, 48.
94. Charles Haine to Haskell Institute, 1905, Box 8, SCF, HR, RG 75, NACPR.
95. Report of Outing Visit, by outing matron Mrs. Stanley, 1919 or 1920, Box 16, SCF, HR, RG 75, NACPR.
96. Superintendent Wise to the assistant supervisor of Indian Employment, April 10, 1913, Box 156, CCF, HR, RG 75, NACPR.
97. Quoted in *Indian Leader*, September 19, 1919, 3.
98. Excerpt from *Indian Leader*, Box 126, Student Case Files, HR, RG 75, NACPR.
99. Report of Outing Trip, 1920, Box 16, SCF, HR, RG 75, NACPR.
100. Child, *Boarding School Seasons*, 85.
101. This is in contrast to the Phoenix Indian School, for instance, where the outing program—due to the racist attitudes of Arizona patrons—was simply a matter of business. Trennert, "Educating Indian Girls," 388.

Chapter Five. Rituals and Recreation

1. *Lawrence Daily Journal*, September 18, 1884.
2. Peairs quoted in David Wallace Adams, *Education for Extinction: American Indians and the Boarding School Experience, 1875–1928* (Lawrence: University Press of Kansas, 1995), 164.
3. Ibid., 166.
4. "Religious Instruction," 1911, Box 18, SCF, HR, RG 75, NACPR.
5. John D.C. Atkins, *Report of the Commissioner of Indian Affairs* (Washington, DC: Government Printing Office, 1886), 225.
6. Files on "Religion" and "Religious Instruction," Box 18, SCF, HR, RG 75, NACPR.
7. Ibid.
8. Ibid.
9. As quoted in Adams, *Education for Extinction*, 168.
10. Interview with Jesse Rowlodge, April 23, 1968, Doris Duke Oral History Collection.
11. Interview with Arthur Sutton, Arapaho, November 18, 1970, Doris Duke Oral History Collection.
12. Ibid.
13. Esther Burnett Horne and Sally McBeth, *Essie's Story: The Life and Legacy of a Shoshone Teacher* (Lincoln: University of Nebraska Press, 1998), 40.
14. Interview with Otis Russell, May 5, 1970, Doris Duke Oral History Collection.
15. YMCA Resolution, 1919, Box 26, SCF, HR, RG 75, NACPR.
16. Ibid.
17. As quoted in Eric P. Anderson, "An Imperfect Education: Assimilation and

American Indians at Haskell Institute, Lawrence, Kansas, 1884–1894" (M.A. thesis, University of Kansas, 1997), 124.

18. Thomas J. Morgan, *Report of the Commissioner of Indian Affairs* (Washington, DC: Government Printing Office, 1890), 291.

19. The Office of Indian Affairs to Superintendent Peairs, March 1920, Box 10, SCF, HR, RG 75, NACPR.

20. Josephine Smith to her sister, 1917, Box 110, Student Case Files, HR, RG 75, NACPR.

21. Thomas A. Britten, *American Indians in World War I: At War and at Home* (Albuquerque: University of New Mexico Press, 1997), 60–61.

22. Ibid., 99–105.

23. Ibid., 147.

24. Superintendent Peairs to Superintendent F. M. Conser, Sherman Institute, July 6, 1918, Box 176, CSA, HR, RG 75, NACPR.

25. Ibid.

26. Britten, *American Indians in World War I*, 66.

27. Letter from Superintendent Peairs to ?, 1918, Box 122, Decimal Correspondence Files, HR, RG 75, NACPR.

28. Britten, *American Indians in World War I*, 149–151.

29. Ibid., 183–187.

30. David Wallace Adams, "Beyond Bleakness: The Brighter Side of Indian Boarding Schools, 1870–1940," in *Boarding School Blues: Revisiting American Indian Educational Experiences*, ed. Clifford E. Trafzer, Jean A. Keller, and Lorene Siquoc, 35–64 (Lincoln: University of Nebraska Press, 2006).

31. Box 8, "Entertainment," SCF, HR, RG 75, NACPR.

32. Ibid.

33. Superintendent Peairs to Superintendent Miller, Indian School, Greenville, California, January 8, 1918, Box 168, CSA, HR, RG 75, NACPR.

34. Haskell School Calendar, 1919–1920, Box 20, SCF, HR, RG 75, NACPR.

35. Superintendent Peairs to Buffalo Bill's Wild West Show, September 16, 1909, Box 8, SCF, HR, RG 75, NACPR.

36. Charles O'Brien, "The Evolution of Haskell Indian Junior College, 1884–1974" (M.A. thesis, University of Oklahoma, 1975), 31.

37. Excerpt from the pamphlet "Haskell Indian Band," 1904, Haskell Institute Records, Kansas Collection, Kenneth Spencer Research Library, University of Kansas.

38. Ibid.

39. Superintendent Peairs to Mrs. Vieux, October 15, 1908, Box 122, Student Case Files, HR, RG 75, NACPR.

40. Commissioner Leupp to Superintendent Peairs, December 8, 1908, Box 143, Correspondence from the Office of Indian Affairs, HR, RG 75, NACPR.

41. Interview with Jesse Rowlodge, April 23, 1968.

42. Box 1, SCF, HR, RG 75, NACPR.

43. Chautauqua pamphlet, June 29–July 3, 1919, Littlestown, Pennsylvania, Box 1, SCF, HR, RG 75, NACPR.

44. John E. Tapia, *Circquit Chautauqua* (Jefferson, NC: McFarland, 1997), 100–101.

45. Superintendent Peairs to the University School of Music, Lincoln, Nebraska, March 8, 1919, Box 3, SCF, HR, RG 75, NACPR.

46. Mrs. J. B. Winslow to Superintendent Peairs, April 14, 1921, Box 1, SCF, HR, RG 75, NACPR.

47. Adams, *Education for Extinction*, 175.

48. Horne and McBeth, *Essie's Story*, 38.

49. Adams, *Education for Extinction*, 177.

50. As quoted in Michael C. Coleman, *American Indian Children at School: 1850–1930* (Jackson: University Press of Mississippi, 1994), 94.

51. Horne and McBeth, *Essie's Story*, 38, 47.

52. Interview with Eli Stover, Creek, January 3, 1970, Doris Duke Oral History Collection.

53. Horne and McBeth, *Essie's Story*, 47.

54. Superintendent Peairs to the Commissioner of Indian Affairs, January 14, 1909, Box 144, Correspondence sent to the Commissioner of Indian Affairs, HR, RG 75, NACPR.

55. Ibid.

56. Report from Superintendent Wise to the Commissioner of Indian Affairs, April 11, 1916, HR, RG 75, NADC.

57. Ibid.

58. The Office of Indian Affairs to Superintendent Peairs, April 8, 1919, Box 9, SCF, HR, RG 75, NACPR.

59. Rev. William P. Ames, "Highlights of Haskell Institute: A Brief Sketch of the Half Century of Indian Education at Haskell Institute, Lawrence, Kansas," 1936, Kansas Collection, Kenneth Spencer Research Library, University of Kansas, 11.

60. Indian Commissioner Jones to Superintendent Peairs, April 27, 1904, Box 139, Correspondence from the Office of Indian Affairs, HR, RG 75, NACPR.

61. Superintendent Peairs to R. O. Marmon, Laguna, New Mexico, June 1, 1905, Box 149, CCF, HR, RG 75, NACPR.

62. Interview with Jesse Rowlodge, April 23, 1968.

63. Horne and McBeth, *Essie's Story*, 43.

64. Box 8, "Entertainment," SCF, HR, RG 75, NACPR.

65. Superintendent Peairs to Supt. J. R. Wise, Chilocco Indian School, December 17, 1908, Box 25, SCF, HR, RG 75, NACPR.

66. Horne and McBeth, *Essie's Story*, 45–46.

67. Ames, "Highlights of Haskell Institute," 25.

68. Benjamin G. Rader, "'The Greatest Drama in Indian Life': Experiments in Native American Identity and Resistance at the Haskell Institute Homecoming of 1926," *Western Historical Quarterly* 35 (Winter 2004): 429–450.

69. Lewis Meriam, *The Problem of Indian Administration*, Institute for Government Research (Baltimore, MD: Johns Hopkins Press, 1928), 326.

70. Rader, "'Greatest Drama in Indian Life,'" 431; Kim Warren, "All Indian Trails

Lead to Lawrence, October 27–30, 1926," *Kansas History: A Journal of the Central Plains* 30 (Spring 2007): 2–19.

71. Warren, "All Indian Trails Lead to Lawrence, October 27–30, 1926," 9, 12; *Indian Leader,* "Haskell Celebration," October 29, November 5, 12, 19, 1926.

72. Speech delivered by Secretary of the Interior Hubert Work, October 30, 1926, Box 1, SCF, HR, RG 75, NACPR.

73. *Kansas City Times,* October 30, 1926.

74. John Bloom, "There Is Madness in the Air: The 1926 Haskell Homecoming and Popular Representations of Sports in Federal Indian Boarding Schools," in *Dressing in Feathers: The Construction of the Indian in American Popular Culture,* ed. Elizabeth Bird, 108 (Boulder, CO: Westview Press, 1998).

75. The paper continued to explain that it was "largely due to the efforts of John Levi, full-blood Cheyenne, and perhaps the greatest all-around Indian athlete in the country, that the subscription campaign was a success. Levi, who was captain of the Haskell football and baseball teams for three years and was named as all-American full-back, took charge of the stadium drive." *New York Times,* October 10, 1926, x3.

76. Bloom, "There Is Madness in the Air," 102–105.

77. Rader, "'Greatest Drama in Indian Life,'" 431.

78. Warren, "All Indian Trails Lead to Lawrence, October 27–30, 1926," 16–17.

79. Rader, "'Greatest Drama in Indian Life,'" 436–437, 449–450. For an in-depth discussion of the changing role of song and dance in native cultures, see Clyde Ellis, *A Dancing People: Powwow Culture on the Southern Plains* (Lawrence: University Press of Kansas, 2003).

80. Adams, *Education for Extinction,* 190.

81. Rader, "'Greatest Drama in Indian Life,'" 436.

82. Warren, "All Indian Trails Lead to Lawrence, October 27–30, 1926," 8.

83. Adams, *Education for Extinction,* 185.

84. Haskell's athletics manager to the *State Journal,* Topeka, Kansas, 1903, Box 192, Correspondence of the Athletic Program, HR, RG 75, NACPR.

85. David Wallace Adams, "More than a Game: The Carlisle Indians Take to the Gridiron, 1893–1917," *Western Historical Quarterly* 32, 1 (2001): 41 pars. Available at http://www.historycooperative.org/journals/whq/32.1/adams.html (accessed June 20, 2007).

86. Ibid., 1.

87. As quoted in Adams, *Education for Extinction,* 188–189.

88. Box 192, Correspondence of the Athletic Program, 1914, HR, RG 75, NACPR.

89. John Bloom, "'Show What an Indian Can Do': Sports, Memory, and Ethnic Identity at Federal Indian Boarding Schools," *Journal of American Indian Education* 35, 3 (Spring 1996): 38.

90. Superintendent Peairs to Maurice Kent, June 1, 1908, Box 7, SCF, HR, RG 75, NACPR.

91. Superintendent Peairs to Louis Corbine, August 27, 1904, Box 192, Correspondence of the Athletic Department, HR, RG 75, NACPR.

92. Horne and McBeth, *Essie's Story,* 46–47.

93. Superintendent Peairs to Charles H. Dickson, February 27, 1908, Box 166, CSA, HR, RG 75, NACPR.
94. Horne and McBeth, *Essie's Story,* 46.
95. Coleman, *American Indian Children at School,* 92.
96. Interview with Eli Stover, January 3, 1970.
97. As quoted in Coleman, *American Indian Children at School,* 92.
98. Interview with Arthur Sutton, November 18, 1970.
100. Ibid., 46.

Chapter Six. Health and the Body

1. Jack White to Estelle Reel, December 4, 1899, Box 136, SCF, HR, RG 75, NACPR.
2. Lewis Meriam, *The Problem of Indian Administration,* The Institute for Government Research (Baltimore. MD: Johns Hopkins Press, 1928), 192.
3. Michael Harkin, "Contested Bodies: Affliction and Power in Heiltsuk Culture and History," *American Ethnologist* 21, 3 (1994): 586–605; Wolfgang Lindig, *Navajo: Tradition and Change in the Southwest* (Zurich: U. Baer Verlag, 1991), 171–180.
4. Brenda J. Child, *Boarding School Seasons: American Indian Families 1900–1940* (Lincoln: University of Nebraska Press, 1998), 38.
5. Affidavit signed by Susie Mars (pseudonym), Box 9, SCF, HR, RG 75, NACPR.
6. Superintendent Fiske to John R. Howard, Superintendent White Earth Agency, February 14, 1911, Box 9, SCF, HR, RG 75, NACPR.
7. Ibid.
8. Ibid.
9. Superintendent Fiske to the Commissioner of Indian Affairs, July 21, 1910, Box 5, SCF HR, RG 75, NACPR.
10. Ibid.
11. Superintendent Fiske to the Office of Indian Affairs, September 22, 1910, Box 5, SCF, HR, RG 75, NACPR.
12. Superintendent Fiske to the Commissioner of Indian Affairs, March 21, 1911, Box 9, SCF, HR, RG 75, NACPR.
13. "Course of Study," Haskell Institute, Lawrence, Kansas, 1911, Haskell Institute Records, Kansas Collection, Spencer Research Library, University of Kansas.
14. Naomi Russell, essay, December 5, 1913, Box 104, Student Case Files, HR, RG 75, NACPR.
15. Health Report by Dr. Van Cleave, January 21, 1914, HR, Records Group 75, NADC.
16. Meriam, *The Problem of Indian Administration,* 332.
17. Martha Wright to Superintendent Peairs, October 30, 1917, Box 132, Student Case Files, HR, RG 75, NACPR.
18. Report by Special U.S. Indian Agent McConihe, November 7, 1908, HR, Records Group 75, NADC.

19. Health Report by Dr. Van Cleave, January 21, 1914.
20. Report by Dr. W. E. Van Cleave, January 7, 1914, HR, RG 75, NADC.
21. Report by Special U.S. Indian Agent McConihe, November 7, 1908, HR, RG 75, NADC.
22. Report by Dr. Joseph A. Murphy, November 12, 1908, HR, RG75, NADC.
23. Ibid.
24. Ibid.
25. Report of Lucretia C. Ross, November 17, 1908, HR, RG 75, NADC.
26. Ibid.
27. Ibid.
28. Report of Dr. Joseph A. Murphy, February 17, 1909, HR, RG 75, NADC.
29. Ibid.
30. Ibid.
31. Ibid.
32. Child, *Boarding School Seasons*, 60–61.
33. Susan Sears Clark to Superintendent Peairs, June 11, 1909, Box 21, SCF, HR, RG 75, NACPR.
34. Superintendent Oliver to Superintendent Peairs, June 3, 1907, Box 166, CSA, HR, RG 75, NACPR.
35. Indian Agent George W. Nellis to Superintendent Wise, September 5, 1911, Box 100, Student Case Files, HR, RG 75, NACPR.
36. J. B. Monroe to the Commissioner of Indian Affairs, September 2, 1913, HR, RG 75, NADC.
37. William Gilluly to Superintendent Fiske, February 28, 1910, Box 176, CSA, HR, RG 75, NACPR.
38. Harkin, "Contested Bodies," 598.
39. Superintendent Fiske to Mr. Jerry Meeker, May 16, 1910, Box 174, CSA, HR, RG 75, NACPR.
40. Dr. Dixon to Superintendent Peairs, December 14, 1900, Box 147, CCF, HR, RG 75, NACPR.
41. As quoted in David Wallace Adams, *Education for Extinction: American Indians and the Boarding School Experience, 1875–1928* (Lawrence: University Press of Kansas, 1995), 133.
42. Report from Superintendent Peairs to the Commissioner of Indian Affairs, July 24, 1903, Box 144, Correspondence sent to the Commissioner of Indian Affairs, HR, RG 75, NACPR.
43. Adams, *Education for Extinction*, 130.
44. Esther Burnett Horne and Sally McBeth, *Essie's Story: The Life and Legacy of a Shoshone Teacher* (Lincoln: University of Nebraska Press, 1998), 40.
45. Dr. Dixon to Superintendent Peairs, April 7, 1900, Box 147, CCF, HR, RG 75, NACPR.
46. Dr. John Alley to Superintendent Wise, January 10, 1912, Box 172, CSA, HR, RG 75, NACPR.

47. Cora E. Tabor to Superintendent Peairs, June 5, 1907, Box 21, SCF, HR, RG 75, NACPR.

48. Superintendent Peairs to Cora E. Tabor, June 10, 1907, Box 21, SCF, HR, RG 75, NACPR.

49. Ibid.

50. Cora E. Tabor to Superintendent Peairs, June 18, 1907, Box 21, SCF, HR, RG 75, NACPR.

51. Report of Dr. Dixon, July 25, 1903, Box 144, Correspondence sent to the Commissioner of Indian Affairs, HR, RG 75, NACPR.

52. Charles E. Banks, General Surgeon, U.S. P.H.S., to Superintendent Peairs, April 17, 1918, HR, RG 75, NADC.

53. Report by Special Physician W. E. Van Cleave, April 10, 1918, HR, RG 75, NADC.

54. Superintendent Peairs to Superintendent John Francis, Carlisle Indian School, April 19, 1918, Box 166, CSA, HR, RG 75, NACPR.

55. Superintendent Peairs to W. S. Coleman, Inspector, U.S. Indian Service, November 18, 1918, Box 12, SCF, HR, RG 75, NACPR.

56. Assistant Superintendent C. E. Birch to Superintendent Peairs, January 27, 1920, Box 12, SCF, HR, RG 75, NACPR.

57. Adams, *Education for Extinction*, 131–132.

58. Child, *Boarding School Seasons*, 59.

59. Dr. C. R. Dixon to Superintendent Peairs, January 23, 1905, Box 148, CCF, HR, RG 75, NACPR.

60. Dr. Joseph A. Murphy to the Commissioner of Indian Affairs, April 27, 1911, HR, RG 75, NADC.

61. Superintendent Wise to Margaret Keith, March 28, 1913, Box 156, CCF, HR, RG 75, NACPR.

62. Report by Dr. W. E. Van Cleave to the Commissioner of Indian Affairs, July 8, 1913, HR, RG 75, NADC.

63. Superintendent Wise to C. B. Lohmiller, Superintendent Fort Peck Agency, August 30, 1913, Box 157, CCF, HR, RG 75, NACPR.

64. Report by Dr. L. L. Culp, February 8, 1917, HR, RG 75, NADC.

65. Child, *Boarding School Seasons*, 59.

66. The Commissioner of Indian Affairs to Superintendent Peairs, January 20, 1909, Box 143, Correspondence received from the Office of Indian Affairs, HR, RG 75, NACPR.

67. Superintendent Fiske to F. A Thackery, Superintendent, Shawnee, Oklahoma, March 15, 1910, Box 176, CSA, HR, RG 75, NACPR.

68. Dr. W. E. Van Cleave to Dr. Joseph A. Murphy, January 21, 1914, HR, R G 75, NADC.

69. Dr. W. E. Van Cleave to Superintendent Wise, January 19, 1914, HR, RG 75, NADC.

70. Report by Special Physician Dr. L. L. Culp, February 8, 1917.

71. Letter from Haskell to A. K. Perry, December 29, 1900, Box 147, CCF, HR, RG 75, NACPR.

72. Child, *Boarding School Seasons*, 67.

73. Dr. Dixon to Superintendent Peairs, January 2, 1905, Box 148, CCF, HR, RG 75, NACPR.

74. Superintendent Fiske to Superintendent Peter Paquette, Navajo Agency, November 10, 1910, Box 132, Student Case Files, HR, RG 75, NACPR.

75. Superintendent Fiske to the Commissioner of Indian Affairs, 1911, HR, RG 75, NADC.

76. Until one of Haskell's employees came to recover his remains, the school had falsely assumed that Callis Peter—not Christian Tehee—had been the victim of the accident. Therefore, Peter's parents had been wrongly notified about their son's death, a terrible confusion that created much pain and grief for the Peter family.

77. *Indian Leader*, November 11, 1915.

78. As quoted in Adams, *Education for Extinction*, 135.

Chapter Seven. Accommodation and Resistance

1. Edward Whale (pseudonym) to Superintendent Peairs, December 17, 1918, Box 126, Student Case Files, HR, RG 75, NACPR.

2. Superintendent Peairs to Superintendent A. S. Wyly, Union Agency, July 28, 1919, Box 126, Student Case Files, HR, RG 75, NACPR.

3. James C. Scott, *Domination and the Arts of Resistance: Hidden Transcripts* (New Haven, CT: Yale University Press, 1990).

4. Esther Burnett Horne and Sally McBeth, *Essie's Story: The Life and Legacy of a Shoshone Teacher* (Lincoln: University of Nebraska Press, 1998), 34.

5. Chuck Haines, "A Brief History of Haskell Institute 1884–1935" (paper prepared by the Wetland Preservative Organization for the Haskell Student Senate and the National Haskell Board of Regents, October 1999), incomplete draft, 5.

6. Report to the Commissioner of Indian Affairs by Special U.S. Indian Agent McConihe, November 14, 1908, HR, RG 75, NADC.

7. Superintendent Peairs to Rev. James Dykema, December 4, 1918, Box 122, Decimal Correspondence Files, HR, RG 75, NACPR.

8. Letter to Henry A. Larson, chief special officer, August 29, 1917, HR, RG 75, NADC.

9. Affidavit by Clarence Thomas, September 22, 1917, Box 116, Student Case Files, HR, RG 75, NACPR.

10. Superintendent Peairs to A. S. Wyly, supervisor of Indian schools, Muskogee, Oklahoma, October 1, 1917, Box 116, Student Case Files, H R, RG 75, NACPR.

11. Lucille C. Abert to Mrs. N. R. Denny, Carlisle Indian School, December 9, 1918, HR, RG 75, NADC.

12. Superintendent Peairs to William A. McKeever, State University, November 19, 1917, Box 24, SCF, HR, RG 75, NACPR.

13. Horne and McBeth, *Essie's Story*, 41.

14. K. Tsianina Lomawaima, *They Called It Prairie Light: The Story of Chilocco Indian School* (Lincoln: University of Nebraska Press, 1994), 157–159.

15. As quoted in Linda Legrade Grover, "Effects of Boarding School Education on American Indian Families: A Qualitative Study of Perceptions from an American Indian Viewpoint" (D.Ed. diss., University of Minnesota, 1999), 139.

16. Ibid., 143.

17. Interview with Otis Russell, May 5, 1970, Doris Duke Oral History Collection.

18. Omer C. Stewart, *Peyote Religion: A History* (Norman: University of Oklahoma Press, 1987), xiii.

19. Ibid., 97.

20. Weston La Barre, *The Peyote Cult*, 5th ed. (Norman: University of Oklahoma Press, 1989), 103.

21. With the spread of peyotism across the plains, gourd rattles became a standard feature of peyote ceremonies. Ibid., 67.

22. Stewart, *Peyote Religion*, 65.

23. Ibid., xiv.

24. Before 1944, the church was called the Oklahoma Native American Church. Ibid., 239–240.

25. Scott, *Domination and the Arts of Resistance*, xi.

26. Ibid., xii.

27. Ibid., 72–73.

28. Horne and McBeth, *Essie's Story*, 40–41.

29. As quoted in Grover, "Effects of Boarding School Education," 140.

30. Amelia Smith to William Smith, October 31, 1907, Box 110, Student Case Files, HR, RG 75, NACPR.

31. William Smith to Superintendent Peairs, November 5, 1907, Box 110, Student Case Files, HR, RG 75, NACPR.

32. Superintendent Peairs to William Smith, November 12, 1907, Box 110, Student Case Files, HR, RG 75, NACPR.

33. Report by Dr. Joseph Murphy, November 12, 1908, HR, RG 75, NADC.

34. J. O. Milligan to Superintendent Peairs, November 30, 1908, HR, RG 75, NADC.

35. Superintendent Peairs to the Commissioner of Indian Affairs, November 30, 1908, HR, RG 75, NADC.

36. Superintendent Peairs to the Commissioner of Indian Affairs, July 26, 1917, Box 6, SCF, HR, RG 75, NACPR.

37. Eric P. Anderson, "An Imperfect Education: Assimilation and American Indians at Haskell Institute, Lawrence, Kansas 1884–1894" (M.A. thesis, University of Kansas, 1997), 88.

38. Superintendent Wise to the Commissioner of Indian Affairs, June 30, 1911, Box 145, Correspondence sent to the Commissioner of Indian Affairs, HR, RG 75, NACPR.

39. Superintendent Wise to W. W. McConihe, Special Agent, Pawnee Agency, May 4, 1914, Box 159, CCF, HR, RG 75, NACPR.

40. Superintendent Peairs to Ada Minesinger [friend of Anna McKiver], St. Ignatius, Montana, August 21, 1922, HR, RG 75, NACPR.

41. Ada Minesinger to Superintendent Peairs, August 14, 1922, HR, RG 75, NACPR.

42. Superintendent Peairs to Ada Minesinger, August 21, 1922, HR, RG 75, NACPR.

43. As quoted in David Wallace Adams, *Education for Extinction: American Indians and the Boarding School Experience, 1875–1928* (Lawrence: University Press of Kansas, 1995), 231.

44. Superintendent Fiske to A. S. Wyly, District Agent, Union Agency, Oklahoma, September 30, 1910, Box 179, CSA, HR, RG 75, NACPR.

45. Scott, *Domination and the Arts of Resistance*, 198.

46. Alice Littlefield, "The B.I.A. Boarding School: Theories of Resistance and Social Reproduction," *Humanity and Society* 13, 4 (1989): 437.

47. Scott, *Domination and the Arts of Resistance*, 201.

48. The Commissioner of Indian Affairs to Superintendent Peairs, June 26, 1906, Box 141, Correspondence received from the Office of Indian Affairs, HR, RG 75, NACPR.

49. Superintendent Peairs to Superintendent S. M. McCowan, Chilocco, Oklahoma, October 26, 1907, HR, RG 75, NACPR.

50. Superintendent Peairs to Mr. J. C. Hart, Pawnee, Oklahoma, July 7, 1920, HR, RG 75, NACPR.

51. Correspondence between Assistant Superintendent Sharon R. Mote (Haskell) and Superintendent R. P. Haas, Shoshone Indian Agency, Ft. Washakie, Wyoming, September 6 and 18 and December 1, 1923, HR, RG 75, NACPR.

52. Superintendent Peairs to Mr. John Tabell, October 12, 1920, HR, RG 75, NACPR.

53. Margaret Tarbell to Superintendent Peairs, October 20, 1920, HR, RG 75, NACPR.

54. E. Townsend to Superintendent Robinson, October 2, 1888, CSRC.

55. Abe Crawford to Haskell's administration, March 6, 1923, HR, RG 75, NACPR.

56. Superintendent Peairs to Wilson B. Charles, September 27, 1909, Box 6, SCF, HR, RG 75, NACPR.

57. Superintendent Peairs to the Commissioner of Indian Affairs, July 15, 1917, Box 6, SCF, HRRG 75, NACPR.

58. Superintendent Wise to W. Opperman, August 1911, Box 6, SCF, HRRG 75, NACPR.

59. Superintendent Peairs to Mr. E. B. Linnen, June 17, 1920, Box 134, Correspondence of the Superintendents, HRRG 75, NACPR.

60. Quoted in Superintendent Peairs to the Commissioner of Indian Affairs, July 15, 1917.

61. Superintendent Peairs to the Commissioner of Indian Affairs, July 15, 1917, Box 6, SCF, HR, RG 75, NACPR.

62. Student petition to Superintendent Robinson, December 4, 1887, CSRC; Student petition to Superintendent Robinson, January 5, 1888, CSRC. From the records, it is not clear what type of dancing the boys refer to, whether indigenous or European-American.

63. Student petition to Superintendent Robinson, May 9, 1888, CSRC.

64. Superintendent Wise to the Commissioner of Indian Affairs, April 11, 1916, HR, RG 75, NADC.

65. C. E. Birch to Superintendent Peairs, October 24, 1919, HR, RG 75, NADC.

66. Ibid.

67. Ibid.

68. Ibid.

69. Scott, *Domination and the Arts of Resistance*, 57–58.

70. Superintendent Fiske to John B. Brown, assistant supervisor, Union Agency, Muskogee, Oklahoma, October 18, 1910, Box 150, CCF, HR, RG 75, NACPR.

71. District Agent A. S. Wyly, Union Agency, Oklahoma, to Superintendent Fiske, September 26, 1910, Box 179, CSA, HR, RG 75, NACPR.

72. J. B. Brown, assistant supervisor, Union Agency, Oklahoma, to Superintendent Fiske, September 22, 1910, Box 179, CSA, HR, RG 75, NACPR.

73. Superintendent Fiske to J. B. Brown, assistant supervisor, Union Agency, Oklahoma, February 4, 1911, Box 179, CSA, HR, RG 75, NACPR. The parents' rejection of Haskell's educational philosophy might have been related to their prior experiences with the Cherokee Nation's own educational system, which gave priority to academic training. Jorge Noriega, "American Indian Education in the United States: Indoctrination for Subordination to Colonialism," in *Genocide, Colonization and Resistance*, ed. M. Annette Jaimes, 379 (Boston, MA: South End Press, 1992); Devon A. Mihesuah, *Cultivating the Rosebuds: The Education of Women at the Cherokee Female Seminary, 1851–1909* (Urbana: University of Illinois Press, 1993).

74. J. B. Smith to Maggie Smith, September 22, 1911, Box 110, Student Case Files, HR, RG 75, NACPR.

75. Horne and McBeth, *Essie's Story*, 47–48.

76. T. W. Hunter to John Presley, October 11, 1910, Box 21, SCF, HR, RG 75, NACPR.

77. The Commissioner of Indian Affairs to Superintendent Peairs, December 14, 1899, Box 136, HR, RG 75, NACPR.

78. Quoted in Grover, "Effects of Boarding School Education," 145.

79. Superintendent Fiske to the Commissioner of Indian Affairs, March 4, 1910, Box 144, Correspondence sent to the Office of Indian Affairs, HR, RG 75, NACPR.

80. Ibid.

81. Superintendent Wise to the Commissioner of Indian Affairs, January 29, 1914, HR, RG 75, NADC.

82. Superintendent Wise to T. J. Ferrar, field clerk, Okmulgee, Oklahoma, November 13, 1912, Box 155, CCF, HR, RG 75.

83. Horne and McBeth, *Essie's Story*, 31.

84. Ibid., 36.

85. Superintendent Wise to Thomas J. Farrar, field clerk, Union Agency, Okmulgee, Oklahoma, March 29, 1913, Box 156, CCF, HR, RG 75, NACPR.

86. Caleb Carter to O. H. Lipps, Superintendent, Ft. Lapwai Indian Agency, Idaho, January 30, 1908, Box 168, CSA, HR, RG 75, NACPR.

87. Superintendent Fiske to Frank J. Van, August 15, 1910, Box 19, SCF, HR, RG 75, NACPR.

88. Interview with Jesse Rowlodge, April 23, 1968, Doris Duke Oral History Collection.

89. Mrs. L. Sparrier to Superintendent Peairs, July 6, 1917, Box 100, Student Case Files, HR, RG 75, NACPR.

90. Frank Selatsee to Superintendent Wise, June 12, 1911, Box 106, Student Case Files, HR, RG 75, NACPR.

91. T. B. Le Sieur to Superintendent Peairs, April 3, 1907, Box 21, SCF, HR, RG 75, NACPR.

92. Joseph Comer to Superintendent Peairs, August 29, 1917, HR, RG 75, NACPR.

93. Horne and McBeth, *Essie's Story*, 52.

94. Jewel Wells to her sister, December 29, 1916, Box 126, Student Case Files, HR, RG 75, NACPR.

95. Josephine Smith to her sister, December 1, 1916, March 2, 1917, March 30, 1917, Box 110, Student Case Files, HR, RG 75, NACPR.

96. Horne and McBeth, *Essie's Story*, 42.

97. Grover, "Effects of Boarding School Education," 112–113.

98. As quoted in ibid., 114–115.

99. Quoted in Adams, *Education for Extinction*, 262.

100. Ibid.

101. Horne and McBeth, *Essie's Story*, 44.

102. Ibid., 44.

103. Adams, *Education for Extinction*, 263.

104. Frederick E. Hoxie, *A Final Promise: The Campaign to Assimilate the Indians, 1880–1920* (Cambridge: Cambridge University Press, 1984), 243–244.

Chapter Eight. Life after Haskell

1. Mrs. Nellie Helgeson to Superintendent Peairs, April 11, 1917, Box 21, SCF, HR, RG 75, NACPR.

2. Clara Toombs to Superintendent Peairs, June 12, 1919, Box 21, SCF, HR, RG 75, NACPR.

3. Dennison Wheelock to Superintendent Peairs, June 13, 1919, Box 126, Student Case Files, HR, RG 75, NACPR.

4. Esther Burnett Horne and Sally McBeth, *Essie's Story: The Life and Legacy of a Shoshone Teacher* (Lincoln: University of Nebraska Press, 1998), 55.

5. As quoted in David Wallace Adams, *Education for Extinction: American Indians*

and the Boarding School Experience, 1875–1928 (Lawrence: University Press of Kansas, 1925), 265.

6. As quoted in Michael C. Coleman, *American Indian Children at School, 1850–1930* (Jackson: University Press of Mississippi, 1993), 179.

7. As quoted in Adams, *Education for Extinction*, 266.

8. As quoted in Coleman, *American Indian Children at School*, 179.

9. Evangeline Johnson-Gover to Superintendent Peairs, December 27, 1917, Box 21, SCF, HR, RG 75, NACPR.

10. Survey form, "Inquiries Relative to Ex-Students of Haskell," 1909, Box 122, Student Case Files, HR, RG 75, NACPR.

11. *Indian Leader*, January 1920, 8.

12. Ibid.

13. Returned Student Survey, January 30, 1917, Box 20, SCF, HR, RG 75, NACPR, 7–8.

14. Ibid.

15. Ibid.

16. Robert Dunlap to Superintendent Robinson, July 15, 1888, CSRC.

17. Horne and McBeth, *Essie's Story*, 50.

18. Genevieve Bell, "Telling Stories Out of School: Remembering the Carlisle Indian Industrial School, 1879–1918" (Ph.D. diss., Stanford University, 1998), 340.

19. Adams, *Education for Extinction*, 294.

20. Superintendent Peairs to Superintendent E. L. Chalcraft, Chemawa, Oregon, July 6, 1908, Box 3, SCF, HR, RG 75, NACPR.

21. Superintendent Peairs to J. B. Walker, February 24, 1908, Box 7, SCF, HR, RG 75, NACPR.

22. The Mescalero Agency to Superintendent Peairs, August 20, 1918, Box 7, SCF, HR, RG 75, NACPR.

23. Eric P. Anderson, "An Imperfect Education: Assimilation and American Indians at Haskell Institute, Lawrence, Kansas, 1884–1894" (M.A. thesis, University of Kansas, 1997), 137.

24. Superintendent Peairs to the Commissioner of Indian Affairs, July 23, 1909, Box 144, Correspondence sent to the Commissioner of Indian Affairs, HR, RG 75, NACPR.

25. Agnes Wright to Superintendent Wise, August 17, 1912, Box 132, Student Case Files, HR, RG 75, NACPR.

26. Charles Dagenett to Superintendent Wise, August 21, 1912, Box 132, Student Case Files, HR, RG 75, NACPR.

27. Agnes Wright to C. E. Birch, January 19, 1914, Box 132, Student Case Files, HR, RG 75, NACPR.

28. Cordelia M. Garvie to Superintendent Peairs, October 15, 1907, Box 8, SCF, HR, RG 75, NACPR.

29. Hattie B. Wright to Superintendent Wise, March 7, 1917, Box 132, Student Case Files, HR, RG 75, NACPR.

30. Superintendent Wise to Hattie B. Wright, March 12, 1917, Box 132, Student Case Files, HR, RG 75, NACPR.

31. George B. Selkirk to C. E. Birch, September 1, 1910, Box 21, SCF, HR, RG 75, NACPR.

32. Ibid.

33. Ibid.

34. Adams, *Education for Extinction*, 295.

35. Wilbert H. Ahern, "An Experiment Aborted: Returned Indian Students in the Indian School Service, 1881–1908," *Ethnohistory* 44, 2 (Spring 1997): 286.

36. Ibid., 290–291.

37. Report on the Business Department, October 29, 1918, Box 3, SCF, HR, RG 75, NACPR.

38. Ibid.

39. John E. Snake to Superintendent Peairs, April 30, 1917, Box 110, Student Case Files, HR, RG 75, NACPR.

40. Correspondence between Haskell and the Underwood Typewriter Company, July–October 1909, Box 8, SCF, HR, RG 75, NACPR.

41. Superintendent Fiske to the Commissioner of Indian Affairs, March 4, 1910, Box 144, Correspondence sent to the Commissioner of Indian Affairs, HR, RG 75, NACPR.

42. Charles E. Dagenett to Superintendent Peairs, May 21, 1917, Box 8, SCF, HR, RG 75, NACPR.

43. Superintendent Peairs to Mr. M. Griswold, manager, General Electric Company, May 17, 1918, Box 8, SCF, HR, RG 75, NACPR.

44. The General Electric Company to Superintendent Peairs, May 24, 1918, Box 8, SCF, HR, RG 75, NACPR.

45. L. G. Moses, "Interpreting the Wild West, 1883–1914," in *Between Indian and White Worlds: The Cultural Broker*, ed. Margaret Connell Szasz, 159 (Norman: University of Oklahoma Press, 1994).

46. Ibid., 178.

47. Superintendent Peairs to Bell Memorial Hospital, Rosedale, Kansas, November 20, 1917, Box 16, SCF, HR, RG 75, NACPR.

48. Hannah Anderson to Superintendent Peairs, April 15, 1919, Box 16, SCF, HR, RG 75, NACPR.

49. Bell, "Telling Stories Out of School," 365.

50. Report on Former Students of H.I. in the Military or Naval Service of the United States, December 26, 1917, Box 109, Decimal Correspondence Files #610, HR, RG 75, NACPR.

51. Bell, "Telling Stories Out of School," 367.

52. John S. Amick, Captain Battery B, to Superintendent Peairs, September 5, 1917, Box 1, SCF, HR, RG 75, NACPR.

53. Superintendent of the Cheyenne and Arapahoe Agency to Superintendent Peairs, April 10, 1917, Box 109, Decimal Correspondence Files #600, HR, RG 75, NACPR.

54. Lydia Partain, April 25, 1917, Box 109, Decimal Correspondence Files #600, HR, RG 75, NACPR.

55. Ebenezer Kingsley to Superintendent Peairs, April 9, 1917, Box 109, Decimal Correspondence Files #600, HR, RG 75, NACPR.

56. James R. Murie to Superintendent Peairs, April 10, 1917, Box 109, Decimal Correspondence Files #600, HR, RG 75, NACPR.

57. George Sharp to Charlotte Presley, September 1917, HR, RG 75, NACPR.

58. Vigil Isidro to Superintendent Peairs, February 1919, HR, RG 75, NACPR.

59. As quoted in Coleman, *American Indian Children at School*, 187.

60. Ibid.

61. Ibid.

62. Horne and McBeth, *Essie's Story*, 49.

63. Ibid.

64. Ibid., 55.

65. Julie Davis, "American Indian Boarding School Experiences: Recent Studies from Native Perspectives," *OAH Magazine of History* 15 (Winter 2001): 20–22.

66. Clyde Ellis, "We Had a Lot of Fun, but of Course, That Wasn't the School Part: Life at Rainy Mountain Boarding School, 1893–1920," in *Boarding School Blues: Revisiting American Indian Educational Experiences*, ed. Clifford E. Trafzer, Jean A. Keller, and Lorene Siquoc, 91 (Lincoln: University of Nebraska Press, 2006).

67. Donald J. Berthrong, "Jesse Rowlodge: Southern Arapaho as Political Intermediary," in *Between Indian and White Worlds: The Cultural Broker*, ed. Margaret Connell Szasz, 223–239 (Norman: University of Oklahoma Press, 1994).

68. Ibid., 224–226.

69. Ibid., 229–234.

70. Interview with Jesse Rowlodge, Background of Informant Section, April 23, 1968, Doris Duke Oral History Collection

71. Ibid.

72. Ibid.

73. Berthrong, "Jesse Rowlodge," 239.

74. Linda Legrade Grover, "Effects of Boarding School Education on American Indian Families: A Qualitative Study of Perceptions from an American Indian Viewpoint" (Ed.D. diss., University of Minnesota, 1999), 154.

75. As quoted in ibid., 161.

76. As quoted in ibid.

77. As quoted in ibid., 181.

78. As quoted in ibid., 177–178.

79. As quoted in ibid., 187–188.

80. As quoted in ibid., 188.

81. Margaret D. Jacobs, "Indian Boarding Schools in Comparative Perspective: The Removal of Indigenous Children in the United States and Australia, 1880–1940," in *Boarding School Blues: Revisiting American Indian Educational Experiences*, ed. Clifford E. Trafzer, Jean A. Keller, and Lorene Siquoc, 224 (Lincoln: University of Nebraska Press, 2006).

82. Brenda J. Child, *Boarding School Seasons: American Indian Families 1900–1940* (Lincoln: University of Nebraska Press, 1998), 100.

83. Grover, "Effects of Boarding School Education," 191–192.

84. David W. Adams, "Beyond Bleakness: The Brighter Side of Indian Boarding Schools, 1870–1940," in *Boarding School Blues: Revisiting American Indian Educational Experiences*, ed. Clifford E. Trafzer, Jean A. Keller, and Lorene Siquoc, 35–64 (Lincoln: University of Nebraska Press, 2006).

85. Grover, "Effects of Boarding School Education," 206.

86. Horne and McBeth, *Essie's Story*, 52–53.

Bibliography

Primary Sources

Archival Collections

Doris Duke Oral History Collection. Western History Collection, University of Oklahoma, Norman.

Kansas State Historical Society, Topeka.

Kenneth Spencer Research Library, University of Kansas. Haskell Institute Records; Kansas Collection.

National Archives–Central Plains Region (Kansas City, Missouri). Records of the Bureau of Indian Affairs; Record Group 75: Records of the Bureau of Indian Affairs; Records on Haskell Indian Nations University, 1884–1954, Box #35/01/01–Box #36/01/12.

National Archives–Washington, DC. Records of the Bureau of Indian Affairs; Record Group 75: Haskell Records; Record Group 75: Records of the Bureau of Indian Affairs; Records on Haskell Indian Nations University, Central Classified Files.

Government Documents

Atkins, John D.C. *Report of the Commissioner of Indian Affairs.* Washington, DC: Government Printing Office, 1885, 1886, 1887.

Browning, Daniel M. *Report of the Commissioner of Indian Affairs.* Washington, DC: Government Printing Office, 1893, 1894, 1895.

Morgan, Thomas J. *Indian Education.* Washington, DC: U.S. Government Publications, 1890.

———. *Report of the Commissioner of Indian Affairs.* Washington, DC: Government Printing Office, 1889, 1890.

Oberly, John H. *Report of the Commissioner of Indian Affairs.* Washington, DC: Government Printing Office, 1888.

United States Senate, Committee on Labor and Public Welfare. *Indian Education: A National Tragedy—A National Challenge.* 91st Cong., 1st sess. Washington, DC: Government Printing Office, 1969.

Newspapers

Denver Times, 1904.

Douglas County Historical Society Newsletter, 1984.

Indian Leader, Haskell Institute, Lawrence Kansas, 1987–1920s.
Kansas City Journal, Kansas City, Missouri/Kansas, 1888.
Kansas City Times, Kansas City, Missouri/Kansas, 1926.
Lawrence Daily Gazette, Lawrence, Kansas, 1885, 1887.
Lawrence Daily Journal, Lawrence, Kansas, 1883, 1884, 1887, 1888.
Philadelphia Public Ledger, 1912.
St. Joseph Herald, 1887.

Secondary Sources

Adams, David Wallace. *Education for Extinction: American Indians and the Boarding School Experience, 1875–1928.* Lawrence: University Press of Kansas, 1995.
———. "Fundamental Considerations: The Deep Meaning of Native American Schooling, 1880–1900." *Harvard Educational Review* 58, 1 (1988): 1–27.
———. "More Than a Game: The Carlisle Indians Take to the Gridiron, 1893–1917." *Western Historical Quarterly* 32, 1 (2001): 41 pars. Available at http://www.historycooperative.org/journals/whq/32.1/adams.html (accessed June 20, 2007).
Ahern, Wilbert H. "An Experiment Aborted: Returned Indian Students in the Indian School Service, 1881–1908." *Ethnohistory* 44, 2 (Spring 1997): 263–304.
Ames, Rev. William P. "Highlights of Haskell Institute: A Brief Sketch of the Half Century of Indian Education at Haskell Institute, Lawrence, Kansas." Kansas Collection, Kenneth Spencer Research Library, University of Kansas, 1936.
Amott, Theresa, and Julie Matthaei. *Race, Gender, and Work: A Multicultural Economic History of Women in the United States.* Boston: South End Press, 1991.
Anderson, Eric P. "An Imperfect Education: Assimilation and American Indians at Haskell Institute, Lawrence, Kansas, 1884–1894." M.A. thesis, University of Kansas, 1997.
Andrews, Thomas G. "Turning the Tables on Assimilation: Oglala Lakotas and the Pine Ridge Day Schools, 1889–1920s." *Western Historical Quarterly* 33, 4 (2002). Available at http://www.historycooperative.org/journals/whq/33.4/andrews.html (accessed October 30, 2007).
Archuleta, Margaret L., Brenda J. Child, and K. Tsianina Lomawaima. *Away from Home: American Indian Boarding School Experiences 1879–2000.* Phoenix: Heard Museum, 2000.
Armstrong, Samuel C. *Indian Education at Hampton Normal and Agricultural Institute.* Hampton, VA: George & Nesbitt & Co. Printers, 1881.
Barman, Jean, and Yvonne Hebert. *Indian Education in Canada.* Vancouver: University of British Columbia Press, 1986.
Barth, Frederik. "Introduction." *Ethnic Groups and Boundaries.* Boston: Little, Brown, 1969.
Bell, Genevieve. "Telling Stories Out of School: Remembering the Carlisle Indian Industrial School, 1879–1918." Ph.D. diss., Stanford University, 1998.
Berkhofer, Robert F. *The White Man's Indian.* New York: Vintage Books, 1978.

Birch, Clarence E. *Methods of Teaching English.* Lawrence, KS, 1914.
Bloom, John. "'Show What an Indian Can Do': Sports, Memory, and Ethnic Identity at Federal Indian Boarding Schools." *Journal of American Indian Education* 35, 3 (Spring 1996): 33–48.
———. "There Is Madness in the Air: The 1926 Haskell Homecoming and Popular Representations of Sports in Federal Indian Boarding Schools." In *Dressing in Feathers: The Construction of the Indian in American Popular Culture,* edited by Elizabeth Bird, 97–110. Boulder, CO: Westview Press, 1998.
Britten, Thomas A. *American Indians in World War I: At War and at Home.* Albuquerque: University of New Mexico Press, 1997.
Buffalohead, W. Roger, and Paulette Fairbanks Molin. "A Nucleus of Civilization: American Indian Families at Hampton Institute in the Late Nineteenth Century." *Journal of American Indian Education* 35, 3 (Spring 1996): 59–94.
Carter, Patricia. "Completely Discouraged: Women Teachers' Resistance in the Bureau of Indian Affairs Schools, 1900–1910." *Frontiers* 15, 3 (1995): 53–86.
Castile, George P., and G. Kushner, eds. *Persistent Peoples: Cultural Enclaves in Perspective.* Tucson: University of Arizona Press, 1981.
Child, Brenda J. *Boarding School Seasons: American Indian Families 1900–1940.* Lincoln: University of Nebraska Press, 1998.
———. "Runaway Boys, Resistant Girls: Rebellion at Flandreau and Haskell, 1900–1940." *Journal of American Indian Education* 35, 3 (Spring 1996): 49–57.
Churchill, Ward. *Kill the Indian, Save the Man: The Genocidal Impact of American Indian Residential Schools.* San Francisco: City Lights Books, 2004.
Coleman, Michael C. *American Indian Children at School, 1850–1930.* Jackson: University Press of Mississippi, 1993.
Cornell, Stephen. "Ethnicity as Narrative." Paper presented at the annual meeting of the American Sociological Association, Los Angeles, 1994.
———. *The Return of the Native: American Indian Political Resurgence.* New York: Oxford University Press, 1988.
———. "The Variable Ties that Bind: Content and Circumstances in Ethnic Processes." *Ethnic and Racial Studies* 19, 2 (1996): 265–289.
Davis, Julie. "American Indian Boarding School Experiences: Recent Studies from Native Perspectives." *OAH Magazine of History* 15 (Winter 2001): 20–22.
DeJong, David H. *Promises of the Past: A History of Indian Education in the United States.* Golden, CO: Fulcrum Publishing, 1993.
Deloria, Vine, Jr., and Daniel R. Wildcat. *Power and Place: Indian Education in America.* Golden, CO: Fulcrum Publishing, 2001.
Ellis, Clyde. *A Dancing People: Powwow Culture on the Southern Plains.* Lawrence: University Press of Kansas, 2003.
———. *To Change Them Forever: Indian Education at the Rainy Mountain Boarding School.* Norman: University of Oklahoma Press, 1996.
Fear-Segal, Jacqueline. "Nineteenth-Century Indian Education: Universalism versus Evolutionism." *Journal of American Studies* 33 (1999): 323–341.
Fink-Eitel, Hinrich. *Michel Foucault.* Hamburg: Junius Verlag, 1990.

Foucault, Michel. *Überwachen und Strafen: Die Geburt des Gefängnisses.* Frankfurt: Suhrkamp Verlag, 1994.
Geertz, Clifford. *The Interpretation of Cultures.* New York: HarperCollins, 1973.
Goddard, Geneva. "A Study of the Historical Development and Educational Work at Haskell Institute." M.A. thesis, Kansas State Teacher's College, 1930.
Goodburn, Amy. "Literacy Practices at the Genoa Industrial Indian School." *Great Plains Quarterly* 19 (1999): 35–52.
Granzer, Mary Loretta. "Education at Haskell Institute, 1884–1937." M.A. thesis, University of Nebraska, 1937.
Green, Donald E., and T. Tonnesen. *American Indians: Social Justice and Public Policy.* Vol. 9. Ethnicity and Public Policy Series. Milwaukee: The University of Wisconsin System Institute on Race and Ethnicity, 1991.
Grover, Linda Legrade. "Effects of Boarding School Education on American Indian Families: A Qualitative Study of Perceptions from an American Indian Viewpoint." Ed.D. diss., University of Minnesota, 1999.
Haig-Brown, Celia. *Resistance and Renewal: Surviving the Indian Residential School.* Vancouver, BC: Tillacum Library, 1988.
Harkin, Michael. "Contested Bodies: Affliction and Power in Heiltsuk Culture and History." *American Ethnologist* 21, 3 (1994): 586–605.
Harroun Foster, Martha. "Of Baggage and Bondage: Gender and Status among Hidatsa and Crow Women." *American Indian Culture and Research Journal* 17, 2 (1993): 121–152.
Hobsbawm, Eric, ed. *The Invention of Tradition.* Cambridge: Cambridge University Press, 1983.
Hoffmann, Robert. "A History of the Commercial Department of Haskell Institute, 1895–1963." M.A. thesis, Pittsburg State University, Kansas, 1964.
Horne, Esther Burnett, and Sally McBeth. *Essie's Story: The Life and Legacy of a Shoshone Teacher.* Lincoln: University of Nebraska Press, 1998.
Horowitz, Donald L. "The Nature of Ethnic Affiliations." In *Majority and Minority: The Dynamics of Race and Ethnicity in American Life,* edited by Norman Yetman, 5th ed., 48–59. Boston: Allyn & Bacon, 1991.
Horsman, Reginald. *Race and Manifest Destiny: The Origins of American Racial Anglo-Saxonism.* Cambridge, MA: Harvard University Press, 1981.
Hoxie, Frederick E. *A Final Promise: The Campaign to Assimilate the Indians, 1880–1920.* Cambridge: Cambridge University Press, 1984.
Hultgren, M. L., and P. Molin. *To Lead and to Serve: American Indian Education at Hampton Institute.* Virginia Beach: Virginia Foundation for the Humanities and Public Policy, 1989.
Hurtado, Albert L., and Peter Iverson, eds. *Major Problems in American Indian History.* Lexington, MA: D. C. Heath, 1994.
Hyer, Sally. *One House, One Voice, One Heart: Native American Education at Santa Fe School.* Santa Fe: Museum of New Mexico Press, 1990.
Jaimes, Annette M., ed. *The State of Native America: Genocide, Colonization, and Resistance.* Boston, MA: South End Press, 1992.

Johnston, Basil H. *Indian School Days*. Norman: University of Oklahoma Press, 1988.

Krush, Thaddeus P. "Some Thoughts on the Formation of Personality Disorder: Study of an Indian Boarding School Population." *American Journal of Psychiatry* 122, 2 (1966): 868–875.

La Barre, Weston, *The Peyote Cult*. 5th ed.. Norman: University of Oklahoma Press, 1989.

LaFlesche, Francis. *The Middle Five: Indian Schoolboys of the Omaha Tribe*. Lincoln: University of Nebraska Press, 1978. First published 1900.

Lindig, Wolfgang. *Navajo: Tradition and Change in the Southwest*. Zurich: U. Baer Verlag, 1991.

Littlefield, Alice. "The B.I.A. Boarding School: Theories of Resistance and Social Reproduction." *Humanity and Society* 13, 4 (1989): 428–441.

Lomawaima, K. Tsianina. "Estelle Reel, Superintendent of Indian Schools, 1898–1910." *Journal of American Indian Education* 35, 3 (Spring 1996): 5–31.

———. *They Called It Prairie Light: The Story of Chilocco Indian School*. Lincoln: University of Nebraska Press, 1994.

Lookingbill, Brad D. *War Dance at Fort Marion: Plains Indian War Prisoners*. Norman: University of Oklahoma Press, 2006.

Matthews, Glenda. *"Just a Housewife": The Rise and Fall of Domesticity in America*. New York: Oxford University Press, 1987.

Medicine, Beatrice. "North American Indigenous Women and Cultural Domination." *American Indian Culture and Research Journal* 17, 3 (1993): 121–129.

Meriam, Lewis. *The Problem of Indian Administration*. The Institute for Government Research. Baltimore, MD: Johns Hopkins Press, 1928.

Mihesuah, Devon A. *Cultivating the Rosebuds: The Education of Women at the Cherokee Female Seminary, 1851–1909*. Urbana: University of Illinois Press, 1993.

Milk, Theresa. *Haskell Institute: 19th Century Stories of Sacrifice and Survival*. Lawrence, KS: Mammoth Publication, 2007.

Nabokov, Peter, ed. *Native American Testimony: A Chronicle of Indian-White Relations from Prophecy to the Present, 1492–1992*. New York: Penguin Books, 1992.

Nagel, Joane. *American Indian Ethnic Renewal: Red Power and the Resurgence of Identity and Culture*. New York: Oxford University Press, 1996.

———. "Constructing Ethnicity: Creating and Recreating Identity and Culture." *Social Problems* 41 (1994): 152–176.

———. "The Political Construction of Ethnicity." In *Majority and Minority: The Dynamics of Race and Ethnicity in American Life*, 5th ed., edited by Norman Yetman, 76–86. Boston: Allyn & Bacon, 1991.

Naylor, Jack C. "A Study of the History of the Vocational Department at Haskell Institute, Lawrence, Kansas." M.Ed. thesis, University of Kansas, 1969.

Noriega, Jorge. "American Indian Education in the United States: Indoctrination for Subordination to Colonialism." In *Genocide, Colonization and Resistance*, edited by M. Annette Jaimes, 371–402. Boston, MA: South End Press, 1992.

O'Brien, Charles. "The Evolution of Haskell Indian Junior College, 1884–1974." M.A. thesis, University of Oklahoma, 1975.

Oxendine, Joseph B. *American Indian Sports Heritage*. Lincoln: University of Nebraska Press, 1995.

Perdue, Theda. "Writing the Ethnohistory of Native Women." In *Rethinking American Indian History*, edited by Donald L. Fixico, 73–86. Albuquerque: University of New Mexico Press, 1997.

Peshkin, Alan. *Places of Memory: Whiteman's Schools and Native American Communities*. Mahwah, NJ: Lawrence Erlbaum, 1997.

Pratt, Richard Henry. *The Indian Industrial School: Its Origins, Purposes and Difficulties Surmounted*. Carlisle, PA: Hamilton Library Association, 1908.

Prucha, Francis Paul. *The Great Father: The United States Government and the American Indians*, vols. 1 and 2. Lincoln: University of Nebraska Press, 1984.

Putney, Diane T. "Fighting the Scourge: American Indian Morbidity and Federal Policy, 1887–1928." Ph.D. diss., Marquette University, 1980.

Qoyawayma, Polingaysi. *No Turning Back*. Albuquerque: University of New Mexico Press, 1964.

Rabinow, Paul, ed. *The Foucault Reader*. New York: Pantheon Books, 1984.

Rader, Benjamin G. "'The Greatest Drama in Indian Life': Experiments in Native American Identity and Resistance at the Haskell Institute Homecoming of 1926." *Western Historical Quarterly* 35 (Winter 2004): 429–450.

Reel, Estelle. *Course of Study for Indian Schools in the United States*. Washington, DC: Government Printing Office, 1901.

Reyhner, Jon, and Jeanne Eder. *American Indian Education*. Norman: University of Oklahoma Press, 2004.

Riney, Scott. *The Rapid City Indian School, 1898–1933*. Norman: University of Oklahoma Press, 1999.

Robinson, Martha K. "Assimilation, Ambivalence, and Resistance: Students at Haskell Institute, 1920–1930." M.A. thesis, University of Kansas, 1996.

Saslow, Harry L. "Research on Psychosocial Adjustment of Indian Youth." *American Journal of Psychiatry* 125, 2 (August 1968): 224–230.

Schirer, Thomas E., ed. *Contemporary Native American Cultural Issues*. Sault Ste. Marie, MI: Lake Superior State University Press, 1988.

Schwingel, Markus. *Pierre Bourdieu*. Hamburg: Junius Verlag, 1995.

Scott, James C. *Domination and the Arts of Resistance: Hidden Transcripts*. New Haven: Yale University Press, 1990.

Spring, Joel. *Deculturization and the Struggle for Equality: A Brief History of the Education of Dominated Cultures in the United States*. New York: McGraw-Hill, 1994.

Stewart, Omer C. *Peyote Religion: A History*. Norman: University of Oklahoma Press, 1987.

Szasz, Margaret Connell, ed. *Between Indian and White Worlds: The Cultural Broker*. Norman: University of Oklahoma Press, 1994.

———. *Education and the American Indian: The Road to Self-Determination since 1928*. Albuquerque: University of New Mexico Press, 1974.

Tapia, John E. *Cirquit Chautauqua*. Jefferson, NC: McFarland, 1997.

Trafzer, Clifford E., Jean A. Keller, and Lorene Siquoc, eds. *Boarding School Blues: Re-*

visiting American Indian Educational Experiences. Lincoln: University of Nebraska Press, 2006.

Trennert, Robert A. "Educating Indian Girls and Women at Nonreservation Boarding Schools." In *Major Problems in American Indian History,* edited by Albert L. Hurtado and Peter Iverson, 381–391. Lexington, MA: D. C. Heath, 1994.

———. *The Phoenix Indian School: Forced Assimilation in Arizona, 1891–1935.* Norman: University of Oklahoma Press, 1988.

Utley, Robert, ed. *Battlefield and Classroom: Four Decades with the American Indian, the Memoirs of Richard H. Pratt.* New Haven: Yale University Press, 1964.

Van den Berghe, Pierre. "Race and Ethnicity: A Sociobiological Perspective." *Ethnic and Racial Studies* 1 (1978): 401–411.

Warren, Kim. "All Indian Trails Lead to Lawrence, October 27–30, 1926." *Kansas History: A Journal of the Central Plains* 30 (Spring 2007): 2–19.

West, Elliott. *Growing Up in Twentieth-Century America: A History and Reference Guide.* Westport, CT: Greenwood Press, 1996.

Williams, Raymond. *Marxism and Literature.* New York: Oxford University Press, 1977.

Winnie, Lucille Jerry. *Sah-Gan-De-Oh: The Chief's Daughter.* New York: Vantage Press, 1969.

Index

Abert, Lucille, 214
abortions, 181
academic curriculum
    contents, 96–97
    English instruction, 97–100
    goals of, 100
    history, 100–102
    literary practices, 102–104
accidents, 208
Adams, Charles, 197
agriculture, 120
Albuquerque Indian School, 251
alcohol, 213
Alcott, Louisa M., 103
allotment, 14, 281n14
alumni
    as cultural brokers and community spokespeople, 269–273
    employment in business, 263–265
    gendered employment, 255–256, 258
    Indian Service employment, 257–263
    letter exchanges with Haskell, 247–248
    marriage, 256–257
    pride in Haskell, 248–249
    "progressive," 251–252
    readjustments after graduation, 249–251
    "returned student problem," 252–255
    surveys of, 253–254
    See also female alumni
American citizenship, 286n10
American Expeditionary Force (AEF), 136, 266. See also World War I
American flag, 135
American Indian Movement, 271
Americanization, 12

American patriotism, 128, 135–138
Anderson, Rose, 123
Apache Indians, 49
Arapaho Indians, 20–21, 271–273
arson, 224
art, 147
assimilation
    altered meaning of, 16
    boarding schools and, 13
    change in public attitudes toward, 14–15
    See also forced assimilation
athletics, 157–165
athletic stadium, 153, 154, 156
attendance. See school attendance
automobile factories, 265

band. See music and musical organizations
banks, 110
Banks, Charles E., 200
Banks, Dennis, 271
bathing, 67–68
Battery B, Field Artillery, 266–267
Bearskin, Lena, 203
Beauregard, Margaret, 30
Bender, Anna, 258
Bible school classes, 130, 171(photo). See also religion and religious education
Birch, C. E.
    accelerated students, 106
    commercial course at Haskell, 108–109
    English instruction, 97, 98
    Haskell's business graduates, 263
    "rebellion" of 1919, 229–230
    on students returning to school, 46
    on vocational training, 111–112

Black, Jay, 76, 105–106
Black Kettle, 74
blacksmithing, 172(photo)
blood degree question, 40–43
boarding schools
    competition between schools for students, 33, 38
    education reform and, 36–37
    effects on Native American culture, 273–275, 276–278
    family resistance to, 35
    founding of, 13, 17–18
    funding, 17–18, 38, 284n24
    health conditions, 33–34, 76, 179–180, 184–185, 210
    as high schools, 36, 37, 95
    Meriam Report on, 16–17
    purpose and philosophy of, 13
    student age limits, 40
    student recruitment, 44–46
    suppression of tribal languages, 74
    unexpected consequences of, 13–14
    World War I and, 137
body
    assimilationist ideology and, 180–181
    sanitation regimen, 67–68
Bonnin, Raymond, 33–34
Bronson, Ruth Muskrat, 243, 270
Buffalo Bill's Wild West Show, 139, 140
burials, 207–208
Burke, Charles, 210
Burnett, Esther
    academic life, 107–108
    accommodation and self-identification, 242, 270–271
    arrival at Haskell, 59
    athletics, 161
    Christmas holidays, 151–152
    contact with home, 233
    dress code, 71
    food, 80
    football, 162
    Haskell as a safe environment, 242
    Indian discipline, 64
    leaving Haskell, 249
    leisure activities of girls, 145
    life at home after graduation, 256
    life story, 31
    male-female relations, 144
    marriage, 145
    military regimen at Haskell, 62, 66–67
    outing experience, 124
    positive memories of Haskell, 277
    on punishments at Haskell, 218, 235–236
    rats at Haskell, 84
    religious education, 133
    school friendships, 85, 88–89, 90
    "slanguage," 84–85
    student dormitories, 82
    on teachers, 245
    teaching career of, 271
    in theater, 150
    trauma at leaving for Haskell, 56
    travel to Haskell, 57–58
    tuberculosis, 197
    unsupervised behavior of students, 212, 215
business education, 37, 94, 95, 108–110, 166(photo), 263–264
business employment, 263–265
butter, 174(photo)

cadet system, 61
Camp Funston, Kansas, 200
Carlisle Indian School, 13, 17, 43, 161–162
Carter, Caleb, 237
cemetery, 21–22, 206
chains, 220
chapel, 168(photo)
Charles, Wilson B., 227
Chautauquas, 142
Cherokee Indians
    education and, 111, 303n73
    Five Civilized Tribes, 35
    mixed bloods, 42
    rejection of Haskell's educational philosophy, 303n73
Cherokee Indian students, 111
Cheyenne Indians, 20–21, 282n29
Cheyenne Indian students, 74

INDEX

Chickasaw Indians, 35
chief matron, 26–27
Child, Brenda, 207–208, 276
Chilocco Indian School
    founding of, 13
    Indian interest in, 31–32
    planning of, 18
    student friendships and shared community, 87
Choctaw Indians, 35, 42
Christianization, 14, 128–135
Christmas, 151–152
churches, represented at Haskell, 130
citizenship, 286n10
civilization-savagism paradigm, 12
civil service, 46
Clark, Susan Sears, 191–192
Cleveland, Vina, 225
clothing and uniforms, 68–73
Cloud, Henry Roe, 16
coaching, 160–161
Code of Religious Offenses, 14
Cody, William ("Buffalo Bill"), 265
Collier, John, 17
Comer, Joseph, 240
Commencement Exercises, 148
commercial course, 108–110, 170(photo)
communicable diseases, 187–189. *See also* influenza; trachoma; tuberculosis
Community Chautauqua System, 142
compulsory school attendance, 37–38
confinement rooms, 221
Congwhio, Lomo, 208
contracts, for student attendance, 39–40
corporal punishment, 23, 61. *See also* punishments
"Course of Study for Indian Schools," 92–93, 160
court-martial system, 61–62
crafts, indigenous, 104
Creek Indians, 35
Culp, L. L. (physician), 204, 205–206
curriculum
    business education, 37, 94, 95, 108–110, 166(photo), 263–264
    commercial course, 108–110, 170(photo)
    health and physiology, 180, 183–184
    nursing program, 117–118, 265–266
    outing program, 26, 113, 118, 122–127
    overview of, 92–97
    reform, 28
    standardized, 92–93
    Superintendent Peairs and, 94–95
    See also academic curriculum; vocational training
Curtis Act, 286n10

Dagenett, Charles, 257–258, 259, 265
Daklugie, Asa, 49
dancing, 146–147, 155, 156
Davis, L., 41
Dawes Act, 14, 136. *See also* General Allotment Act of 1887
Decoration Day, 152
Deloria, Ella, 243, 270
Deloria, Vine, 74
"demarcation line," 83
demerit system, 62
dental hygiene, 205–206
depression, 195
desertions, 211, 231, 234–237
Dewey, John, 16
diet, 76–81, 187
Diné Indians, 17, 65, 250. *See also* Navajo
dining hall, behavior in, 81–82, 143–144
discipline
    Lucille Abert on, 214
    bodily, 180–181
    court-martial system, 61–62
    at Haskell, 23, 227
    military system, 60–63, 65–67
    See also punishments
diseases
    child mortality at Haskell and, 21, 22, 208–209
    epidemics, 200–202
    health conditions at Haskell and, 187–189
    students' hiding sickness from authorities, 194–195
    See also influenza; pneumonia; trachoma; tuberculosis

domestic education, 116, 117, 170(photo), 171(photo)
domestic science cottage, 118–119
Dorchester, Daniel, 26
dormitories, 82–84, 173(photo), 185, 188–189
Douglas, Mrs., 227, 228, 229
dress code, 68–69, 71
Dull Knife, 282n29
Dunlap, Robert, 255

Eastman, Charles, 103
education
    Cherokee Indians and, 111, 303n73
    Native Americans and, 47–50, 241–242
    See also boarding schools; Indian education
elopements, 235
employment
    in business, 263–265
    difficulties finding, 255
    in entertainment, 265
    gendered, 255–256, 258
    in the Indian Service, 257–263
    military service, 266–269
    nursing, 265–266
English instruction, 97–100
English-only policy, 73–74
enrollment. *See* student enrollment
Ensign, Charles, 201
entertainment business, 265
epidemics, 200–202
essays, 104
Esther Home for Indian Girls, 95
Eufaula Boarding School, 271
expulsions, 43–44, 225–226, 238–239
eye diseases. *See* trachoma

factory work, 265–266
families
    effects of boarding schools on, 275–276
    "progressive," 251–252
    resistance to student attendance, 35–36, 45–46
    valuing of education, 47–50
    See also parents

farming, 120
female alumni
    gendered employment, 255–256, 258
    marriage, 256–257
    nursing, 265–266
female education, 116, 117–120
female students
    athletics, 164–165
    clothing, 70–71
    expulsion for sexual activity, 181, 183
    gendered behavior, 143–144
    gendered vocational training, 114–120
    gymnastics, 176(photo)
    homesickness and desertion, 234–235
    labor and, 113, 114
    leisure activities, 145, 176(photo)
    outing program, 122, 123–126, 127
    overcrowding in dormitories, 188
    physical condition, 187
films, 139
fires, 28, 224
Fiske, H. H.
    alumni employment in business, 265
    medical practice at Haskell, 194
    sexual activity of students, 181–183
    student clothing, 70, 72
    student homesickness and desertion, 232, 234
    visually impaired students, 204–205
Five Civilized Tribes, 35, 111
flag pledge, 135
Flying Earth, Eva, 266
Folsom, Cora, 195
food, 76–81, 187
football, 153, 157–160, 161–162, 163, 166(photo), 174(photo)
forced assimilation
    clothing and uniforms, 68–73
    English-only policy, 73–74
    military regimentation, 60–63, 65–67
    sanitation regimen, 67–68
    See also assimilation
Fort Lapwai Agency, 259
Fort Lapwai Indian Sanatorium School, 198
Fort Marion, 13

Fort Sill, Oklahoma, 266
Franchise Day, 135–136
Freeman, Mary J., 227
friendships, 85–90
Fuller, Lizzie, 50–51

gambling, 214
games, 145–146
Garvie, Cordelia, 260
gender, vocational training and, 114–120
gendered behavior, 143–144
General Allotment Act of 1887, 14, 136. *See also* Dawes Act
General Electric, 265–266
Genoa Indian School, 13
geography instruction, 100
Geronimo, 49
Ghost Dance, 129
Golden, Gertrude, 244
gonorrhea, 181
Grabowskii, Arthur, 22–23, 24, 61
graduation rates, 37
grandparents, resistance to student attendance, 35–36
Grant, Ulysses S., 14
Griggs, Lucy Logan, 75
Grover, Linda, 274, 277
guardhouse, 219–220, 221
Gullet, Fannie, 42–43
gymnasium, 175(photo)
gymnastics, 176(photo)

Haines, Chuck, 212–213
hair cutting, 68
Hampton Institute, 13
Haskell, Dudley Chase, 18, 19
Haskell, Harriet Kelsey, 27
Haskell, John, 18
Haskell Indian Orchestra Band, 142. *See also* music and musical organizations
Haskell Institute
   academic life, 105–108
   additions and expansions, 23, 25
   alumni survey of 1919, 253–254
   American patriotism, 128, 135–138

   athletic stadium, 153, 154, 156
   attendance, 21, 23, 25, 28, 29, 43, 46
   bodily transformation of students, 180–181
   campus, 19, 168(photo)
   cemetery, 21–22, 206
   chapel, 168(photo)
   competition between schools for students, 33
   contract for attendance at, 39–40
   curriculum (*see* academic curriculum; curriculum)
   daily program, 91–92
   desertions, 211, 231, 234–237
   dining room, 81–82
   discipline (*see* discipline)
   dormitories, 82–84, 173(photo), 185, 188–189
   early years, 19–29
   employment of alumni, 258–259
   English-only policy, 73–74
   ethnic diversity, 28
   expulsions, 43–44, 225–226
   extracurricular and cultural activities, 138–143
   family resistance to student attendance, 35–36
   fires, 28, 224
   food and nutrition, 76–81, 187
   founding, 13, 18–19
   funding, 23, 27
   goal and philosophy of, 29, 111
   graduation rates, 37
   growth of interest in, 30–31
   health conditions (*see* health conditions)
   health investigation of, 186–187
   as a high school, 37, 95
   holiday celebrations, 150–152
   homecoming of 1926, 153–157
   hospital, 22, 175(photo), 196
   imprisonment, 23, 61, 219–220, 221
   library, 103, 169(photo)
   medical care, 187, 193–194
   military system, 60–63, 65–67
   motto, 278

Haskell Institute, *continued*
  naming of, 19
  opening ceremony, 20
  outing program, 26, 113, 118, 122–127
  parental visits, 232
  parents' rejection of, 303n73
  prejudices against, 35
  punishments (*see* punishments)
  quarter-centennial celebration, 153
  "rebellion" of 1919, 229–230, 231
  religion and Christianization, 128–135
  renaming policy, 74–76
  reputation of, 30–31
  sanitary facilities, 83
  sanitation regimen, 67–68
  Small Boys Building, 173(photo)
  small children at, 40
  sports and athletics, 157–165
  student accommodation to, 241–242
  student age limits, 40
  student agendas for applying to, 53–55
  student enrollment, 31, 32
  student labor, 19–20, 110, 112–114
  student mortality, 21, 22, 206–209
  student petitions, 227–229
  student population composition, 34–35
  student population fluctuations, 38
  student recruitment, 24–25, 31, 32, 35, 38–39, 45, 46
  student resistance to, 211–217, 222–224, 228–231
  students' arrival at, 59–60
  students perceive positively, 240
  summer vacations, 53, 237–238
  superintendents (*see* superintendents of Haskell Institute)
  teachers, 243–245, 258–259, 270, 271
  theatrical productions, 148–150
  travel to, 56–58
  uniforms and clothing, 68–73
  water supply, 28
  working conditions of students, 185–187
  World's Fair exhibits, 147–148
Haskell & Wood architectural firm, 18–19

health conditions
  accidents involving students, 208
  affecting communicable diseases, 187–189
  at boarding schools, 33–34, 76, 179–180, 184–185, 210
  dental hygiene, 205–206
  in dormitories, 82, 83–84, 185, 188–189
  parental concerns with, 191–193
  student petition about, 228–229
  trachoma, 185, 192–193, 202–204
  tuberculosis, 179, 184, 185, 188–191, 194, 196–198
  See also diet; diseases; working conditions
health investigations, 186–187
health services, 187. *See also* medical care
Helgeson, Nellie, 247
Henry, Lillian, 110
Hiawatha (Longfellow), 103
hidden transcript, 212
high schools, 36, 37, 95
Hill, Eli, 39–40
history education, 100–102
holidays
  celebrations of, 150–152
  patriotic, 135–136
homecoming of 1926, 153–157
home economics, 117
homemaking arts instruction, 116
homesickness, 195, 231–232, 233, 234
honor roll system, 63
Hopi Indians, 65, 283n5
hospitals, 22, 175(photo), 196
Howard Institute, 17
hozho, 65
Hudspeth, Myrtle, 51–52
Hudspeth, W. E., 51
Hyer, Sally, 64

immigration, 282n22
Indian Appropriation Bill of 1883, 17–18
Indian Boyhood (Eastman), 103
Indian Citizenship Act, 138

Indian education
    civilization-savagism paradigm, 12
    colonial period, 11–12
    creation of a pluralistic society and, 17
    implementation of vocational training, 15, 16
    Thomas Jefferson Morgan and, 27
    original federal policy, 12–13
    reformed notions of assimilation and, 15–16
    reform of, 36–37
    See also boarding schools; Indian school system; reservation schools
Indian Employment Bureau, 257
Indian Employment Office, 259
Indian Leader (newspaper), 103, 248
Indian Legends and Superstitions, 105
Indian New Deal, 17
Indian policy
    allotment of tribal lands, 14, 281n14
    Christianization, 14
    principal components of, 12–15
Indian School Rules of 1898, 40
Indian School Service, 257
Indian school system
    attendance, 17
    the civil service and, 46
    number of employees in, 47
    number of schools in, 47
    superintendent of Indian schools, 46–47
    See also boarding schools; Indian education
Indian Service
    employment in, 257–263
    racism in, 42
individualism, 110–111
industrial training, 177(photo)
    purpose of and emphasis on, 110–112
    reorganization and expansion, 120
    student labor, 110, 112–114
    See also vocational training
influenza, 200–202
interracial marriage, 256–257
intertribal marriage, 256–257

involuntary recruitment, 31
Isidro, Vigil, 268

Jackson, Helen Hunt, 103
jail, 219–220, 221. *See also* prison
Janis, Fannie, 51, 52
Johnson, Robert, 121
Johnson, W. R., 33
Johnson-Gover, Evangeline, 251–252
Jones, W. A., 40–41, 94, 113, 116–117

Kaibab Indian School, 34
Kansas City Star (newspaper), 234
Kansas City Times (newspaper), 155
Keck, Katherine, 227–228
Kidder, Marion, 39
kindergartens, 40
Kiowa Indian Agency, 36

labor
    traditional divisions of, 115
    See also student labor
LaFromboise, Rose, 218
land allotment, 14, 281n14
land disputes, 282n29
La Pointe, Sophia, 30
"lateral sanctions," 65
laundries, 185–186
Lawrence, Mary, 35
Lawrence Daily Journal (newspaper), 18
Learnard, E., 18
leaves of absence, 53, 237
LeCroie, Henry, 105
Leonard, Oscar E., 26, 27
Leupp, Francis E.
    blood degree question, 41
    business department at Haskell, 94
    commercial course at Haskell, 109
    critic of off-reservation boarding schools, 44–45
    health conditions at Haskell, 190
    Indian Employment Bureau, 257
    music at Haskell, 141–142
    parental consent for child's school enrollment, 52

Levi, John, 157, 296n75
library, 103, 169(photo)
linguistics, 97
Lippincott, Joshua A., 20
literary societies, 102
literature, 102–103
Little Wolf, 282n29
Little Wolf, Tom, 208
Little Women (Alcott), 103
living conditions
    in dormitories, 82, 83–84, 185, 188–189
    See also health conditions; working conditions
Lomawaima, K. Tsianina, 87
Longfellow, Henry Wadsworth, 103
Lumpmouth, Carrie, 272

malnutrition, 187
manual training. *See* vocational training
marriage, 145, 256–257
Marshno, Mary, 201
Martin, Mary, 266
Marvin, James, 19, 20, 22, 23, 128, 130
matrons, 82–83, 116–117, 227–228, 244
McGilbery, Charles, 54–55
McKiver, Anna, 221–222
medical care, 187, 193–194
Memorial Day, 152
Menominee Reservation, 35
mental health, 195
Meriam, Lewis, 16
Meriam Report
    condemns jail punishment, 220
    Haskell's athletic stadium criticized, 154
    outing program criticism, 127
    overview, 16–17
    student health conditions, 179, 180
    students' diet and nutrition, 76, 187
    working conditions of students, 185–186
Mescalero Agency, 258
Meserve, Charles Francis, 21, 27, 50, 69, 82
mess halls, 81–82
Methods of Teaching English (Birch), 97
Midsummer Night's Dream, A (Shakespeare), 150

military service, 266–269. *See also* World War I
military system, 60–63, 65–67
Milligan, J. O., 220
Mitchell, George, 271
mixed bloods, 42
Morgan, Thomas Jefferson
    American patriotism, 135
    goals of Indian education, 100, 102
    impact on Indian education, 27
    Indian education reform, 36, 37
    opposition to emphasis on vocational training, 16
    renaming policy, 74
mortality, of students, 21, 22, 206–209
movies, 139
Murphy, Joseph A., 188, 190, 203, 220
music and musical organizations, 140–143, 169(photo)

Naismith, James, 183–184
naming process
    in indigenous societies, 75
    See also renaming policy
National Origins Quota System, 282n22
Native American Church, 129, 216–217
Native American culture
    consequences of the boarding school system for, 273–275, 276–278
    crafts, 104
    cultural values, 64–65
    effects of World War I on, 138
    homecoming celebration of 1926, 153, 154, 155, 156
Native American languages
    decline of, 274–275
    suppression of, 74
Native Americans
    American citizenship, 286n10
    cultural values, 64–65
    education and, 47–50, 111, 241–242, 303n73
    notions of learning, 11
    as teachers, 243–244
Native American women
    athletics, 164–165

sexist visions of, 115
World War I and, 137
See also female alumni; female students
Navajo Indians, 17, 65, 250. *See also* Diné Indians
Navajo Indian students, 33, 163
Neido, Mary Poafpybitty, 50
newspapers, 103
normal department, 28, 94
nurses and nursing, 117–118, 189–190, 265–266
nutrition, 76–81

"objective" instruction, 98–99
Office of Indian Affairs, 257
  racism in, 42
  school system supervised by, 47
Ojibwe Indians, 207–208, 274–277
Ojibwe Indian students, 31
Ojibwe language, 274–275
"Old Haskell Will Be There," 159–160
O'Neil, Patrick, 55
orchards, 212
Osage Indians, 71
Ottawa Indians, 20
outing programs, 26, 113, 118, 122–127, 293n101

parents
  complaints about children's punishment, 219
  concerns about student health, 191–193, 209–210
  conflicts with children over school enrollment, 50–52
  death of a student and, 206–208
  desertion of a student and, 235
  Haskell's treatment of tubercular children and, 198–199
  military service of children and, 267–268
  rejection of Haskell's educational philosophy, 303n73
  student attendance and, 35–36, 45–46
  student complaints about Haskell and, 226–227
  support for children at Haskell, 232
  support for enrolling students, 52–53
  visits to Haskell, 232
patriarchy, 115–116
patriotism, 128, 135–138
Patterson, Florence, 210
Pawnee Indians, 20–21, 267–268
Peairs, Harvey
  alumni employment, 258, 259
  alumni war veterans, 268
  athletics at Haskell, 160–162
  children's games at Haskell, 145–146
  Christmas holidays at Haskell, 151
  commercial course at Haskell, 108, 109
  effects of World War I on Haskell, 137, 138
  employment for alumni nurses, 265, 266
  expulsion of students, 225–226
  fires at Haskell, 224
  as Haskell Institute's superintendent, 28–29
  Haskell's curriculum, 94–95
  Haskell's farm, 120
  Haskell's quarter-centennial celebration, 153
  health conditions at Haskell, 189, 190–191, 192
  homecoming celebrations of 1926, 154
  influenza epidemics, 201, 202
  interactions with parents, 53
  Katherine Keck as matron, 228
  on learning through object lessons, 96
  medical care for students, 196
  movies at Haskell, 139
  music at Haskell, 141, 143
  outing program, 122, 123
  punishment of students, 219, 220–221
  religion at Haskell, 128, 131
  school overcrowding and, 189
  seen positively by students, 240
  on social behavior of children, 146
  student clothing and uniforms, 69, 70
  student desertions, 211
  student dormitories, 83
  student enrollment, 30

Peairs, Harvey, *continued*
  student labor, 111, 114
  student population composition, 35
  student population fluctuations, 38
  student reading, 102–103
  student recruitment, 33, 39, 45
  students' attitudes toward, 33
  students' diet, 78
  student use of tobacco, 213
  student use of traditional costumes, 143
  as superintendent of Indian schools, 46–47
  trachoma-infected students, 204
  tubercular students, 198, 199
  unsupervised behavior of students, 214
Peltier, Leonard, 271
Perry, Arleigh, 207
Peter, Callis, 208, 300n76
petitions, 227–229
peyote religion, 129, 134, 216–217, 272–273
Phoenix Indian School, 293n101
physical education, 157–165
physical exercise, 187, 188
physiology, 180, 184
pledge of allegiance, 135
pneumonia, 200, 202, 228–229
poems, 222
Polingaysi Qoyawayma, 283n5
Pollock, William, 258
Ponca Indians, 20
pool halls, 214
Pottawatomie Indian students, 38
poverty, 31
powwows, 156
Pratt, Richard Henry, 13, 18, 26
prayer routine, 222–223
Price, E. J., 261
primary education, 36, 167(photo)
prison, 23, 61. *See also* jail
profane language, 214
Protestant ideology, 12
psychological problems, 195
public transcript, 212
Puckskino, Frank, 204–205
Pueblo Indians, 64–65

Pueblo Indian students, 163
pulmonary consumption, 196–198
pulmonary tuberculosis, 196–198. *See also* tuberculosis
punishments, 23, 61, 62, 218–222, 235–236

Qoyawayma, Polingaysi, 283n5
Quain, Charles, 208
Quapaw Indians, 71
quarter-centennial celebration, 153

racism, 42, 282n22
Ramona (Jackson), 103
rape, 182–183
rats, 84
reading, 102–103
"rebellion" of 1919, 229–230, 231
recruitment raids, 31. *See also* student recruitment
Red Cross, 266
Red Eagle, Mary, 88, 119
Red Wolf, 49
Reece, James, 208
Reel, Estelle, 15, 37, 92–93, 160
religion and religious education, 128–135
renaming policy, 74–76
reservation schools
  compulsory attendance, 37–38
  primary education at, 36
  See also Indian education; Indian school system
restaurants, 80
"returned student problem," 252–255
Rice, Carrie, 201
Richmond, Mildred, 119, 238
Roberts, Henry E., 261
Robinson, Charles
  court-martial system at Haskell, 61–62
  as Haskell's superintendent, 24–25, 26
  Indian leaders' praise for, 49
  outing program, 26, 122
  student labor, 112–113
  student recruitment, 24–25, 32
Ross, Lucretia, 189–190
Ross, Tom, 80

Rowlodge, Jesse
   academic life, 105
   business education, 110
   as a cultural broker and tribal leader, 272–273
   food at Haskell, 79–80
   Hiawatha play, 149–150
   Indian identity from Haskell, 216
   life story, 271–273
   music at Haskell, 142
   Native American Church, 217
   reasons for attending Haskell, 54
   school friendships and shared community, 86–87, 88, 89
   student clothing, 71, 72–73
   summer life, 237–238
   Sunday routine at Haskell, 132
runaways. *See* desertions
running, 163
Russell, Naomi, 184
Russell, Otis, 87–88, 121–122, 133, 216
Ryan, Will Carson, Jr., 16

Sac and Fox Sanatorium, 198
Saint Mary's Hospital, Minneapolis, 266
Salem Training School, 17
sanatoriums, 198
Sandoval, Adelia, 32–33
sanitary facilities, 83
sanitation regimen, 67–68
Santa Fe Indian School, 33, 64–65
Schanadore, Mrs. Jamison, 123
school attendance
   compulsory, 37–38
   contracts for, 39–40
   family resistance to, 35–36, 45–46
   government schools, 17
   Haskell Institute, 21, 23, 25, 28, 29, 43, 46
   See also student enrollment
science curriculum, 100
"scientific racism," 41
scrofula, 196, 228–229
Scudder, Horace E., 100–101
secondary education. *See* high schools

Selkirk, George, 261–262
Sells, Cato, 95
Seminole Indians, 35
sewing and tailoring, 170(photo)
sexual activity, 181–183
sexually transmitted diseases, 181
shorthand class, 166(photo)
Short History of the United States (Scudder), 100–101
Shoshone Indians, 64
sign language, 87
Sisseton Agency, 261–262
"slanguage," 85
sleeping porches, 82
Small Boys Building, 173(photo)
Smith, Josephine, 136, 242
Smith, William, 219
Smith & Sargent, 19
Smoot, Mrs., 106
Snake, John E., 263–264
Snedden, David, 16
social evolutionism, 41, 42
socialization, athletics and, 164
socials, 144
solitary confinement, 221
Song of Hiawatha, The (play), 148–150
"sore eyes." *See* trachoma
Sosseur, Louise, 123
Spanish Influenza, 200–201, 202
speakers, 139
Split Ax, 49
sports, 157–165
Spybuck, Roy, 208
Standing Rock reservation, 234
Stanup, Grace, 194
Star Hawk Society, 272
Stewart, Irene, 250–251
Stewart, Omer C., 216
stories, traditional, 105
Stover, Eli, 145, 162–163
streptococci pulmonitis, 201
student enrollment, 30, 32
   age limits for, 40
   blood degree question, 40–43
   factors affecting, 31

student enrollment, *continued*
  parents' support for, 52–53
  parent-student conflicts over, 50–52
  See also school attendance; student recruitment
student labor
  at Haskell, 19–20, 110, 112–114
  working conditions, 185–187
student recruitment, 24–25, 31, 32, 35, 38–39, 44–46. *See also* student enrollment
students
  academic life, 105–108
  accelerated, 106
  accidents, 208
  accommodation to boarding school life, 241–243
  agendas for applying to Haskell Institute, 53–55
  American patriotism, 128, 135–138
  arrival at Haskell, 59–60
  athletics, 157–165
  bodily transformation, 180–181
  clothing and uniforms, 68–73
  complaints to parents about Haskell, 226–227
  conflicts with parents over enrollment, 50–52
  crimes and offenses, 224–225
  cultural and extracurricular activities, 138–143
  dental hygiene, 205–206
  desertion, 211, 231, 234–237
  desire to visit homes, 236–237, 239
  diet and nutrition, 76–81, 187
  discipline (*see* discipline)
  diseases (*see* diseases)
  early enrollees at Haskell Institute, 20–21
  English-only policy, 73–74
  essays and writings, 104
  ethnic awareness of, 215–216
  expulsions, 43–44, 225–226, 238–239
  friendships and social ties, 84–90, 241
  games, 145–146
  gendered behavior, 143–144
  health conditions, 33–34, 179–180, 187–189 (*see also* health conditions)
  hiding sickness from authorities, 194–195
  holiday celebrations, 150–152
  homesickness, 231–232, 233, 234
  indigenous cultural values and, 64–65
  labor and, 19–20, 110, 112–114
  leaving Haskell, 249
  medical care, 187, 193–194
  military system, 60–63, 65–67
  mortality, 21, 22, 206–209
  overcrowding in dormitories, 188–189
  parental support, 52–53, 232
  petitions, 227–229
  positive views of Haskell, 240
  primary grade, 167(photo)
  psychological problems, 195
  punishments, 23, 61, 62, 218–222, 235–236
  reading, 102–103
  readjustments after graduation, 249–251
  "rebellion" of 1919, 229–230, 231
  religion and Christianization, 128–135
  renaming, 74–76
  resistance to Haskell, 211–217, 222–224, 228–231
  rift with home communities, 239–240
  sanitation regimen, 67–68
  sexual activity, 181–183
  small children, 40
  social activities and male-female relationships, 143–147
  summer vacations, 53, 237–238
  table manners, 82
  teachers and, 243–245
  trauma of separation and travel to school, 56–58
  unsupervised behavior, 211–215
  working conditions, 185–187
  See also alumni; female alumni; female students
summer vacations, 53, 237–238
superintendent of Indian schools, 46–47
superintendents of Haskell Institute
  Arthur Grabowskii, 22–23, 24
  Oscar Leonard, 26, 27

INDEX 329

James Marvin, 19, 20
Charles Meserve, 27
Harvey Peairs, 28–29
Charles Robinson, 24–25, 26
J. A. Swett, 27–28
John Wise, 42–43
See also Fiske, H. H.; *and individual superintendents*
survival of the fittest, 158
Sutton, Arthur, 120–121, 132–133
Swett, J. A., 27–28
syphilis, 181

table manners, 82
Tabor, Cora, 198, 199
Tanner, Peter, 209
Taos Pueblo, 32
Tarbell, Margaret, 225–226
Taylor, John, 55
teachers, 243–245, 258–259, 270, 271
Tehee, Christian, 208
temperance, 104, 184
theater, 148–150
Thomas, Clarence, 214
time, conceptions of, 66
tobacco, 213
toilets, 83
Tongue River School, 260–261
Toombs, Clara, 248
towel system, 185
trachoma, 185, 192–193, 202–204
track team, 163
traditionalists, 35
tribal lands, allotment policy, 14, 281n14
tuberculosis, 179, 184, 185, 188–191, 194, 196–198
Tucquinn, Teresa, 25

Underwood Typewriter Company, 265
uniforms. *See* clothing and uniforms
Ute Indians, 34

vacations, 53, 237–238
Valley, Annie, 198
Valley, Maud and Mamie, 198–199
Van Cleave, W. E., 187, 200, 204, 205

vaudeville, 265
Vieus, Osie, 141
vision impairments, 204–205. *See also* trachoma
Vivia, Alice, 106–107
vocational training, 172(photo), 177(photo), 178(photo)
 in agriculture, 120
 boys and, 120–122
 early implementation of, 15, 16
 emphasis on, 93–94, 96
 gendered curriculum, 114–120
 popularity in America, 111–112
 See also industrial training

wages, of student workers, 113, 123
Wahpeton Indian School, 271
Wakarusa River, 212–213
Walker, Suzie, 74
war veterans, 268–269, 286n10
Washington, Booker T., 139
Wa-Ya-Wa-Ble (play), 148
Webster, Sophia, 208
Wells, Jewel, 119–120, 242
Whale, Edward, 211
Wheelock, Dennison, 140–141, 248–249
Wheelock, Frances, 125–126
White, Jack, 179
Whitefox, Lottie High, 88, 107
White Wolf, Harry, 206
Wild West shows, 139, 140, 265
Williams, John, 23, 24
Winnie, Lucille
 athletics at Haskell, 162, 164
 clothing at Haskell, 68
 food at Haskell, 78
 graduation, 245
 Haskell's socials, 144
 life story, 269
 military system at Haskell, 66
 perceptions of Haskell, 269
 wages for labor, 113
Wise, John R.
 alumni employment, 260–261
 commercial course, 110
 dancing by students, 146–147

Wise, John R., *continued*
   Haskell's guardhouse, 221
   nursing program, 117–118
   outing program, 122
   student clothing, 70–71
   student desertion, 235, 236
   student enrollment, 42, 43
   student labor, 113–114
   student social life, 146
   trachoma-infected students, 203–204
Wolf, Harry White, 21
Wolf Face, 49
Work, Hubert, 16, 154–155
working conditions, 185–187

World's Fairs, 140, 147–148
World War I, 136–138, 266–269
Wright, Agnes, 259
Wright, Hattie, 260–261
Wright, Martha and Marie, 186

Yazza, Pahhe, 208
Yellow Bear, John, 221
YMCA Rocky Mountain Student Conference, 134
Young Men's Christian Association (YMCA), 80, 130, 131, 134, 167(photo)
Young Women's Christian Association (YWCA), 130, 131, 177(photo)

www.ingramcontent.com/pod-product-compliance
Lightning Source LLC
Chambersburg PA
CBHW051535230426
43669CB00015B/2612